HISTORY OF THE OLD TESTAMENT

IV

VOL. IV

HISTORY OF THE
CLAUS SCHEDL

OLD TESTAMENT

THE AGE OF THE PROPHETS

alba house

A DIVISION OF THE SOCIETY OF ST. PAUL

STATEN ISLAND, NEW YORK 10314

First published under the title: **Geschichte des Alten Testaments** by Tyrolia-Verlag, Innsbruck, Austria

Library of Congress Cataloging in Publication Data

Schedl, Claus.
History of the Old Testament.

Translation of Geschichte des Alten Testaments.
Includes bibliographical references.
CONTENTS: v. 1. The ancient Orient and ancient Biblical history.—
v. 2. God's people of the covenant.—v. 3. The golden age of David. [etc.]
   1. Bible.   O. T.—History of Biblical events.
I. Title.
BS1197.S3213   221.9   70-38990
ISBN 0-8189-0231-0 (set)
ISBN 0-8189-0209-4 (v. 4)

Nihil Obstat:
   Donald A. Panella, M.A., S.T.L., S.S.L.
   Censor Librorum

Imprimatur:
   Joseph P. O'Brien, S.T.D.
   Vicar General, Archdiocese of New York
   April 5, 1971

Designed, printed and bound by the Fathers and Brothers of the Society of St. Paul as part of their communications apostolate.

THE THEOLOGIAN AND
THE OLD TESTAMENT

BY theologian we understand not merely the professional theologian who studies the Bible in connection with his vocation in order to qualify himself for the exercise of his office, but every believer for whom the Bible is an interesting and venerable document of the history of the ancient Eastern mind and religion. The Bible is not the private literature of a specially elect band of devotees, but the life book of God's people. It is in this book that the Word of God, binding on all men, has become flesh.

Just as the person of Christ "who, though he was in the form of God, did not count equality with God a thing to be grasped, but emptied himself, taking the form of a servant, being born in the likeness of men" (*Phil.* 2, 6-7) is the key to all theology, it is also the only approach to the Bible. Just as the God-man Jesus spans a mighty dichotomy in his person, by uniting what appear to be strictly disparate elements in one divine-human unity, so the word of the Bible is filled with a dynamism which surpasses human measurement. Are we now about to do away with this involvement in the sphere of human affairs by advancing a theology of the word of the Bible that concentrates too heavily on the overpowering splendor of that Word which was in the beginning with God and which is incapable of being incorporated into "the shards of letters"? [1]

Not at all. Just as the man who repudiates Christ's bodily

---

1. Origen, *Commentary on St. John,* Migne, PG 13, 29B-32B.

existence and ascribes only a phantom human existence to the Incarnate Word is guilty of seriously misinterpreting Christ, so the man who refuses to recognize the fact of the Incarnation entirely misses the mystery of Scripture. Just as Christ was a true man of his times, speaking the Galilean dialect and wearing the dress of his century, so every word in the Bible is spoken in a concrete, unique, and historical setting. This very fact determined its fate. The dust of centuries has grown heavy upon it. The Word has made its way into history, as every other, earlier or later, profane document of history.

If we mean to approach this word, we must face the difficult task of entering into all the stipulations of historical development and not rest comfortably in our secure position by pointing to the fact of inspiration. Whoever wishes to approach the Bible in a scientific manner necessarily takes on the total load of a profane exegesis. The Old Testament is a written document of the Ancient Near East, and it has undergone a development over the course of more than a thousand years before reaching its present form. For the most part it is written in the Hebrew language. A scientific examination of the Old Testament, therefore, becomes impossible without the study and knowledge of this language. The man who bases his approach only on translations is always something of a stranger to the concrete call of the revealed word; for every translation is, in some respects, a betrayal. Only the original text is inspired, and not the translations, no matter how venerable they might be.

The Old Testament is also a literary document. Thus we are also obliged (and it would be a serious error to omit this task) to approach the text in terms of the principles of philology and literary criticism in order to critically test every passage. But a literary criticism always runs the danger of being too removed from life and reality, unless it constantly keeps in sight the *Sitz im Leben* — its position in actuality.

The written document thus appeals to the mute witnesses of ancient history, which are made articulate by archaeological excavation. Philology, literary criticism, archaeology, and the history of the Ancient Near East are the guideposts for this profane exegesis; without them we are irrevocably lost in the realm of unreality, and we miss the full "incarnation of the Word." The personal religious conviction of the investigator plays no role in this. In fact, we might go so far as to claim that if there were one ideal technique for carrying out this methodology of examination, then the results of a study by an atheistic philologist and a believing theologian would be completely in agreement. And, in practice, to a large extent, this is exactly what happens.

But if we mean to rest content with this *profane exegesis,* we fail to recognize the inexhaustible reality of the Bible word. Profane exegesis must be enlarged upon, not only as a mere supplement, but as an ultimate fulfillment, by "pneumatic" exegesis. The primary source of Scripture is at once both human and divine. If one of the pillars is missing here, the whole construction collapses in ruin.

This is not the place to fully treat on the nature of inspiration,[2] although the study of Scripture wanders about blindly without a clear idea of it. Both Church and synagogue have always attested to the fact that the Bible contains God's word. Disagreements were only on questions concerning how the authorship of Scripture was to be ascribed to God, and how it was possible to speak of human authorship. The Patristic age [3] was fond of parables: the Holy Spirit, it was claimed, used the human author like a musical instrument (organ, flute, lyre, etc.). Though it is an attractive metaphor, it runs the risk of considering human cooperation too exclusively in terms of a dead "instrument," without any proper activity of its own. When God overshadows a human author, he does not extinguish human existence; he elevates it into greater light, into a freedom untrammeled by sin. Inspiration is the elevation of the human faculties. If God calls upon man to compose a book, he directs this call to a concrete, historically qualified man, who, under the divine impulse, takes up the historical source material available and forms it into a unity that has been revealed to him. In this process, it is only too easy

---

2. A. Merk, *De Inspiratione S. Scripturae,* Biblical Institute, Rome 1951.
3. Cf. J. Schildenberger, *Vom Geheimnis des Gotteswortes,* 1950, p. 17.

to recognize the awkward hand of the human author, who was obviously not always an accomplished literary artist. But it is from this very defect that God's power sounds its clearest note. Thus the word formed by man becomes the true "bounty of the divine Word." [4] We can then speak of personal literary style, power of poetic expression, artistic or faulty composition without thereby calling into question the divine reality of inspiration.

Once the divine origin of Scripture is properly grasped, there are some ponderable conclusions. The basic concept of this book is divine and grandiose. It lays bare the deepest abysses of sin and judgment; but it also discloses the glories of forgiveness and grace. There is nothing superficial or monotonous about this book. It sounds depths of such great dimensions that they shine like lightning "from the beginning to the end of days." This book was not composed without a plan; it storms along towards its goal. The "shards of the individual words" announce the irresistible and passionate arrival of the Eternal Word. The words are all oriented towards *the* Word. The Old Testament is the "educator towards Christ." Thus, if you tell how you look at Christ, I will tell you how you read the Old Testament. The ultimate understanding of Scripture comes only from faith and Spirit. Once a man has tasted the "sweetness of the word" (*Ps.* 34, 8), he is awake to the "passion of the divine." Since the Spirit who has inspired this book is passion and love, the man who has once experienced this "divine taste" can never again turn away. Even the mighty waters of boredom, which every study necessarily involves, will not be able to destroy this love. The final object of theological instruction does not consist in the imparting of knowledge, but in the development of the "theological eros." If this succeeds, the small spark becomes a conflagration which can inflame the entire world.

Thus we raise our voice in a complaint which is perhaps also an accusation: Why is there so much weakness and fragility in Christianity? Obviously, because the word has been dulled. We are taken up with New Testament exegesis and frequently

---

4. Origen, *Commentary on Jeremiah*, Migne, PG 13, 544C.

lose ourselves in spiritualistic conclusions. The bread of the Old Testament is not broken enough. And still the Catholic Church is, much more than we dare to realize, *the* Church of the Bible. The liturgical missal is almost exclusively Old Testament in its sung texts. If we would remove the Old Testament from our liturgy the Church would be without song. Take away the powerful readings from Law and Prophets from the liturgical year, and Christianity is made incomplete. The Old Testament is neither old nor ancient; it is a living reality in our midst. But how many of us recognize the power coming from this book? Today, more than ever, we must call upon the tidings of the Old Testament, in order to recognize the hand of Yahweh in a world on the verge of collapse. Yahweh is a God of history, and he directs the chaos of human history towards a goal and purpose he has set.

The concluding words of this introduction are taken from Origen, one of the greatest Scripture scholars and interpreters of the Greek Church, and for that matter, the whole Church: "If we have once admitted that these writings owe their origin to the creator of the world, we must be convinced that whatever is encountered by those who examine into the fundamental meaning of the world will also be met with in the study of Scripture. The further we progress in reading, the higher the mountain of mysteries towers above us. And just as a man who sets out upon the sea in a tiny ship is unafraid so long as he is close to the land but, when he gradually approaches the high seas and the waves begin to swell and he begins to be lifted high upon their crests or, when they gape open and he begins to be swarmed under into the abyss, it is then that his spirit is seized by a monstrous fear and anxiety for having entrusted such a tiny ship to such monstrous floods — this is the experience we seem to have when, from the smallness of our merit and the narrowness of our spirit we dare to approach so wide a sea of mysteries." [5]

5. Origen, *Homily on Genesis.*

CONTENTS

SECTION ONE
ZEAL FOR YAHWEH

SECTION THREE
UNDER THE HAMMER OF BABYLON

ABBREVIATIONS

AASOR	Annual of the American School of Oriental Research
ABEL	F. M. Abel, *Géographie de la Palestine* (Études Bibliques), Paris, vol. I, 1933, vol. II, 1938
AfO	E. Weidner, *Archiv für Orientforschung*, Graz
AJA	American Journal of Archaeology
ANEP	J. P. Pritchard, *The Ancient Near East in Pictures relating to the Old Testament*, Princeton Univ. Press, 1954
ANET	J. P. Pritchard, *Ancient Near Eastern Texts relating to the Old Testament*, Princeton Univ. Press, 1955
AnglTR	Anglican Theological Review
Ann. PEF	Annual of the Palestine Exploration Fund, London
AnOr	Anacleta Orientalia, Rome
Ant.	Flavius Josephus, *Antiquitates Judaicae, Jüdische Altertümer*
AO	Alter Orient
AOB	H. Gressmann, *Altorientalische Bilder zum Alten Testament*, Berlin/Leipzig, 1927
AOT	H. Gressmann, *Altorientalische Texte zum Alten Testament*, 1926
APAW	Abhandlungen der Preussischen Akademie der Wissenschaften, Berlin
ARM	Archives Royales de Mari, Paris
Arch	Archaeology
ArOr	Archiv Orientálni
AT	Altes Testament
ATD	Hentrich and Weiser, *Das Alte Testament Deutsch*, Göttingen
BA	The Biblical Archaeologist
BASOR	Bulletin of the American Schools of Oriental Research

BB	Bonner Bibelkommentar
Bibl	Biblica
BiblArch	The Biblical Archaeologist
BibLex	H. Haag, *Bibellexicon*
BibLit	Bibel und Liturgie
BHK	R. Kittel, *Biblica Hebraica*, adapted by Stuttgart, 1954
BJRL	K. Galling, The Bulletin of the John Rylands Library
BK	M. Noth, *Biblischer Kommentar, Altes Testament,* Neukirchen
BRL	Biblisches Reallexicon
BZ	Biblische Zeitschrift, Neue Folge, Paderborn
BZAW	Beihefte zur ZAW
CalwK	Calwer Kommentar: Die Botschaft des Alten Testaments, Stuttgart
CBQ	The Catholic Biblical Quarterly
ClamB	Pirot-Clamer, *La Sainte Bible,* Latin and French text with both exegetical and theological comment, Paris
DB	Vigouroux, *Dictionaire de la Bible,* Paris, 1861-1912
DBS	Supplément au Dictionaire de la Bible, Paris, 1926
DOT	Winton-Thomas, *Documents to the Old Testament*
EB	Echter Bibel, Würzburg
EinlAT	O. Eissfeldt, Einleitung in das Alte Testament unter Einschluss der Apokryphen und pseudepigraphen sowie der apokryphen und pseudepigraphenartigen Qumrān-Schriften. Entstehungsgeschichte des Alten Testaments, Tubingen, 1956
EnchBibl	Enchiridion Biblicum. Documenta ecclesiastica Sacram Scripturam spectantia, Rome, 1956
EncMikr	Encyklopaedia Mikra'it. Encyclopaedia Biblica. Thesaurus rerum biblicarum, Hebrew University, Jerusalem, 1950
EphThLov (ETL)	Ephemerides Theologicae Lovanienses
ET	The Expository Times
EvT	Evangelische Theologie
FF	Forschungen und Fortschritte, Berlin
Fs	Festschrift
GAV	H. Schmökel, *Geschichte des Alten Vorderasien,* Leiden, 1957

GTT	J. Simons, *The Geographical and Topographical Texts of the Old Testament*, Leiden, 1959
GVA	A. Moortgat, *Geschichte Vorderasien bis zum Hellenismus*, Munchen, 1950
HAT	Handbuch zum Alten Testament
HistM (HM)	Fritz Kern, *Historia Mundi*, 1952
HUCA	Hebrew Union College Annual, Cincinnati
IEJ	Israel Exploration Journal, Jerusalem
IntBib	The Interpreters Bible. A Commentary in twelve volumes, New York
JAOS	The Journal of the American Oriental Society
JBL	The Journal of Biblical Literature
JEArch	Journal of Egyptian Archaeology
JerB	Jerusalem Bible
JNES	The Journal of Near Eastern Studies
JSS	The Journal of Semitic Studies
KAT	E. Sellin, *Kommentar zum Alten Testament*, Leipzig
KB	Keilschriftliche Bibliothek
LexVT	L. Koehler — W. Baumgartner, *Lexicon in Veteris Testamenti Libros*, Leiden, 1953
LXX	Septuaginta
Migne, PG	Migne, *Patres Greci*
Migne, PL	Migne, *Patres Latini*
MiscBibl	Mischellania Biblica
MT	R. Kittel, *Masoretischer Text nach der Biblica Hebraica*, 1954
NouvRevThéol	Nouvelle Revue Théologique
OLZ	Orientalische Literaturzeitung, Leipzig
Or	Orientalia, Rome
PEQ	Palestine Exploration Quarterly, London
PG	Migne, *Patres Greci*
PL	Migne, *Patres Latini*
RA	E. Eberling and Br. Meisnner, *Reallexicon der Assyriologie*
RB	Revue Biblique, École Biblique, Jerusalem
RCB	Rivista di Cultura Biblica
REHM	Die Bücher der Könige, Echter Bibel, Würzburg, 1949
RSR	Recherches de Science Religieuse

Rev HistRel	Revue de l'Histoire des Religions, Paris
SAT	Gunkel — Gressmann, *Die Schriften des Alten Testaments*, Göttingen
ST	Studia Theologica
TGI	K. Galling, *Textbuch zur Geschichte Israels*, Tubingen, 1950
ThLZ	Theologische Literaturzeitung, Leipzig
ThZ	Theologische Zeitschrift, Basel
TTZ	Trierer Theologische Zeitschrift
UM	C. H. Gordon, *Ugaritic Manual*, Rome, 1955
VD	Verbum Domini
VT	Vetus Testamentum
WTJ	Westminster Theological Journal
ZAW	Zeitschrift für Alttestamentliche Wissenschaft
ZDMG	Zeitschrift der Deutschen Morgenländischen Gesellschaft
ZDPV	Zeitschrift des Deutschen Palästinavereines
ZKT	Zeitschrift für Katholische Theologie, Innsbruck
ZTK	Zeitschrift für Theologie und Kirche

ZEAL FOR YAHWEH

"How long will you go limping with two different opinions? If the Lord is God, follow him; but if Baal, then follow him" (1 K 18, 21).

THE golden age of David had found a sorry end in the division of the kingdom and the schism of the national faith. The next stroke was delivered by the Egyptian Pharaoh Shishak in the fifth year (926-25) of Rehoboam (1 K 14, 25). Jerusalem was preserved from siege and destruction only when Rehoboam plundered the treasury of Solomon and delivered its treasures as tribute to the Egyptians. Among other booty, the two hundred golden shields of Solomon fell victim to the enemy's greed. Rehoboam had bronze shields made to take their place, a sorry symbol of the mighty change in the political situation.

The era of the divided kingdom for Israel and Judah which now begins can be rightly called the "age of the prophets." At every climax and turning point in this history there stands the figure of a prophet, rising up to judge and condemn, but also to pronounce oracles of salvation and redemption. Various attempts have been made to interpret the individual phenomena of Hebrew prophecy, to isolate its roots and origin. The study of prophecy is, today more than ever before, at a turning point. The one-sided derivation of the prophetic charism from an ecstatic and mantic movement of the eleventh century is now a thing of the past.[1] The letter achives of Mari, a city state on the middle Euphrates, dating from the time of Hammurabi (c. 1700

---

1. The more recent positions taken by scholarship on the prophets are presented by G. v. Rad, ThAt II: *Die Theologie der prophetischen Uberlieferungun,* Munich (1960), 22.

B.C.), are already familiar with the phenomenon of "prophet."
A mantic figure (*muhhum*) makes known to the king the divine
decisions he has received in a dream.[2] This is strongly reminiscent
of the prophets Nathan and Gath at David's court. Egyptologists
can point to similar phenomena in the course of Egyptian history.[3]
It follows that the Biblical prophets, in the externals of their
function and appearance, are the subject of pointed similarities
with the world about them. The contrary would be a source of
great surprise. In the course of our presentation thus far we have
had frequent occasion to refer to the Old Testament's roots in
the ambient of the Ancient Near East. In this comparison, it is
not the points of similarity which surprise us, but the sudden and
almost unexpected points of contrast and difference which assert
themselves. Fundamentally, it is Israel's faith in God which explains all the points of contrast. Israel's God is a God who
speaks and reveals himself. He lays hold of men in order to
announce his word through them. This divine activity sometimes
assumes the form of ecstatic phenomena; but once again it is
not the external phenomena that are the decisive factor, but rather
the word of God that is announced. This can take place within
the framework of cult or outside it.[4] It follows that the charism
of prophecy is not the special privilege of any state or calling.
God raises up men wherever he needs them. In terms of linguistic
analysis it has not yet been definitively explained whether the
Hebrew word for prophet *nabi'* is to be considered of an active
formation ("the caller") or a passive formation ("the called").[5]

---

2. W. v. Soden, *Die Verkündigung des Gotteswillens durch prophetisches
   Wort in den altbabylonischen Briefen aus Mari*, WO (1950), 397.
3. G. Lanczkowski, *Ägyptischer Prophetismus im Lichte des alttestament-
   lichen*, ZAW 70 (1958), 31-38.
4. More recent OT scholarship has rediscovered this cult; but it is not
   a sufficient explanation for the phenomenon of prophecy. H. H. Rowley, *Ritual and the Hebrew Prophets*, JSS 1 (1956), 338-360.
5. ThWNT VI, 796ff. The Greek word *pro-phetes* does not mean to "say
   in advance, to foretell," but rather to "speak in someone else's
   place, to represent." It is thus equivalent to "herald." — The Egyptian
   origin of the word has also been suggested: *nābi'* from *nab-i'o*
   "lord, one honored, reverend." ZAW 75 (1961), 100.

Actually, the Biblical prophets were really callers and announcers of God in the midst of an era of moral and political collapse. This they could be only because they were first called. Instead of involving the present discussion in a lengthy semantic and conceptual propaedeutic, we shall let the pages of our history speak for themselves, for it is in them that the word of God is revealed by human speech.

CHAPTER I

THERE WAS WAR BETWEEN JUDAH
AND ISRAEL
(931 — 880)

THE century of history which begins with the division of the kingdom and the schism of the national faith finds Palestine in a state of external and internal dissolution. There could be no more penetrating commentary on this fact than the constantly recurring words of our historian: "And there was war continually between the kings of Israel and Judah." [6] The divided kingdoms now had to face the serious business of asserting their political rights in the vastly different interplay of national and international relations in the Ancient Near East. Their kings had to address themselves to new economic and social problems, and primarily to new religious difficulties which now arose to jeopardize the very existence of their nations.

1) REHOBOAM FORTIFIES HIS TERRITORY (931/30 -- 914)

It seems that the Southern Kingdom was the first to recover from the blow dealt by the Egyptian invasion. The crisis of the

---

6. 1 K 14, 30; 15, 6, 7, 16, 32.

times dictated immediate action. Like it or not, Rehoboam had to accept the actual division of the kingdom as a *fait accompli* and adapt to the new political situation. The territory of the northern tribes must be regarded as definitively lost. After the Egyptian invasion, the southern territory with its coastal stretch as far as Gerar had to be abandoned to the Egyptian sphere of influence. Judah was thus thrown back to her own mountain territory. In an effort to protect what was left of his territory, Rehoboam systematically set about the construction of boundary fortresses (2 Ch 11, 5ff.).[7]

On the edge of the "lowland" (*sephelah*), which forms the southern part of the coastal plain, he refortified the ancient fortress triangle [8] of Lachish, Mareshah, and Gath, as protection against attack from this quarter and to bar any military approach into the mountain countries in the direction of Hebron. The rest of

---

7. G. Beyer, *Das Festungssystem Rechabeams*, ZDPV 54 (1931), 113, 114.

8. Neither in Kings nor in Chronicles is there mention of Shishak having captured and destroyed any cities in Judah. It would appear that he was satisfied with the high tribute payment offered by Rehoboam and withdrew from Jerusalem. Excavation has only confirmed this very concise account in 2 Ch 12, 1-12. The other Judaean cities were also made to feel the force of the Egyptian invasion: with the exception of Jerusalem and the cities of the mountain districts, every excavated city exhibits a stratum of debris caused by destruction, dating to the end of the tenth century. Rehoboam thus had to rebuild on top of ruins in Lachish and the other sites. G. E. Wright, *Israelite Samaria and Iron Age Chronology*, BASOR 155 (1959), 28; *Ibid., Judaean Lachis*, BA 18 (1955), g-17; — DBS III, 359. I visited this triangle of fortifications on March 21, 1959 and found it a strangely desolate region. The special map I had referred to it by the Arab name *hârûs*, "laid waste." A Jewish Kibbutz has been established at the foot of the mound at Lachish. According to the settlement planning, Lachish is to become an agricultural outpost. Mareshah is generally identified with Tell Sandahannah (Arabic corruption of Santa Anna, a Church dating to Byzantine times), a trapezoidal hill jutting up and dominating the landscape, even in modern times it is a strategic frontier outpost (DB III, 336). — Gath is the home of David's body-guard, who probably incorporated this Philistine city into his kingdom. It is situated in the rolling plain as an outpost for the fortifications established along the edge of the mountains.

his fortifications along the margin of the coastal plain are typical valley barricades. The Valley of the Oak (Elah), through which the Philistines made their way in the days of Goliath, was to be closed by the fortress cities of Azekah, Socok, and Adullam.[9] They served to protect the hinterland in the direction of Bethlehem. The fortress of Zorah was to control the valley of the Sorek, while the city of Aijalon controlled the valley of the same name. Each of these valleys affords an easy access to Jerusalem, and thus, from the first days of Israel's possession of the country, they served as a favorite quarter of invasion, for hostile forces making their way eastwards from the coastal plains, and were frequently the scene of important battles.

Nor did the mountain heights remain unfortified. A string of fortresses from south to north: Ziph, Adoraim, Beth-Zur, Tekoa, Etam, and Bethlehem [10] were to form an outer circle of defense and also serve as a series of bulwarks to protect the capital city of Jerusalem against attack from this quarter.

Each of these cities was under the control of a military commander who is called *nagid*. The ancient sacral title "shepherd and leader of the people" thus takes on a new military-technical meaning. Rehoboam wisely entrusted much of this power to his own sons and thereby established his family as a dynasty (2 Ch

---

9. Azekah = *Tell zakariyah;* the citadel stood on the top of the hill, like a stronghold for final · refuge in time of war. G. E. Wright, *Biblical Archaeology* (1958), 148 − DBS III 369.

10. Ziph = *tell Zif,* some 3 mi from Hebron; Adoraim = Dura, 4-5 mi SW of Hebron; Tekoa = *Ḥirbet Tequ,* 5 mi S of Bethlehem; Etam = *Ḥirbet et-Hoh,* 2 mi SW of Bethlehem. These locations are identified only by surface information. In Beth-Zur, since 1931, there have been American trial ditches (DB III, 341), but it was not until 1957 that the work could be taken up once again under the direction of O. R. Sellers. The excavation report is to be found in BA 21 (1958), 71-76. / R. W. Funk, *The 1957 Campaign at Beth-Zur,* BASOR 150 (1958), 8-20. The excavations make it clear that Rehoboam made use of the already existing walls dating from the Bronze Age and built nothing more than a citadel. Modern *Ḥirbet et-Tubeiqah,* 4 mi N of Hebron, on the right hand side of the modern highway. On June 20, 1951, I walked around in the area. The ancient sites are uninhabited and half-wilderness.

11, 23). In order to be prepared for the events of war, he assembled a supply not only of military material, shields, and lances, but also established a series of provisions dumps, which he supplied primarily with wine and oil.

The southern kingdom thus took on the appearance of a well built fortress. Accordingly, Rehoboam must have been a very energetic ruler. This we might suppose already on the basis of the infamous popular assembly at Shechem which took place in the year 931, and during which the self-assured young ruler mockingly declared that his little finger was thicker than his father's loins, and threatened to chasten them with scorpions rather than mere whips (1 K 12, 10ff.). These military preparations are unthinkable without the full exploitation of the entire populace.

In the system of fortification, the northern boundary remained open. Rehoboam had not abandoned all hope that the rebellious northern tribes might one day return to their allegiance to the scepter of David. But it was precisely along this open boundary that the fiercest internecine struggle was doomed to break out, a war between brothers.

2) THE OPEN NORTHERN BOUNDARIES OF JUDAH

During his lifetime, Rehoboam handed over far-reaching authority to his son and heir Abijah (2 Ch 11, 22),[11] who was descended, on his mother's side, from Gibeah, the ancient fortress city of Saul (2 Ch 13, 2). This explains his interest in protecting the northern boundary of the kingdom. It seems that, once he had become king (914/13 — 912), Abijah initiated the attack. He succeeded in throwing back Jeroboam's general troops, and controlling the southern half of the mountain country of Ephraim. The cities of Bethel, together with their "daughters," [12] Jeshanah

---

11. Reference to God as Father: *'abî-yahu*, "My father is Yahweh!" Abbreviated to Abijah, Abiam. Cf. Abias.

12. "Daughters" is the word used to describe cities founded from a mother city or settlements dependent upon it. The city itself is called "mother" (metropolis = "mother city"). — The excavations at Bethel have produced abundant material from the Middle and Late Bronze Age, Roman and Byzantine eras, but no evidence from the Iron Age. An-

together with her "daughters," and Ephron together with her "daughters" were incorporated into the kingdom of Judah (2 Ch 13, 19).

Jeroboam's kingship, which had been acclaimed with such great enthusiasm, could not survive this constant series of political and military failures. Even the Philistines, the ancient hereditary enemy of Israel, had seized upon the occasion of the Egyptian invasions to throw off the yoke of Israel. Some decades later the Philistine city of Gibbethon [13] was the scene of a fierce but apparently undecisive battle. Gibbethon is situated almost half-way between the two fortress cities of Ekron in the west and Gezer in the east. It is possible that the Philistines were attempting to occupy the Israelite territory of Gezer, and that their attack was repulsed by Solomon's fortress city there; or, conversely, it might have been Israel in an attempt to annex the Philistine city of Ekron, just as Judah had occupied the city of Gath.[14]

It was before the gates of Gibbethon that the fate of the first short-lived dynasty of the Northern Kingdom was decided. Jeroboam's rise and collapse is sufficiently explained in terms of the at first favorable but rapidly deteriorating political situation of his time, but the underlying causes which only find their expression in the larger history of the world about him become visible only in the work of the prophets. Every king has a prophet for

---

cient Bethel (Israelite) is generally identified with the modern Arab village of Beitin — a fact which makes excavation extremely difficult. For the excavation accounts, cf. J. L. Kelso, BASOR 137 (1955), 5-10; 151 (1958), 3-8.

---

13. Ancient Canaanite settlement, occupied by the Philistines, probably to be identified with Gob, where David's soldiers already fought (2 S 21, 18). Modern Tell el-Malat, 2 mi east of Aqir and 2 mi west of Gezer. Cf. Simons, GTT #795, 894. — Gezer, ancient Canaanite city, conquered by the Egyptians and later given to Solomon as a wedding present. Solomon built the city into a fortress; the towers have been excavated; similar excavation has unearthed a gate similar to those in Megiddo and Hazor. Y. Yadin, *Solomon's City Wall and Gate at Gezer*, IEJ 8 (1958), 80-86. — G. E. Wright, *A Solomonic City Gate at Gezer*, BA 21 (1958), 103-104. DBS III, 396.

14. Noth, GeschIsr, 207.

his counterpart who, opportunely or inopportunely, asserts the prerogatives of God. Thus Jeroboam himself had once been encouraged by the words of the prophet Ahijah [15] from Shiloh (1 K 11, 29) to take a stand against Solomon. But his religious politics set him more and more at variance with the prophetic circles. They soon came to look upon him only as the rebellious king who was leading Israel into the service of alien gods (1 K 14, 9). In a time of crisis, when his son was mortally sick, Jeroboam once again thought of the prophet from Shiloh, who had once announced a favorable oracle. He did not go himself, but he sent his royal spouse to Shiloh. Even though she entered the prophet's house disguised as a simple woman from among the people, Ahijah, even in his blindness, recognized her by an interior inspiration. Rather than words of comfort and healing, he had to announce the oracle of Yahweh's threat: "The boy will die." Why? Because Jeroboam, as *nagid,* that is, shepherd and ruler of Israel, chosen by Yahweh himself, had not been true to his calling. Instead of leading Israel to Yahweh, he had led Israel to the service of the golden bulls. This sin is so great that it can be expiated only by extermination. As the "sin of Jeroboam" (1 K 14, 16) it will continue to gnaw at the body of the people, until Israel, as a people, has ceased to be. Under the burden of this dread decision, Jeroboam's wife makes her way back to Tirzah. The moment she arrived at the threshold of her house, the child died (1 K 14, 1-8).

It is surprising to note that in the middle of the Book of Kings there is a whole chapter devoted to the prophet Ahijah. But it is precisely in this insertion of the prophetic chapter that the theological interests of our historian are visible. It is the prophet who gave the political course of events their divine depth of meaning. Thus Ahijah suddenly made his appearance to encourage Jeroboam in his position against the king. He immediately disappears from focus for the rest of Jeroboam's reign. Only on the occasion of the wife's prayer for her sick son do we

---

15. The name *'ahî-yahu* ("My brother is Yahweh") proves that God was considered the "great brother."

discover that the aged prophet is still living in Shiloh, and that he is now blind. Jeroboam was the greatest disillusionment of his life. It is almost a reenactment of the tragedy between Saul and the prophet Samuel. The same prophet who announces the divine choice must also pronounce the sentence of judgment. Jeroboam was not only in rebellion against Solomon; he also revolted against Yahweh. The 22 years of Jeroboam's reign end in a political and religious collapse (1 K 14, 22). His son and successor Nadab [16] (910-909) is allowed to reign for only two years (1 K 15, 25). When he attempted to subdue the rebellious Philistines, and was laying siege to the fortress city of Gibbethon, he was struck down by Baasha, who then had himself proclaimed king and set about the extermination of the entire royal family. The ruling position of the tribe of Ephraim was thus definitively broken, the "glory of Ephraim": Baasha was from the tribe of Issachar (1 K 15, 25-30).

Baasha ben-Ahijah [17] (909-8 — 886) was certainly not inclined to tolerate Judah's extension of her territory along the open northern boundary without resistance. He did not attack at once, since he first had to establish his authority at home and abroad. A treaty with Ben-Hadad I of Damascus greatly relieved the strained relationship with the Aramaeans which had prevailed since the days of Solomon (1 K 15, 9). Baasha thus had a free hand to deal with Judah. Throughout the entire 24 years of his reign, there were constant border disputes with Judah, but a decisive confrontation was attempted only towards the end of his reign in the year 887-86.[18] He occupied not only the aban-

---

16. Abbreviated form for Nadab-Yahu, "Yahweh has shown himself prodigal."

17. The name cannot be fully interpreted. Comparison with personal names from Tadmur (Palmyra) would suggest an abbreviation: *Ba‘* (= *ba‘al*) -*ša’* (= *šemeš*), evidence for a sun cult: "God is the Sun!" *EncMikr* II, 303.

18. The dating in 2 Ch 15, 16; 16, 1 obviously involves a scribal error: "There was no war until the 35th year of Asa .... There was war in the 36th year of Asa." Baasha died already in the 26th year of Asa (1 K 16, 3). Since, moreover, the war was preceded by ten years of peace, which date from the 15th year of Asa, the year in which

doned districts in the mountain country of Ephraim, but also attempted to bar any further penetration on the part of Judah by establishing a boundary fortress at Ramah. Ramah is only 7 mi north of Jerusalem and controls not only the north-south traffic along the principal trade routes, but is also in a perfect position to keep the Judaean capital under constant observation and in perpetual stalemate. Baasha's coup struck home. There was an immediate reaction from the court at Jerusalem.

In an attempt to free his capital city from this hostile threat, Asa (912-11 — 871), Rehoboam's successor, attempted to dissolve Baasha's treaty with Aram. "Asa took all the silver and the gold that were left in the treasures of the house of the lord and the treasures of the king's house, and gave them into the hands of his servants; and King Asa sent them to Ben-Hadad I of Damascus, saying, 'Let there be a league between me and you . . . . Go, break your league with Baasha King of Israel, that he may withdraw from me' " (1 K 15, 18ff.).

For the Aramaeans this was an opportunity which could not be passed by. Damascus' trade interests demanded access to the Mediterranean. The route over the mountain passes of Lebanon was too difficult in those days. The obvious commercial route, dictated by nature herself, led southwards to the Jordan sources, and from there along the "highway by the sea," along the sea of Gennesaret, across the great plain and to the Mediterranean coast. But all these territories were under Israelite control. At the time there was a peace treaty between Aram and Israel. It appeared more desirable to occupy the territory in question than to respect the questionable alliance with Israel. Accordingly, Ben-Hadad I declared war upon Israel, and attacked the cities along the sources of the Jordan: Dan, Ijon, and Abel-Beth-Maacah, penetrating as far as the Lake of Gennesaret, and even took the city of Chinneroth,[19] and laid siege to the whole district of the

---

he acceeded to power and the year of the Kushite campaign, the beginning of the war coincided not with the 36th but with the 26th year of Asa. Baasha died in the year of the campaign. Instead of 35 and 36 we should read 25 and 26. — Rehm, Vol. II, 368.

---

19. Modern Tell el-'Oreime near Capernaum. Named after a divinity, like

tribe of Naphtali (1 K 15, 20). Even though there is no explicit mention of the fact, this campaign might well have seen the capture of the fertile provinces of Golan and Bashan, east of the Lake of Gennesaret. Under the pressure of these attacks, Baasha must have interrupted the construction of his fortifications along Judah's boundaries. He withdrew into his capital city Tirzah, where he did not long survive defeat. Asa of Judah quickly seized the opportunity. The building material which had been assembled for the fortification of Ramah he now took for himself, for the construction of the two fortresses Geba-Benjamin and Mizpah (1 K 15, 22). Excavation has cast new light upon this tragic conflict.[20]

---

many other Canaanite cities. A. Jirku, *Gab es eine palästinisch-syrische Gottheit Kinneret?* ZAT 72 (1960), 69 believes that it is a reference to a goddess of the "lyre" (= *kinneret*). The city would then have given the Lake its name, rather than vice versa. — Even though the name is not specifically mentioned, excavation does show that Hazor, too, was sacked and destroyed by Ben-Hadad. The ruins in Level IX are identified as dating from this time. One object of interest is the discovery of a stylized stone horse head with a solar disk and the cross insignia upon its forehead, the symbol of the thunder god Hadad. The excavation report: Y. Yadin, *The Third Season of Excavation at Hazor, 1957*, BA 21 (1958), 30-47; Illustration on p. 45.

---

20. Geba'-Benyamin is, according to LXX, identical with Gibeath-Benjamin, Saul's capital city, which is tentatively identified as Tell el-Ful, 3 mi N of Jerusalem, on the right hand of the main road. Excavations in the years 1922-23 unearthed a Migdal, a fortified citadel dating from the time of King Asa, BASOR IV (1924) — Simons, GTT # 893 DBS III, 404. — *Mispah* means simply "look-out, observation post." It is frequent as a place name, generally in conjunction with a proper name, such as Mizpah-Gilead. A. Alt, ZDPV 69 (1953) represents the opinion that the location fortified by Asa had previously been called Ataroth, but after the erection of this outpost in Mizpah (called simply "outpost") which was meant to serve as lookout against the Northern Kingdom, the older place name was dropped. Accordingly, Alt identifies the location with *hirbet atarah*. Simons, GTT 324, note 141, rejects this explanation as untenable and advances his own opinion that ancient Mizpah and Ataroth were two distinct though neighboring places. Most scholars identify Mizpah with *tell en-Nasbeh*, 6 mi from Jerusalem, just to the left of the highway. The excavated ruins

This completed Judah's belt of border fortifications. But at what price? Israel had gone over to her archenemy Aram, the outlying provinces of Golan and Bashan had been definitively lost, Upper Galilee was occupied by the enemy; at the same time, the Philistines were revolting along the coastal plains. Baasha's reign can only be seen as a further step downward in the Northern Kingdom, not only in politics, but also in religion. King Baasha's counterpart was the prophet Jehu ben Hanani. Despite the bloody extirpation of the house of Jeroboam, prophetic circles had looked to him for the restoration of the pure Yahweh cult. As shepherd of Israel (*nagid*) this would have been his most important office. But he "walked in the sins of Jeroboam"; he and his house were also destined to hear the word of Yahweh's rejection (1 K 16, 1-4).

Ben-Hadad I of Damascus appears to have been successful in his activity against his northern Aramaic neighbors. The details of the campaign have escaped our investigation; only the so-called Melkart-Stele [21] is left to testify to Ben-Hadad's importance in Northern Syria. This stele portrays the god Melkart in a walking posture, carrying an axe over his shoulders with his left hand, while in his right hand he has a looped cross, the sign of life. Beneath the figure of the god stands the following inscription:

"MONUMENT WHICH BAR-HADAD, SON OF TAB-RAMMON, SON OF HADYON, KING OF ARAM, ERECTED IN HONOR OF THE GOD MELKART. HE CONSECRATED TO HIM THIS STELE AND HARKENED TO HIS VOICE."

---

of the fortifications are impressive even today. The city walls were almost 20 feet thick at the top and even thicker at the base. There were towers at regular intervals. In many places the wall rose to a height of over 22 feet. The gate opened towards the NE. Long banks of stone seats bordered the walls of the tower chambers and the entry court; here, at the gate, the town elders used to sit. G. E. Wright, *Biblical Archaeology* (1958), 148. There is a good reconstruction of the ancient fortifications.

---

21. Discovered in 1940 in a village some 6 mi N of Aleppo in the midst of Roman ruins. It might well have come from an Ancient Syrian temple in the near vicinity. Text and illustration in Winton Thomas, DOT 239, illustration 15.

On the basis of the script form, this stele has been dated from the middle of the ninth century.[22] Bar-Hadad is merely the Aramaic form of the Hebrew name Ben-Hadad.[23] Consequently, this discovery casts some light on the figure of the Biblical Ben-Hadad.[24]

3) "PIOUS" QUEEN MOTHER AND CULT OF THE MOTHER GODDESS IN JUDAH

Despite the defection of the northern tribes, David's dynasty had succeeded not only in asserting their claim to the remaining districts of Judah and Benjamin, but also in erecting an impressive circle of fortifications. This was possible only because the Southern Kingdom was spared the plague of a contested succession to the royal throne. This political guarantee, however, did not preserve the Kingdom from religious collapse.

Rehoboam, in his religious politics, followed the example of his father Solomon, who, in deference to his pagan wives, had erected pagan sacrificial heights in the neighborhood of Jerusalem (1 K 11, 7). Since, at the court of Jerusalem, the queen mother always enjoyed a place of special prominence and a variety of privileges, it was these royal ladies who exercised the greatest influence on the religious developments of the country. They bore the title *g^ebirah,* approximately equivalent to "exalted lady." [25] It might be interpreted as a literary evidence of their position that these "elevated ladies" are mentioned by name. "His (Rehoboam's) mother's name was Naamah from Ammon" (1 K 14, 21). "His (Abijah's) mother's name was Maacah, a

22. W. F. Albright, *A Votive Stele erected by Ben-Hadad I. of Damaskus to the God Melcarth,* BASOR 87 (1942), 23-29.
23. A. Jepsen, *Zur Melqart-Stele Barhadads,* AFO 16 (1952/53), 315-317.
24. W. F. Albright, *The Near East and Israel,* JBL 59 (1940), 102-110.
25. Here, too, the Bible is similar to the world of its time. The queen mother occupied a position of special privilege in other courts of the Ancient Near East as well. In Ugaritic she was called *rabitu,* "the great" — VT 8 (1958), 103-106. Among the Hittites she was called *tavananna.* G. Molin, *Die Stellung der Gebirah im Staate Juda,* ThZ 10 (1954), 161-175.

daughter of Absalom" (15, 2). — Or finally: "The name of his (Asa's) (grand-) mother [26] was Maacah, the daughter of Absalom" (15, 10).

It was primarily under the official protection of these highly placed ladies that, even in the kingdom of Judah, the Canaanite paganism continued to gain ground. Already under Rehoboam, and thus shortly after the religious splendor of Solomon's reign, the process of religious decay had begun in the Southern Kingdom: "For they also built for themselves high places (*bāmôt*), and pillars (*massebôt*), and Asherim (*ªšerîm*) on every high hill and under every green tree. And there were also male cult prostitutes (*qadeš*) in the land" (1 K 14, 23).

In this brief statement we find the characteristic monument of Canaanite religion which posed a most serious threat to the Yahweh religion. "High places, pillars, Asherim," words which were only too well recognized by the ancient readers and needed no further description in the text. It is only the excavations of recent years that enable us to form some picture, not yet definitive but at least strongly probable, of the implications these words once had for religious practice. Previous excavations in Palestine had already shed some light on Canaanite temple sites and religious practices; but these discoveries have all been outdated by the finds at Hazor [27] which was excavated in four campaigns, 1955 — 1958. Hazor is mentioned in the Book of Joshua (11, 10), where it is called "the queen of all the kingdoms (of Canaan)." The excavations certainly substantiate this information. At its cultural

---

26. The Hebrew text refers to her also as simply '*ēm*, "mother." Since biblical terms for family relationship are often presented in simplified form (e.g. "brother" can also mean "cousin"), the word no doubt stands for "grandmother" here. Why Asa's mother was not guardian we cannot determine. Probably the energetic old lady refused to give up her position of honor and continued to function in the royal court.

27. The standard account of the excavations at Hazor is: *An account of the first Season of Excavation*, Jerusalem (1958). — Hazor II: *Second Excavating Time Report*, Jerusalem (1959). Both are the work of Y. Yadin and his collaborators. There is an account with extensive illustrations in Y. Yadin, *EncMikr* III (1958), 257-269. *Ibid.*: *The Rise and Fall of Hazor*, Arch 10 (1957), 83-92.

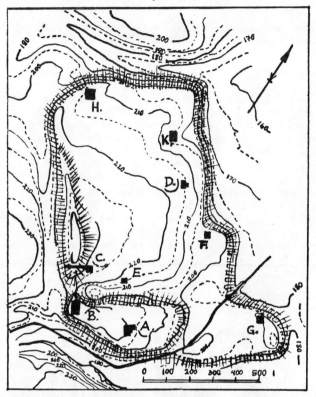

Excavations at Hazor, BA 19 (1956), 5; 22 (1951), 3.
A. Pillared court (Ahab); B. Citadel; C. Stone Pillar Temple; D. E. Buildings from various strata; F. "Temple of the Dead"; G. Fortifications; H. Temple Site; K. City Gate.

peak, the city must have numbered 40,000 inhabitants, certainly a cosmopolitan city of the greatest magnitude in those days. Joshua destroyed the city and Solomon had it rebuilt. Ahab and other kings refortified it, until, under the assault of the Assyrians, it sank forever into a heap of ruins. The excavators uncovered 21 cities from the earliest beginning around 2700 B.C. up to its complete destruction around 150 B.C. Here we are interested primarily in the finds which cast light upon the Canaanite religion and thus the battle between the prophets and the inroads of Cana-

anite cult. Accordingly, we must direct our attention to four areas
of excavation:

a) *The Stone Pillar-Sanctuary* (*massebôt*):

Excavation field C extends, towards the west, to the great earthen wall
with which, in the Middle Bronze Age (2000 – 1600 B.C.), the city
was surrounded. At the foot of this wall there was a sanctuary, whose
west wall was contiguous with the city walls. The entrance was at the
eastern side. Entering here, the devotee was treated to an astonishing vista:
against the western wall stood the basalt statue of a god seated on a
throne, holding a goblet in his right hand. In itself, this would not be
so astonishing, since statues of divinities are to be expected in temples.
But to the left of this statue stood a series of five stone pillars, basalt,
rounded at the top, not unlike large gravestones such as we find in our
modern cemeteries. Only the middle pillar bore some symbolic signs,
chiseled into it, two open, extended, praying hands, and above them the

Stone pillar sanctuary in Hazor, *EncMikr* III, 267.

crescent moon and the solar disk. Beside the last pillar, a basalt lion was still keeping vigil. At the divinity's right hand were bowls and dishes, apparently for sacrificial purposes. This temple gives evidence of two strata of construction. In the more ancient stage, stone benches ran the length of the walls. All around the temple there were a series of what appear to be quarters for the attendant priests. In one of these a potter was at work. Witness to this is the well-preserved potter's wheel. Here too the cult objects were preserved. A very well-preserved cult mask was discovered, as well as a standard of which we shall have to speak more fully below. On the basis of these finds we can arrive at some idea of what we are to understand by the pillars (*massebôt*) in the text. The sun and moon and praying hands chiseled upon the basalt are obviously astral symbolism. The divinity to which they must be ascribed can be determined only from the finds in field H.

b) *The "Temple of the Dead" (Excavation Field F):*

This title is misleading, since there is no clear evidence that the temple was devoted to the cult of the dead; it is, however, quite certain that it was located above a subterranean necropolis with a labyrinth of chambers and passage ways.[28] In one of these burial chambers excavators discovered a treasure trove of 500 jars. Our attention is drawn primarily to the temple court, in the midst of which stood a basalt block, five tons in weight, as altar. On the northern side of the court there was an elevated area constructed of unhewn stone, apparently the "sacrificial high places" (*bāmah*) in the proper sense of the word. An incense stand was also discovered. The court was divided into a series of rooms, in which great stone jars and ceramic products of the finest Mycenean work were discovered, as well as a bronze axe and an incense spoon of alabaster in the form of a hand. A statue of a god seated on a throne, likewise of basalt, also made its appearance. This excavation cast new light on our knowledge of the "high places" (*bāmah*). The name "sacrificial high places" is certainly not restricted to mountains and hilltops. The "temple of the dead" is not situated on a high place; it is found in the lower city. Sacrificial high places thus refer to a heap of unhewn stone upon which the sacrificial gifts were deposited as an exposition throne.[29]

c) *The Great Temple (Excavation Field H):*

Like the other temples, this structure was also destroyed by Joshua when

---

28. Y. Yadin, *Further Light on Biblical Hazor,* BA 20 (1957), 41ff. More detailed account: *EncMikr* III, 265.
29. Y. Yadin, *Further Light on Biblical Hazor. Results of the II. Season,* 1956 BA 20 (1957), 44ff. – *Ibid.: The III. Season of Excavation at Hazor,* 1957, BA 21 (1958), 31ff. – *EncMikr* III, 269.

the Israelites took possession of the country. The rafters of the structure caught fire and, in their collapse, buried the entire array of cult objects under their ashes, so that the furnishings of the temple were preserved up to the time of excavation. Dating from the time of Joshua, we can recognize a succession of four distinct temples. The most ancient, erected on the virgin soil, belongs to the Middle Bronze Age (18th century B.C.). This was followed, at the beginning of the Late Bronze Age I, around 1600 B.C., by a second temple built on the same scale. In Late Bronze Age II, around 1400 B.C., this was followed by a more recent temple structure, which was restored around 1300 B.C. Without embarking upon a more thorough discussion of individual particulars, we can restrict our discussion to the two architectural types. The temple structure destroyed by Joshua we shall call Temple I — excavations establish a further subdivision between Ia and Ib —, and we shall refer to the two older temples (IIa and IIb) as simply Temple II.

Temple I we might also call the Solomonic temple. For this is the first occurrence in Palestine of the tripartite temple structure: an antechamber, holy place, and holy of holies, or sanctuary. The dimensions of this structure are proportionately small, 78 ft. in length and 53 ft. in width. The signs from the inner sanctuary are particularly conclusive. A toppled basalt pillar was discovered there, 4 ft. high and 1½ ft. square. On the front was engraved a solar symbol, a round disk with a cross in it. Beside it was discovered a basalt basin, almost 3 ft. in diameter, for the water which was used in the cult. Between the pillar and the basin lay two basalt blocks, which gave evidence of slight impressions on their upper surface. These might have been the libation altars upon which oil and wine were poured. At the entrance to the inner sanctuary, excavation laid bare the basalt statue of a throned god, with a goblet in his hand. For determining the type of Canaanite cult, there are four bronze statuettes which are particularly conclusive: a masculine divinity, a bull, and two feminine divinities. They are all constructed in such a manner that they could be raised on a wooden base.

The second room, the Holy, finally yielded the key as to what god this temple had been dedicated to. Among the debris, excavators discovered the remnants of a shattered basalt statue of a god. It is quite possible that, upon taking the city of Hazor, the Israelites shattered this idol. Two characteristic pieces of the statue had survived: the statue's breast, which was adorned with a solar disk marked with a cross, and the base of the statue, which represented a bull. This is the first time that excavation had discovered a Canaanite cult image, not perfectly preserved, but at least recognizable in its essential characteristics. The storm and sky god Baal-Hadad was conceived of as standing upon a bull, holding a thunderbolt and a sheaf of lightning in his hands.

The antechamber also yielded some archaeological surprises. At the entrance stood two pillars, which recall the pillars later erected by Solomon at the entrance to the temple of Jerusalem. Here, too, was discovered the "lion pit." This is not a reference to a cage for animals, but rather a deep trench in which an almost 6½ ft. long lion orthostat of basalt had been buried. Was this the work of the conquerors or the last of the devotees? At all events, this statue, together with an as yet undiscovered companion piece, was surely meant to function as guardian of the entrance into the inner sanctuary.

Temple II: this tripartite Temple I had been preceded by a much simpler structure, with a single principal chamber about the dimensions of the inner sanctuary. The temple house faced onto a court, in the midst of which had been erected a square "high place" (*bāmah*), which was surrounded by altars. A canal supplied the necessary water. A clay figure in the form of an animal liver attests to the practice of divination in this temple.[30]

If we now return to the preliminary thesis of our investigation, we shall understand it much better in terms of recent archaeological finds: "And they built for themselves high places, and pillars, and asherim . . ." (1 K 14, 23). Stone pillars with solar symbols, altars and "high places," statuettes of male and female divinities, particularly the figure of a bull — these are characteristic of the Canaanite religion not only prior to the Israelite penetration into Canaan, but also the same symbols by which the Yahweh religion is always severely threatened in eras of descendancy. The battle fought by the prophets was, primarily, a battle against the gods of Canaan. Corresponding to the shift and development in the area of religious practices concerned, new aspects keep coming to the fore. Jeroboam made it the characteristic sign of his reform to introduce the bull symbol into the national religion of his kingdom and thus brought the worship of the one God Yahweh, who suffered no other beside himself, dangerously close to the cult of the Canaanite storm, thunder, and sky god Baal.

Yahweh was still venerated, no longer as the invisible God who thrones above the Ark of the Covenant, but as the God who makes his way upon the bull. The Canaanization of the Yahweh

---

30. Y. Yadin, *The Fourth Season of Excavation at Hazor*, BA 22 (1959), 6ff.

faith was thus in full progress. It was only natural for this fundamental transformation in the divine image to lead to the rapid introduction of Canaanite cult into Israel. Sacrificial heights and stone monuments throughout the countryside, as described in Scripture, are a clear witness to this state of affairs.

During the time that the exalted lady Maacah was ruling for her son in his minority, it was not primarily the bull cult that was involved in Judah, but rather the cult of the great mother goddess Asherah, a cult, as we might well believe, which was very dear to the heart of the queen mother. The ancient Yahweh cult was, of course, still practiced, or, perhaps better, "tolerated"; the protection and sympathies of the highly placed queen mother, however, were directed to a quite different objective. After the two years' reign of Abijah, the queen mother (grandmother) ruled 15 years during the minority of her grandson Asa (911 — 896 — 2 Ch 15, 10). During this time she had ample opportunity to introduce her favorite religious ideas. Even in Jerusalem she erected an "abominable image of Asherah" (1 K 15, 13). "Abominable image" [31] is, naturally, the expression used by our historians, but for the queen mother it was an expression of deepest piety and devotion.

d) *The Goddess Asherah* [32]

Under this name, from the most ancient times, throughout the Syro-Palestinian area, a female divinity was widely venerated. Traces of this divinity are to be found in ancient names for persons. In the cuneiform letters from Tell el-Amarna, the residence of the heretical Pharaoh Ikhnaton, we find mention of an *'abdi-'ăsirta* or *'abdi-'ašrat*, that is, a servant of the goddess Asherah. The veneration of this goddess in Palestine is attested to by an ostracon from Taanach. The inscription was first read as *'uban 'aširat*, "finger of Asherah"; an expression which corresponds to the "finger of God" in the Bible (Ex 8, 15; 31, 18 etc.). Further investigation has established the reading "prophet (*nabî*) of Asherah." It was only

---

31. The Hebrew word *miphléset* occurs only in I K 15, 13 and 2 Ch 15, 16. Its meaning is uncertain. Kohler, LexVT 552 translates it "abominable cult-image, terrible image"; JerB, Rois 88 translates "canopy(?)."
32. For a fuller account of Asherah, cf. *EncMikr* I, 786-788, the source for the above account.

the great discoveries in Ugarit which made it possible to cover the skeleton of this hereditary name with flesh and blood. Today we know that Asherah was not some second-rank goddess, but that, in the Canaanite pantheon, she enjoyed a position of primary authority. Her full honorary title was *'atiratu-yammi,* "she who strides upon the sea"; accordingly, she was particularly venerated by Phoenician seafarers.[33] She was worshiped as consort and throne-consort of the supreme god El, father of god and men. She was thus the mother of gods and men, a dignity expressed by her title *qoniyyad ha'elim,* "creatrix of the gods." The gods are her sons. The myth numbers some 70 of them. By reason of her primary position in the Canaanite pantheon she is called simply "mistress" or "the goddess" (*'elat*), just as El is the masculine god *par excellence.* The residence of El was located "at the source of the two rivers," [34] "in the midst of the great deep." This led to the obvious extension of the title to El's female consort, "she who strides upon the sea."

In the text discovered in Ugarit, Asherah plays a two-fold role. She is mother and mortal enemy to her children at one and the same time, giving life and destroying life. Her male consort El accordingly chased her into the desert wilderness, where she gave birth to terrible monsters, who have names like "devourer" and "annihilator." These monsters had horns like oxen and humps like buffalo and enjoyed mysterious powers. In the course of a hunt, the young god Baal comes upon them. He is seized with a desire to destroy them. A broken section of a clay tablet has destroyed the details of their combat. Baal, at all events, is overcome: "Thus Baal fell like an ox, and Haddu collapsed like a bull." [35]

On the other hand, it is once again this same Asherah who visits El in his palace in order to prevail upon her royal consort to supply a palace for the young Baal. Upon her intercession, a temple palace is actually

---

33. Evidence is furnished by the excavations in Naharijah, along the coast some 12 mi N of Haifa. M. Dothan, *The Excavations at Naharijah,* IEJ 5 (1955), 126-127; 6 (1956), 14-25. A sacrificial high-place (*bāmah*) was unearthed, where "Asherah of the sea" had been worshipped.

34. There are cosmological concepts behind this, just as in the Babylonian creation epic *Enuma elish* (I, 52ff.). There were two abysses functioning as primordial principles: the salt water ocean as the personification of all hostile elements, encompassing the globe like a huge serpent, and the sweet water ocean under the earth, from which the waters of life spring up. El and Asherah thus belong to the most primordial gods. W. R. Farmer, *The Geography of Ezekiel's River of Life,* BA 19 (1956), 18. — R. Follet, *El in alveo duarum abyssorum,* VD 34 (1956), 280-289.

35. Albright, *RelIsr* 100.

built for Baal, of gold and silver. Upon the completion of the building, Baal gives a banquet for his brothers, the "seventy sons of Asherah," for eight days.[36]

Asherah thus belongs to the type of the great mother divinities, both giving and destroying life. In Canaanite myth, she has a corresponding figure in the younger god Astarte, consort and beloved of Baal, as well as her sister Anat.[37] The three goddesses are so similar that their individual traits, over the course of history, have merged into a single figure, the great mother goddess. According to the sacrificial text from Ugarit, cattle were offered to her in sacrifice; she also had a slave of her own, with the epithet qadeš, "the consecrated one," who is also called "fisher of Asherah." There is also mention of a handmaiden of Asherah.[38]

For the cult of Asherah rejected in the Bible, one cult object was so characteristic that it was simply called ašerah. This was a common expression in ancient times. Everyone knew what it meant. For us, unfortunately, this is no longer the case; we are forced to conjecture. At all events, we are dealing with a wooden cult object which could be felled and burned like a tree, and which was erected on the high places beside the incense altars (hammanîm) and stone pillars (massebôt). Babylonian counterparts suggest wooden emblems for Canaan as well.[39] Other scholars think in terms of an "asherah tree," planted beside the high altar as a sign of fertility; hence the prohibition: "You shall not plant any tree as an Asherah beside the altar of the Lord your God" (Dt 16, 21).

What is to be understood by the abominable image of the Asherah which the queen mother had set up is not easy to say. Jerome, in the Vulgate translation, already introduced a whole explanatory sentence for the one Hebrew word miphléset: "Ne esset princeps in sacris Priapi et in luco ejus quem consecraverat" (1 K 15, 13). He explained the unknown Asherah cult in terms of the Priapus cult practiced in the Propontis during his time. Priapus was venerated as the god of masculine sexual power. In his honor they erected wooden statues, rough finished and painted

---

36. *Ibid.*, 103.
37. Cf. Vol. I, p. 181ff.
38. *EncMikr* I, 787.
39. Albright, *RelIsr* 93.

red.[40] While this interpretation is not essentially alien to the Canaanite religion, it could hardly be the correct interpretation of *miphléset*. The discovery at Hazor [41] would suggest rather a sort of standard. The excavated Canaanite temples do, of course, date back to the pre-Israelite era, but, by reason of the persistence of cultic phenomena, knowledge acquired in these discoveries can

Standard of the Serpent Goddess: Bronze, silvered; 13th cent. before Christ: found in Hazor, BA 20 (1957), 43.

40. These were basically rough blocks of wood carved with defective instruments (sickel, knife, hatchet) in such a way that only the head and the phallus area were finished, while the other parts of the body were left undeveloped. The country figurines were daubed with red lead, perhaps symbolic of blood. As the ugly son of Dionysus and Aphrodite, Priapus belongs to the realm of primitive, uncouth fertility magic. Paulys, *Realencyclopädie der Classischen Altertumswissenschaft*, XXII, 2 (1954), 1914-42.

41. Y. Yadin, *Further Light on Biblical Hazor*, BA 20 (1957), 43, Fig. 8.

also be applied to Israelite times. In the stone pillar temple excavation has yielded a squared standard of bronze, pointed on the bottom, and adorned with silver figures; in the middle, roughly stylized, the face of a goddess, with two wounded serpents to the right and to the left, the sickel of the moon over her head together with a third stylized serpent. The pointed end apparently served to fix the shaft in a wooden pike. The goddess in question was obviously a fertility deity, as the serpent and lunar sickel would seem to testify. Such standards were borne in procession in honor of the deity, and the rest of the time they were apparently erected in the sacred precinct. That the "abominable image of Asherah" was in this form is, of course, only a speculation.

The extent to which the Asherah cult figured in daily living can be well understood by the vast quantity of small Asherah-Astarte figurines in clay which are unearthed at almost every Palestinian excavation. There must have been some process of mass production, since excavation has yielded models which were apparently the basis of a wide-scale multiplication and distribution. The figurines display a naked, standing female figure, hands crossed over her breast.[42] Were these figurines meant to serve as fertility charms, as amulets for expectant mothers, a source of help and comfort during labor? At all events, the reference to the great mother goddess is inescapable.

The conclusion that all this was a reference to fertility symbolism is unavoidable in terms of the simple statement: "There were also male cult prostitutes (consecrated devotees) in the land" (1 K 14, 24). This was a very particular consecration and sanctification. The goddess Asherah herself bears the honorary epithet "holiness" (qudšu). In like manner, those who were completely dedicated to the service of "her holiness" were also called "sanctified" ("consecrated devotees") (qadeš). What was the "holiness"

---

42. Pritchard, ArchOT (1958), 122ff. Catalogues some 300 pieces from the most recent investigations. Illustrations.
43. Albright, RelIsr, 93 — I. E. S. Edwards, A Relief of Qudshu-Astarte-Anath in the Westminster College Collection, JNES 14 (1955), 49-51. Nude goddess standing upon a lion with a lotus blossom in her right hand and a serpent in her left. Inscription: the name Qudshu.

involved here? Since Asherah was mother goddess and giver of life, her cult was involved with the sacred mystery of life, life in its totality, as it is expressed in the blossom and decline of nature, in the fertility of herds and flocks, in the blessing of children. The rhythm of life was felt to be accomplished and promoted by the constantly repeated union of the divine pairs.

It is not without reason that Asherah's throne consort El is called "the bull" [44] and the young Baal bears the epithet Aliyan, the "young bull." [45] In cult it was the divine act of impregnation, begetter of all life, that was performed as a sort of sympathetic magic.[46]

4) REFORMS OF KING ASA BEN-ABIJAH

It must remain the sad accomplishment of the queen mother Maacah, that, during her regency (912/11 — 897) she officially opened the door to the cult of the mother goddess Asherah. It is, in human terms, certainly quite understandable that the sensuous and intoxicating cult of the great mother should arouse much greater sympathy than the austere Yahweh faith, with its lack of tangible image and its hard moral imperatives. In Jerusalem itself, she erected "an abominable image of the great mother goddess who strides upon the sea." Her example was followed throughout the land. The officially proscribed Canaanite cult of the high places broke out everywhere in the land. It is one of

---

44. In the Danel Epic from Ugarit, the hero prays for a son:
   "Will you not bless him, El, Bull, my Father?
   make him happy, O Creator of creatures?
   Then will there be a son in his house,
   an offspring within the palace."   Pritchard, ArchOT 120.

45. H. Cazelles, VT 10 (1950), 231. *'aleyn* derived not from the root *l'y* "to be strong," but rather *l'h* "young bull" (cf. Accadian *littu* "cow," Biblical Leah, "young cow, heifer" used as a person's name). — Fully mature life is symbolized by the God Mot, the god of the ripe grain and of the underworld. The name is not to be derived from *mawet* "death," but from the root *mth* "to be fully grown" (*mētîm* — "men"). T. Worden, *The Literary Influence of the Ugaritic Fertility Myth on the OT*, VT 3 (1953), 273-297.

46. *Sex, Fertility and Religion,* in Pritchard, ArchOT 124.

the paradoxes of history that in the midst of this decaying Yahweh faith the young King Asa should have grown up to be a reformer of the Yahweh religion. We are reminded of the prophet Samuel, who, despite the sorry abuses in the sanctuary at Shiloh, which cried to heaven for vengeance, became the champion and hero of the pure Yahweh faith.

When, in the year 897, after 15 years of his mother's regency, the young Asa [47] came into power (2 Ch 15, 10), he found himself in a most unenviable situation. What was his position to be against the great lady who had protected his crown? The prophet Azariah ben-Obed [48] became his tireless advisor, the very conscience of the young ruler (2 Ch 15, 1, 8). In trenchant words he unmasked the unholy state of affairs. Where was Yahweh? Certainly still in his temple. But who went to see him there? The land had grown pagan. Unless some attempt was made to stem the inroads of Canaanitism, Yahweh must surely withdraw from his people. "The Lord is with you, while you are with him. If you seek him, he will be found by you, but if you forsake him, he will forsake you" (2 Ch 15, 2ff.).

The penitential preaching of the prophet would not, apparently, have been sufficient of itself to accomplish this reform activity to any great extent. Asa first of all had to establish his position as king. The involuntary occasion for this work was afforded by the invasion of Zerah the Ethiopian (2 Ch 14, 8-14). Was this a new predatory campaign from Egypt, like the invasions under Pharaoh Shishak? Scholars have thought in terms of Shishak's son Osorkon I. But thus far it has been impossible to establish the identity of the two names Zerah and Osorkon. Accordingly, it could hardly be a pharaonic campaign against Palestine.[49] Is Zerah to be identified as a subordinate Nubian prince who was established in Gerar [50] after Sheshonk's campaigns? It

---

47. The name is not clearly explainable. Perhaps Aramaic "doctor" or Arabic "patience, mercy." *EncMikr* I, 467.
48. *'azar-yahu* "Yahweh has helped"; Obed is an abbreviated form for Obed-yah, "servant of Yahweh."
49. P. Montet, *L'Egypte et la Bible*, (1959), 44.
50. Gerar has till now been identified with Tell-Gemmeh, some 7 mi S of Gaza (DBS III, 353). The site is an imposing ruin mound, over-

is true that the land of Cush, modern Nubia (Ethiopia), played a significant role in late Egyptian history. But this possibility is less favorable, since the name Cush and Cushite (Ethiopian) was never restricted to the southern Nile country. According to Habakkuk (3, 7) Cushites were encamped in the neighborhood of Midian, on the Arabian peninsula. Egyptian sources speak of Cushite tribes established as nomads from the coast of the Red Sea as far as Palestine. With the collapse of the Solomonic empire, southern Palestine presented an open frontier. The energetic Beduin chieftains must have seen this as a welcome invitation to penetrate into the unprotected territory and establish themselves. It appears that Zerah established his position in Gerar, from which point he made regular raids into the Judaean territory. The weakness of the Jerusalem government, under the control of a woman, was not calculated to win any particular respect from him. The identification of the inroads, not as an Egyptian campaign, but rather as the inroads of south Arabian Beduins, is further confirmed by the name of the invader, Zerah, that is, "splendor, shining light," which is best derived from south Arabia.[51] Zerah and his hordes made their way as far as the fortress of Mareshah. The young king Asa himself took the field at the head of the Judaean army,[52] defeated the Cushite in the valley

looking the Wadi Gaza. It was partially excavated in the adventurous dig by Pythian-Adams in 1922. Because of a band of salt smugglers there was trouble with the police. This incident only demonstrates what an important commercial position the city occupied along the road from Egypt and the central part of the Southern country. C. C. McCrown: *The Ladder of Progress in Palestine*, 1943, 120-123. — The military activities described above would, however, seem to suggest a more inland position for Gerar. The Mosaic Map and the *Onomasticon* of Eusebius (60, 3) would suggest *tell eš-šeri'ah*, 13 mi SE of Gaza, which overlooks the Wadi of that same name. Y. Aharoni, IEJ 6 (1956), 26ff. identifies Gerar with *tell abu hurierah*, 4 mi away from *tell eš-šeri'ah*. Simons, GTT #369.

51. *EncMikr* II, 942: Zerah.
52. The numbers in Chronicles are generally wrongly interpreted, resulting in impossible figures such as 300 "thousand" men from Judah or 280 "thousand" men from Benjamin. The Cushite would thus have had an army of a million, and 300 chariots. But if we translate

north of Mareshah, pursued him as far as Gerar, and returned home with rich spoils in camels and sheep. His military success was interpreted as a victory from Yahweh: "They were broken before the Lord and his army" (2 Ch 14, 13).

Under the impetus of this victory, Asa was able to proceed to his reform. First of all, he removed his (grand-) mother from her position as "exalted lady" (g^ebirah). The "abominable image of Asherah" he had cut down and burned in the Kidron Valley. The sacrificial high places in the country were destroyed, the "consecrated" cult prostitutes, male and female, were banished. In the 3rd month of the 15th year, the desecrated altar of Yahweh was reconsecrated, libations and votive offerings were brought into the temple and, accompanied by the most solemn sacrifices such as once took place on Sinai, the covenant with Yahweh was renewed (1 K 15, 9-15; 2 Ch 15, 1-18). The kingdom of Judah had once again found its way back to its true mission in the world. It could exist only in terms of the covenant; otherwise it must collapse. This religious reform was followed by a reform in domestic politics. The fortress construction received new attention and the army was reorganized. Economic welfare and peace soon followed. "He had no war in those years, for the Lord gave him peace" (2 Ch 14, 6).

5) HANANI CRITICIZES THE ARAMAEAN POLICY

After ten years of peace, the war (described above) broke out along the open northern boundaries of Judah. King Asa placed his confidence in the high art of diplomacy, and attempted to purchase the help of the Aramaeans, whereupon they immediately attacked the northern districts of the Kingdom of Israel and forced Baasha to give up the fortification of Ramah. This policy, however, did not meet with approval in the prophetic circles. It seemed a

---

'eleph in its older meaning of "clan levy," and not in the later meaning of "thousand," the narrative takes on historically possible dimensions. Such a levy or company consisted of about ten men. Thus Judah supplied a force of 3000 and Benjamin 2800. The number of the Cushite soldiers is, however, corrupt. For a fuller treatment cf. Vol. III, 264ff.

perfectly reasonable policy to dissipate the enemy's strength by forcing a war on two fronts. But the "seer" (rô'eh) Hanani was courageous enough to reproach the victorious king for having failed in his faith. Had not his victory over the Ethiopian hordes been won in the name of Yahweh? And surely now the same Yahweh of hosts would also free him from the threat of Baasha's invasion. What point was there in buying the help of a pagan king, and this with the treasures of the temple of Yahweh? The confrontation was more than the king could bear. He became angry and had the seer cast into prison and put into the torture chamber (2 Ch 16, 10).[53] The fate of the great Jeremiah thus has a sad precedent, as, for the first time, we see the spectacle of conflict between king and prophet lurking ominously on the horizon of a gloomy history. Human reason and blind obedience to the direction of Yahweh stand at cross purposes.

Seen as a whole, the reign of King Asa was a success, both in politics and in religion. According to the judgment of the theologian of history, he approaches the image of his forebear David: "Asa did what was good and right in the eyes of the Lord his God" (2 Ch 14, 1). One point remains, however, to qualify this general encomium: he did not completely root out the cult of the high places, since he left them standing in the country (2 Ch 15, 17).

This brings us to the problem of unity of cult in ancient Israel. There is no one easy line of solution. But one thing is certain: unity of cult is not the final product of the late royal era; it dates back to Mosaic ideals. It is possible to distinguish three phases of development.[54] Already upon the entrance into the Promised Land, the practice of a single, if not geographically determined, cult site was established. With the destruction of Shiloh, Israel lost her cult center. From that time, we note the

---

53. *Bet-hammahpeket,* literally, "house of the beam," where prisoners were kept in stocks. Köhler, LexVT 500.
54. B. Uffenheimer, *On the Question of Centralisation of Worship in Ancient Israel,* Tarb 28 (1959), 138-153. Accordingly the description of cult sites in Deuteronomy is to be dated shortly after the desert period.

plurality of cult sites. The sacrificial high places (*bamôt*) were regarded as legitimate sacrificial sites. With the building of the temple in Jerusalem, the situation changes. Now there is a well defined effort to carry out the laws of an earlier period in their fullest measure. Asa's reform is only one milestone along the long road that leads to the unqualified cult unity of Jerusalem. He succeeded in doing away with the pagan high places, but not with the high places dedicated to the Yahweh cult.

Asa's last years were darkened by a disease which he suffered in his feet. But in this sickness he did not turn to God for help, as Jeroboam had done when his son was sick; he turned to the doctors for help, and for this he is reproached by the Chronist (2 Ch 16, 12).[55]

Asa left to his son Jehoshaphat a kingdom well secured both within and without. The boundaries were protected by a ring of fortresses, and the few open positions along the northern frontier were closed. Within, the inroads of paganism had been turned aside, and the covenant with Yahweh had been renewed. Thus it seemed that the Davidic heritage in the Southern Kingdom was definitely established.

The Northern Kingdom of Israel, on the other hand, presents the picture of a mutilated body, bleeding from many wounds. The territory northeast of Lake Gennesaret, Golan and Baashan, had been completely lost, Upper Galilee was under Aramaean occupation, and along the coastal plain the Philistines were once again shaking off the yoke of Israel. The royal dynasty, in all this up and down of historical change, did not afford a constant point or support; succession to the throne itself was swept along into the self-destruction of power politics. The short-lived dynasty of Jeroboam had been cruelly rooted out already in its second member. The dynasty of Baasha was destined for no better fate.

Elah [56] the son of Baasha, was murdered on the occasion of

---

55. The Chronist has harmonized the picture of Asa. W. Rudolph, *Der Aufbau der Asa-Geschichte* (*2 Ch 14-16*), VT 2 (1952), 367-371.

56. *'elah* "oak": names of trees frequently used for personal names. Cf. *tamar* "pine." *EncMikr* I, 297. Elah became king in the 26th year of Asa and died in his 27th year. This is at most a year and a half

a palace revolt in Tirzah (885), in the course of a drinking bout, by Zimri,[57] captain of a chariot division (1 K 16, 8ff.). When the troops, who were encamped in siege of the Philistine city of Gibbethon, heard this news, they acclaimed the commander of the army, Omri, as king (16, 16). Omri broke off the siege and made his way towards Tirzah, in order to attack his rival. Since Zimri had no other escape, he set fire to his own palace and perished in the flames. But Omri had not yet won the day. One faction of the people acclaimed a certain Tibni ben-Ginath (885/4 — 881) king. The already weakened Northern Kingdom was thus involved in a war of succession. It was only after the natural death of Tibni, a point which receives particular stress, that Omri succeeded in reuniting Israel [58] and leading it to new prosperity (881/80).

---

by our reckoning, and perhaps as little as a half year (886/5). *EncMikr* I, 296.

57. The full form *zimri-yahu* has been discovered on a seal. D. Diringer, *Le iscrizioni antico-ebraiche palestinesi,* Florence (1934), 43, 211. The name is interpreted on the basis of similarities with Southern Arabic as "my shield" or "my judge." Cf. the west-semitic names Zimri-abum, Zimriperah ("My shield — judge — is the father — the moon god).

58. Omri became sole ruler in the 31st year of Asa (881/80); the total sum of 12 years for his reign includes the 5 years in which he shared the throne with Tibni (I K 16, 23).

CHAPTER II

FRIENDLY RELATIONS BETWEEN
ISRAEL AND JUDAH (880 – 841)

THE PROPHET ELIJAH

EVEN though the Book of Kings devotes only seven verses to the reign of Omri (1 K 16, 21-28), it was he who redirected the course of internal and external politics. In the Assyrian sources there is frequent mention of Bit-Humri, the house of Omri, in reference to the kingdom of Israel. The constant state of war with the brother kingdom of Judah was quickly changed into a treaty of friendship, which was then sealed by the intermarriage of royal offspring. Omri's main accomplishment was the construction of a new capital sity, Samaria, a move which greatly strengthened the internal resources of his kingdom, since Samaria remained the capital until the destruction of the Northern Kingdom. The rise of Omri thus represents an important turn in the history of the kingdoms of Israel and Judah.[1]

---

1. Under the influence of the theocratic interpretation of history, Omri's history is kept entirely in the background. There is no evaluation of his significance in world history. C. F. Whitley, *The Deuteronomic Presentation of the House of Omri*, VT 2 (1952), 137-152.

1) IN QUEST OF A NEW CAPITAL

By the establishment of Jerusalem as his capital city, David had created a firm nucleus of power for his kingdom. Jerusalem was royal property and belonged to none of the Twelve tribes. For a kingship which was to be exercised over all the tribes, this was no mean advantage. In bringing the Ark of the Covenant to Jerusalem, David had made his capital city the religious focus of the people of the covenant. The division of the kingdom and the defection of the northern tribes changed this situation. Jerusalem remained the capital of the Southern Kingdom, but it was no longer situated in the protection of the interior; suddenly it became a frontier city for the Southern Kingdom. A transfer of the official government to Hebron, where David had been anointed king over Judah, would have been quite understandable in terms of political expediency. But despite the dangers inherent in their unprotected position, the kings of Judah retained Jerusalem as their capital city, up to the end of the Southern Kingdom.

a) *Shechem — Penuel — Tirzah*

The development of the Northern Kingdom was quite different. Jeroboam first chose Shechem [2] for his capital. He wished to present the figure, not so much of a revolutionary, as rather the restorer of the old order. Since the time that Joshua, after the entrance into the Promised Land, had renewed the covenant of Yahweh at Shechem, between the two mountains of Ebal and Gerizim, Shechem remained the "navel of the Land" (Jg 9, 37),[3] the focal point of the people of the Twelve tribes. Its favorable location along the principal routes made Shechem, by its very nature, the "uncrowned queen of the land."

---

2. The name means "two shoulders," a reference to the position between the two mountains Ebal and Gerizim. In the Egyptian sources it is called Sakmani. There is a good account of Shechem, history and archaeology, in BA 20 (1957), 2-32: a. extra-Biblical sources, b. Biblical sources, c. archaeology.
3. "Navel of the Land," BA 20 (1957), 2. — Ezekiel applies the description to Jerusalem. The hosts of God are mustering for a mighty confrontation around Zion, the navel and focal point of the world (Ez 38, 12).

On the occasion of the disputed popular assembly at Shechem, the city was still in its first blossom. Excavations have shown that it was set torch to, shortly afterwards, and partially destroyed, probably by Aramaean hordes. At all events, Jeroboam had to rebuild Shechem (1 K 12, 25). The city gate, towers, and guardposts were in ruins. Jeroboam cleared away the debris, and rebuilt the walls and gates.[4]

Under the pressure of the predatory campaign from Egypt, Jeroboam withdrew into Transjordania, and transferred his government to Penuel (1 K 12, 25),[5] a site consecrated by the patriarchal history. But such a remotely situated capital was hardly a happy choice. After the political situation had quieted, Jeroboam did not return to Shechem, which appeared to be too open to attack; he chose in its stead the much less accessible city of Tirzah for his residence (1 K 14, 17), some 10 km northeast of Shechem. Tirzah had been excavated, in several sessions, since the second world war.[6] The most ancient strata dates back to the Chalcolithic. In the Bronze Age, the city attained its first great blossom. Towards the end of the Late Bronze Age, it was destroyed by the inroads of the Israelites. The new Israelite houses are, in comparison to the well-constructed Canaanite dwellings, very poor and primitive. When the city was raised to the dignity of capital, a rage of building activity must have ensued. The fortifications were strengthened and a citadel and royal quarters were erected in the city. In the valley floor, at the foot of the city hill, there are abundant springs, which, from the most ancient times, have been an invitation to settlement.

The valley opens towards the Jordan and thus assures a rapid line of communication towards the east and north. Traffic with the west proved difficult because of the steep ascent of the mountain terrain. Tirzah thus

---

4. In Shechem, modern village of *tell-balata,* there have been three expeditions: 1913/14 and 1926/27 under the direction of Prof. Sellin and since 1957 under the American Drew-McCormick Expedition. BA 20 (1957), 20-32. Cf. Simons, GTT #578.

5. Probably *tulul ed-dahab* ("gold hill") on the northern bank of the Jabbok, not far from the border of the Jordan plain. Simons, GTT, #415.

6. Under the direction of R. de Vaux, École Biblique, Jerusalem. Current excavation reports in RB, since 1947. Cf. also R. de Vaux, *The Excavations at Tell el-Farah and the Site of the ancient Tirzah,* PEQ 88 (1956), 125-140. The identification with Tirzah is thus practically certain. An uncompleted building there seems to point to the transfer of the residence to Samaria. Tirzah's decline corresponds with the rise of Samaria. Cl. Schedl, *Tirzah, die alte Hauptstadt Israels,* BibLit 24 (1956/57), 168-172.

afforded a position of security in times of crisis, but as a capital city it was not a very successful choice.

b) *The Founding of Samaria*

After Omri had been acclaimed king in the camp at Gibbethon (885), he immediately set out for Tirzah, in a series of forced marches, in order to attack his rival Zimri. Since Zimri saw no possible escape, he set torch to his own palace and perished in the flames (1 K 16, 17). Omri reigned only six years from Tirzah (1 K 16, 23). For his far-reaching plans, the city of Tirzah was not well situated. Around the year 880 he set about searching for a new capital. "He bought the hill of *šômerôn* from *šemer* (Shemer) for two *kikkar* of silver and he fortified the hill and called the name of the city which he built *šômerôn,* after the name of the owner of the hill" (1 K 16, 24).[7] Samaria presents a much more favorable position than the previous capital cities of Shechem, Penuel, and Tirzah. Surrounded by a fertile plain, the city hill rises in the middle, its foot forming a crossroads for the trade route from south to north, and east to west. From the top of the hill, looking to the west, the Mediterranean Sea is visible. This fact can be symbolically interpreted. Omri had withdrawn the capital city of Israel from the isolation of the country's interior and chosen a location which nature itself had marked for dominion. As excavation has shown, Omri did not purchase an unsettled or empty hill. There was already a small village settlement on the location, which Omri systematically rebuilt into a royal city. This city, up to the time of its destruction by the Assyrians and its reconstruction in Samaritan, Hellenistic, and Roman eras, had experienced a long and rich history. It is

---

7. *šômerôn*: the Hebrew form can hardly be derived from *šemer*. The interpretation of the name, as it often happens, is a popular rather than a scientific reconstruction. Accadian: *Samarina,* Aramaic: *Samerain.* Simons, GTT #882. The Hebrew interpretation is based on the concept of "outpost, lookout," which fits the location well enough. It is actually possible to overlook a considerable portion of the surrounding country from this point of vantage (*samar* — "overlook, guard").

important to give at least some outline of the history of the building activity of the Israelite kings, as witnessed to by the excavated
ruins, and interpreted in the light of the Bible text.

In period I, the top of the hill, a flat surface of some 540 x 270 square
ft. was surrounded by a wall 5 ft. thick.[8] On the western side there was
a royal palace, and on the north side the so-called ivory house,[9] and a
great court to the south. This relatively small reconstructed area forms
the royal city or acropolis. The residential area expanded towards the
northeast, similar to the growth of Jerusalem under David and Solomon.

In period II, the city heights were fortified by casemates in the north,
west, and southwest. These were built partially of the older city walls.
The system of casemates consists of two parallel walls, joined together
by supplementary walls, resulting in a series of chambers. The distance
between the parallel walls was 23 ft. The outer walls were over 5 ft.
thick, while the inner wall measured almost 4 ft.

In period III, the royal palace and the ivory house were completely
rebuilt, apparently after a catastrophic destruction. Periods IV and V
show evidence of rebuilding and constant improvement. A thick stratum
of charred remnants and debris, in which the ivory tablets were discovered,
proves that the city was thoroughly and violently destroyed.

Now to relate this mute testimony of the excavation to the living account of the Books of the Kings. After some oscillation in the dating,
it is possible, today, with reasonable accuracy, to assign period I as the
city of Omri and Ahab. Omri had acquired the location and begun
the construction. The six years of his reign were not sufficient time to
complete the work. Thus it was his son and successor Ahab who, like
a second Solomon, functioned as the great building master. It is to him,
accordingly, that we must ascribe the construction of the city walls and
the palace. This first city was overrun and destroyed by the Aramaeans.
Jehu, upon his succession to power, undertook to rebuild the royal city.
He fortified it with the greatly strengthened casemate walls (period II).
Periods III – V, with their various rebuildings and constant improve-

---

8. On history and excavations, cf. G. E. Wright, *Samaria*, BA 22 (1959),
   62-78.

9. The name is based on the wall and furniture decorations which were
   ivory carved to represent various themes: cherubs, trees, drinking
   stags, etc. The style of the work would suggest indirect Egyptian
   influence, perhaps by way of Phoenicia. The art of palace building,
   as well as the style of decoration, made its way into Israel from
   Tyre. The artistic symbolism was also imported from Tyre. In
   Zengrili excavations have unearthed the model for the winter and
   summer house. R. O. Barnett, *Phoenicia and the Ivory Trade*, Arch
   9 (1956), 87-97. In Megiddo ivory was a royal monopoly.

ments, belong in the eighth century, in which, under Jeroboam II, Samaria experienced a new period of ascendancy, until it was eventually destroyed by the Assyrians.[10] Period I in Samaria corresponds to contemporary strata in Megiddo and Hazor, where excavation yielded such splendid capitals for stone pillars.[11] Such an expensive building activity, embracing the whole of the Northern Kingdom, was possible only as the result of a flourishing economy and a settled politics. The architects and stone masons came from Phoenicia. Lebanon furnished the precious cedar wood, just as it had in the days of Solomon.

c) Winter Residence in Jezreel

Side by side with Samaria, Jezreel [12] appears as the second capital city of the Northern Kingdom. A. Alt represents the opinion that Jezreel was the capital city of the kingship which was founded on the strength of the Israelite tribes, whereas Samaria remained an independent Canaanite city state, which was united to the kingdom of Israel only by a personal union.[13] This position, at first examination, would appear to offer a good explanation for the existence of two capital cities; closer examination, however, shows that it is too artificial. The Northern Kingdom was not a double monarchy, consisting of Israel and Canaan. Jezreel was only the winter residence to which the royal family retired during the cold season.

The name of the city Jezreel is to be found in no ancient Egyptian or Accadian source, and this would argue for a new Israelite establishment.

---

10. Stratification according to G. E. Wright, BA 22 (1959), 77.
    from 3000: village settlement
    870-842: Period I, Omri and Ahab
    842-810: Period II, Jehu
    810-750: Period III, Jeroboam II
    750-735: Period IV, first Assyrian destruction.
    735-721: Period V, second Assyrian destruction.
    NB.: Our system of chronology would have to change some of these dates.
11. K. Galling, Bibl. Reallexicon, 442 and A. Parrot, Samaria, die Hauptstadt des Reiches Israel, (1957), 47, assign Per. I to Omri and Per. II to Ahab, a position that can hardly be defended in view of Wright's arguments.
12. yizre'ēl "May the God El give seed (zera'), i.e. fertility." A prayer for the blessing of children and agricultural fertility. Cf. Jer 31, 27. Similar name forms abound in the pagan world of the time. Accadian: zera-šubši "May he (God) awaken seed!" Adad-lu-zerum "May the God Hadad be for him (give him) seed." EncMikr III, 626.
13. Alt, Kleine Schriften III, 258-302.

According to Joshua 19, 18, some clans of the tribe of Issachar had established themselves in the neighborhood of the Canaanite city of Shunem, where they founded the new settlement of Jezreel. Since it was situated in the midst of a fertile country,[14] on one of the most important crossroads in Palestine, it quickly developed into a city of great prominence. In Saul's day, it was already one of the most important cities of the kingdom (2 S 2, 9). It was Jezreel which witnessed the decisive battle in the Philistine war, on the mountain of Gilboa (1 S 29, 11; 2 S 4, 4). Under Solomon, Jezreel was the capital of the fifth administrative district (1 K 4, 12). The city thus had a long and lively history behind it when Ahab began the construction of his winter residence. The site had not yet been excavated, since the Arabic village Zerin is located directly above the ancient ruins. Ostraca finds, however, confirm the fact that the site was settled from the Iron Age down to the present time.[15] On the evidence of Biblical texts, it appears that Jezreel was a walled city, with towers and royal palaces.

In the administration of his kingdom, Ahab followed the patterns set by Solomon. The kingdom was already divided into twelve districts (*medînôt*). With the collapse of the Solomonic kingdom, this system obviously must have suffered. Ahab re-established it and set up a system of administrators or prefects. In the event of war, these officials were to undertake the military leadership of their levy (cf. 1 K 20, 14-19). This system effectively curtailed the influence of the great family heads (*sheikhs*), a fact which greatly contributed to popular unrest and, apparently, hastened the collapse of the whole system.

2) TREATY WITH TYRE

The friendly relationship which David had established with Tyre [16] Omri now renewed by the marriage of his son Ahab with

---

14. In Scripture: Plain of Jezreel (*yizre'el*); today simply *'Emek*, plateau. In antiquity it was a rich producer of grain, but in the Arab period it was a malaria infested swampland; territory occupied by the raids of the tribe of Ibn 'Amr; acquired by Qeren Qayemet and systematically cultivated by the Israelite pioneers; today a rich paradise once again. Cf. N. Tzori, *An Ancient Site in the Emek*, PEQ 89 (1957), 82-96.

15. *EncMikr* III, 627; Simons, GTT #901.

16. Tyre, the city on the rock island (*sôr*), had taken Sidon's place as

Jezebel, the daughter of the Tyrian King Ethbaal.[17] The Phoenicians were obviously concerned only with the economic and commercial advantages such a treaty could guarantee. For their commercial enterprises, peaceful passage through the Israelite territory was an absolute necessity, in order to have ready access to the markets of inner Asia. Israel herself, from the time of Solomon, had become a great commercial center for the whole of Asia Minor. Omri and Ethbaal continue this tradition. There were no military considerations involved in their alliance; neither during the extensive Aramaean wars which followed, nor in the campaign against Ashur do we find any Tyrian contingents. The Phoenicians had little interest in the politics of the Ancient Near East. They were primarily concerned with the sea and their commerce with western nations. It was there that they established their most lasting achievement, a mighty thalassocracy. In this undertaking, they were concerned primarily with maintaining a peaceful relationship with the hinterland. Ethbaal, to judge from the accounts of Menander of Ephesus,[18] must have been a very enterprising ruler. Like Omri, he had seized power by force. As high priest of the goddess Astarte, he had seized possession of the throne and extended the sphere of Tyrian domination along the coast northward beyond Gebal. As the northernmost outpost of his power, he established the city of Auzia. He also sent colonists across the sea into Lybia.[19]

The growth from a Tyrian city state into a Mediterranean world empire also seems to have been accompanied by religious

---

mistress of the Phoenician coastal cities. Despite this fact, people continued to refer to the "country of the Sidonians" (1 K 17, 9) when they spoke of the Phoenicians.

---

17. In LXX Jethebaal, according to Menander Ithobalos, Phoenician Ittoba'al. The meaning is probably not "Baal is with him," but rather "Baal really exists." A militant confession of faith which fits the priest of Astarte very well. *EncMikr* I, 749, 790.
18. Menander's work is only partially preserved in Flavius Josephus, Ant. VIII, 312.
19. *EncMikr* I, 791.

The God Hadad, hurling a lightning-bolt, standing on a bull. Found in Arslan-Tash, *EncMikr* II, 788.

upheaval.[20] The Canaanite agricultural religion was no longer equal to the demands of universal empire. King Hiram I [21] was apparently the man responsible for introducing the new sun religion. The

20. J. Morgenstern, *The King-God of the Western Semites and the Meaning of Epiphanes*, VT 10 (1960), 139-197 presents many arguments that are stimulating, some that are fantastic.

vegetation cycle of blossoming and dying nature was replaced by the cycle of the rising and setting sun. The earlier storm god Hadad became the sun and sky god Baal-Shamem, and in the place of the youthful god Tamuz-Adon we find the newer god Melkart. Asherah, the former throne consort of Hadad, is now venerated side by side with the newer god Melkart. Under this new configuration, the Tyrian religion set out to acquire a position for itself. The so-called Melkart-stele [22] bears witness to the spread of this cult among the Aramaeans as far as Northern Syria. In Israel, Queen Jezebel introduced the new cult and pressed for a decisive confrontation with the Yahweh cult. The name Melkart means "king of the city." But what city? An earlier opinion held that Melkart had been first the city god of Tyre, from which position he gradually expanded his territory. Since the discoveries at Ugarit, however, it is clear that the "city" involved is the underworld.[23] The Canaanite gods were not local gods, but rather cosmic divinities, and Melkart is thus "king of the underworld." In the solar system he symbolizes the dying, setting sun, whereas Baal-Shamem incorporates the youthful, rising sun. Their relationship is that of father and son. The younger divinity arises like the phoenix from the ashes of the elder, in a continual process of dying and return. Since this is a solar religion, the pillars of sunrise and sunset also have an important role to play. Every day Melkart makes his way into the underworld, passing between the two western pillars, in order to reappear next morning, as the newly born phoenix, radiating through the eastern pillars, which close again after his passage. This myth was imitated in the cult. The annual equinoxes became the festival of Melkart's waking. On this occasion the king personified the divinity. When the first rays of the rising sun fell between the two solar pillars of the temple,

21. J. Liver, *The Chronology of Tyre at the Beginning of the First Millennium B.C.*, IEJ 3 (1953), 113-120 (Hiram 979/78 — split of the Kingdom).

22. For fuller information, cf. above page 16.

23. R. Dussaud, *Melkart d'apres de recents travaux*, RHR 151 (1957), 1-21; W. F. Albright, *A Votive Stele erected by Ben-Hadad of Damascus to the God Melcarth*, BASOR 87 (1942), 23-29.

and shone upon the sacred precinct, where the king sat upon his divine throne, they surrounded him with divine radiance. He became the epiphanes, the apparition of god among his people. Granted that this representation of the Tyrian religion is open to question in individual details, it is, at all events, quite certain that, together with Tyre's political and economic influence, the new gods of the great sea power made their way into the countries of the allies.

The treaty with Tyre enabled Israel to ride the crest of Tyrian economy. Tyrian merchants, artisans, and artists thronged into the country. Together with them came Melkart and Asherah.[24] With all the means at her disposal, Queen Jezebel attempted to find a permanent place for the new religion. The alliance with Tyre is thus represented in two quite different lights. In terms of politics and economics, it was a stepping stone to an unheard of prosperity; but in the sphere of religion it led Israel to the edge of doom. The real issues involved in this era are strikingly expressed by the names of the two principal figures: Jezebel,[25] "Where is the Lord (God)!" (meaning, Melkart), and Elijah (u), "My God is Yahweh!"

---

24. Ahab had an Asherah erected in Samaria, together with a temple in honor of Ba'al (Melkart) (1 K 16, 33).

25. The name is a composite of two elements: *'i-zébel*. The second element *zebel* has been interpreted on the basis of the West Semitic *zabulu*, "lord, prince." It is frequently found in the Ugarit texts in the phrases "Lord of the country" or "Lord of the sea." In Phoenician it is used in personal names, such as *zabul-hadad* "the storm god Hadad is Lord": *ba'al-zabulu* "Baal is lord." — The first element *'i* has been interpreted as an abbreviation for *'ᵃbi*; hence "my father (God) is Lord." B. Meisler, *Lesonenu* 15 (707), 39 thinks it more probable that the *'i-* is a contraction of the older form *'ayyeh*, "where?" W. F. Albright, *An Ostracon from Calah and the Northern Israelite Diaspora*, BASOR 149 (1958), 34. The word thus would be a confessional formula, which would be most fitting for this unsettled era: "Where is the lord (God)?" The answer to this question is the name *'ēli-yahu*, "My God is Yahweh."

3) CONFRONTATION BETWEEN BAAL AND YAHWEH

a) *The Elijah Cycle*

"In solitary grandeur, this prophet, the most grandiose and heroic figure in all the Bible, stands head and shoulders above his contemporaries. His image was captured in saga, but never in history." This is how Wellhausen [27] sums up his judgment on Elijah. There is hardly a reader of the Bible, whether he reads for piety or scientific motivation, who can escape the greatness of this solitary figure. Not only does he go beyond the limitations of common humanity; he also towers above the measure of the man of God as it is known in previous Biblical history. Was Elijah actually a superman of heroic stature? [28] Or was it really the saga which produced such an image of the prophet? How can we distinguish between history and saga? Kittel [29] will not even raise the question: "Elijah's history is completely veiled in the miraculous, and it stems from an ancient and reliable source. To reinterpret it along rationalistic lines, as Hitzig has done, is an offense against good taste and the spirit of Hebrew antiquity. It must be taken — in so far as it is well attested — just as it is, and we must always remember that Elijah is a magnificently original prophetic figure, a man of God, filled with the Spirit of Yahweh, glowing with zeal for Yahweh's cause and fully aware of the power of his God which works within him. Even the most narrow

---

26. W. Michaud, *Les Cycles d'Elie et d'Elisée,* Bible et Vie Chretienne 2 (1953), 76-99. Mirjam Prager, O.S.B., *Elias und Elisäus.* Practical introduction to 1 K 17 − 2 K 13, 22. There is also a good presentation of the present state of scholarship on the subject of Elijah, with a discussion of the prophet's continued effect upon the Church (Carmelite Order), in worship (Mass in honor of St. Elijah), in the Jewish religion, Koran and iconography. *Elie, le prophet,* vol. I (1955): *Selon les écritures et les traditions chrétiennes,* vol. II (1956): *Au Carmel − dans les Judaisme et l'Isram.* In "Les Études Carmelitaines."

27. Wellhausen, *Geschichte* 73.

28. Pfeiffer, IntrOT 404: "A superman of heroic stature, contemplated by a reverent popular imagination through the haze of legend."

29. R. Kittel, *Geschichte* 316.

historical approach could not, for a single moment, cast doubt upon the fact that Elijah actually was a man of wonders, a man who succeeded in doing most extraordinary things — a powerful and compelling personality — a man to whom everything was willing to yield, a man who had even the most extraordinary and mysterious powers at his disposal. We must also consider his strange entrance upon the Old Testament scene, his lightning-like and abrupt appearance and departure, and, not least of all, his bold religious idealism. It was only natural that, in terms of all this, the wonder-struck eyes of his people should see something most extraordinary in everything Elijah did and experienced. What could be more natural that everything he actually did should be elaborated, in the mouths of the people, into the proportions of saga? The two elements can no longer be adequately distinguished."

In its admiration for the great Elijah Old Testament criticism is united, but in the evaluation of the individual sources, the opinions are less unified. Where as one group of scholars finds it quite obvious that the figure of the historical prophet can now be grasped only through the veil of saga and legend, others refuse to reckon with the possibility of legendary tradition in the Bible. The way it is written is the way it happened. These opposing views seem to have somewhat relaxed in our day. Since, on the basis of form-history investigation, scholars have learned to distinguish various literary genres in the Bible, the mystery of inspiration has also been seen in a new light, without sacrificing any of the truths of faith. Scripture is certainly not the product of a mechanical dictation on the part of God, to the complete exclusion of all human activity; rather, the Spirit of God made use of human forms of expression and tradition, both oral and written, making them the vehicles of the content of revelation. In order to have a proper grasp of the content of revelation, we must first examine the human form involved, the "spiritual vessel," to see how it couches its message. The testimony of tribal traditions is one thing and the testimony of written documents is quite another. These might be annalistic sequences of events, but they can also be masterpieces of historical composition, highly artistic and bearing the stamp of deep psychological and theological reflection. Free poetic composition can also be the vehicle of inspiration. In terms of principle, accordingly, there is nothing to prevent the "lives of the saints" functioning as a body for the incarnation of the Word, provided we can definitely establish the fact that such a genre has actually been at work.

If, accordingly, on the conservative side, the possibility of legend tradition had been taken into account, it is equally true that, on the other hand, from the critical point of view, concepts of saga and legend have been subjected to a fresh analysis. Saga and legend are not, after all, the one-sided product of devout and reverent poetry. They can contain a very deep level of historical experience, to a degree that can hardly be reached by the historico-critical methods of investigation. The "typizing" saga is much more in keeping with the potential of expression proper to an ancient people that is the sober recital of historical fact. "It would be a very premature conclusion for the historico-critical science of history to claim that it controls the only way to understand the history of Israel, particularly if it were to deny all foundation in 'actual' history to everything that Israel has recorded in its sagas." [30] Saga and legend have a real historical value and content.

The most difficult question is the problem of recognizing the fact that legend and saga actually underlie a given text; that is, that we are faced with a spiritualized representation of an event, a narrative which proceeds from meditation. Obviously, the mere appearance of the miraculous is not sufficient to characterize an account as legend.[31] For the God of the Bible, the miraculous is the most natural thing in the world. The God who has created all the universe and chosen Israel for his people truly has the power to supply his representatives on earth with the credentials of miracle. The God of Israel is a God of miracles, a God who can always, and everywhere, do anything he wills. It follows that the distinction between legend and sober history is a very difficult undertaking. It is not a process that can be hurried; each individual

---

30. G. v. Rad, ThAT I 147f.
31. Pfeiffer, IntrOT 404: "What marks the Elijah stories as legends is the supernatural background manifested in numerous miracles."

account must be examined to determine its point of view. If the scholarly conclusion points to the existence of legend,[32] this is no constriction on the word of God; quite the contrary, we become its true and obedient servant, and only thus do we arrive at a proper understanding.

As we have already discussed in greater detail, the Books of Kings, which are the only sources for Elijah, are the product of several streams of tradition: court, priestly, and prophetic tradition. All of them had an independent literary form prior to the composition of Books of Kings, and the author of the Books of Kings welded them into a higher unity, in his theology of history. The court circles are responsible for the annalistic accounts of the history of the kings of Israel and Judah; the priestly circles contributed accounts of the temple building and court reform. In the midst of these more objective and sober accounts, the narratives of the prophets Elijah and Elisha form an independent bloc of quite different character. We shall first treat the "biography of Elijah."

The principal part of Elijah's activity falls within the reign of King Ahab. In 1 K 16, 29 his accession to power is introduced by the stereotype formula: "In the thirty-eighth year of Asa King of Judah, Ahab-ben-Omri began to reign over Israel, and Ahab-ben-Omri reigned over Israel in Samaria twenty-two years (874/73 — 853)." The concluding formula for Ahab's reign does not occur until 1 K 22, 39: "Now the rest of the acts of Ahab ... are they not written in the Book of the Chronicles of the Kings of Israel?" Between these two termini, a variety of traditional material has been incorporated. One bloc is formed by the religiously passionate account of the life and work of Elijah, a narrative in which the prophet is constantly represented as the adversary of the apostate king; another bloc is the history of the Aramaean wars, in which Elijah is not even mentioned (20, 22, 1-38). It is impossible that both accounts have the same origin. The history of the Aramaean wars reminds us rather of the "biography of David." [34] There is a feeling for precise observation, psychological precision, objective narrative with great pains to do full justice to persons and events. One gets the impression that these chapters represent a selection from a more extensive chronicle of the reign of Ahab.[35] Our historian has selected the sections

---

32. It is a generally acknowledged fact that the older forms of the lives of the saints are richly adorned with legend. Surely the same factors must have been operative in the Old Testament saints.

33. Cf. Vol. III, 279: Sources of the Books of Kings.

34. *Ibid.*, 45.

35. Robert-Feuillet, IntrOT 445f.

he needed in order to present the necessary background for his story of the prophet Elijah.[36]

For the history of Elijah, too — and modern scholarship is generally agreed on this point — he also made use of a "life of the great prophet" which was already circulating among the prophetic circles. He did not merely take over this work mechanically; he freely worked it into his overall presentation. These chapters, accordingly, present the impression of "selective excerpts from the life of Elijah." [37]

The presentation is a work of art, a masterpiece from the best period of northern Israelite prose literature, written in purest Hebrew.[38] The principal figure Elijah is like an icon. Only the essential features are outlined; whatever is secondary remains unstressed. He stands in his "glorious isolation" [39] opposed to a hostile and rebellious world. The flaming gold background of the icon is the fire of Yahweh that consumes him. The name of the prophet itself is not the private name of an individual, but rather a confession of faith.[40]

Despite all this, in presenting this extremely compact picture, our historian does not lose anything of his historical grounds. Between the time of the events themselves and their first literary composition, hardly a single generation has passed. Some 40 years after Elijah's death, and thus already around the year 800 B.C., the Elijah cycle, the "Life of the Great Prophet," must already have been in existence.[41] The disciples of the prophet preserved the heritage of their master and handed down his "life,"

36. C. Fohrer, *Elia*, AThANT 31 (1957), 5-96, examines more closely into the development of the tradition. He distinguishes six original narratives and six anecdotes and demonstrates a deliberate parallel structuring of historical motifs with Moses, thereby accentuating the theological significance of Elijah for the development of religion in the OT. He claims that Elijah established the Yahweh cult on a new foundation. Though there is some room for discussion in his source criticism, he has obviously found the correct key to the history of the tradition.
37. Robert-Feuillet, IntrAT 446: "Extraits d'une biographie."
38. Pfeiffer, IntrOT 403.
39. Robert-Feuillet, IntrAT 448.
40. *EncMikr* I, 337 explains the name.
41. Pfeiffer, 403; De Vaux, *Rois* 12.

until, around the time of the prophet Jeremiah, 600 B.C., or shortly after the destruction of Jerusalem (586), it found its way into the Books of the Kings.

b) *The Man From Tishbe in Gilead*

Without preparation, like a lightning bolt from a clear sky, the man from Tishbe in Gilead makes his appearance.[42] Neither father nor family nor prophetic vocation are described. The first thing that the Bible records of him is "that he spoke." It is the word which makes him prophet: "Now Elijah the Tishbite, or Tishbe in Gilead, said to Ahab..." (17, 1). Perhaps this mention of the prophet's birthplace in Gilead is already the key to understanding his activity. The Transjordanian tribes had certainly not completely shared in the cultural and economic development of the tribes which had settled in Canaan. They thus retained something of their originally nomadic life which dated back to the days of Moses. In terms of religion, too, they could not possibly have been so subject to the enticement of the Canaanite Baal religion as their brother tribes west of the Jordan. These facts, however, do not seem a sufficient basis for explaining Elijah's religious mission. Elijah did come from the edge of the steppe country, and his clothing was a simple cloak of hide, cinctured with a leather belt; but still his nomadic origins are not clearly demonstrable. He did not fight on the side of the Beduins, announcing the ancient civilization as an ideal; his mission was to battle for the rights of the one God Yahweh. His activity was prompted not by the cultural advancement of his age, but by his people's defection to the gods of Canaan. The derivation of his spiritual heritage from a nomadic culture is already charged with the concept of a developing history of religion. It was to this great prophetic figure that the promulgation of monotheism has frequently been ascribed. Elijah is represented as one of the

---

42. Identified as early as the Byzantine pilgrimage accounts with Ḥirbet el-Istib (NW of Aglun). *Mar Elias* is in the vicinity. Since, however, there have been no materials dating to the Iron Age, the identification remains questionable. Simons, GTT #897.

very first thinkers who hit upon the concept of ethical monotheism. "For the age of Moses represents the position that, together with Yahweh, there are other gods, although their veneration is forbidden to the Israelites. Elijah, in the passion of his zeal for the God of Israel, would thus represent a more advanced tradition. There is absolutely no other God beside Yahweh. Yahweh is the one true God." [43]

It is true that the religion of Israel has experienced an interior and exterior development; but today we are not so inclined to look upon the Mosaic era in such a primitive light as was customary before the great discoveries in the cultures of the Ancient Near East.[44] Elijah belongs not to the first creators of monotheism, but rather among the great reformers. Without the background of Mosaic monotheism, his activity cannot be explained. He is so dependent upon Moses that he can rightly be called a second Moses. Moses' work was about to be shattered in rebellious Israel's defection to the bull cult. When Moses, returning from the sacred mountain, saw the idol of the golden calf, he shattered it in his holy wrath and completely destroyed the rebels with blood and sword. Elijah's battle was simply a fight against the resurrection of the bull cult.

"The ancient sentiments of the Mosaic era are all alive in Elijah. It is a spirit in which Yahweh, whose true vassal he was, surrounded by the youthful love of Israel, was chosen and acclaimed, with a resounding and jubilant ovation, as the one and only God of the people. If, in the times that followed, this violent dedication to Yahweh began to swell into a mighty storm which swept away not only the Tyrian Melkart, but all the other Canaanite 'Baals and gods' and all the gods of the pagans, it was Elijah's merit that he is the first to take up the battle." [45]

The spiritual homeland of Elijah is not to be identified with the Rechabites. "These were a tribe-like union (and thus not a

---

43. Balla, *Die Botschaft der Propheten* (1958), 50.
44. Cf. Vol. II, p. 223ff.
45. Gressmann, 265. — F. Spadafora, *Mose ed Elia*, RBib 5 (1957), 305-328 interprets the history of both figures and their spirituality in terms of the NT.

'sect') and even in an agricultural civilization — on religious grounds — they held to their nomadic way of life. They refused to live in houses, that is, in village or city communities; they tilled no fields, they cultivated and drank no wine, in order to have long life in the country in which they dwelt as aliens (Jr 35, 6ff.). They were thus the proponents of a radical Yahweh faith . . . . They are the spiritual descendants of the Jehonadab mentioned in Jeremiah 35, the man whom Jehu took up into his chariot, recognizing him as a man dedicated to the 'zeal for Yahweh' (2 K 10, 15ff.). This is not to imply that the nomadic union came into existence only in Jehu's day, at a correspondingly late age." [46] In the case of Elijah, however, this affected position against agricultural civilization is not to be found. He is not involved with the antithesis between steppe and civilization, but rather with the opposition between Yahweh and Baal.

Elijah's spiritual relatives are the ancient Nazirites, and the Nebiim inspired by God. Elijah stands in the closest relationship to the prophetic community, but there is nowhere any evidence that he has come from these circles. Like Amos after him, he could very well have been called out of his normal life and profession, to become the warrior and herald of the one God Yahweh.

c) *Drought and Famine*

Elijah makes his entry into the fate of Israel with an oracle of threat: "As the Lord the God of Israel lives, before whom I stand, there shall be neither dew nor rain these years, except by my word" (17, 1). Just as suddenly as he makes his appearance, the announcer of this doom disappears. The threatened catastrophe sets out upon its death-dealing course.

The Palestinian farmer and shepherd has always been dependent upon the timely advent of the early and late rains.[47]

---

46. G. v. Rad, ThAT I, 71ff.

47. On the occasion of my last visit to Palestine in Fall of 1958 the early rain, that is, the first rain in the Fall, had not fallen. As a result the fall sowing could barely be made. In the Negeb, huge tractors managed to turn up and turn over the hard earth and the seed was actually sown, but it perished for lack of moisture. In Jordania entire

Over the rains no man has ever had power; God alone was able to bestow rain — and thus the blessings of the fields. It is only his command that is acknowledged by the cloud-bearing winds with their blessing of rainfall. In such a world the withholding of the annual rain and the consequent drought and famine would necessarily lead to a crisis in the area of faith. The people's need would make it very clear just who was the true Lord of heaven.

This is the point at which Elijah makes the ultimate challenge. Now it is to be decided whether Baal or Yahweh has power. Baal, of course, had always been venerated as the god of the life cycle, constantly renewed and ever verdant. Elijah's threatening word claimed that it was not Baal, but rather Yahweh, who has the keys to the flood gates of rain. Catastrophic droughts have frequently occurred in Palestine. But the drought that marked Elijah's appearance on the public scene led to a great religious confrontation. In somewhat the same way, the Egyptian plagues had frequently overrun the country of the Nile; but it was only the plague that occurred in Moses' day that produced the ultimate religious confrontation. Mute nature needs prophetic interpretation to be properly understood.

After pronouncing his oracle of threat against King Ahab, Elijah took flight. Faced with the overwhelming power of the Baal religion, he feared for his very life. He went into hiding at the Brook Cherith [48] in Transjordania, and even the king's spies could not discover his hiding place. The account of his sojourn there is richly embroidered with the miraculous. Ravens used to bring him bread every morning and meat [49] every evening (17,

---

herds of sheep and cattle had to be slaughtered because the wells had all dried up. The steely blue sky of Palestine, which is such a source of charm and enticement to visitors from the rainy north, can also be a fearsome spectacle. In an effort to avoid the recurrence of such a disaster, the new State of Israel plans to use the waters of the Jordan and the Yarkon for agriculture.

---

48. Perhaps identical with Wadi Jabis. Literally: "the deeply cut (brook)." Abel, Geogr. II, 684.
49. The Greek text!

2-7). As we have already pointed out, we do not mean to set any boundary to God's miraculous powers. Just as God, on the exodus from Egypt, provided Israel with manna from heaven every morning and with the flesh of the quail (Ex 16, 8, 12), he obviously has the power to provide for his prophet's daily food through the agency of ravens. As a matter of fact, even today there are a good many ravens in this region, and, whenever they can, they will fly off with chickens, rabbits, eggs, or bread.[50] The prophet could thus have maintained his life from the leavings of their meals. The Hebrew text actually speaks of "ravens" (*'orebîm*); but this term could also refer to humans, dark-skinned Beduins, who provided the fugitive with the necessities of life while he was in hiding. For more than a thousand years after Elijah, Arabic literature has referred to dark-skinned inhabitants of the Jordan lowlands as "ravens." [51]

When the water in the brook of Cherith dried up, Elijah made his way further into Zarephath in the territory of the Sidonians.[52] He probably hoped that the mountain torrents flowing down from mighty Lebanon would still contain a little water even in the midst of the drought. He discovered not only drought, but also famine. The Greek historian Menander of Ephesus also speaks of a great drought and famine which plagued the Phoenicans in the days of King Itobaal of Tyre, whose daughter Jezebel had been married to Ahab.[53] Before the city gates, Elijah met a woman whom he recognized, by her clothing, as a widow. She was gathering wood [54] in order to prepare a final meal for herself

---

50. Médebille, ClamB III, 669.

51. M. S. Seale, *The Black Arabs of the Jordan Valley*, ET 68 (1956), 28ff. There is the further question of whether or not the Hebraic consonant text *'rbym* should not be read simply as *'arabîm*, "Arabs," rather than *'orebîm*, "ravens."

52. Cuneiform *Sariptu*. Köhler, LexVT 817. According to Luke 4, 26 Sarepta; today a Lebanese village Saragand, half a mile S of Saida, ancient Sidon, lying on a lofty mountainside along the coast. I visited the location on June 30, 1951.

53. FlavJos., Ant. 8, 13, 2.

54. According to Augustine and Caesarius of Arles the widow is the

and for her son. The prophet called to her, asking for a drink of water. As she went to get the water he also asked her to bring him a piece of bread. At this, the widow was forced to confess that her provisions had all run out. Elijah, however, promised her in the name of Yahweh, the God of Israel, that the meal in the jar would not run out and the oil in the cruse would not fail until the rain came again (17, 14). The woman believed the prophet's word, and the miracle took place.

Despite the presence of the man of God, the widow's son died (17, 17-24). She felt that it was precisely because of the presence of the prophet that he died. If he had not come, God would have overlooked her sins. The presence of the man of God is equivalent to the presence of God himself, insofar as it has made public her sins and punished them with the death of her son.[55] Elijah was also very much struck by the misfortune. He dealt very boldly with God. Was this poor widow also to be involved in his own personal misfortune (17, 20)! Then he stretched himself upon the child three times,[56] called upon the name of Yahweh, who gives life, and the boy came back to life.

It is precisely these miracle accounts which have been, one-sidedly, relegated into the realm of poetic legend by negative criticism. The story takes place far from the story teller, in a distant country, in order to achieve greater credibility.[57] Miracle is ever the darling of legend. And in the case of many legends of the saints that is a point well taken. But simply because a

---

type of the pagan world who are called to the Faith. The two pieces of wood that are laid upon her are a symbol of the cross, the source of unfailing nourishment for the Church. De Vaux, *Rois* 96 (JerB).

---

55. Death here is not a physiological experience. It really begins to be this when Yahweh abandons the person, and thus it is intimately bound up with sin. G. v. Rad, ThAT I, 386.

56. Literally: "he measured himself out to the measure of the boy" (17, 21). Augustine and Bernard see this as a reference to the Incarnation of Christ who accommodated himself perfectly to the measure of humanity and thus brought new life to humanity. De Vaux, *Rois* 97 (JerB).

57. Gressmann 261.

miracle account is present in a story does not mean that it has
to be considered legend and invention. What else could it be? —
The miracle of the multiplication of the bread and the raising from
the dead is, at all events, to be ascribed to faith in the living
Yahweh, by whom Elijah swears (17, 12).

d) *Divine Judgment on Carmel*

Meantime, the drought had assumed such serious proportions
that King Ahab himself and his chief steward Obadiah went out
in search of water (18, 1-6). Elijah came up to the chief steward
and told him to announce his arrival to the king. Obadiah was
afraid to do this. Ahab had ordered a thorough search into all
the most remote corners of the country, to capture this prophet
of doom and have him put out of the way. Popular faith in the
prophet's powers is revealed by Obadiah's answer: "As soon
as I have gone from you, the Spirit of the Lord will carry you
whither I know not; and so, when I come and tell Ahab he
cannot find you, he will kill me, although I your servant have
revered the Lord from my youth" (18, 12). Only Elijah's oath
which he takes upon Yahweh *seba'ôt,* the God of hosts, sets the
steward at ease.

The scene in which the encounter between the two antagonists
takes place, is not only a masterpiece in the art of literary presentation, but it is also charged with tragedy. Each man sees the
other responsible for the destruction of Israel. Ahab speaks first: "Is
it you, you troubler of Israel?" [58] Elijah says in reply: "I have
not troubled Israel; but you have, and your father's house"
(18, 18). The prophet is pressing for a decisive confrontation. He
proposes the verdict of Yahweh himself, on Carmel. The king
agrees to the proposal.

We might ask precisely why Carmel should be chosen as
the scene for this confrontation.[59] The territory of Carmel was

---

58. Jonathan said the same thing to Saul — 1 S 14, 29.
59. A. Alt, "Das Gottesurteil auf dem Karmel" (Kleine Texte II, 135-
    149) sees the confrontation in terms of the contemporary political
    situation and thereby achieves some important new perspective. This
    involves a distinction among the various sources. He completely ig-

not situated in the original territory settled by the Israelite tribes. It was a sparsely settled wooded district, surrounded on every side by plains which, in theory but not in fact, had been occupied by the tribes of Israel. Until the Davidic-Solomonic era, the Canaanites were able to maintain their sovereignty in this territory. Perhaps it was on these very heights of Carmel that they venerated a sort of Baal of the covenant (*ba'al b^erît*). It was only under David that an altar to Yahweh was erected on this site. After the split in kingdom and national faith, the Yahweh altar was abandoned. Now we know that Solomon actually mortgaged Israelite territory to the King of Tyre.[60] The fact that Solomon had the city of Megiddo on the eastern spur of Carmel built up as a boundary fortress, leads us to suspect that the Plain of Acco had been abandoned to Phoenician influence. If, accordingly, in Ahab's day the district of Carmel was subject to Tyrian sovereignty, the proposal of a divine judgment on this site is an even more logical conclusion than before. At the boundary line between two political spheres of power, we are now to witness a decisive confrontation: which is the true God? The Tyrian Baal, under the protection and patronage of Queen Jezebel, had won many partisans and worshipers in many districts of Israel. On the other hand, the champions of Yahweh's sole sovereignty were being persecuted and handed over to death. From every worldly point of view, the Yahweh faith was close to extinction.

From all sides, people and priests of Baal streamed to the heights of Carmel. In the eyes of many of them, this may have been a normal rogation procession [61] begging for the blessings

---

nores the account of the drought and makes the Carmel story an independent unit. The result is indeed a very compact picture, but the text criticism is rather arbitrary. What is more, I should be inclined to find more in the narrative than a "saga-like precipitate of an historical event." — K. Galling, *Der Gott Karmel und die Ächtung der fremden Götter*, Geschichte und AT. Fs. A. Alt (1953), 105-125.

---

60. Vol. III, 357.
61. Something similar is recorded of Itobaal, King of Tyre. The Greek historian Menander is quoted in Josephus, Ant. 8, 13, 1. — Cf. *EncMikr* I, 790.

of rain. The forces of heaven were regularly placated by great sacrifices on the high places. Tradition has identified the place of sacrifice as *el-Muhraqa* [62] on the south peak of Carmel, a high altar built by nature herself. From this vantage point, the entire plain of Sharon is visible, all the way to the white coastal dunes, where the vista is lost in the blue sea. To the north, lies the Plain of Jezreel bordered on every side by the Galilean mountain country. Across a chain of hills, the eye catches a glimpse of the Tyrian Sea.

At this place, where the world seems to be so distant and God so close, the altars of sacrifice were erected.[63] "On the one side stand the prophets of Baal, 450 in number, and on the other side Elijah all alone; but behind him is the powerful figure of Yahweh. The prophets of Baal begin their ceremony in the morning. The rite begins — or so we must imagine it — with a long series of dances and prayers which last several hours. Gradually the dancing becomes more impassioned, and the prayers grow louder. By now it is midday. The dances have turned into meaningless motion, and the prayers have become a series of shrieks that defy interpretation. The priests are no longer in full possession of their senses; with swords and knives they wound their own bodies. In this manner they carry on for several hours. Finally, from all their physical and psychic excitement, they are on the verge of collapse, staring blankly about them, foaming at the mouth. Their whole behavior is not unlike that of a madman. Dancing, according to the Hebrew expressions, is described as hobbling on both knees;[64] such hobbling dances are described by

---

62. There is a church there today, attended by the Carmelite Fathers. Formerly a place of pilgrimage for Christians of all denominations as well as Mohammedans, today it is a favorite vacation area for the younger class in Israel. On March 31, 1951 I visited the location after crossing diagonally over the Plain of Jezreel. Magnificent wild flowers and panorama. At twilight, back to Haifa by auto.

63. The following version is from Gressmann, 262.

64. Gressmann's interpretation is only one of many, according to the various interpretations of the verb *pôseḥîm*, participle from the root *pāsaḥ*, and the noun *seʿappîm*. The Vulgate translates it freely: "Usquequo claudicatis in duas partes?" — "how long will you limp

Heliodorus in his description of Tyrian seafarers; they leap and skip, now darting upwards with sudden jumps, now squatting close to the floor and whirling around with the whole body, like possessed men. According to 18, 21, this hobbling (leaping) dance must have been a characteristic trait of the Baal religion: 'To limp on both knees' is equivalent to 'to serve Baal.' Since this Baal was the Tyrian Melkart, these hobbling dances must have come to Samaria from Tyre together with his cult, and in Samaria they appear to have enjoyed a temporary vogue. Between the description of the morning and afternoon scene, Elijah's contempt is masterfully inserted; he makes open mockery of Baal and the priests. The greater the fury of his opponents, the more disdainful the manner of Elijah, who is fully conscious of the omnipotent strength of his God. Until nearly evening, the time at which the food offering was customarily offered, he waits patiently. Then, with the help of the assembled people, he rebuilds the ancient altar of Yahweh. Only then does he step forward and speak a short prayer. Immediately the 'fire of Yahweh,' that is, lightning, falls down from the sky. The battle has been decided. Yahweh has conquered; all the people acclaim the praises of Yahweh and his prophets. The false priests of Baal are seized and slaughtered at the brook of Kishon . . . . By his masterful presentation, our historian has heightened the tension in the minds of his audience, up to the final moment. With masterful strokes he has sketched the wild, sensuous intoxication characteristic of the Baal religion as the somber background against which the spiritual superiority

---

in both directions?" According to Köhler LexVT 769 *pāsaḥ* means "to limp, to be lame," and *se'appîm* are crutches made from branches of a tree. — Rehm, EB II 191 thinks this is a reference to his irresolute conduct, seeking help from both Yahweh and the pagan gods, relying as it were on two different crutches. R. de Vaux, *Les prophètes de Baal sur le Mont Carmel.* Bull. du Musée de Beyrouth 5 (1941), 7-20 has demonstrated, however, that this limping on two crutches is a typical element of the Tyrian Baal cult. The reference is to a wild dance, such as is described by Heliodorus in his *Ethiopica* IV, XIII, 1. Cf. above in the text. The quotation is thus an ironical and figurative expression for: "How long will you be fascinated by the Baal dances?"

of the Yahweh religion stands out in all its glory." — This is Gressmann's eloquent retelling of the story. Not only are we in the presence of a masterpiece of poetic narrative, but we are also swept along, in this noble account, into those anxious hours in which the Yahweh faith was fighting for its very existence. At all events, the miracle at Carmel completely broke the further penetration of the Tyrian Baal cult.[65]

The slaughter of the priests of Baal at the brook of Kishon — a terrible carnage — was certainly redeemed by the religious context of the situation. Elijah himself, as the text clearly states (18, 40), was in full agreement. But before we can arrive at a proper evaluation, we must also take into account the political point of view. The Tyrian control of the country was an unbearable oppression in the mind of the people. The fact that this "blood bath" at the brook of Kishon [66] was possible is only further evidence of the extreme bitterness which had already accumulated in the heart of the nation. Moreover, we must also point out the fact that the annihilation of devotees to the bull cult, by sword and blood, already had a precedent in Moses (Ex 32, 27). Elijah, in this point too, was simply imitating the zeal of the great Moses.

While the people were engaged in the bloody work of revenge at the brook of Kishon, Elijah cast himself upon his face, on

---

65. Elijah's words of mockery are a reference to the Tyrian Baal Melkart: "He is lost in contemplation" (*sîaḥ*): Herakles of Tyre (BAAL) was also called the "philosopher": he was reputed to be the inventor of purple and seafaring. — "He is busy, he is on a journey" points to the god of merchants and sailors. "He is sleeping and will have to be awakened" is a reference, finally, to the awakening of Melkart, an annual celebration which took place in Jan./Feb. The festival was also carried to Carthage. A huge pyre was set ablaze, in the belief that the god perished in the flames. But when the flutes began to sound the god would reawaken from his sleep to renewed life. Médebielle, ClamB II, 675 — R. Dussaud, *Melqart d'après de recents travaux*, RHR 151 (1957), 1-21. Melkart as a purely Canaanite god, one of the sons of Baal, one of the "sons of the gods."

66. At *Tell el-Kassis,* located near Kishon. H. Junker, *Der Graben um den Altar Elias. Eine Untersuchung über die kultische Überlieferung von 1 K 18, 29-38.* TTZ (1960), 65-74.

the mountain heights, and begged for rain.[67] When his servant came back from looking towards the sea for the seventh time, he saw a little cloud like a man's hand over the sea.[68] Elijah jumped up. The sky turned dark and the storm appeared. But the prophet, too, is seized by the storm wind of God. He fled before the horses of the royal chariot into Jezreel.[69]

e) *Elijah on the Mountain of God* (1 K 19, 1-18)

This unexpected triumph was followed by an equally unexpected setback.[70] When Jezebel heard of Yahweh's day of vengeance on Carmel, she swore a two-fold vengeance. The threat she spoke to the prophet is unsurpassed for its classical brevity, its recognition of her adversary, and its estimation of her own greatness:[71] "If you are Elijah, I am Jezebel!" [72] Meantime Elijah seized the opportunity to take flight and save his life. This time he took the route towards the south, left his serving boy behind at Beersheba, while he himself went on a day's journey further into the wilderness, where he lay under a broom tree,[73] tired not

---

67. This scene is narrated in immediate connection with the divine judgment, but this involves some difficulty. When the priests of Baal are overcome, Elijah is located by the Brook of Kishon (18, 40), but he is on top of Carmel when he prays for rain (18, 41ff.). This could hardly have happened on one and the same evening, and the miracle occurred at the time of the evening sacrifice. It is possible that the execution was entrusted to servants acting on the prophet's orders, while he himself made the prayers for the rain. (18, 40: "And he ordered; seize them . . . .)

68. It was the writers of the Carmelite Order and not the early Church Fathers who first interpreted this cloud as being the Virgin Mary who was to bring salvation to the world in the seventh age of the world. De Vaux, *Rois* 103 (JerB).

69. Karmel to Jizreel approximately 15 mi.

70. Gressmann 267 thinks that ch. 19 cannot possibly be the continuation of ch. 18. He argues for the existence of two totally independent cycles of saga, and places the wandering in the wilderness before the judgment of Yahweh on Carmel.

71. *Ibid.*, 267.

72. Greek translation.

73. Hebrew *rôtēm*, "broomtree — *genista*" not juniper (*juniperus Juni-*

only of the long day's journey, but also weary of his continued struggle without issue: "It is enough; now, O Lord, take away my life; for I am no better than my fathers" (19, 4). Death would have been salvation for him. But then the angel of Yahweh (*mal'ak yahweh*)[74] called to him: "Arise and eat" (19, 5). He arose and saw, near his head, a cake baked on hot stones, and a jar of water.[75] He arose and ate and — went back to sleep. A second time an angel woke him. After eating a second time, he walked, in the strength of this food, forty days and forty nights until he reached Horeb, mountain of God.[76]

There he spent the night, apparently in the same cave [77] in which Moses had once looked upon the glory of Yahweh passing by (Ex 33, 22). What follows next is unsurpassed in its dramatic sense of climax. All manner of fearful things are set loose, all the powers of nature are unshackled, just as in the great day of the Law upon Sinai. A mighty storm wind, rending the mountains, breaking the rocks into pieces — but Yahweh was not in the storm wind. After the storm an earthquake — but Yahweh was

---

perus). In the Southern country this tree is frequently encountered, some 13-15 feet in height, with thick network of branches and small leaves. It affords a sparse but (in this desert region) most eagerly sought shade.

---

74. "The personified help of Yahweh for Israel." For more detail cf. G. v. Rad, ThAT I, 285.

75. *'uggat resāphîm,* literally "bread of the glowing stones." A fire was built over a bed of pebbles, then when the fire had burned down, the ashes were brushed aside and the dough was placed on the glowing stone, covered with ashes, and baked. E. W. Heaton, *Biblischer Alltag. Zeit des Alten Testaments* (1959), 61.

76. Mountain of the legislation (Dt 4, 10-15) identical with Sinai (Ex 19, 1-23). "Forty" is a general time reference, perhaps a reminiscence of the forty years of wandering in the desert. The distance between Beer-Sheba and Sinai is about 210 mi in a straight line, and some 300 mi allowing for a detour around the Aqaba. A camel caravan covers the distance in 10-14 days. Garofalo 144.

77. According to tradition, a cave immediately under the peak of Jebel Musa. Verses 19, 9b-11a are from a later hand with the exception of verse 14f.

not in the earthquake. After the earthquake fire — but Yahweh was not in the fire. After the fire — a still, small voice (19, 11-13).

When Elijah recognized the ineffable calm that followed the storm, he left his cave, prepared to meet his God. The loosing of the elements was only the advance guard of the scene to follow. Immediately he became aware of the divine presence: "Behold, there came a voice to him" (19, 13). It said: "What are you doing here, Elijah?" Then the prophet must have finally poured out all the bitterness of his soul before Yahweh: "I have been very jealous for the Lord, the God of hosts; for the people of Israel have forsaken thy covenant, thrown down thy altars, and slain thy prophets with the sword; and I, even I only, am left; and they seek my life, to take it away" (19, 14). — It is hardly possible to imagine a more somber reckoning. Failure and nothing but failure in his "zeal for Yahweh." The account must have worked like a summons upon Yahweh who is "a jealous God, visiting the iniquity of the fathers upon the children to the third and the fourth generation of those who hate me; but showing steadfast love to thousands of those who love me and keep my commandments" (Ex 20, 5f.). For this God of Sinai, who calls himself 'el qanna,[78] "jealous God," it could not possibly be a matter of unconcern that the people bound to his covenant have not been true. The prophet's account of Israel's defection from the covenant of Yahweh could only produce a jealous and passionate fire.

This theophany has been variously interpreted. The fact that God appeared, not in the storm-driven elements, but rather in the midst of great calm, is supposed to be a gentle admonition to Elijah who sought to root out the Baal cult in a wild frenzy of activity; this is not God's way.[79] Yahweh is quite different from the storm and thunder god Baal, who is represented with a sheaf of lightning and a thunderbolt;[80] Yahweh

---

78. Older form 'ēl qannô. The fundamental meaning of the verb qinnē' and the noun qin'āh is "to be zealous, zeal" or rather "to be jealous, jealousy." Hence it serves well as an expression of a passionate and uncompromising love that will tolerate no rival. Albright, *From Stone Age to Christianity*, 306.

79. Rehm, EB II, 195.

80. Médebielle, ClamB III, 679.

surpasses all the elements of nature; he is the quiet and abiding foundation of being that underlies all things.

But, in my opinion, the sense of this theophany lies in a quite different direction. It is not spoken as an admonition to the prophet. Elijah had taken up the sword on Carmel, and now Yahweh, from the very mountain of God, sends out a three-fold sword that will drink blood until it has accomplished the vengeance of God. From without, the sword of the Aramaean Hazahel of Damascus will rage against Israel; within the sword of Jehu will have no rest until it has cut out all the roots of Ahab's seed; whatever remains is destined to the sword of Elisha's prophetic word (19, 15-18). The theophany is thus not meant to chide the prophet; quite the contrary, it is a full endorsement of his zeal in behalf of Yahweh's sole kingship. The theology of history reaches a climax at this point, a climax which makes it possible to understand the frequently horrifying history of the kingly era. The leitmotifs are covenant (berît) and Yahweh's zeal (qin'at yahweh). God is not an uninterested spectator to political and social evolution; in his passionate love he takes a most active role.[81] When his covenant is broken, he looses the messengers of his judgment of wrath, to bring Israel back to the love of her first days. Reconfirmed in his vocation, Elijah returned from the mountain of God with a three-fold mission, which was at once judgment and election, and once more set about preparing the triumph of the one God Yahweh who suffers no other god besides himself, throughout the later course of Israelite history.

First of all, Elijah cast the cloak of prophetic vocation upon Elisha ben-Shaphat,[82] from Abel-Meholah,[83] who was out plowing in his field. "He took the yoke of oxen, and slew them, and boiled their flesh with the yokes of the oxen, and gave it to the

---

81. This is not to introduce later theological history interpretations into the story of Elijah. On the Mesha Stele which dates from the same century the subjugation of Moab is explained by the fact that "the god Chemosh was angry against his land." When his anger turned away, Moab was once again victorious. In the back and forth of history it was God's hand that was recognized. The difference between Israel and Moab in this respect is simply their different conception of God. Winton Thomas, DOT, 196.

82. Depending on the way 'lyšᶜ is broken down, there are two possible interpretations of the name: a. 'ēl-yaša', "God saves, redeems." Cf. Yesă'-Yah "Yahweh saves." b. 'ēli-ša', "my God is strong, powerful, noble." From the root šuᵃ'. The name occurs on ostraca and seals. South Arabic and Ugaritic parallels. EncMikr I, 358.

83. Location not clearly defined. According to Eusebius, it is 10 Roman

people, and they ate. Then he arose and went after Elijah, and ministered to him" (19, 21). By this establishment of the prophetic succession, the continuation of the prophetic word was assured. The word of God becomes the measure of all activity. And though it be only a tiny remnant, such as the seven thousand who did not bend the knee before Baal (19, 18), preferring to listen to the Word, it is precisely in this human impotence that we see a clear manifestation of the one power which abides all reversal and every attack, inviolate amid the confusion of human history and the insecurity of human thrones.

f) *Conscience Incarnate* (1 K 21)

Ahab would have been only too delighted to acquire the vineyard of Naboth, which bordered on his palace in Jezreel, in order to turn it into a vegetable garden (*gan-yaraq*). He was prepared to make any payment required, in money, or by exchange of a better vineyard. Naboth, on the other hand, could not be induced to sell the heritage of his fathers at any price. Vexed and sullen, Ahab returned to his house, lay down on his bed, and refused to eat or drink.

At this point his wife Jezebel came to see him. She began spinning her deadly web. There are two kingly ideals in conflict here. Ahab was ready to respect the will of his subject as clearly established by tradition. For Jezebel, however, the will of the king was the only law: "Do you now govern Israel?" (21, 7). In Ahab's name, she wrote letters (*separîm*) probably on papyrus, sealed them with the royal seal,[84] and sent them to the elders

miles from Beth-Shan; thus identified as *Tell Abu-Sifri* in the SE corner of the Plain of Beth-Shan. There are no Iron Age remains, however. Simons, GTT #567-568. Others suggest Abel-Meholah in Transjordania. Albright identifies it with the city of Jabilima mentioned in the Amarna letters, in northern Gilead. BASOR 89 (1943) 15. In Epiphanius' "Life of the Prophet" and also in the Jewish Haggadoth, the birthplace of both Elisha and Elijah is given as Gilead. *EncMikr* I, 38.

84. For more detail on seals, cf. *EncMikr* III, 68-86, with abundant illustration. In the older seals Phoenician influence is obvious; this con-

and foremost citizens of Jezreel. In these letters she accused Naboth of the two-fold crime of blasphemy and high treason. The court was summoned to sit at the city gate. Hired false witnesses, sons of Belial, made their appearance. There was no counter-testimony. Naboth was stoned to death. A deed worthy of the daughter of the Tyrian priest-king Ethbaal, who had made his way to the throne over the corpses of his relatives.

No sooner had the crime been committed and the welcome news received from Samaria, than Jezebel told Ahab to make his way to Jezreel and claim the vineyard as royal property. The camouflage was successful. In the eyes of formal justice, Ahab was perfectly justified. But there were still prophets in Israel. Elijah also made his way to Jezreel. Once again the two met, king and prophet. The troubled conscience manifested itself: "Have you found me, O my enemy?" (21, 20). Elijah immediately answered, quite without fear: "You have committed murder," although the Ten Commandments clearly state "Thou shall not kill" (*rassah*). The crime called out to heaven for vengeance, and Elijah was the messenger of God's avenging justice. Just as the dynasties of Jeroboam and Baasha had been rooted out, so was the house of Ahab to be annihilated because of this bloody crime. Upon that very piece of ground on which Naboth was stoned to death, the dogs would come to lick the blood of Ahab and Jezebel (21, 21ff.). Ahab had allowed himself to be led into a serious crime; Jezebel's influence over him was too great. After his terrible deed, he once again listened to the prophet. In sackcloth and ashes he did penance. Because of his contrition, the execution of the divine verdict was deferred (21, 28).

4) REORGANIZATION OF THE KINGDOM OF JUDAH

Since the first split of the kingdom, there had been constant war between the kings of Israel and Judah. Omri embarked upon a new policy. Instead of constant hostility, he established an abiding peace between the brother kingdoms. First of all, Judah was to

firms the Biblical data on culture exchanges. G. R. Driver, *Hebrew Seals*, PEQ 87 (1957), 183: winged griffin with the name of the owner.

dissolve its ruinous alliance with Aram, and Israel was to guarantee the frontier against Judah. This established the prerequisite for the economical and political development of both kingdoms. Under the excellent rulers, Ahab of Israel [85] and Jehoshaphat of Judah,[86] the two kingdoms achieved a position of prominence within the Ancient Near East which recalls the empire of Davidic-Solomonic days. Since, however, the subsequent ascendancy of Ashur completely altered the political balance of power, these "middle kingdoms" were destined to enjoy only a short blossom.

Jehoshaphat (870 — 845) was a ruler with great plans, both brilliant and energetic. In this respect he was fully the equal of his great contemporary Ahab. Both men succeeded in establishing a new position of respect for their kingdoms. The distinction lay only in their confession of faith: Jehoshaphat was a devotee and reformer of the pure Yahweh faith. Ahab, on the other hand, was a broad-minded politician who made room in Israel for even the foreign gods from Tyre. In the third year of his reign (867)[87] Jehoshaphat began carrying out his political and religious program of reform (2 Ch 17, 7).

---

85. The name *'aḥab* occurs frequently: false prophet in Babel (Jer 29, 21): seal inscription from Lachish "*lešebna (ben) 'aḥ'ab*"; Shalmaneser's inscription "*a-ḥa-ab-bu (mât) sir-'i-la-a-a*," i.e., "Ahab of the land of Israel." The interpretation of the name is contested: **a.** term of relationship: "Brother (*'aḥ*) of the father (*'ab*)," because the image of the uncle had taken new form in the newly born nephew. — b. Theophoric name: "My brother is the father (God)." Reference to God as the great brother was a frequent practice in many other name formations, e.g. Ahimelek, "my brother (= God) is king." — C. M. Noth thinks the name is derived from an Arabic root of uncertain meaning. *EncMikr* I, 195.

86. *yᵉho-šaphat* "Yahweh has held judgment." This might possibly be a reference to some historical event which occurred at the child's birth.

87. Chronology: The synchronism with 1 K 22, 41 presents some difficulty. Jehoshaphat's accession corresponds to the fourth year of Ahab, the fifth year according to our reckoning. The succession to the throne occurred at the New Year, which fell one month later in the Northern Kingdom since Jeroboam I. On Jeroboam's calendar reforms, cf. S. Talmon, VT 8 (1958), 48-74.

a) ADMINISTRATION REFORMS: A properly functioning administration and economic prosperity go hand in hand. Solomon had
divided the kingdom of Israel into twelve administrative districts,
in which Judah was not included. Jehoshaphat, in his turn, divided
the kingdom of Judah into twelve administrative districts, with
district governors (*n^essîbîm*) at their heads.[88] The southern territory (Negeb) was organized with Beersheba as the administrative
center, the wilderness of Judah (*midbar yehûdah*), as well as
the newly acquired districts in the mountain country of Ephraim
were formed into administrative units. Keeping pace with these
administrative developments, there was an intensive colonization
of the Negeb and the Arabah. The western districts also included
Philistine cities which had been incorporated into the empire
(2 Ch 17, 11).

b) MILITARY PREPARATION: Rehoboam had already had the
foresight to establish a circle of fortifications around his kingdom,
and Asa had continued the process; it was Jehoshaphat who put the
final touch on these works. He improved the ancient fortifications,
established new ones, and strengthened them with casemate walls.
There are two types of fortifications which must be distinguished:
fortresses in the strict sense of the word, with garrisons and
chariot divisions, and the less fully fortified store-cities [89] (2 Ch
17, 12-13). The army organization was also influenced by the
reform. David had already maintained a bodyguard, thereby establishing the basis of a standing army. Jehoshaphat built upon this

---

88. Many authors think that the district divisions described in the Book
    of Joshua (15, 21-63; 18, 21-28; 19, 1-9) show literary influence from
    the lists of Jehoshaphat and not those of F. M. Gross. — G. E.
    Wright, *The Boundary and Province List of the Kingdom of Judah*,
    JBL 75 (1956), 212-226.
89. From Jehoshaphat's time we date the fortifications in Ramath-Rahel
    south of Jerusalem, as well as those in Azekah. There are further
    evidences of his building activity in Cades-barnea. The Negeb was
    strongly settled in MB. Agriculture and animal industry were flourish-
    ing. Then there is a long lacuna until Iron II. Here we once again
    find abundant material, suggesting an extensive cultivation. Cf. N.
    Glueck, *The Age of Abraham in the Negeb*, BA 18 (1955), 2-9. —

foundation and, in Jerusalem, he maintained a standing army of "men of valor," mighty heroes (2 Ch 17, 13). Together with this professional army, in the event of war, he could also rely upon the levy of the "clans" (*bêt-abôt,* literally "houses of the fathers"). The command of the clan levies was no longer in the hands of the individual sheikhs; Jehoshaphat appointed five generals over the levies from Judah and Benjamin. The account in 2 Chronicles 17, 13ff., is an important source for the manner of warfare in those times, as well as the makeup of the army and the conscription lists. The foundation of the conscription levy continues to be the clan (*bêt-abôt* or *'eleph*), which is led by a commander (*gibbor hayil,* hero of strength). A company of several clans was led by a captain (*sar*). Judah supplied three "divisions." Commander Adnah was in charge of 300 clan levies, Jehohanan 280, Amasiah 200; this gives a total field strength of some 7800 men. The tribe of Benjamin supplied 2 "divisions." Eliada was in charge of 200 and Jehozabad 180 tribal levies, a total of some 3800 men. Understood in these terms, the Biblical numbers are quite reasonable. But if the word *'eleph* is translated as "thousand" instead of "tribal or clan levies," the result is a series of figures which, in the context of Ancient Near Eastern politics, can only be a monstrosity. The professional army was equipped with the most modern weapons of its time, the war chariot, while the tribal and clan levies were largely composed of foot soldiers.

c) REFORM OF THE JUDICIARY (2 Ch 19, 5): Prior to this time, less serious legal contentions were settled within the clan or tribe. Only the more serious cases came before the royal judge. Jehoshaphat's reform consisted in the appointment of the Levites to a judiciary position. The fortified cities also became centers for the administration of justice. A college of judges, consisting of Levites and, apparently, some of the elders, was established in the

---

Jehoshaphat's building activity can be identified in the Buqeah, the high valley lying in the middle of the wilderness of Judah on the northern end of the Dead Sea. Irrigation works and defense installations still preserved. J. T. Milik, *Explorations in the Judaean Buqeah,* BASOR 142 (1956), 5-17.

administrative capitals. Jerusalem supplied the court of final instance, composed of priests, Levites, and elders. For religious
litigation, there was the high priest, and for cases which touched
the crown, there was the "prince of the house of Judah." The
law which was thus administered was not a merely humanitarian
law, subject to change according to the whim and fancy of the
current power; it was a divine law. "Now then, let the fear of
the Lord be upon you; take heed what you do, for there is no
perversion of justice with the Lord our God, of partiality or taking
bribes" (2 Ch 19, 7). The reform of the judiciary which was thus
accomplished presents many points of similarity with the judiciary
of Egypt in the days of the New Kingdom. As in David's time,
we are probably not to think in terms of any direct adoption of
Egyptian judiciary practices. It is more probable that Egyptian
norms and practices were passed on to the Israelites by means
of the Egyptian administration established in the land of Canaan.

d) RELIGIOUS REFORM: Hand in hand with the military preparations and the economic advances, we find a religious reform.
Asa had laid the foundation for this in his battle against the Asherah cult. Jehoshaphat wanted to achieve new depth in religious
life and knowledge. At the same time, in the Northern Kingdom
of Israel, we witness the disintegration of the Yahweh faith by
the Tyrian Baal cult as promoted by Queen Jezebel. Under the
pressure of persecution, many Levites emigrated towards Judah,
where they formed the nucleus of a reform movement. The disintegration of the Yahweh faith in the Northern Kingdom was
balanced by its renewal in the Southern Kingdom. It was carried
out under the sign of "sword and book," with Jehoshaphat sending a mixed commission, composed of Levites and military commanders (*sarîm*) through the cities of Judah. The Levites carried
the "lawbook of Yahweh" (*sepher tôrat-yahweh*) and instructed
the people in the formal elements of Yahweh's law. The soldiers'
sword provided unmistakable emphasis for the words of the
Levites. The remaining pagan "high places" were destroyed, and
the cult prostitutes were driven from the land. The Levites were
to instruct the people in the "law of God" (2 Ch 17, 7-9). This
term "law of Yahweh" obviously does not refer to the Pentateuch

as a whole, since, in its present form, it was not yet completed. Most likely it refers to the Book of Deuteronomy in its earliest form (Ur-Deuteronomium). In Deuteronomy 17, 18 the king is admonished "when he sits on the throne of his kingdom, to write for himself in a book a copy of this law, from that which is in charge of the Levitical priests."

Even if this reform was carried out as the will of the king, it still contributed to enriching the religious consciousness and the purity of the Yahweh faith. North and South, despite their political alliance, are separated by an insurmountable religious opposition. On the one hand there is persecution and the threatened annihilation of the Yahweh faith, as Baal of Tyre is raised to the throne; and on the other hand the total banishment of the remaining Baal cult and the solemn enthronement of the one God Yahweh.

5) MOAB AND EDOM: ALLEGIANCE

Moab had taken advantage of the confusion which followed upon the political division of Israel to withdraw from the Davidic-Solomonic empire and reassert her autonomy. Omri and Ahab, however, as the Mesha Stone testifies,[90] had once again subjected Moab: "Omri was king over Israel and had humbled Moab many days; for Chemosh was angry against his country. His son (Ahab) followed him and said: I will humble Moab . . . . Omri had made himself master of the country of Madabah, and Israel dwelt there during his reign and half of the reign of his son, forty years." [91]

In order to solidify his conquest of Moab, Ahab had the ruins of Jericho rebuilt as an outpost against Moab. This construction, as judged by the sparse testimony of excavation, was restricted to

---

90. The only lengthy Moabite inscription, discovered in 1868. Since the Arabs thought there was treasure hidden in the black basalt stone, they shattered it. Still preserved today in the Louvre at Paris. Erected by King Mesha as a victory memorial in the heights sanctuary in Qeriho. Gressmann, AOT 440, Hebrew transliteration, Galling, TGI 47. Moabitic is the same language as Hebrew with only small dialectal differences.

91. General number, useless for chronology. Galling, TGI 48.

the fortification of a citadel, or rather a fortified tower. It was on this occasion that Heli offered his two sons as a building sacrifice[92]: "He laid his foundation at the cost of Abiram, and set up its gates at the cost of his youngest son Segub" (1 K 16, 34).

Edom had been subjugated under David's general Joab in a bloody campaign (1 K 11, 14ff.). The kings were driven out and Israelite officials were established in their place. Towards the end of Solomon's reign, Hadad who had fled into Egypt, returned from exile and reestablished kingship in Edom. This restoration cannot have lasted very long; under Jehoshaphat it was once again a Jewish official who ruled over Edom. Edom's defection occurred only after the death of Jehoshaphat (2 K 8, 20).

The actual extent of Judah's sovereignty thus no longer extended from "Beersheba to the mountains of Ephraim" (2 Ch 19, 4); but Edom had been subjugated as a vassal state, and the Arab tribes continued to pay their tribute (2 Ch 17, 11). The internecine conflict with the Northern Kingdom had given way to a treaty of friendship. Israel had reestablished the allegiance of Moab and renewed her treaty with Tyre. The splendor of the Solomonic kingdom seemed to have returned, even though his crown was now split into two halves. All the preparations were thus made for united action against the enemies pressing down from the north.

---

92. Rehm, EB II, 189 thinks that these were not building sacrifices, but rather are to be considered as tragic accidents. Both sons perished during the construction, a fact which was interpreted as a fulfillment of the curse pronounced by Joshue. — On the other hand, on the basis of excavation, it would appear that we are dealing with a genuine sacrifice, such as were characteristic of the Canaanites. A remarkable confirmation of this view is furnished by the discoveries in the vicinity of the Northern Gate of Tanis; archaeologists discovered the skeleton of an adult bedded in the sand and the skeleton of a child in a jar. This can be regarded as all but absolute confirmation of the fact that human sacrifice was involved in the building of Jericho. Foundation sacrifices were discovered in Megiddo, Taanach, Gezer, Tirzah, and other cities in Palestine. P. Montet, *L'Égypte et la Bible* (1959), 99.

6) THE WARS WITH THE ARAMAEANS

a) SYRIAN FREE TRADE ZONES IN SAMARIA: The Aramaeans were not satisfied with their possession of the territory along the sources of the Jordan and their section of Upper Galilee; they also won the right to free trade [93] in Israel's new capital city of Samaria (1 K 20, 34). With this acquisition they had practically the whole route from Damascus to the Western Sea under their control. It is evidence of Omri's weakness that he had to submit to this imposition. With the establishment of his sovereignty, however, he was making continual inroads into the Aramaean sphere of influence. His son Ahab was in a position to take up a counterattack and regain the territory sacrificed by his father.

b) SIEGE OF SAMARIA (c. 860): We can only conjecture as to the manner in which the siege of Samaria was lifted. Probably the Syrians felt the threat of Israel's gradual economic and military advance. The energetic Ahab lost no time in laying claim to the territories lost under the reign of Baasha. Ben-Hadad II of Damascus, a son of the Ben-Hadad who had fought with Baasha (1 K 20, 34), assembled a force of 32 "kings" (sheiks), to bring Israel to her knees. Damascus had, apparently, assumed sovereignty over the smaller Aramaean states, and thus, after the collapse of the Davidic-Solomonic empire, represented the most significant power between Egypt and Mesopotamia. Only Israel, tiny and weakened by strife, stood in the way of Syria's plans for empire. It seems that Ben-Hadad II, in order to put an early end to Israel's threatening rise to power, directed his initial attack against Samaria. He would be satisfied with nothing more, and nothing less, than the total subjection of Ahab.

---

93. Trade colonies established in foreign countries go back to most ancient times. In the Ancient Assyrian Kingdom, for example, there was a colony in Kanes (Kultepe) in Asia Minor near Kaisari. The merchant class occupy a quarter of their own (bazaar) on the edge of the city. The Phoenician colonies in the Mediterranean were probably of the same kind.

The political correspondence contained in 1 K 20, 1-12, has retained something of the tensions of those times. Ben-Hadad II meant to reduce the king to a position of impotence. Accordingly, he demanded the surrender of the royal harem, together with the royal sons and daughters, and all the gold and silver. Ahab would have been prepared to make any sacrifice for himself and for his house in order to rescue the city from the enemy siege. But there was an end to his willingness to comply. Ben-Hadad II simply went too far in his demands. He required that the whole city be given over to plunder. Ahab took council with his elders. The result: "The demands are unacceptable"; hence the threatened response: "The dust of Samaria shall not suffice for handfuls for all the people who follow me." In answer we have Ahab's measured words, as an expression of his equally confident self-assurance: "Let not him that girds on his armor (for battle) boast himself as he that puts it off (after victory)." The time for battle had come.

In ancient military practice, such decisions were not reached by purely rational deliberation. Together with the military commander there were prophets and seers. Israel shared this general practice, excepting that in Israel, since ancient times, it had been the priests and prophets of Yahweh who announced the decision. Ahab too listened to the words of a man of God who advised him to start the battle with the servants of the governors of the districts. The fact that Ahab's forces were arranged in terms of district levies presupposes the fact that the administrative divisions inaugurated by Solomon had been preserved. This bold attack was rewarded by a totally unexpected and speedy victory. Ben-Hadad II did well to save himself by horse. The chariots and horses captured in the battle were destroyed. For Israel this was a mighty victory. The Aramaeans had been repulsed from the Israelite heartland. The further battles of this campaign were fought along the frontier.[94]

---

94. Y. Yadin, *Some Aspects of the Strategy of Ahab and David* (I K 20; 2 S 11), argues that the word *sukkôth* (1 K 20, 12, 16) does not mean "huts, tents," but the strategically important location Succoth in

c) THE BATTLE AT APHEK (c. 860): This battle was followed by a feverish time of preparation on both sides. One year later, at the time that kings generally set out for war, that is, in the spring, the two opposing forces met at Aphek, east of the Lake of Gennesaret (1 K 20, 22-43). Once again, it was a man of God (1 K 20, 28) who announced victory in the name of Yahweh. The Aramaeans had said that Israel's God was a mountain god, and that is why they had lost the battle of Samaria. Now they meant to force a battle in the plain. According to the words of the man of God, the battlefield itself was to be a proof of God's power. Israel's God is also the Lord of the plains.

The Aramaeans were repulsed and withdrew into the fortress of Aphek. The pursuing Israelites undermined the city walls and brought them down. Ben-Hadad II, in his attempt to hide, fled from one chamber into another. Only the hope that Israel's kings would be mild masters encouraged him to yield to the victor. Ahab did indeed hope to put an end to the long-standing state of war between Israel and Aram, by the exercise of clemency. Accordingly, he called Ben-Hadad II his "brother," received him into his chariot, and agreed to a very sympathetic peace treaty. Ben-Hadad II was to return the occupied territories and also grant Israel the right of free trade in Damascus. This was at once a very moderate and extremely clever political move. The prophetic circles, however, were not in agreement with this compromise. According to their opinion, Ahab should have continued the war without interruption and shown no mercy. From Aram Israel could look for nothing but eventual ruin. A young prophet gave the king a dramatic demonstration of this fact. He deliberately suffered a wound in the forehead, bandaged it, and came before the king and asked for a judgment. He was supposed to have kept guard over a prisoner, but the prisoner escaped because of his carelessness. The king's judgment was short and clear: "You shall die." Then the young prophet tore the bandage from his

---

Transjordania. If this view is correct, then it is possible to distinguish two phases of the campaign on the basis of the text: Ben-Hadad sent the conditions of surrender to Ahab. When Ahab refused them, he went on to besiege Samaria.

forehead and Ahab recognized him as a prophet. It was for Ahab that the penalty of death would be invoked. He returned to Samaria resentful and sullen, despite his glorious victory [95] (1 K 20, 35-43).

d) THE ASSYRIAN THREAT FROM THE NORTH: It is surprising to note that so decisive an event as the military campaign of the Assyrians is not even mentioned in the Books of Kings. Particularly since this is an event which seems to have equal significance for the overall religious picture. Yet, from profane sources, we know that in the war against the Assyrians, Israel played a decisive role as one of the most powerful allies.

It is one of the whimsical accidents in the play of human history that the year of Israel's political split, which signalled the eventual collapse of the Solomonic empire, should also have begun the ascendancy of the New Assyrian Kingdom [96] (c. 930 — 612). The Assyrian annals recommence their narrative with Ashur-dan II (932 – 910). It is he who claims the glory of having reestablished the political, economic, and military organization of his country. Like Israel, he claims his battle against the Aramaeans as his proudest achievement. The Aramaeans had established themselves, not only in Syria, but also in Mesopotamia, where they were threatening the Assyrian kingdom. Ashur-dan's campaign against the Aramaeans was not, however, blessed with any lasting success. It was only his son and successor, Adad-nirari II (919 – 889), who succeeded, after six fierce campaigns, in conquering Nisibis, the capital city of the remnant state of Hanigalbat, dating from the Hyksos era, and making it an Assyrian province. As a consequence of this victory, a great number of neighboring states were forced to pay tribute. After

---

95. Chronology: According to 1 K 22, 1, we get the impression that the battle of Aphek was followed by three years of peace, after which occurred the decision at Ramoth-Gilead. The two events are not, however, to be connected so closely. The siege of Samaria and the battle at Aphek date from the beginning of Ahab's reign. Then there must have been several border disputes and hostile raids, until finally, under the threat of impending Assyrian peril, both sides made a peace treaty which lasted only three years, that is, until the return of the Assyrians. *EncMikr* I, 198 (article: Ahab).

96. H. Schmökel, *Geschichte des Alten Vorderasien*, Handbuch der Orientalistik, vol. II, section 3, 247ff. "The history of ancient Israel no longer stood in the isolation of 'sacred history'... entered into the main stream of world history." Pritchard, ArchOT 127.

the conquest of Babylonia, he called himself "king of the whole," "king of the four ends of the earth." His fame as a warrior was equalled by his fame as a mighty hunter, against such prey as lion, aurochs, and elephant. This gives us some indication of the peculiarity of Assyrian politics. War was fought with unheard of cruelty. The Assyrian soldier is never intimidated by the difficulty of the terrain. His power seems to grow with the opposition. The enemy is quartered, splayed, impaled, and the severed heads are heaped together in a pyramid of skulls. Defenseless women and children are carried off to slavery or burned in the ruins of conquered cities. Cruel mass executions and vast depopulation must all be enlisted in the one objective of establishing the world sovereignty of the god Ashur. "There is a bloody consistency to this century of continuous reign of terror, which establishes the type for the apocalyptic horror of the Bible. It was terror which forced the countless disunited peoples, tribes, and cities to bow before the Assyrian yoke; fear and terror preceded the arrival of their army, and often the mere appearance of their troops was enough to win tribute from the most distant country." [97]

Adad-nirari's son Tukulti-Ninurta II (888 – 884) represents the type of the ambitious and reckless adventurer who dies young and still, in his few years, leaves magnificent accomplishments behind. The energetic young king undertook a great campaign of pursuit and reconnaissance, with occasional military confrontations, a route of some 900 miles through the whole of Mesopotamia. He was followed by the mightiest ruler of the century. Ashur-nasir-pal II (883 – 859). History has not presented a consistent picture of this man. On the one hand, he is cruel to the point of sadism, a scourge of the people, slaughtering hecatombs of men, driving tens of thousands from their homes, spreading Ashur's terror with a terrible virtuosity. On the other hand, we see him as a clever administrator, the wise organizer of his empire, administering the provinces, territories, and districts of his country, building cities and temples, establishing storehouses, digging canals, promoting agriculture, undertaking a far-reaching military reform based on the introduction of a powerful cavalry, and, in his capital city of Calah (Nimrud), and particularly in his palace, presenting artists from all over the world with unparalleled opportunity.[98]

It was thus a mighty heritage to which Ashur-nasir-pal's son Shalmaneser III (858 – 824) succeeded, but his military fortunes were unequal to his father's. His further penetration into Syria was blocked by the powerful

---

97. *Ibid.*, 249.

98. *Ibid.*, 251. — E. Michel, *Die Texte Assur-nasir-apli* II, WO (1957), 313-321. Prayer of repentance to Istar in severe illness. Confession of sin and prayer for the mother of the gods to make intercession with the supreme god. W. V. Soden, *Herrscher im Alten Orient* (1954), 77.

alliance of the "twelve kings" which had meantime been established. In the face of their common peril, the twelve kings had forgotten their own individual differences.

The leadership of this alliance was undertaken by Ben-Hadad II of Damascus [99] (1 K 20, 1). It was, perhaps, the far-seeing policy of Ahab which had spared his opponent after the battle at Aphek precisely in view of this Assyrian peril, refusing to humble the mighty king and making a friend of him instead. Shortly thereafter, we find the two kings Ahab of Israel and Ben-Hadad of Damascus, standing side by side in their common cause against the Assyrians. The decisive confrontation took place at Qarqar (853), north of Hamath on the Orontes. Shalmaneser, in his inscription, boasts of a powerful victory, but the reality was somewhat less pretentious.

---

99. Chronology: In the Assyrian texts he is called Adad-idri, which occasions a problem still not adequately explained. The first half of the name is written as the ideogram *IM*, which admits of various readings; a. IM = bir, *ben* (son); *idri = hadar*; the name Bir-Hadar is supposed to be identical with Bir-Hadad (hebr. Ben-Hadad). b. *IM* = Adad-Hadad; *idri = Hebrew 'ezer*, and thus the king's name would not be Ben-hadad, but Hadad-'ezer (The God Hadad has helped). This is a contradiction between Bible and cuneiform sources. According to the Bible, Ahab's opponent was a Ben-Hadad (1 K 21, 34), son of the Ben-Hadad who took the cities from Baasha. There was a Ben-Hadad in power even during the time of the prophet Elisha (2 K 8, 7). Yet it is hardly likely that we are to insert the name of Hadad-'ezer between the last two Ben-Hadad's and identify him with the unnamed "King of Aram" in the battle of Ramoth-Gilead (1 K 22, 31). — c. The answer to this puzzle appears to lie in the assumption that the Damascene kings, upon their accession to the throne, all added the name Bar-Hadad (son of the God Hadad) to their personal names. This was cause enough for the Israelites to refer to any king of Damascus, whether his name was Hadad-'ezer or anything else, simply as Ben-Hadad. *EncMikr* II, 156-157. — Winton Thomas, DOT 48, thinks that Ahab's opponent in the battle was actually Hadad-'ezer, son of Ben-Hadad I, whom we, following the Bible, count as Ben-Hadad II. — A. Jespen, AFO 16 (1952/52), 315-317, dates Ben-Hadad's reign 885-860, with some possible leeway on both sides. Ben-Hadad II = Hadad-'ezer must be inserted between the years 860 and 842.

In the monolith inscription, we read (line 79)[100]:

"They became afraid of the terror emanating from my position as overlord, as well as of the splendor of my fierce weapons.... I crossed the Euphrates another time at its flood on rafts of goatskin.... I received tribute from the kings on the other side of the Euphrates.... I departed from the banks of the Euphrates and approached Aleppo. They were afraid to fight and seized my feet. I received silver and gold as their tribute and offered sacrifices before the Adad of Aleppo. I departed from Aleppo and approached the two towns of Irjuleni from Hamath.... I captured his royal residence. I removed from them his booty, his personal possessions. I set his palaces afire. I departed from Agarna and approached Karkara, the city of his royal residence. I destroyed, tore down, and burned Karkara. He brought along to help him 12-00 chariots, 1200 cavalrymen, 20,000 foot soldiers of Adad-idri of Damascus, 700 chariots, 700 cavalrymen, 10,000 foot soldiers of Irhuleni of Hamath, 2000 chariots, 10,000 foot soldiers of Ahab the Israelite,.... 1000 camels from Gindibu, from Arabia.... These twelve kings rose against me for a decisive battle. I fought them with the mighty forces of Ashur, which Ashur, my lord, has given to me, and the strong weapons which Nergal, my leader, has presented to me and I did inflict a defeat upon them between the towns Karkara and Gilzau. I slew 14,000 of their soldiers with the sword, descending upon them like Adad when he makes a rainstorm pour down. I spread their corpses everywhere, filling the entire plain with their widely scattered soldiers. During the battle I made their blood flow down the hur-pa-lu of the district (the plain?). The plain was too small to let all their souls descend into the nether world; the vast field gave out when it came to bury

---

100. Galling, TGI 45; Winton Thomas, DOT 46ff.; Pritchard, AET 276; Gressmann, AOT 340; E. Michel, *Text of Shalmaneser* III, WO (1955), 137-157; (1956), 221-232. The stele is illustrated in Pritchard, ArchOT Fig. 51. It is called the Kurkh-stele, after the location of its discovery, some 30 mi S of Dijarbekir on the banks of the Tigris. Shalmaneser is doing homage to the emblems of his gods: winged sun, moon, and stars. The text describes the battle of "Karkara."

them. With their corpses I spanned the Orontes before there was a bridge. Even during the battle I took from them their chariots, their horses broken to the yoke."

The number twelve, in reference to the allied kings, is a formality. In the text, eleven are mentioned. Their military strength is recorded in higher figures, in other inscriptions.[101] Even if the numbers are, obviously, not to be taken literally, they still give the impression of a great, united campaign against Assyria, mounted by a coalition of middle powers. Beginning with Cilicia in Asia Minor, and including the various Aramaean states in Syria, as far as Ammon in Transjordania, all were united against their common enemy. Even an Arabian sheikh provided a thousand camel troops. The strongest levy came from Ben-Hadad of Damascus, who, in truth, must be considered the motive power behind the alliance. Next to him stands Ahab of Israel, with his 2000 chariots and 10,000 soldiers. We must presume that, although there is no specific mention of the fact, the levy of Judah is included in this figure.

The battle at Qarqar shows the kingdom of Israel in its full military strength. This was possible only as the result of a deliberate and long-standing preparation. Ahab here follows the path of Solomon, building fortresses and store-cities. The clearest example of this is furnished by the excavations of Hazor. The great building with its many columns appears to have been simply a storeroom. The magnificence of the governor's palace is still evident today in the stupendous capitals, which adorned the entrance. Like Solomon, Ahab also carried on a large-scale traffic in horses and chariots. Quite probably, in addition to supplying his own needs, he was in a position to furnish his allies with material. Nothing could have been more important in this time of crisis, with the menacing thunderhead threatening from the north, than for the alliance to have remained together. But hardly had the Assyrians been turned aside in the battle at Qarqar —

---

101. The monolith inscription gives 14,000 enemy soldiers, the Nimrud obelisk 20,500, the Bull Inscription 25,000, the Assyrian text 29,000. Galling, TGI 47m.

their losses must have been considerable since it is five years
before they reappear on the military scene — the alliance of the
twelve fell to pieces, and the forces that necessity had joined in
friendship once again took up their bitter quarrels. In the same
year, 853, there was a decisive battle between Aram and Israel
at Ramoth-Gilead.

e) AHAB FALLS AT RAMOTH-GILEAD (1 K 22, 1-38): Ahab
was pressing for a decisive confrontation. He prevailed upon
Jehoshaphat of Judah to undertake a common cause with him
against the Aramaeans. It seems that Ben-Hadad II after his
defeat at Aphek, had refused to give up the occupied city of Ramoth-Gilead. This was a thorn in Israel's side. The occupation of
the Transjordanian crossroads city also implied control of the trade
routes. Before Ahab took the field, in keeping with Israelite custom, he asked the prophets for advice.[102] There were 400 such
prophets, and with one mouth they proclaimed the victory of
his expedition. Jehoshaphat was not satisfied. For his own part,
he wanted to consult a prophet of Yahweh. He turned to the
single representative, Micaiah.[103] His name is itself a battlecry:
"Who is like Yahweh?" He would not make common cause with
the schismatic prophets. He had little influence upon Ahab, because he was always foretelling doom. This time too, he had no
encouraging report: "I saw all Israel scattered upon the mountain,
as sheep that have no shepherd" (1 K 22, 17). Then he described
his vision from Yahweh, God of hosts, whose throne is surrounded by the whole host of heaven. In order to destroy Ahab,
Yahweh had sent forth a lying spirit in the mouth of all the
prophets, so that they would prophesy victory while Yahweh
himself was planning doom. Zedekiah, the leader of the band
of prophets, came up and struck Micaiah on the cheek, and made

---

102. S. Yeivin, *Social, religious and cultural trends in Jerusalem under
the Davidic Dynastie,* VT 3 (1953), 149-166. The court prophets are
not typically Israelite. They also appear in Canaanite and Aramaean
courts. The distinction here, as elsewhere, is in the God they worship. — E. Jenni, *Die politischen Voraussagen der Propheten,* ATHANT
2 (1956), 5-118.

103. Cf. the name *Mi-ka-el,* "Who is like God!"

iron horns as a symbol of Israel's invincibility. Ahab, too, refused to listen to the prophet of Yahweh; he had him cast into prison to await the king's victorious return from battle.

Still, the prophecy left Ahab uneasy. Before the battle, he took off his royal robes, in order to fight incognito. Ben-Hadad II had given these orders to his soldiers: "Fight with neither small nor great, but only with the king of Israel" (1 K 22, 31). The attacking forces thus centered about Jehoshaphat, whom they recognized by his royal robes as king, and they were pressing him hard. When Jehoshaphat cried out in the confusion of the battle, they recognized him as king of Judah, and withdrew from the pursuit. At that point, an archer in the enemy ranks struck Ahab between the scale armor and the breastplate. Mortally wounded, the king would not yield. Propped up in his chariot facing the Tyrians, he remained in the front ranks of his fighting troops, while his life blood drained away. By evening he was dead. About sunset a cry went through the army, "Every man to his city, and every man to his country!" (1 K 22, 36). Ahab was carried back to Samaria and buried there. His chariot was washed in a pool and dogs licked up his blood, while the harlots washed themselves in the water (1 K 22, 38).

CHAPTER III

THE FALL OF OMRI'S DYNASTY
THE PROPHET ELISHA

ISRAEL'S defeat at Ramoth-Gilead and Ahab's death resulted in the most serious consequences. The history of the Ancient Near East has frequently witnessed the truth of the old proverb: "The tyrant's death is the hope of the oppressed." Moab, accordingly, now began to shake off the yoke of Israel. The energetic Mesha, king of Moab, took up the counter-offensive, and occupied Israelite territory. There were also internal difficulties with the allied kingdom of Judah, occasioned by the construction of the fleet.

1) THE FLEET'S DISASTER

Ahaziah ben-Ahab [1] (853/52) was faced with the difficult mission of reestablishing order in his kingdom after the defeat. The Aramaean peril was still to be reckoned with, and Moab was shaking off the yoke of Israel. Moreover, the construction of a fleet in Ezion-Geber led to differences with the allied kingdom of Judah. For this venture, Jehoshaphat was absolutely dependent

---

1. According to 2 Ch 21, 17, also called Jehoahaz, the divine name being transposed. In LXX and Vulgate Ohozias.

upon the help of Israel, as well as the support of the seafaring Phoenicians. Accordingly, he reached an agreement with Ahaziah with respect to building the fleet (2 Ch 20, 36). Ahaziah seemed to have stipulated some claim to a share of the trade profits, which Jehoshaphat refused. Further negotiations proved unnecessary when the departing fleet was shipwrecked on the cliff of Ezion-Geber (1 K 22, 49). The entire undertaking had, from the outset, found disfavor with the prophet Eliezer, who branded every treaty between Judah and the schismatic Israel — and this included a trade agreement such as the building of a fleet — as an insult to Yahweh (2 Ch 20, 37). The destruction of the fleet was interpreted as a divine judgment.

Ahaziah (853-852) had no time to solve these pressing problems. Unfortunately, he fell through the lattice in his upper chamber and sustained severe internal injuries. In his desperate sickness, he could find no better counsel than to send a messenger to Ekron [2] to consult the god Baal-zebub [3] concerning his fate

---

2. J. Naveh, *Khirbet el-Mukanna: An Archaeological Survey*, IEJ 8 (1958), 87-100. Ancient Ekron is not to be identified with the modern village Kafr 'Ekron, but with the tell of Muqanna.

3. *ba'al-zebûb*: ancient Canaanite God, taken over by the Philistines. Principal sanctuary in Ekron. Derivation of the name not entirely certain: a. from a place name Zebub, similar to the Ba'al of Pe'or. — b. God of the flies (*zebûb*) since the fly was his sacred animal or perhaps because he warded off the flies as demons and bearers of pestilence. — c. Ugarit tablet V, AB, describing the monsters fought by the Goddess Anat, mentions a certain *śbb*, evidence of the fact that we are dealing with an ancient name, and not simply a misinterpretation of a modern concept. — Since the NT and Rabbinic texts (Mt 10, 24-27; Lk 11, 15-19) use *ba'al-zebûl* as the name for the devil, scholars have supposed that this is simply another name for *ba'al-zebûb*. In terms of religious history there is ample precedent for expecting the gods of defeated nations to be demoted to the position of devils. But in the Canaanite pantheon *ba'al-zebûl* was an expression of honor and reverence. The root *zbl* means "to be elevated": a. of things, "a high place, palace, residence." In this sense it occurs frequently in the Bible (1 K 8, 13; 2 Ch 6, 2; Is 63, 15; Ps 48/49, 15). — b. of persons, "highness, prince, ruler." Frequent in the Ugaritic texts: *zbl ym* "prince of the sea"; *zbl ba'al ars* "the high lord of the world," which is understood to include the underworld, the abode of the dead

(2 K 1, 1). The prophet Elijah met this messenger as he was on his way and sent him back to the king with Yahweh's own answer: he must die.[4] He was permitted to reign only two years.[5] He was followed by his brother Joram-ben Ahab.

2) ELIJAH'S "ASCENSION" (2 K 2, 1-18)

The account of Elijah's "ascension" belongs, in terms of its literary genre, not to the Elijah cycle as such; it must be taken, rather, as an introduction to the Elisha cycle and is thus to be compared to the introductory vocation visions of the other prophet.[6] Since the account of Elijah's ascension soon formed the nucleus of a most prolific legend cycle, it is worthwhile to examine the sober contents of the text.

It is a well known fact that, shortly before their last breath, dying people are seized by an inexplicable sense of unrest. They want to get up and walk away. A similar unrest seized upon the prophet Elijah. He thought that death was near. Since he, like

---

(Barrois II, 326). — The interpretation *Ba'al-zebûl* as "Lord of the (dead men's) abode" might be suggested in this connection from the context. The one consulting this god is knocking at the gates of the underworld and asking the god of the underworld to give him an oracle on his fate. If *Ba'al-zebûl* was actually the god of the underworld, it was only a short step to identifying him with the devil. For his ancient worshipers however he was not a demon, but the "God (*ba'al*) of majesty (*zebûl*)." — *ba'alzebûl* is thus an honorific epithet for *ba'al-zebûb*. EncMikr II, 287, 907.

---

4. The account of the fire falling from the sky and consuming the men sent to take Elijah prisoner (2 K 1, 9-16) might be merely a legendary midrash, designed to emphasize the inviolability of the man of god. Cf. also J. Steinmann, *Elie le prophète*, Étude Carmélitaines, I (1956), 112 (Amplification Midrashique).
5. Chronology: The chronological data present some problems. Ahaziah became king in the 17th year of Jehoshaphat (1 K 22, 52) and died in his 18th year (2 K 3, 1). Ahaziah reigned two "regnal years," at least half a year and at most a year and a half. The contradictory dating in 2 K 1, 17 is open to attack on textual grounds: it is lacking in LXX.
6. "C'est un cas d'exstase prophétique." J. Steinmann, *Elie le prophéte*, Étude Carmélitaines, I (1956), 113. Comparison with the visions of the prophets Micah, Amos, and Isaiah.

a second Moses, had striven for the unicity of Yahweh against
the Baal cult, he wanted to die in the same place that Moses
died. From Nebo, Moses had been permitted to look into the
Promised Land before he died "upon Yahweh's command" (Dt
34, 5). He was buried in the valley, in the land of Moab, across
from Beth-Peor. But no one knows the location of his grave, down
to our own day (Dt 34, 6). Where Moses once died and was
buried [7] Elijah also wanted to die. Accordingly, he set out from
Gilgal in the mountain country of Ephraim, passed through Bethel
on his way to Jericho, from where he crossed the Jordan River
and entered the Fields of Moab. The sons of the prophet knew,
by some sort of secret knowledge, that their master was now
leaving them once and for all. Elijah wanted to have no witnesses.
He refused every invitation to escort him; only Elisha his faithful
servant would he permit to accompany him upon his last journey.
In this hour of farewell, Elisha claimed for himself the hereditary
right of the firstborn, two-thirds of his master's spirit (Dt 21,
17). But the spirit of a prophet is not something which a human
person, even a chosen soul, can freely lay claim to. It is God's
prerogative to give the spirit to whomever he wills. That is why
Elijah in the face of death, can do nothing more than bid Elisha
wait for a sign from God: "You have asked a hard thing; yet,
if you see me as I am being taken from you, it shall be so for
you; but if you do not see me, it shall not be so" (2 K 2, 10).

The text speaks of a "being taken up" (*luqqah*). This Hebrew verb,
laqqah, like the English word "take," has a wide variety of meanings and
is used, in the Bible, in the most varied senses. The concordance of Lis-
owski lists almost a thousand passages: to take something (in the hand),
to take a wife (marry), to take a city (conquer), to take (seize) someone, etc. The proper word must be selected on the basis of context, if
we are to correctly establish its specific meaning. Now it is clear that
laqah can also mean "die" in the sense of "be taken off." [8] Even today we
sometimes use the expression: he was carried off by death.

---

7. Moses' death is also surrounded by legend: the story is told that he
   was buried directly by God or by the hands of angels. The text, however, explicitly refers to the men who performed this last service for
   Moses (Dt 34, 6).

8. Ez 33, 6 uses the word *laqah* in the sense of "to be killed, violently
   carried off."

If the text uses the expression: "Elijah was taken off" (carried off), this does not mean to say that Elijah was spared the pain of death and was taken up into heaven body and soul. What happened at Elijah's last moment on earth stands outside the narrow framework of this world. Seen from without, it is a lonesome death, somewhat east of the Jordan; but in the eyes of prophetic intuition, it is a tremendously dramatic and spiritual event. Elijah had made everything depend upon whether or not his servant Elisha would "see something" (2, 10). And Elisha actually did see his master's fate in the hereafter. "As they still went on and talked, behold, a chariot of fire and horses of fire separated the two of them. And Elijah went up by a whirlwind into heaven" (2, 11). In much the same manner, Elisha himself later opened the eyes of his servant and "he saw, and behold, the mountain was full of horses and chariots of fire round about Elisha" (2 K 6, 17). There is no need to wonder at this. The whole description is in perfect keeping with contemporary presentations of God's majesty. Israel's God is not a solitary God; he is God of hosts. His name is Yahweh-Sabaot. The element proper to his apparition in this world is fire; so it was at Carmel, at Horeb, and finally at the "ascension" of Elijah.

The sober meaning of "Elijah's ascension" is this: Elisha, in prophetic vision, with his eye open to the other-worldly realities of life, was privileged to see Elijah's return to God. Does not this description go beyond the current representations of the hereafter common to that ancient era? It is true that the conception of an underworld, sheol, where the departed led a somber and shadowy and wretched existence, was a predominant element, a very moving expression of human unredemption. But, side by side with this conception, we note some evidence of a new light which already testifies to the soul of the departed being taken up to God. Thus, Psalm 48/49, 15 proclaims, on the one hand, the inevitability of human death, while on the other hand it proclaims man's victory over death: "God will ransom my soul from the power of sheol; for he will receive me." The psalmist sees the same word, *laqah*, which describes Elijah's being "taken away." Finally, Ps 72/73 climaxes in the hope of being lifted up to God. At the end of this sorrowful life on earth, "thou wilt receive me to glory" (Ps 72/73, 24). Side by side with the somber representation of sheol, we thus find a faith in a blessed and luminous existence with God after death. It is true that this testimony comes rather

late in Scripture; but the new discoveries from Ugarit [9] already testify
to the existence, among the ancient Canaanites, of a belief in a blessed
Elysium, a blessed life with God. For a man like Elijah, who was all
afire for Yahweh, the somber darkness of sheol would not be a fitting
place. He was carried up to God in the midst of storm. The fact that
God's intervention in human activity was experienced as a storm is already
familiar from the vision accompanying the call of the prophet Ezekiel
(1, 4-5).

The Biblical narrative is so completely under the influence
of "being taken up to God" that there is no word of Elijah's burial.
And yet we must presume that Elisha buried his departed master
in the neighborhood of Moses' grave, across the Jordan. One
priceless heirloom he took with him, Elijah's cloak. Coming to
the Jordan, he did as Elijah had done, striking the waters with
the cloak, and immediately the water parted to one side. Then
the sons of the prophet, who were waiting across the river, realized
that the spirit of Elijah had passed into Elisha. Elisha discouraged
any attempt to discover Elijah's mortal remains. The fifty men
who set out to search found nothing. Thus, the location of Elijah's
burial is shrouded in the same silence of mystery as the grave of
his great forerunner Moses.

For the centuries to follow, Elijah became the type of the great prophet
who was to return at the endtime, preparing Israel for the dawn of God's
kingdom. He is thus described primarily by the prophet Malachi (4, 5-6):
"Behold I will send you Elijah the prophet before the great and the
terrible day of the Lord comes. And he will turn the hearts of fathers
to their children and the hearts of children to their fathers, lest I come
and smite the land with a curse."
In his song of praise on men of old, Sirach (48, 1-12) includes Elijah,
the hero of God. The narrative of the Book of Kings is here contained in
a verse form. Sirach also draws on the prophet Malachi: "You are
ready at the appointed time, it is written, to calm the wrath of God
before it breaks out in fury, to turn the hearts of the fathers to the sons,
and to restore the tribes of Jacob . . . ." The Book of Maccabees contains
no new material regarding the narrative of Elijah's departure into heaven.
The manner in which we are to interpret Elijah's return to earth
has been clearly explained by Christ himself, and with the most astounding
simplicity. In his day, the belief in Elijah's eventual return had become

---

9. M. Dahood, Bibl 42 (1961), 236.

a common popular motif. At the Paschal meal, even today, Jews will set a cup for Elijah and leave the door half open. No one is allowed to look out to see whether Elijah is already there. But Jesus will have none of this pious legend. He says quite simply: "Elijah has already come" (Mt 17, 10). By this he means John the Baptist. Accordingly, the prophetic text regarding Elijah's return is to be understood in a typal sense; it offers no foundation for any wild fancy of the imagination.

Nor does the Book of Revelations (11, 3-13), in referring to the two great witnesses who are to appear before the endtime, mean to say that one of them will be Elijah in person. The whole section is filled with symbolism. It means only to say that, before the great judgment at the end of human history, God will once again call forth witnesses, who will arouse mankind as did the prophet Elijah.

3) MOAB'S VIOLENT RAGE AGAINST ISRAEL (2 K 3, 27)

After the disastrous battle at Ramoth-Gilead (853), Moab [10] had revolted. Joram ben-Ahab was forced either to accept the revolt as a *fait accompli* or intervene with military action. He chose war (c. 850). The most obvious course would have been an attack from north of the Dead Sea, with Jericho as the point of support. Since, however, there was still a state of war with Aram, Joram would thus have been engaging on a two-front campaign. Moreover, he would have had to negotiate Mesha's newly erected border fortifications. These considerations prompted him to attack from the unfortified south. This was possible only because Jehoshaphat was his ally and Edom was subject to the sovereignty of Judah. The approach through the desert country of Edom occasioned great difficulty. Lack of water was the most serious problem. A most unfortunate choice of route: word was already passing through the army that "Yahweh has called these three kings to give them into the hands of Moab" (2 K 3, 10). In this time of crisis they turned to a prophet. Elisha was present in the camp. Called before the king, he had no kindly words for him. His prophetic rage against the treaty of Judah and the schismatic Israel burst into words. Only after a minstrel had come

---

10. J. A. Thompson, *The History of Biblical Moab in the Light of Modern Knowledge*, ABR 5 (1956), 119-143. — Roland E. Murphy, *Israel and Moab in the Ninth Century*, CBQ 15 (1953), 409-417.

to soothe his anger, did the hand of Yahweh descend upon him. He instructed the army to dig trenches in the bed of the Wadi, and in the morning they would be full of water. Next morning, the sun reflected in the water, and when the Moabites saw the water red as blood, they concluded that the three kings had begun fighting among themselves. They approached the camp to carry off the spoils, but the allies attacked them, repulsed the Moabites in a fierce battle, laid waste to the land, sowed the fields with stone, stopped up the wells, chopped down all the fruit trees, and forced their adversaries back to their capital city of Kir Hareset [11] (2 K 3, 25).

The siege was a hard one. Slingers took up their position all around the fortress. Mesha attempted to break through the siege opposite the king of Edom, with 700 of his best armed troops. He was beaten back. In his terrible hour of crisis, he sacrificed his own son and successor as a holocaust on the city walls. The Biblical account says that "there came great wrath upon Israel" (*kesseph gadôl*), so that they withdrew and returned to their own land (2 K 3, 27): this no doubt means that the Moabites, with the courage born of their final despair, fell upon the besieging armies with desperate fury and forced them to withdraw (2 K 3, 4-27).

That the campaign against Moab was unsuccessful is further witnessed by the Mesha inscription,[12] the only major written document from the era of the kings. It breathes a spiritual atmosphere which is not too alien to the Biblical world. King Mesha's war chronicle is, like the Biblical narratives, completely saturated with the religious point of view. The historical event is accomplished by the divinity, in Israel by Yahweh, in Moab by Chemosh. When Chemosh was angry with his people he gave them

---

11. Also called Kir-heres, or simply Kir-Moab (a city of Moab), identified with modern el-Kerak, on the ancient king's highway of Transjordania, some 18 mi S of Arnon. Today: 16,000 population, some 2000 orthodox Christians. From Amman it can be reached by auto-route, about 61 mi.
12. Cf. above page 74. Text, Gressmann, AOT 440-443; Galling, TGI 47-49; Winton Thomas, DOT 195ff., Table 9; Pritchard, ANET 320.

over to their enemy. After his wrath had been appeased, the people's fate also changed for the good. It was Chemosh who drove out the enemy and took up his residence in the conquered cities.[13] Even the military procedures are no different from Israel's. Mesha, too, invoked the blood ban (*herem*): "I took the city of Nebo and killed all its people, seven thousand men and boys, and women and girls and maid-servants, for I have sworn to Ashtar-Chemosh to destroy it" (*hrmth* — line 17). In sharp contrast to the Biblical narrative, Mesha puts great stress on the first-person pronoun; he gives a list of all his accomplishments, what cities he conquered, what cities he rebuilt.[14] In the full pride of his victory he proclaims: "Israel is once and for all destroyed."

Moab was not content with her successes on the far side of the Dead Sea. In alliance with Ammon and Seir, that is, Edom, she carried the attack into the heartland of Judah (2 Ch 20, 14-30). From Engedi the army meant to pass through the wilderness of Judah up the Ascent of Ziz [15] (2 Ch 20, 16) into Judea. King Jehoshaphat turned to Yahweh; as the enemy approached, he decreed a prayer service in the temple of Jerusalem, begging for salvation from his terrible crisis. The spirit of the Lord fell upon Jahaziel ben-Zechariah (2 Ch 20, 14), foretelling help from God and salvation from their peril. Jehoshaphat and his army marched through Bethlehem into the steppe of Tekoa. As they approached the hostile camp, the battle, contrary to all expectations, had already been decided. The invaders had fallen

---

13. This was a commonplace of Ancient Near Eastern theology, especially the gods' involvement in human fate. Cf. Morton Smith, *The Common Theology of the Ancient Near East*, JBL 71 (1952), 136-147.
14. At the excavations in Dibon (Mesha stele line 21) a great amount of grain was unearthed. Carbon-testing dates it from the year 1020 to 680 B.C. Moab must have been a fertile grain-producing land in those days. Cf. W. L. Reed, *A Recent Analysis of Grain from Ancient Dibon in Moab*, BASOR 146 (1957), 6-10; BASOR 133 (1954), 6-26; Bibl 35 (1954), 402-404.
15. Modern *wadi hasāsa*: "The road zigzags across an impressive pass down into the springs of En-geddi." Th. Fast, *Zwischen der südpalästinischen Wasserscheide und dem Toten Meer*, ZDPV 75 (1960), 120.

into a serious quarrel and begun fighting among themselves. There was little left for the men of Judah to do. They put all the survivors to death and carried off a great quantity of spoils. As a memorial to this act of salvation, the valley was named "Valley of Blessing and Praise" (*'emek berakah*) (2 Ch 20, 26). It seems that Judah was secure from this direction for some time, for "Yahweh gave Jehoshaphat rest roundabout" (2 Ch 20, 30).

4) DESCENDENCY OF THE KINGDOM OF JUDAH

The 25 years of Jehoshaphat's reign (870 — 845) began as a promise of general blossom. The alliance with Israel assured the economic progress of the country; the military and judicial and religious reforms provided an unparalleled internal strength for the kingdom. In the judgment of history he lives on as a successful, fortunate, and also pious king, who walked in the footsteps of David. And yet the end of his rule inaugurated the inevitable collapse which darkened the last years of his reign. The alliance with Israel was never approved by the prophetic circles. Because of his failing health, during his last years (849/48) he shared his kingdom with his son Jehoram.[16] In order to avoid any quarrels in the succession to the throne, he sent out princes to rule in fortified cities throughout the land.

No sooner had Jehoshaphat been interred in the royal tomb and Jehoram officially recognized as sole ruler(845) than he had all his brothers murdered, in order to secure his throne. Since he was married to Ahab's daughter Athaliah, the treaty of friendship with Israel was still very much in effect. Certain changes in the surrounding political situation, however, severely strained relations

---

16. Chronology: This follows from the synchronism in 2 K 8, 16, according to which the fifth year of Jehoram of Israel is synchronous with the first year of Jehoram of Judah and the 22nd year of Jehoshaphat. The synchronism in 2 K 1, 17 is not in LXX and thus cannot be used as a solid argument, on the basis of textual criticism. Jehoram was co-regent with his father Jehoshaphat from the 22nd to the 25th year of his reign. Since probably the year of the co-regent's accession to power was also officially counted, the sharing of power would have taken place in the year 849/848.

between the two kingdoms. Moab had succeeded in freeing herself from Israel's yoke. What was to prevent the enslaved Edomites from casting off the chains of Judah? In the war against Moab, an Edomite contingent had fought under the command of the Judaean governor. Shortly afterwards, Edom revolted from Judah and created a king of her own (2 K 8, 20).

Jehoram, in an effort to put down the revolt, set out towards the south with a chariot force. The decisive battle took place at night. The Edomites succeeded in surrounding the army of Judah and beat them (2 K 8, 21). The text is not precise in locating the position of this battle.[17] Edom's revolt, at all events, was a heavy blow to Judah's economy. Not only the mines and the shipyards, but the entire caravan trade with Arabia was lost.

Nor was this all. After the bulwark had fallen, the door was open to further raids by robber hordes. The attacks of the Philistines, Arabs, and Cushites (2 Ch 21, 16ff.) probably had some connection with the renewed campaigns of the Assyrians. We cannot exclude the possibility that, by reason of his obligation as an ally, Jehoram of Judah might have sent a contingent against Shalmaneser in the year 845. This would leave Judah itself without adequate military protection. Such an opportunity would obviously be used by the heretofore tribute-paying tribes to make a series of raids. It is possible that Assyrian agents may have been active in promoting these diversions. At all events, the robber hordes succeeded in overrunning Jerusalem itself. They plundered the royal palace, captured the wives and children of the king. Only the youngest of the king's sons survived, Jehoahaz (2 Ch 21, 16).

This continuous series of severe misfortunes led the prophetic circles to renew their opposition to the religious defection of Jehoram ben-Jehoshaphat. In the "letter of Elijah" [18] (3, 16) we

---

17. And he went to s'yr (8, 21). a. Soar on the southern end of the Dead Sea was Moabite and thus cannot be the correct identification; b. si'or, 4 mi N of Hebron, is too far into the Judaean territory; c. hence, correct to se'ir-Edom. This makes it simply a general reference, "somewhere in Edom." Simons, GTT, #914.

18. Criticism has attributed the letter to Elijah — justifiably, on the basis of chronology.

have a clear expression of this: "Thus says the Lord, the God of David your father, 'Because you have not walked in the ways of Jehoshaphat your father, or in the ways of Asa King of Judah, ... and have led Judah and the inhabitants of Jerusalem into unfaithfulness, the Lord will bring a great plague on your people...'" (2 Ch 21, 12-25). The purity of Jehoshaphat's heritage was gone. Under the influence of his wife Athaliah, a true daughter of Jezebel, Jehoram had reintroduced the cult of the high places into Judah, and thus led Judah into religious adultery and shame (2 Ch 21, 11). When Jehoram fell mortally ill — at the end of two years, his bowels came out because of the disease and he died in great agony — the people interpreted this as God's own sentence. He was buried in the city of David, but not in the royal tombs. Neither was he buried with a solemn funeral pyre (2 K 8, 24; 2 Ch 21, 20).

5) DESCENDENCY OF THE KINGDOM OF ISRAEL

a) "FIVE KINGS I DEFEATED ...": Whether the great majority of the Aramaean principalities of Syria, the Phoenician cities, and also the two kingdoms of Israel and Judah wanted to admit it or not, they had no freedom of choice against the ascendant power of Assyrian supremacy. Only under the powerful pressure from the north could they manage, from time to time, to overlook their mutual grievances and oppose the Assyrian with a united front. According to the Assyrian sources, Hadad-Idri (Ben-Hadad II) was the rallying point of this resistance. Together with him the text speaks of Irhuleni of Hamath, as well as the "twelve kings" of the sea coast. This anti-Assyrian coalition had succeeded in stopping the further penetration of Shalmaneser III in the battle at Qarqar (853). The Assyrian inscriptions boast of a victory, but it was obviously a defeat. No sooner was the peril turned aside than the ancient quarrels revived among the parties to the alliance. Israel and Judah made common cause in battle against Aram, at Ramoth-Gilead. Ahab fell in this battle (853). Five years after the battle of Qarqar, in the year 848, when Shalmaneser III once again crosses the Euphrates, the coalition of twelve under the leadership of Ben-Hadad is formed for a second time. Although the inscriptions make no explicit mention of the fact, Jehoram of Israel and Jehoram of Judah must have both taken part in the war. This time, too, they succeeded in breaking the advance of the Assyrian, before Hamath. Shalmaneser III, however, unwilling to accept defeat, renewed the attempt three years later (845), with a much stronger army. He had no better success, however, in breaking the resistance of the western countries. It was only the bloody revolution in Damascus and Samaria that changed the political situation.

b) "WHY DID THIS MAD FELLOW COME TO YOU?" (2 K 9, 11). Just as after the battle at Qarqar (853), once again after the threat of Assyrian invasion was turned aside in the year 845, the old border disputes between Aram and Israel flared up anew. Once again it was Ramoth-Gilead. After the tragic death of Jeroham ben-Jehoshaphat, as described above, his one remaining son who had survived the Arab raids followed him, at the age of 22, on the throne of Jerusalem — Ahaziah (842/41 — 2 Ch 21, 17, 22, 1; 2 K 8, 25). He kept faith with the covenant with his uncle Jehoram ben-Ahab, and sent a Judaean contingent[19] to Ramoth-Gilead (2 K 8, 28). The war dragged on. At first it seemed a successful venture for Israel, since Ramoth-Gilead passed into Israelite possession, but Jehoram was wounded and withdrew towards Jezreel to recover. The command over the frontier garrison at Ramoth was entrusted to Jehu (2 K 9, 14). Hearing of his uncle's wounds, Ahaziah of Jerusalem went to visit the wounded warrior in Jezreel. Meantime, the fate of Ramoth-Gilead ran its course.

A son of the prophets, sent by Elisha, appeared in the camp. Jehu [20] was sitting in the council of his officers (*sarê hahayil*:

---

19. The text: "And Ahaziah together with Jehoram entered into the war" (2 K 8, 28) does not necessarily mean that Ahaziah himself took part in the battle. He sent auxiliary troops but did not go to Jezreel until hearing of his uncle's wound.

20. Short form for *Yahu-hu'* "Yahweh-HE!" A name proclaiming that "Yahweh *is*" (i.e., "is the great one in Israel," or "it is Yahweh who has sent the child.") Cf. the change from Yehoshua to Yeshuah, to Jesus. In Assyrian documents he is called *Ya-u-a. EncMikr* III, 473.

2 K 9, 5). "I have an errand to you, O commander." — The two men withdrew to the house. Then the young man took a vessel of oil, poured it over Jehu's head, proclaiming in the name of Yahweh: "I have anointed you king over the people of the Lord, over Israel." He ordered him to execute the judgment of God over the godless house of Ahab. Then he tore open the door and fled. The officers witnessed his strange behavior with astonishment. When Jehu came back out, they joked about him: "Is all well (šalôm)? Why did this mad fellow come to you (mešugga')?" Jehu refused a direct answer: "You know the fellow and his talk." But they would not be put off: "That is not true; tell us now." Jehu admitted that the young prophet had anointed him king. This was the necessary spark. They all took up the cry: "Jehu is king" (malak yehu', 9, 13), spread their cloaks for a carpet before him, and sounded the trumpets (šophar).

c) JEHU'S RIDE (841): The events that follow are closely crowded. To keep any traitor from spreading the news outside, Jehu had the city gates closed. He himself, with a detachment of chariot warriors, raced in wild haste towards Jezreel. From the city gates, the guards observed the approaching multitude. Horsemen were dispatched to meet him. These were forced to ride behind him and did not return to the city. When the watchman realized that it could only be Jehu, because he was "riding so furiously" (9, 20), Jehoram made ready his chariot to go to meet him. They met at the vineyard of Naboth. "Is it peace, Jehu?" (šalôm) — "What peace can there be, so long as the harlotries and the sorceries of your mother Jezebel are so many?" — Then Jehoram cried "treachery!" and turned to flee, but Jehu drew his bow and shot Jehoram between the shoulders, so that the arrow pierced his heart and he died. His corpse was cast upon the ground in Naboth's fields.[21]

---

21. Jehu belonged to Ahab's body-guard (2 K 9, 25), and had thus heard Elijah's words of threat. Bidkar was Jehu's chariot companion — he is called šališ, "the third one." The war chariot was occupied by the driver, the warrior, and his squire.

Meantime, Ahaziah, King of Judah, had also made his escape, in the direction of Beth-haggan. Jehu had him hotly pursued. He was overtaken on the Ascent of Gur which is by Ibleam, and struck down there. He made his way as far as Megiddo, where he died.[22] His corpse was carried to Jerusalem (2 K 9, 21-29).

Jehu's entry into Jezreel borders on the grotesque. Jezebel had painted her eyes and adorned her head. She was looking out the upper window and when she saw Jehu's approach she cried out to him: "Is it peace (*šalôm*), Zimri, murderer of your master?" (9, 31). Calling him Zimri was an act of contempt on her part; Zimri had also killed his master Elah. Jehu had only the briefest answer for her: "Who is on my side? Who?" Two or three eunuchs took Jezebel and cast her down from the window. Her blood spattered on the wall and the horses trampled her corpse. When Jehu, later that same night, had them search for her body, they found only the skull and feet and the palms of her hands. The dogs had eaten the rest — a most gruesome fulfillment of Elijah's threat (2 K 9, 30-37).

d) LETTERS TO SAMARIA (2 K 10, 1-14): Jehu had managed, by his bold and energetic attack, to kill the two kings and to overrun the fortress city of Jezreel. But he had not yet won his game. He had no assurance that his *coup d'état* would be particularly welcome in Samaria, and that there would not be any opposition to the murder of the king. To ascertain the situation there, Jehu sent a first letter, loaded with irony, to the commanders of the army, the elders of the city, and the princely house of Samaria. He pointed out that they had chariots and horses, fortified cities and weapons. They need only select the best and fittest of of their master's sons and set him on his father's throne, to fight against Jehu. Their answer was couched in the most subservient tones: " We are your servants, and we will do all that you bid us.

---

22. 2 Ch 22, 9 presents a different version. Ahaziah was hiding in Samaria and had to be hunted out first. He was carried before Jehu, who had him killed. The account in 2 K 9 deserves greater credence by reason of its clarity and familiarity with the geography involved. The Chronist is recording only a schematically abbreviated report.

We will not make any one king." Jehu then sent a second
missive, demanding a gruesome blood bath. He would be content
with neither more nor less than the heads of the seventy sons
of the king. His order was carried out, the severed heads were sent
in baskets to Jezreel. There Jehu had them heaped into two
piles before the city gates.

Meantime, all unsuspecting, the royal princes of Jerusalem
had set out to visit their wounded uncle in Jezreel. All forty-
two of them were cut down by the fountain of Beth-eked (2 K
10, 12-14). Thus was the house of Omri completely annihilated.

e) ZEAL FOR YAHWEH: On his way back to Samaria, Jehu
met Jehonadab ben-Rechab and took him up into the chariot:
"Come with me, and see my zeal for Yahweh" (2 K 10, 15).
The Rechabites formed a special group within the Israelite tribes.
They traced their origin to the Kenites (1 Ch 2, 55). Even after
the occupation of the Promised Land, they held to their old
Beduin life, drank no wine, and preserved the purity of the Yahweh cult (Jr 35, 6-14). Since Jehu — in spite of all his bloody
excesses — was about to annihilate the Baal cult together with
the schismatic dynasty and reestablish Yahweh's position as the
only God, it was only natural that the sons of Rechab should
be on his side.

Samaria opened her doors. Jehu entered as the new master.
It was not yet clear what his position would be towards the Baal
cult. At first it seemed that he would walk the familiar path of
the house of Ahab. He convoked a great feast in honor of Baal.
This could only be interpreted as a victory feast after his accession to power. It is true that his invitation to the prophets,
priests, and servants of Baal was bound up with a threat of capital
punishment if they should fail to appear. The fact that the temple
of Baal was filled from one end to another does not argue the
presence of all the people faithful to Baal, but only the spiritual
leaders. The temple area was proportionally rather small and
could be occupied only by the cult servants. Jehu had the cult
vestments distributed, in order to begin the sacrificial service.
Meantime he had the temple surrounded by 80 soldiers. On a
given signal, they all fell upon the assembled faithful and cut

them down. Then they dragged out the furnishings of the temple, burning what could be burned, and shattered the stone altars; the temple was then demolished and turned into a latrine (2 K 10, 18-27). This was a mortal blow to the Phoenician Baal cult. It was never again reestablished. We have further evidence of this fact from the ostraca remains of Samaria. From this time onward, there are no further names compounded with the suffix -baal. Jehu, however, for all his zeal, did not take the final step. The bull cult at Dan and Bethel, inaugurated by Jeroboam, was not destroyed. And thus the sorry wound of a divided faith continued to fester.

6) SEQUEL IN JERUSALEM (841)

The political alliance between Israel and Judah had been confirmed by the marriage between Jehoram ben-Jehoshaphat and Athaliah, the daughter of Ahab.[23] Athaliah's mother Jezebel had introduced the Tyrian Baal cult into Israel, and now her daughter attempted to do the same in Judah. She seems to have been just as energetic as her mother. She succeeded in exercising a great degree of influence over her husband, so that "Jehoram walked in the way of the kings of Israel and did what was evil in the sight of Yahweh" (2 K 8, 18). The cult of the high places was reestablished (2 Ch 21, 11). Jerusalem itself housed the temple of Baal (bêt habba'al — 2 K 11, 18). The reform work inaugurated by Asa and Jehoshaphat was severely threatened by the machinations of Athaliah. If this was true during the lifetime of her royal consort, it was even more serious after Athaliah had seized sole power for herself alone.

After Jehu had annihilated the "seed of Omri" in the Northern Kingdom, Athaliah did her part in Jerusalem (841/40 — 836). Whatever survived of the "royal seed" (2 K 11, 1) she had put to death, and seized full power for herself. Jehosheba, the sister

23. H. J. Katzenstein, *Who were the parents of Ataljah?* IEJ 5 (1955), 194-197, thinks that Athaliah was Omri's daughter, raised as an orphan at Ahab's court; hence her name "daughter of Ahab." Not convincing.

of the murdered Ahaziah and the daughter of Jehoram, did, however, succeed in escaping Athaliah's bloody vengeance. She hid Ahaziah's infant son Joash, together with his nurse, in the bed chamber (2 K 11, 2). When Joash was seven years old, Jehoiada (836) thought the time was ripe for a *coup d'état*. He very cleverly set to work. In order to avoid all suspicion, he chose a Sabbath day for his stroke. First he assured himself of the faithfulness of the royal bodyguard. He secretly convoked the commanders of the hundreds, of the Cares,[24] as well as various sheikhs (tribal heads) from outside Jerusalem, called simply "the people of the land" (*'am ha'ares* — 2 Ch 23, 20), as well as Levites.[25] To these he presented the young king. The plan had been laid, down to the least detail. When the guard was relieved, the departing garrison was not to withdraw, but rather to occupy the key positions. The soldiers off guard were divided into three divisions, each with its appointed task. The one group was to hold the royal palace in check and, at the same time, cover the approach to the temple from the south. The second group was to occupy the Sur Gate, a position which cannot be accurately determined. The objective of the third group is given differently in 2 Kings 11, 6 and 2 Chronicles 23, 4. According to Chronicles, it is to stand with the priests and Levites who are keeping watch at the threshold of the temple tower; that is, to lend additional strength to the normal watch. The expressions used in the Book of Kings would seem to point in the same general direction, excepting that their position is given in more precise terms, "a third at the gate behind the guards" (2 K 11, 6). The relieving watch was charged with the

24. Foreign mercenaries like the Keretites and Peletites in the days of David. Cf. the "Swiss Guard."
25. *'am ha'ares* means, in NT parlance, "the poorer classes," but in the era of the Kings it was equivalent to the "country gentry." It was a collective expression for the ruling classes outside Jerusalem, people who were bound to the royal house by a long tradition and frequently exerted considerable influence in determining the succession to the throne. Leaders of the various districts, royal officials, and sheikhs. No property qualifications. L. A. Snijders, *"Volk des Landes" in Juda,* NTTs 12 (1958), 241-258.

personal protection of the king's body. Anyone who attempted to break through the ring of guards about the person of the king was to be immediately cut down. Jehoiada distributed the weapons which were stored in the temple. When all the guards were at their post, he led forth the young king, put the crown upon his head, and anointed him king.[26] All present began applauding and crying out: "Long live the king!" The ceremony took place near a "pillar" (2 K 11, 14), probably one of the temple pillars called Boaz and Yakin which was symbolic of the abiding power of David's dynasty.[27]

When Athaliah heard the people's shouts and the sound of the trumpets, she hurried into the temple. The sight that greeted her there stopped her short. A royal coronation. She tore her clothes and cried out: "Treachery!" At a sign from the high priest Jehoiada she was seized, dragged outside the temple area, and cut down with the sword. The coronation ceremonies climaxed in a renewal of the covenant (*berît*), the covenant with God on the one hand (Yahweh — king, people) and the royal covenant on the other hand (king — people). They swore that, from that time on, they would be, unreservedly, the "people of God" (*'am l^eyahweh*). After the coronation and anointing in the temple, the young king was escorted into the palace. There he sat upon the throne of his fathers and received the homage of his subjects.[28] During the minority of the young ruler, the high priest Jehoiada acted as regent.

---

26. According to 2 K 11, 12 the high priest also bore witness (*'ēdût*) to the king, probably on the "book of the Law of Yahweh" (*sēpher tôrat yahweh*) upon which the young ruler was obligated.
27. Cf. Vol. III, 332ff. — H.-J. Kraus, *Archäolog. u. topograph. Probleme Jerusalems*, ZDPV 75 (1960), 140 argues that the "column" (*'ammûd*) was a stone pedestal between the temple entrance and the altar, a place of natural preeminence generally reserved only for the king's worship alone.
28. The Israelite kingship did actually have a sacral character. By his anointing the king enjoyed a higher rank than the levites and could thus exercise priestly functions. It is precisely on the basis of their consecration that the pious kings always exert a reforming influence on the cult. VT (1957), 433-435.

In their enthusiasm for this "new covenant" the people stormed into the Baal temple and tore it down. Images and altars were demolished, and Mattan, the priest of Baal established by Athaliah, was put to death (2 K 11, 18). Thus, in Judah too, the seed of Omri was rooted out. The new dynasty could begin. Athaliah had broken into the temple of Yahweh and devoted all the votive offerings to the service of the Baal cult (2 Ch 24, 7). It was the high priest Jehoiada who outlined the financial plan for the restoration of the temple. He counted on the cooperation of the Levites. Since the cult regulation established by David, the Levites' primary responsibility was the cult service, but now they were also to cooperate actively in the maintenance of the temple. One portion of the "church tax," that is, the regular duties imposed by Moses, was now to accrue to the building project. Among these was the head tax which every Israelite more than twenty years of age was obliged to pay, to the amount of half a shekel, as a contribution to the service in the sanctuary (Ex 30, 12-16); this also included the ransom of the firstborn (Nb 18, 16) as well as spontaneous contributions. The portions of the sacrifices and tithes accruing to the priests and Levites were untouched by these new regulations, excepting that the Levites were commanded to collect these taxes from all Israel (2 Ch 24, 5). They were in no great haste to do so. The plan seems not to have been carried out primarily because the Levites refused to undertake the responsibility of collecting the money (2 Ch 24, 6). Obviously the Yahweh cult in the temple was reestablished during this era; the temporary restoration seemed, as it so often does, to turn into a lasting solution. But, in the 23rd year of his reign (814/13), Joash took matters into his own hands. He supported Jehoiada's financial plan, which was counting solely on the regular prescribed income, and also established what might be called a free-will "building fund." He had a chest (*arôn*) set up in the temple, into which contributions could be made. When the chest was full, the money was counted and weighed, in the presence of the high priest and the king's secretary. The contributions were so abundant that they soon sufficed for the purchase of building materials, wood and hewn stone, and for a satisfactory wage for the builders. The surplus was used to purchase cult objects (2 K 12, 5-17; 2 Ch 24, 4-14). The high priest Jehoiada died at a patriarchal age, which is expressed by the symbolic number of 130 years (2 Ch 24, 15). It remained his abiding accomplishment that he renewed the Davidic kingdom and the temple cult. Soon after his death, however, the opposition gained in strength.

CHAPTER IV

"IN THOSE DAYS YAHWEH BEGAN
TO CUT OFF PARTS OF ISRAEL"
(2 K 10, 32)

WHAT the songs of Omri had built up by their energetic political activity was quickly and bloodily destroyed. With the extermination of the Tyrian Baal cult, there was an end to the friendly trade relationships with the Phoenician cities. Israel and Judah relapsed into their former political isolation. It was only the ancient hereditary enemy in Damascus who gained. But first there was the far-reaching Assyrian peril from the north.

1) JEHU PAYS TRIBUTE TO ASHUR (841)

Shalmaneser III had not abandoned his obective of once and for all subjugating the Aramaeans of Damascus together with the twelve allied kings. In the 18th year of his reign (841) he crossed the Euphrates for the 16th time. This time, the situation was far more favorable than on any of his previous campaigns. A mysterious *coup d'état* had taken place in Damascus (2 K 8, 7-15). As to the role played by the prophet Elisha the text is not clear. At all events, Ben-Hadad was already a sick man when Elisha came to Damascus. When he learned of the prophet's coming, the sick man sent Hazael to meet him with rich presents, inquiring what would be his fate. Would he recover or must he die? The prophet's answer was two-fold, yes and no. It was no mere conventional attempt to calm the king's apprehension when the prophet said: "Go, say to him, 'You shall certainly recover!' " (8, 10). Normally, Ben-Hadad would have recovered, provided . . . . Hazael fixed his gaze and stared at Elisha, until he was ashamed and wept: "Yahweh has shown me that he shall certainly die" (8, 10). Is this to be understood as an encouragement to regicide, or was the prophet merely exposing the secret plans of Hazael? At all events, the prophet began to weep because he had also seen in his vision that this man could bring only suffering and humiliation upon Israel. Elijah had been commanded on Mount Horeb to go and anoint Hazael king over Aram (1 K 19, 15). His disciple Elisha now met with this marked man; there is, however, no mention of a royal anointing. Hazael returned to Damascus, took a coverlet, dipped it in water, and spread it over the king's face until he suffocated. Then he had himself proclaimed king.

This revolution must have taken place between the two Assyrian campaigns, in the years 845-841. In the account of the campaign of 845, Ben-Hadad is still at the head of the middle powers, but in the accounts of the campaign of 841 we read of "Hazilu,[1] the son of a nobody," [2] that is, a usurper who had seized the throne by violence. Hazael had no time to reconstitute the old alliance. He was forced to face the Assyrian attack alone. The decisive battle took place in the Antilebanon, on the slopes of Senir. Hazael was forced to withdraw to the fortifications of Damascus. Shalmaneser did not succeed in taking Damascus, but he did lay waste to the whole countryside, forcing his way, burning and pillaging, as far south as Hauran, where he crossed the Lebanon and immortalized his achievements in an inscription on Cape *Ba'ali-ra'si*.[3] Here he also accepted tribute from the Tyrians

---

1. "God has looked upon" (complete the sense by adding: "the lowliness of his handmaiden and sent a son"). *EncMikr* III, 87.
2. Gressmann, AOT 344.
3. A rocky promontory jutting sharply above and directly above the sea;

and Sidonians and the *Ya-u-a mar Hu-um-ri-i,* that is, Jehu of Israel.[4] The account of this campaign is preserved both in the Assyrian royal annals and on the black obelisk.[5] Shalmaneser attended by a great number of defeated warriors, captured chariots, and destroyed cities. On the obelisk, we have a record, in relief with an accompanying text, of Jehu's homage, the only surviving representation of an Israelite king. Jehu bows low at the feet of Shalmaneser, his forehead touching the ground. He is wearing a beard, a long, fringed tunic, girt in the middle, and a sleeveless cloak. He is followed by 13 men, who can be recognized as Hebrews by their dress, all bearing gifts: "Gold, silver, a golden basin, a golden vase, a golden goblet, a golden bucket, a staff for the king's hand (?) . . . ." [6]

Three years later, in his grim and sullen tenacity, Shalmaneser set out upon a new campaign against Damascus, hoping finally to subjugate the city. This time, once again, he was unsuccessful. He did, however, once again succeed in laying waste the entire country and receiving tribute from the cities of Tyre, Sidon and Byblos.[7]

For the time, Ashur's powers were spent. Internal political unrest stood in the way of any further military expeditions. This

---

in earliest antiquity a narrow road had been cut along the rock. Egyptian, Babylonian, and Assyrian conquerors have all left inscriptions in the stone. Situated N of Beirut, on the Nahr el-Kelb (Dog River). — The ancient roads lay half-way up the cliff, while the modern route is cut along its base. Gressmann, AOB 146.

---

4. Despite this overthrow, the Assyrian sources refer to Jehu as a "son of Omri," and call the land simply the "land of Omri."
5. Gressmann, AOT 343; Pritchard, ANET 280; Galling, TGI 47; Winton Thomas, DOT 46.
6. Gressmann, AOT 343; Pritchard, ANET 280; Winton Thomas, DOT 48 (with illustration of the obelisk). Shalmaneser had the black obelisk erected in his newly founded capital city of Calah (Nimrud) as a monument to his victory. Today it is in the British Museum. The black obelisk was discovered in 1846 by Lagarde in Nimrud, and after two years of wandering, by way of India, it reached London. Pritchard, ArchOT 144. — New texts from Shalmaneser were discovered in Ashur. R. Follet, VD 30 (1952), 227-233.
7. Black Obelisk, lines 102-104, AOT 343.

finally gave Jehu and his opponent Hazael time to recover. In describing the twenty-eight years of Jehu's reign (841/40 — 814), the Book of Kings makes mention of no individual details, since "the rest of the acts of Jehu, and all that he did, and all his might, are they not written in the Book of the Chronicles of the Kings of Israel?" (10, 34). It would appear from this brief notice that Jehu did have some successes to record. Where the written records are silent, the mute stones begin to speak. Jehu was responsible for the new fortifications at Samaria, the surrounding of the city with a double casemate wall.[8] The cities of Megiddo and Hazor show evidence of intensive building activity in this same era.[9] We must suppose some similar activity on the part of his rival in Damascus. When both parties had recovered their strength, the ancient quarrel broke out anew. Jehu may well have won many victories over the Aramaeans (2 K 10, 34), but under his son and successor Jehoahaz, Israel passed completely under the sway of Damascus.

2) ISRAEL UNDER THE RULE OF DAMASCUS — JEHOAHAZ OF ISRAEL (814/13 — 798) AND JOASH OF JUDAH (836/35 — 797)

The prophet Elisha wept when he proclaimed Hazael of Damascus king over Aram. Why? He had proclaimed such magnificent accomplishments that Hazael exclaimed his own unworthiness: "What is your servant, who is but a dog, that he should do this great thing?" (2 K 8, 13). Elisha, however, had a premonition that this man had been chosen to be the scourge of God, the waster of Israel. "In those days the Lord began to cut off parts of Israel" (2 K 10, 32).

The ascendancy of the Aramaeans of Damascus was made possible only by the simultaneous collapse of the great Assyrian empire. A previous break in the succession of world empires had furnished David with an opportunity to establish his own kingdom in the middle country. He had no significant opponent, either in Mesopotamia or in Egypt. The appearance of Shalmaneser

---

8. BA 22 (1959), 74, 77.
9. *EncMikr* III, 262.

spelled the end of the many small autonomous middle kingdoms.

"How it happened that this restless figure, successful in the face of all his reverses, who never tired of proclaiming his accomplishments in a countless series of inscriptions, was forced, in his old age, to witness the revolt of almost all the ranks and cities of his empire and even the treason of his son, and finish out his days in solitude in the one residence left to him at Calach, can only be conjectured. Was it the result of dissatisfaction with his philo-Babylonian politics; was it the immense pressure of his taxation and the drain upon his country's resources from his many wars? Twenty-seven cities united to oppose him. The many resettled peoples, who now made up the population of vast stretches of Assyrian territory, welcomed the hour of their deliverance. But the old lion would not give in. He died in solitude like his great ancestor Tukulti-Ninurta I — condemned, perhaps, by an everlasting justice for all the monstrous havoc which he had spread over the countries of the Ancient Near East." [10]

The civil conflict in the Assyrian royal house was resolved by the victory of Shamshi-Adad (823-810). He was sufficiently occupied with welding together his collapsed kingdom. After his early death, he was followed by his son Adad-nirari III (809-728), still in his minority, with his mother Sammuramat, a wise and energetic daughter of Babylon, ruling as regent for four years. She is the Semiramis who is famous in legend for her extraordinary beauty and of whom the Greeks report the most marvelous and wonderful things, such as the construction of the "hanging gardens," a war against Africa, and a campaign to India. When Adad-nirari himself took over the rule, there was no reason to change the course established by his mother. The forces and material assembled by his mother made it possible for him to set out immediately upon a most impressive and richly rewarding campaign into Syrio-Palestine, as a result of which he conquered the "rebels against his father" and forced them back into subjection.[11] In the time between the last campaign of

10. Schmökel, GAV (1957), 257.
11. Ibid., 259.

Shalmaneser III, in the year 835, and the first campaign of Adad-nirari, in the year 805, Hazael and his son Ben-Hadad III of Damascus had time to enrich themselves at the expense of Israel (2 K 8, 13).

a) THE LOSS OF TRANSJORDANIA (2 K 10, 22-33): Jehu had begun the revolt against the house of Omri in the camp at Ramoth-Gilead (841). The state of war with Aram continued after his seizure of power. Both sides, of course, had been so weakened by their resistance to the Assyrian conqueror that it was, at first, simply a matter of the customary border disputes and outlaw raids, which seemed to have been rather successful for Jehu. In the "Chronicle of the Kings of Israel" there must be some more explicit account of these victories (2 K 10, 34). The work has, unfortunately, not survived. Towards the end of Jehu's reign, however, Hazael succeeded in making a significant break-through. Not only Ramoth-Gilead was captured, but the entire district of Transjordania was overrun: "From the Jordan eastward, all the land of Gilead, the Gadites, and the Reubenites, and Manassites from Aroer which is by the valley of the Arnon" (2 K 10, 33). Jehu could not have survived the defeat by any great length of time. Many authorities are of the opinion that he fell in these battles. Under his son and successor Jehoahaz (814/13 — 798), the humiliation of Israel at the hands of Aram reached its climax. To this era we must assign the accounts of the Aramaean raids, the siege of Samaria, and the attack upon Jerusalem.

b.) ARAMAEAN RAIDS [12] (2 K 6, 8-23): After the defeat in Transjordania, the west lay open to Aramaean raiding parties. Burning and pillaging, they made a series of rapid and devastating attacks. Elisha's prophecy about Hazael proved true: "I know the evil that you will do to the people of Israel; you will set on

---

12. The account in 2 K 5-7 is, in our present text, fitted into the reign of Jehoram, an era in which Aramaean attacks as described there could hardly have been a danger. The text speaks in general terms of "the king of Israel and the King of Aram," without mentioning any names. In the actual course of history such events must be attributed to the reign of Jehoahaz, Jehu's son.

fire their fortresses, and you will slay their young men with the sword, and dash in pieces their little ones, and rip up their women with child" (2 K 8, 12). The prophet Elisha enlisted his prophetic knowledge in the service of national events. Whether it was clairvoyance or some similar phenomenon, at all events the prophets always told the king when and where the Aramaeans would make their attack. On the basis of this warning system, the Israelites were able to make their way to safety. The king of Aram had no other explanation for this than to accuse some of his highly placed officials of espionage and treason. The courtiers, however, pointed to the mysterious knowledge of the prophets. Accordingly, Hazael sent a special raid to capture Elisha and render him harmless.

The prophet was staying in the city of Dothan [13] (2 K 6, 13). The raiding party arrived with horses and chariots and a great army; they came by night and surrounded the city. Next morning, when the servant of the man of God looked out and saw the city surrounded, he could only break out in lamentation. Elisha, however, did not lose faith; he was not alone in facing this enemy. He had invisible chariots and horses of fire (6, 17) at his disposal. When the Aramaeans opened the attack, the outcome was a surprise to everyone. Elisha went to meet the enemy and convinced them that they were fighting at the wrong place. Elisha directed them further towards the fortress city of Samaria. They realized immediately that they had fallen into a trap. The king of Israel was minded to have the invaders cut down on the spot. But "father Elisha" (6, 21) ordered him to give them royal hospitality and send them on their way.

c) THE SIEGE OF SAMARIA (2 K 6, 24—7, 20): The Aramaeans' feeling of strength is adequately demonstrated by the fact that after the petty raids, they now undertake to storm the capital city of Israel itself: "Afterward Ben-Hadad King of Syria

---

13. Excavation report in J. B. Free, BASOR 131 (1953), 16-20; 135 (1954), 14-20; 139 (1955), 3-9; 143 (1956), 11-17. Ashes and charcoal, tested by carbon-14, date the destruction towards the end of the ninth century, the time of the Aramaean attacks.

mustered his entire army and went up, and besieged Samaria"
(2 K 6, 24). Since the Syrian kings all assumed the royal epithet
"son of the god Hadad" (Ben-Hadad) immediately upon their
accession to the throne,[14] this reference to a Ben-Hadad in the
story of the siege of Samaria is nothing more than a reference to
the then reigning king of Damascus. The siege is actually to be
ascribed to Hazael, since it was he who "cut off pieces" [15] from
Israel in east and west (2 K 10, 32; 13, 22).

The siege dragged on. Famine broke out. Even the foods which
were generally considered unclean had to be eaten. Prices quickly
mounted to an inflationary level.[16] Two women agreed to slaughter
their children for a meal. When they had already eaten the son of
the first, the second woman refused to surrender the child. Their
quarrel was taken to the king for a decision; he happened to be
passing by in his inspection of the city walls. In his great sorrow
and horror, he rent his garments. The people noticed that he
was wearing a penitential garment. He had made every attempt
to turn aside God's wrath by religious practices. Strangely enough,
his anger was now directed against the prophet Elisha. Apparently
it had been the prophet who had encouraged the king to resist the
attack. Now he was to atone for his poor counsel. Without further
delay, the king sent the executioner to dispose of Elisha. Elisha
had a presentiment of this approaching doom, and locked the
gate to his house. When the king himself approached, he had
these bitter words for the prophet: "This trouble is from Yahweh.
Why should I fight for Yahweh any longer?" (6, 23). Against
this failing faith of the king, the prophet holds out a clear promise
of Yahweh's immediate assistance. On the very next day there

---

14. *EncMikr* II, 156.
15. But if we take Ben-Hadad as a personal name, then it can only have
been Ben-Hadad III, Hazael's son (2 K 10, 25). On the subject of
the identification of Ben-Hadad III, cf. *EncMikr* II, 157.
16. An ass's head, which was otherwise never eaten, cost 80 shekels, a
quarter of "pigeon dung" even cost 5 shekels. The interpretation of
ḥiryyônîm as "pigeon dung" is uncertain. Hence, other readings have
been proposed: *ḥarsônîm,* an onion-like plant, called "milkstar" or
"star of Bethlehem." EB II, 219 — *ḥarubbîm,* "carob." ClamB III,
720.

would be an abundance of food and water. The captain on whose hand the king leaned said, in mockery, that even if Yahweh were to make windows in heaven, the prophet's words could hardly be fulfilled. And yet, by some unexplainable circumstance, next day witnessed the turning point. Over night the besieged camp had been seized with a sudden panic. There was a noise of horse and chariot in the air. The Aramaeans thought that the Hittites and Egyptians [17] were coming to relieve Israel. For fear of a surprise attack they had broken in wild flight, leaving weapons and food behind them. The still, abandoned camp had an uncanny effect on the anxious city. Lepers had announced the withdrawal of the enemy. The king was afraid of an ambush. Finally, he dispatched scouts on the last remaining horses to reconnoiter the situation. When they returned and confirmed the fact that the Aramaeans had withdrawn, the famished populace burst through the city gates and seized the food and spoils in the camp. In this mass exodus of hungry people, the mockers who had doubted the prophet's word, were trampled at the gate.

Excavation has proved the existence of a far-reaching destruction in Samaria around the year 810. The entire casemate system needed, subsequently, to be completely restored. It is, of course, hardly possible to determine whether this destruction dates back to the siege or to a different attack, not mentioned in the Bible.

d) ARAMAEAN ATTACKS UPON JERUSALEM (c. 814): After the siege of Samaria, Hazael prepared for a new campaign. He made his way along the coastal plains, where he occupied the city of Gath, built as a frontier fortress by Rehoboam, and turned to attack Jerusalem itself. The then king of Jerusalem, Joash, bought his freedom at the price of a mighty tribute. The votive offerings, all the gold from the temple and palace treasuries, were all delivered to the enemy, whereupon he went his way in peace. Judah, however, was exposed to the attack of her now rebellious neighbors (2 K 12, 18-21; Am 1, 6).

---

17. Hittites, and Land of Hattu are general names for the petty states allied against the Assyrians, from Asia Minor as far as Palestine. Thus the black obelisk. ANET 280. — Instead of Egypt (*misráim*) others read Musru, a Hittite successor state in Cilicia. ClamB III, 721.

These reverses in foreign policy also created a new internal situation. As long as Jehoiada was alive, domestic policy was directed by the adherents of Yahweh. After the national defeat, however, the "princes of Judah," who had secretly remained faithful to the ancient Baal cult, asserted their claim to power. The cult of Baal and Asherah once again raised its head. Then Zechariah, the son of Jehoiada, was seized by the Spirit of God. He came before the people and said: "Thus says God, 'Why do you transgress the commandments of the Lord, so that you cannot prosper? Because you have forsaken the Lord, he has forsaken you' " (2 Ch 24, 20-22). In order to be rid of this unwelcome voice of conscience, they had the prophet stoned, with the connivance of the king, in the "court of the house of the Lord" — "between the altar of holocaust and the temple court" (Mt 23, 35; Lk 11, 51). The kingdom of Judah thus suffered a devastating blow, in both religion and politics.

Nothing gives a better picture of the desolate position of Israel around 800 B.C. than the sober statement: "There was not left to Jehoahaz an army of more than fifty horsemen and ten chariots and ten thousand foot men (better, ten "clan levies")" (2 K 13, 7). Ahab, at the battle of Qarqar, in the year 853, had been able to muster a force of 2,000 chariots and 10,000 warriors. Of all this, only a small remnant was left. Bowed under the yoke of Damascus, both Judah and Israel began to look to a redeemer (*mošía*) (2 K 13, 5). The tragic contradiction of history lies in the fact that this redeemer from the Syrian yoke was expected to arise from the restoration of Assyria, and it was Ashur herself who would spell the doom of both Damascus and Samaria.

3) THE ELISHA CYCLE

"There is no doubt but that free poetic composition and folk saga have mixed with reality. But it is much more difficult here, than in the case of Elijah, to separate the two discordant elements." Thus writes R. Kittel in his history of the people of Israel.[19] His

---

18. Again: not "thousand" but "ten": *'eleph* means "clan levies."
19. II (1922), 329.

statement gives a clear outline of the problems which the Elisha cycle poses for the history of tradition. What the Second Book of Kings has to say about the prophet Elisha is obviously composed in a great variety of literary forms. In accordance with the underlying literary form, the historical value of the documents concerned is also quite varied. The value of a chronicle is one thing, a deliberate attempt to record objective facts of history; but the value of popular accounts is something quite different — a certain tendency towards fable is always in evidence; finally, the historical value of free poetic composition is quite different still.

In terms of a comparison with the Elijah cycle, it is not difficult to establish fundamental differences in the Elisha narratives. We are struck by the rather peculiar fact that, on the one hand, the Elisha narratives are much more closely bound up with the political events of their day than are the stories of the Elisha cycle, and on the other hand, they also assume the proportions of a "life of the saints." Despite these essential differences, the two cycles have much in common. The "oil miracle" and the raising of the dead men are told of both prophets (1 K 17, 8-24; 2 K 4, 1-37). This leads many scholars to believe [20] that the Elisha cycle is only an artificial anthology of legends which grew up after the pattern of the great master Elijah, to celebrate his disciple Elisha. It would thus be an *editio minor,* a poor second edition of the Elijah cycle,[21] a version which has lost much of its original poetic power.

If, on the other hand, on the basis of a conservative defense position, without taking literary genre and history of tradition into account, the narratives of Elisha's mighty deeds are interpreted too literally,[22] this will hardly bring us closer to the historical reality than would the so-called extreme, negative criticism. The truth can obviously be ascertained only by combining the two approaches. Even the most cursory examination makes it

---

20. Pfeiffer, IntrOT 417: "The Elisha cycle is an artificial literary product."
21. *Ibid.,* "In fact, Elisha is an editio minor of Elijah." 407/8.
22. K. Fruhstorfer, *Die Wunder des Eliseus,* (1941).

obvious that the Elisha cycle is based upon the existence of several strata of tradition.

a) "FIORETTI": This is the Italian word used to designate those stories told of St. Francis of Assisi which are the product of his school of disciples and are, in many respects, permeated with legend. Though there are some two millennia between Elisha and the Poor Man of Assisi, we must not overlook the similarity between the two lives. In both schools of disciples, the image of the master was preserved in an abiding literary form. The Franciscan school of disciples had woven a "bouquet" (*fioretti*) to the memory of their founder. The narratives which owe their origin to the circle of young prophets who followed Elisha are not essentially different in form.

Although he was originally a farmer by vocation, after Elijah cast his cloak upon him, Elisha remained in the closest contact and relationship with the prophetic brotherhoods. He served Elijah up to the time that the master was taken away. In fact, it was precisely Elijah's death that occasioned the prophetic vocation of his disciple Elisha. That is why the account of Elijah's being taken up (2 K 2, 1-18) is not a part of the Elijah cycle as such; it must rather be understood as an introduction to the Elisha cycle. Elisha had asked for two thirds of his master's spirit, the hereditary right of the first born. Upon him now rested the spirit (*rûaḥ*) of Yahweh, making him a man of God (*'îš ha'elohîm*) and capable of extraordinary deeds. The spirit is that mysterious power which emanates from God and accomplishes wonders in the world. Everywhere the man of God makes his way, wonders and miracles are the evidence of his coming.

In Jericho he restored the water (2 K 2, 19-22). The mockery of the boys from Bethel was quickly punished (2, 23-25). The poor widow of a son of the prophets, whose son would have otherwise been sold into slavery, was helped by the miracle of the oil (4, 1-7). In the great famine he "sweetened" the poisonous food (4, 38-41) and miraculously multiplied the bread (4, 42-44). What was to keep this man of God, whose very name means "helper in time of need" (*'eli-ša* — God helps), from discovering the lost axe, even though it had fallen into the water (6, 1-7).

These accounts give a vivid picture of the poor life of the prophetic brotherly communities, entirely devoted to the service of Yahweh. They lived a common life, but they were married. At times of drought, they suffered the most bitter want. They gathered the last weeds from the field, plants that were not usually eaten, and almost died from hunger. The widow of the prophet was about to sell her two sons into slavery to pay her debts. Her poverty is further accentuated by the fact that the axe with which she was going to chop wood along the Jordan was borrowed property. Even though Elisha's life comprised a much broader sphere of activity, he was always available, within this smaller circle of his disciples, to alleviate whatever sufferings he could. No wonder then, that within this circle of disciples the memory of the master should continue to live as the object of stories and fond recollections.[23] Critical scholarship [24] has established the fact that this cycle already existed around 750, that is, some 50 years after Elisha's death, with its abundant evidence of popular oral influence.

b) "THE HOLY MAN OF GOD" AMONG HIS PEOPLE: Although the prophetic brotherhoods were intimately bound together, Elisha was not a permanent member. We find him constantly on the move, keeping watch on the faith of Yahweh among the people: now he is with the brethren in Jericho, Bethel, Gilgal; then we find him in Samaria at the royal court and once again enroute to Shunem and on Mount Carmel. Gehazi seems to have been his constant companion. Obviously, Elisha must have rested from his journeys from time to time. "Behold now, I perceive that this is a holy man of God who is continually passing our way" (2 K 4, 9), said the woman from Shunem. He had a small room made for him on the roof of her house, and furnished it with bed, table, stool, and lamp. To show his gratitude for such hospitality, Elisha prayed for her to have a son. But when her son, after he had grown, died of a sunstroke, he brought him back to life and returned him to his mother (2 K 4, 8-37). When, on the occasion of a famine, the same woman from Shunem, on the prophet's advice, migrated into the country of the Philistines, and then returned home after the famine to find her property in the possession of strangers, it was the same man of God who represented her at court (8, 1-7).

There is no evidence of this kind and generous conduct in the narrative of the leprous Syrian captain Naaman (2 K 5, 1-27). This event took place in the days of the Aramaean raids. On one such occasion an Israelite maiden had been captured, and taken by Naaman as a slave girl into his home. She brought news of the miraculous activity of this man of God in the foreign land. Naaman thought that he might buy his health with gold and silver. Equipped with a royal letter, he made his way to Samaria where he wanted to be healed. When the king of Israel read the letter, he rent his clothes, because he feared the makings of a diplomatic incident. Then Elijah took charge. The Syrian was to come and recognize the fact that there was a prophet in Israel (5, 8).

---

23. W. Reiser, *Eschatologische Gottessprüche in den Elisa-Legenden*, Thz 9 (1953), 321-338, argues that the individual oracles from the prophetic bands of the last years of the 9th century were uprooted and worked into the Elisha cycle. This could be done without serious deformation because the eschatological era was believed to be present in the great master.

24. Robert-Feuillet, IntrAT 452; Pfeiffer, IntrOT 408.

When the leper appeared before the prophet's house, Elijah did not come out, nor did he extend his staff or stretch himself out upon the man, as he had done in calling the dead to life. Nothing of this sort occurred. He had Naaman informed that he should bathe in the Jordan. He consented to do so, only against his will, and he was made clean. Greatly moved by this miraculous healing, Naaman confessed that there is no other God beside Yahweh alone, the God of Israel. Elijah refused every form of recompense: It is God's work to heal a man. His servant Gehazi, however, decided to take advantage of a favorable opportunity. He hastened after the Syrian and demanded rich gifts for himself. For his avarice, he was himself stricken with leprosy.

As distinguished from the narratives of the kings, whose deeds are set forth in sober series, like a chronicle, these two miraculous narratives betray the popular bent for "fable." The individual scenes are portrayed with the greatest attention to detail, and the person of the actors is clearly drawn. Something of a life long disappeared begins to stir once more in its imperishable vitality. In concentrating on the larger historical horizon, our ' narrator must neglect the details of daily life. He can speak only in generalities of the king of Aram. But these popular narratives produce an almost timeless effect, incomparably close to life and reality. They have preserved the image of this "holy man of God, who is continually passing by" (2 K 5, 1-27) bringing the distant and jealous God of Sinai into the very midst of human affairs.[25]

c) ISRAEL'S CHARIOT WARFARE: In a much different tone from these timeless narratives of his wanderings and miracles, other accounts portray Elisha in the midst of the political and national activities of his day. Returning from the mountain of God, Elijah had cast the cloak of prophetic vocation upon Elisha as he was plowing in the fields (1 K 19, 19). Elisha immediately abandoned his work, together with his house and land, not to seek out Yahweh in the solitary wilderness, but rather to prepare a way for Yahweh's sword of vengeance in the historical circumstances of his day (1 K 19, 17).

Elijah's last prophetic words were directed to Ahaziah of Israel (8, 53). His departure from earth must have followed shortly afterward, perhaps around 850. The dynasty of Omri, which had threatened Elijah's destruction, was still in power; Jezebel's policy still protected the Baal cult. After Elijah's death

---

25. Fleming James, *Personalities of the OT* (1939), 193.

it was his disciple Elisha who took an equally zealous stand against the inroads of paganism. No wonder that, on the occasion of the campaign against Mesha of Moab (c. 850), Jehoram of Israel heard these angry words: "What have I to do with you?[26] Go to the prophets of your father and the prophets of your mother" (2 K 3, 13). All his wrath against the house of Ahab breaks out in these words. He would not even have come to see Jezebel's son were it not that Jehoshaphat, the king of Jerusalem, faithful to Yahweh, was also a participant in the campaign. Since Elijah's day, little had changed. The impassioned and tenacious position of the prophet is still the same. In Elijah's day, on Carmel, the battlecry had sounded "Up Baal; up Yahweh!" Now, before this wilderness campaign, the same fundamental decision flared up again. Elisha represents himself as one who "stands before the face of Yahweh of Sabaot, the God of hosts" (3, 14), who will suffer no other god beside himself.

Elisha could hardly have been alone in his contention that the house of Ahab, by reason of its defection from the Yahweh faith, had lost every claim to the royal crown. In very truth, the royal house was ripe for terrible vengeance, and, little by little, the hour draws near for the most bloody revolution of all the Old Testament. It was Elisha's doing to set the spark. He had had a hand in the revolution in Damascus (2 K 8, 7-15); he had sent one of his disciples into the camp at Ramoth-Gilead, to anoint Jehu, who then swept away the house of Ahab in his wild fury (2 K 9, 1-13). Must we find some way to save the prophet's honor, and claim that these actions were dictated by the necessity of the moment? It was not Elisha, after all, but rather the Rechabites, whom Jehu received into his triumphal chariot. Later prophets passed a devastating sentence over the bloody day of Jezreel (Hos 1, 4). Elisha's position towards the new dynasty is quite friendly. But it is, nonetheless, rather surprising that we have no individual scene reported for the long years of Jehu's reign (841/40 — 814), no single story of a meeting between Jehu and Elisha. Is this some tacit evidence of the fact that the prophet

---

26. Here an expression of sharp refusal.

kept his distance from this man of blood? Or have our modern sensitivities grown too soft to appreciate the hardness of that era in which the Yahweh faith was fighting for its very existence?

Only when the Aramaean wars flare up again under Jehu's successor Jehoahaz (814/13 –– 798) is Elisha once again in evidence, and he is active wherever there is an opportunity to defend his people against the enemy, as can be seen from our previous treatment of the Aramaean crisis. What Elisha meant for Israel's king and people is evident once again at the hour of his death. Jehu's second successor and grandson Joash went to visit the prophet on his deathbed. He wept and cried out: "My father, my father! The chariots of Israel and its horsemen!" [27] (2 K 13, 14). The life of the prophet is, for Israel, equivalent in value to a well equipped army. The pitiable condition of the national defense has already been clearly expressed by the earlier statement that there were only ten chariots and 50 warriors surviving (13, 7). What would happen now that Elisha too was dying?

But the dying prophet aroused himself to a final exhortation. He had the king bring him a bow and arrow and shot one, two, three arrows. This symbolic action he accompanied with these words: "The Lord's arrow of victory, the arrow of victory over Syria!" (13, 17). The salvation (*tᵉšû'ah*) which Elisha proclaimed in the last moments of his life does not have any messianic overtones in the strict sense; it simply proclaims eventual victory over the Aramaeans. But since this salvation is the work of Yahweh,

---

27. MT plural, LXX and Vulg. singular. *pāraš* means neither "chariot driver" nor "rider," but simply, literally, "horse-man," a name applied to anyone who has anything to do with horses. In the earlier royal era, *pāraš* refers to the man on the chariot, either the driver or the warrior. It was Ashur-nasir-pal (884-859) who first introduced the cavalry as a new weapon. K. Galling, *Der Ehrenname Elisas und die Entrückung Elias*, ZTK 53 (1956), 126-148, gives this translation: "Israel's chariot corps and their teams" (*rekeb yisra'el ûpharašaw*) and thus relates the title to the Aramaean divinity *RKB-EL*, a god who is called "lord of the war chariot." If this interpretation is correct, then the title takes on a deeper meaning, bound up with contemporary events. For the Aramaeans it was the god of the war chariots, but for Israel it was the prophet with his victorious faith in Yahweh.

the prophet's last words are still a confession of faith in Yahweh, the God of history, who directs the confusion of human politics towards his own eternal goal.

And thus a life lived in a wildly chaotic age had turned into a clear explanation at its end. According to the accounts contained in the Book of Kings, Elisha's activity extended over a period of fifty years. Very little of this activity has actually been handed down to us. And even this little knowledge is the product of a variety of sources, which, in the composition of the Book of Kings, are not always perfectly stitched together:[28]

a) *Fioretti from the circle of disciples*: Elijah's taking up (2, 1-18), the miracle of the water (2, 19-22), the mocking boys (2, 23-25), the miracle of the oil (4, 1-7), death in the pot (4, 38-41), the multiplication of the bread (6, 1-7), Elisha's grave (13, 20-21).

b) *Popular accounts*: the woman from Shunem (4, 8-37; 8, 1-6), Naaman (5, 1-27), the king's servants (6, 8-23), the siege of Samaria (6, 24-7, 20).

c) *Chronicle accounts*: the campaign against Moab (3, 4-7), Hazael of Damascus (8, 7-15), the history of Jehu (9, 1-10, 36), Elisha's death (13, 14-21).

The historical value of the individual collections must be evaluated in different terms. In the chronicle accounts, at least, there is an historical nucleus, no matter how much it has been elaborated by the addition of legendary details; whereas the other narratives must be the product of religious imagination and not the echo of a superior personality.[29] But when, in such an evaluation, the element of miracle is introduced as a literary criterion — since it is a miracle it must be a legend — the entire structure of the argument is open to attack. After all, miracle accounts can be just as historical as mere chronicle narratives with no mention of miracles, especially given the deeply developed Old Testament concept of God. Thus, miracle as such cannot be introduced as a literary criterion. Neither can we draw any valid conclusions

---

28. According to 2 K 6, 23, the Aramaeans no longer make their way into the country. But the immediately following section describes a new Aramaean attack with the siege of Samaria.

29. Pfeiffer, IntrOT 407.

based on the variety of sources. All of them together present a very moving picture of the strong prophetic personality of Elisha. His activity was not confined to the narrow circle of the prophetic brotherhoods; the royal court is open to him and he journeys throughout the length and breadth of the land; always and everywhere he is prepared to bring help, wherever it is needed. It is no wonder that the various spheres in which he was active have all preserved his image, in somewhat different tones, as a heritage for the generations to come. All share the common conviction that it was Elisha who once again made room for the Lord God of Hosts, Yahweh Sabaot, in Israel. His appearance forms one of the great turning points of Old Testament history. The inroads of the Phoenician Baal cult had been, once and for all, turned aside by Elijah and the faithful guardian of his testament, Elisha. In these stormy centuries of war, where the Yahweh faith was fighting for its very existence, the prophets Elijah and Elisha have their own important share in the warlike impetuosity at which our later, and somehow more hypocritical generation frequently takes scandal. Scripture, however, has honored both men with the glorious title "Israel's chariot and its horsemen" (2 K 2, 12; 13, 14).

* * * *

An era of history has thus come to its close. Under the two energetic rulers Ahab of Israel and Jehoshaphat of Judah it seemed as if the splendor of the Davidic-Solomonic era would be restored. From the gulf of the Red Sea as far as Phoenicia, the power of the allied double kingdom had held sway. Israel has incorporated Moab, and Judah Edom as vassal states. Arab tribes were paying tribute. In the war against Ashur it was "Israel," which we are obviously to understand as including the kingdom of Judah as well, who represented the strongest military power in the alliance of the twelve.

It was not the change in world politics, the rise of the great Assyrian empire, to which the prophetic historical writings ascribe the collapse and eventual fall of the kingdoms of Israel and Judah. In the prophetical conception of things, the fabric of the empire, so magnificent seen from without, was already rotten in its core, where the Baal cult was eating away at its life's marrow. That is why Yahweh had determined to "cut off parts of Israel" (2 K 10, 32). One blow followed another. Bloody civil wars of extermination, military threats and plundering from without at the hands of the strongly resurgent hostile neighbors. The end of the ninth century finds Israel and Judah in a state of deepest humiliation.

In the midst of these not always entirely clear political situations, we find the prophets. They were not retiring or unworldly mystics and ecstatics, a point of view which might have found some support in earlier scholarship; they are everywhere very much in evidence, whether called or not called, wherever there is a question of asserting Yahweh's divine rights in the life of individuals or in the nation as a whole. The messianic idea is nowhere evident. All their religious powers are enlisted in the service of preserving the monotheistic faith. While the fate of the other prophets of the ninth century is only touched upon incidentally in the swift passage of history — they appear to proclaim some divine oracle and then immediately disappear — the Books of the Kings devote considerable space to the two great zealots for Yahweh's glory, the prophets Elijah and Elisha. It is only against a detailed exposition of the history of this century that their life can be appreciated in its proper frame of reference; without this orientation it is a picture without a substance.

THE TERRIBLE SPLENDOR
OF THE GREAT DRAGON

THE title "The Terrible Splendor of the Great Dragon" is not a free invention; it is adapted from the Assyrian documents. Salmanassar, for example, refers to himself as the "Great Dragon, the only power within the four rims of the earth, overlord of all the princes, who had smashed all his enemies as if earthenware, the strong man, unsparing, who shows no mercy in battle." These words are taken from the throne inscriptions and, more than any other text, portray the thinking of the Assyrian rulers. The title "Great Dragon" (*ušumgal*) also occurs in the prologue to the Code of Hammurabi, but it has always been a favorite title of the Assyrian kings. Their armies which, over the course of two centuries, crushed the then known world, were preceded in battle by the "terrible splendor of the god Ashur," as we continually read in the various chronicles of the wars.

The fate of the tiny kingdoms of Israel and Judah is inseparably bound up with the rise and fall of the Great Dragon. The kingdom of Israel was utterly crushed by the Assyrians and ceased to exist; of the kingdom of Judah, only a "miserable hut in the cucumber field" (Is 1, 8) remains. In these hard times, in which the Old Testament people of God were tortured as never before, the line of prophecy flowed more richly than at any other age. It is precisely within the period of Assyrian peril that we date the appearance of the great prophets Amos, Hosea, Isaiah, and Micah. All of them are foretellers of doom, but even more so they are the heralds of salvation. All of them stand under the terror and splendor of the great dragon; but they do not speak of weakness and yielding: in their own impotence it is the all-power of Yahweh which appears, and in the face of his terrible splendor even the great dragon disappears like an idle dream. This is the great leitmotiv of the prophetic vision of history, its balance between human and divine, between glory and despair.

CHAPTER V

REESTABLISHMENT OF THE DAVIDIC - SOLOMONIC KINGDOM

THE formation of an empire in the territory of the Syro-Palestinian middle country was possible only when the giants along the Nile and the Euphrates-Tigris were slumbering. This was the case in the first half of the eighth century. It is true that, at the beginning of this century, Assyria does make an entrance — and play the savior — in Palestinian history, but, in the latter half of the century, Assyria falls prey, in domestic and foreign politics alike, to a long period of weakness which makes possible the restoration of the Davidic-Solomonic empire.

1) THE "SAVIOR" FROM THE NORTH (2 K 13, 5)

It is one of the contradictions of history that the kingdoms of Israel and Judah, humbled under the yoke of Damascus, seek salvation exclusively from that power which was destined to annihilate Israel and bring Judah to the very brink of destruction. The awaited "savior" (*môšia'*, 2 K 13, 5) was none other than the Assyrian king Adad-nirari III (811-783). His name is already a battlecry: it means "the god Hadad saves." [3] When he was fully

---

1. ANET 276b.

grown, after his mother Semiramis' regency during his minority, Adad-nirari took the reins of government into his own hands and immediately set out to follow the footsteps of his great predecessors and reestablish Ashur's sovereignty in the western countries. His primary objective was to subjugate the city of Damascus, frequently humbled at the hands of Ashur, but never captured.

a) CONQUESTS OF THE LORD (*mari*) OF DAMASCUS (805): According to the Assyrian annals [4] Adad-nirari was at work in the western countries in the years 805-802. Hazael of Damascus (c. 844-801) had laid his victorious hand not only on Israel, Judah, and the Philistine cities, but he was also attempting to extend his power towards the north where he was bringing pressure to bear against the Aramaean state of Hamath, a former ally. It seems that Hamath's cries for help afforded the Assyrian with his long sought for occasion to interfere.

Adad-nirari crossed the Euphrates in its flood stage [5] in the fifth year of his reign (805). The states of Northern Syria immediately subjected themselves before the terrible splendor of Ashur and kissed the royal feet. Adad-nirari then concentrated his attack upon Damascus. The "Lord" (*mari*) [6] of Damascus capitulated and paid one hundred gold talents and one thousand silver

---

2. The title is first encountered in the hymns to the gods and was reserved for the mightiest gods of the Babylonian pantheon. With the expansion of royal power, there was little hesitancy in assuming the original divine titles as part of the king's titulature. Terror emanates from the king as well as from the dragon. With some reservations the Assyrian title can be compared with the Egyptian Uraeus K. Tallquist, *Akkadische Götterepitheta*, 34. − ANET 276b, note 2. − *ušumgallu* I (from *UŠU = ediššu*, "alone, lonely," and *GAL* "big") "sole ruler, tyrant"; *ušumgallu* II (from *UŠU = bašmu* and *GAL*) "huge, venomous serpent, dragon, one of the evil spirits." Fr. Delitzsch, *Assyrische Handwörterbuch* (1896), 145.

3. *EncMikr* I, 723.

4. RLA 429: Eponymenkanon CBI.

5. ANET 282.

6. The original source does not record the name of the ruler; he is referred to simply as *mari*, that is "my ruler" (cf. mon-seigneur). Probably Hazael was still in power and not his successor Ben-Hadad III, DOT 52.

talents in tribute.[7] An inscription from Nimrud [8] mentions much higher figures: 20 talents of gold, 2300 of silver, 300 of copper, 5000 of iron, as well as rich clothing, an ivory bed, other furniture with ivory inlay, and many precious statues of deities. Since the surrender took place in the palace, we must presume the conquest of the city. It seems that Adad-nirari retained the "Lord" of Damascus as king under Assyrian command.

The Assyrian boasted that, during this campaign, he subjugated Tyre, Sidon, the land of Humri (Israel), Uduma (Edom) and Palastu (Philistia). This is confirmed by the annals entry for the year 802 which speaks of an "advance to the western sea." [9] After these successes, Adad-nirari withdrew into Assyria. Israel was liberated from the pressures of Damascus and free to develop her own domestic affairs.

b) OSTRACA FROM SAMARIA: Under Aramaean pressure, the territory of the kingdom of Israel had practically shrunk to the mountain country around Samaria. After the defeat of the tyrant at Damascus, Israel gradually recovered. Evidence of this, among other sources, is furnished by the Ostraca discovered in the storehouses near the royal palace at Samaria.[10] There are some 75 potsherds, written with a reed pen and black ink. The script is clear and fluent, proof of the fact that the art of writing was well established in Samaria. The individual words are separated by strokes or points. The content is very sober: invoice lists of old wine and pure oil. Generally the place of origin, the name of the carrier, and the content of the consignment are noted. The places of origin are not restricted to a narrow radius of some 6 mi from Samaria,[11] but they

---

7. AOT 345, DOT 51.

8. AOT 344, DOT 51.

9. RLA 429.

10. In the excavations from 1908-1910, 25 pieces were unearthed. Since they were discovered in the vicinity of Ahab's palace, they were dated to his era. Further excavations in the years 1931-1935 made it possible to arrive at a more precise date. W. Thomas DOT 204 fluctuates between Jehu, Joahaz, and Jeroboam II. Eamon O'Doherty is in favor of Jeroboam II: *The Date of the Ostraca of Samaria*, CBQ 15 (1953), 24-29. — *EncMikr* I, 723 argues for Joahaz, a solution that probably best corresponds to the context of the time and the excavation information.

11. DOT 205.

extend as far as the Lake of Gennesaret.[12] The Ostraca, unfortunately, do not exhibit any royal names, only the regnal year: for example: "In the tenth year — for Shemaryau of Beeriam [13] one bottle of old wine, two bottles from Raga ben Elisha, one from Jeda'yau, etc."

The dates run from the ninth to the seventeenth year of an unnamed king. The greatest probability favors Jehoahaz (814/13 — 798). His tenth year is contemporary with the military campaign of Adad-nirari (805). Accordingly, the potsherd evidence would confirm the impression that after the pressure from Aram had been withdrawn, the royal administration was reestablished with Samaria as a central point. Shipments from the crown properties as well as the immediate territory of Samaria itself, and even distant Galilee, continued to flow into the royal residence.

For the religious development of the Northern Kingdom, the personal names of these Ostraca are particularly significant. The common Old Testament formations with ab- (father), ah- (brother), 'am- (uncle) are also to be found on the Ostraca. The divine name is given as El-, Baal, and Jau (Yau- Yahu, Yahweh). The names compounded with Baal do not necessarily point to the Caananite cult, since, at David's time, Baal was still a word in good standing. When, however, we meet with a name such as 'egel-yau, "Yahweh is a young bull," [14] this is a clear reference to the bull cult as practiced in the Northern Kingdom. It was still the Yahweh of the days of Moses who was worshiped there, but now — and it is precisely this that constitutes the "sin of Jeroboam" — under the symbol of a bull, whose images had been set up in the national sanctuaries at Bethel and Dan. This is a surprising confirmation of the judgment passed by the Books of Kings over Joash and Jehoahaz: "They did evil in the sight of the Lord and walked in the way of Jeroboam" (2 K 13, 2, 11).

c) REVOLT IN JERUSALEM, KING JOASH MURDERED (797): It seems that Damascus soon recovered from the Assyrian attack and began to avenge herself on all the Assyrian vassals. Jehoahaz of Israel was expelled from his recently acquired territories [15] (2 K 13, 25). Aramaean raiding parties made their way as far as Judah, where they fell upon Jerusalem and "destroyed all the princes of the people from among the people, and sent all their spoil to the king of Damascus" (2 Ch 24, 23ff.). To make the catastrophe complete, several questionable elements — Zabad,

---

12. *EncMikr* I, 158, article: *Ostrakon*, with illustrations.
13. "Well of the Lake," probably located along Lake Gennesaret.
14. DOT 206.
15. B. Meisler (MAZAR), JPOS 22 (1948), 117-133.

son of an Ammonite woman, and Jehozabad, son of a Moabite woman — made a conspiracy against King Joash of Judah and murdered him in "Beth-Millo" (2 K 12, 21), "in his bed" (2 Ch 23, 25). Was this merely an internal house revolt, with the sons of foreign women doing away with their aged father in order to succeed to power? This would certainly be possible. Actually, however, the murderers did not succeed to power; it was Amaziah who ascended the throne and, contrary to the schismatic religious policies of his father, held to the ancient faith of Yahweh.

d) "Savior" FOR THE SECOND TIME: It was not until Adadnirari defeated the forces of Damascus at Man-su-a-te [16] in his second expedition in the year 796, that Israel could breathe in peace. This location has been identified in the neighborhood of Baalbek. If this is correct, then the Assyrian attack seems to have been directed, on this occasion, against the Aramaean possessions in the fertile plain between Lebanon and Antilebanon. It would follow that Aram's power was now restricted to the tiny territory immediately surrounding Damascus.

Against such a weakened state of Aram, Israel could now proceed with real success. The prophet Elisha had proclaimed that King Joash would be victorious over Ben-Hadad III when he bade him shoot the victorious arrow of Yahweh three times (2 K 13, 14-19). Joash won back not only the cities which had been lost on northern Galilee, but he also restored the Transjordanian provinces to Israelite sovereignty and thus laid the way for a new era of glory (2 K 13, 25). Amaziah of Judah was also in a position to attack Edom and thus force an access to the Southern Sea. After the Aramaean pressure had subsided, Palestine experienced the revival of those very laws of political intercourse which, already under David and later under King Ahab, had swiftly led to the formation of a great middle empire.

e) "CEDAR AND THISTLE" (793): After his accession to power, Amaziah's first objective was to reestablish the domestic

---

16. Eponymn list, RLA II, 429. — The name occurs on ostracon 16, evidence of the fact that wine was shipped to Samaria even from

tranquility.[17] Blood had twice been shed. The pagan reaction had soiled its hands with the blood of the prophet Zechariah; in return, the priests and prophets faithful to Yahweh could hardly have been entirely unconnected with the murder of King Joash — a situation not unlike the earlier story of Jehu. Appealing to the Law of Moses, Amaziah punished only the murderers themselves, without demanding punishment for their sons who were all soiled with the same guilt by their clan allegiance. This seemed to have secured a favorable balance in domestic politics (2 K 14, 5-6; 2 Ch 25, 1-4).

In his foreign politics, Amaziah followed the example of David, insofar as this was possible for the remnant state of Judah. He wanted to win back free access to the mines and the seven harbors occupied by the Edomites. This was not possible without a war. Accordingly, he made careful preparations for a campaign. In Judah and Benjamin the general conscription was carried out along clan lines (*bêt-abôt*). The young men from twenty years upwards were forced to appear before the drafting commission. The result was a military strength of 300 clan levys (*'eleph*), some 3000 men (2 Ch 25, 5). In order to be certain of his success, and at the expense of a thousand talents (gold or silver?) engaged the services of an Israelite auxiliary corps of one hundred squads, some thousand men. A "man of God" raised such a mighty storm of protest against the hiring of Israelite mercenaries that Amaziah felt himself forced to dismiss the auxiliaries before setting out upon his campaign. They returned home in fierce anger (2 Ch 25, 6-10).

Amaziah came upon the Edomites in the Valley of Salt,[18] where he defeated them, winning the fortress of Sela, which he renamed Joktheel (2 K 14, 7). This brief report of the war is far from clear. The Valley of Salt has been identified in Wadi el-Malih, in the territory south of Beersheba. Accordingly, the Edo-

---

Coelesyria. *EncMikr* III, 483.

17. *'amas-yahu* "Yahweh is strong," or "Yahweh makes strong." Cf. Is 40, 26. The name occurs on a signet ring of unknown origin. *EncMikr* I, 439.

18. *ge-hammelah*, modern Wadi el-Malij, in the Negev east of Beer-sheba.

mites had extended their sphere of sovereignty very near to Judah. After his victory, Amaziah pursued the defeated enemy into their home country east of the Arabah sink, where he conquered the fortress city of Sela. This city is generally identified with the later Nabataean capital city of Petra (Sela = rock), but perhaps it is to be identified with the mountain fortress es-Sela' located some 18 mi south of the Dead Sea, a location which still preserves' the ancient name. It had been established as a frontier fortress, to protect the access to the Edomite heart country. The mounds of ruins would seem to confirm this conjecture.[19] Amaziah thus succeeded in throwing back the Edomites into their own tribal territory. He thereby cleared the way for his successor Azariah to capture the harbor of Elath on the Southern Sea.

The renaming of a conquered city was frequent in the Ancient Near East. Frequently the new name would conceal some symbolic meaning. Joktheel is approximately equivalent to "may God destroy!" [20] The victor also carried off the gods of the Edomites as booty to Jerusalem, an act for which the prophets severely rebuked him (2 Ch 25, 14-16). Amaziah had only followed the common practice of the Ancient Near East, in accordance with which the gods of the vanquished are made to serve the God of the victor.

Israelite auxiliary troops which had been sent home by Amaziah indemnified themselves by plundering the territory of Judah: this led to civil war between the Northern and the Southern Kingdoms. After his successful campaign against Edom, Amaziah was quite ready to take up the quarrel with Israel. He challenged Joash to battle: "Come, let us look one another in the face" (2 K 14, 8), that is, "Let us take each other's measure in battle." Joash, meantime, had achieved a few successes at the expense of Aram, and felt himself clearly superior to the presumptuous claims of Judah. This position he expressed in his diplomatic answer, couched in the form of a parable: "A thistle on Lebanon says to a cedar on Lebanon, saying, 'Give your daughter to my son for a wife'; and a wild beast of Lebanon passed by and trampled

---

19. *es-Sela* near *et-Tafileh*. *EncMikr* III, 767.
20. 2 Ch 25, 13 treats Sela not as a proper name, but merely as a general term: "rocky heights," from which the prisoners were cast down.

down the thistle" (2 K 14, 10). Amaziah had no response. The two kings "looked each other in the face" at Beth-Shemesh. The forces of Judah were struck an annihilating blow, and Amaziah himself was taken prisoner. Joash took Jerusalem by storm, had the city walls torn down, from the Ephraim Gate to the Corner Gate, a distance of some 400 cubits. He also plundered the temple and the palace. In order to further reduce the position of the conquered enemy, he demanded hostages. This was the end of the proud dream: Judah was now more or less a vassal state of Israel.

In Jerusalem, this led to a reorganization of the government. When they learned of Amaziah's capture, the "people of Judah" (2 K 14, 21) raised his sixteen year old son Azariah to the throne. After his release, Amaziah retained his royal title, but the actual rule was in the hands of his son, with the result that their regnal years overlap. Comparing regnal years,[21] we also notice that Joash of Israel, prior to his departure for the war, had established his son Jeroboam II as his coregent. Accordingly, the battle between the "cedar and the thistle" can be precisely dated in the year 793. The two contemporaneous young rulers, Jeroboam II of Israel (794-754) and Azariah of Judah (792/91 — 740) brought their kingdoms to a final period of blossom before the great catastrophe.

2) FROM HAMATH TO THE STEPPE SEA

a) Jeroboam II, "savior of israel" (794-754, co-regent

---

21. Chronology (For greater clarity cf. the tables in the appendix): Amaziah's year of accession is the second year of Joash of Israel (2 K 14, 1). Joash ruled for 16 years (2 K 13, 10). Accordingly, both kings ruled simultaneously for 14 years. But since Amaziah ruled for 29 years (2 K 14, 1), his first 14 years coincide with the last 14 years of Joash, and his last 15 years with the first 15 years of Jeroboam II. Amaziah must accordingly have died in the 15th year of Jeroboam. But the text records his death in "the 27th year" (2 K 15, 1). It follows from this that Jeroboam must have been co-regent with his father for 12 years (27-15 = 12). The dating is misleading in that the record of the regnal years includes both the years of sole rule and those of the co-regency. Only the available synchronisms make the proper interpretation possible.

UNTIL 783): In normal usage, the word "savior, redeemer" has already acquired a religious if not messianic meaning. For the total overall view of history in ancient times, however, it is characteristic for earthly kings, in their connection with the pivotal points of time, to be designated as "savior and redeemer" (*môšîaʻ*); nor is this true only in the case of pious kings, faithful to Yahweh. Even the Assyrian king Adad-nirari is called "savior." Mesha, king of Moab, calls himself simply "savior" (*mešaʻ*). The word "savior" has accordingly, a primarily political meaning. But since politics and religion were not to be separated, the religious meaning is always included. Every event in history was referred to God or to the gods. In Israel it was Yahweh who always sent a savior in times of crisis. In this series of savior figures, Jeroboam II now takes his place. "The Lord saved them (*yôšîʻem*) by the hand of Jeroboam ben-Joash" (2 K 14, 27). Since the author of the Books of Kings is primarily interested in stressing the religious significance of Jeroboam's activity, his involvement with the larger picture of world history is restricted to a fragmentary minimum. He loves contrast. With lightning-like strokes, we catch a brief glimpse of Jeroboam's political magnitude, only to hear the sorry sentence: "He did evil in the eyes of Yahweh" (2 K 14, 24).

It is clear that, after these various reverses, Transjordania was once and for all freed of the Aramaean yoke. The prophet Amos (6, 13) could point to the victorious battles at Carnaim in Bashan and Lodebar in Gilead. Accordingly, Jeroboam had recovered the fertile provinces of Bashan and Gilead. He was not content with these successes. Like David, he carried the battle into the enemy's own country. Damascus, which had so frequently humbled Israel, was now conquered by Jeroboam. With the defeat of Damascus, the way was open to Northern Syria. The conquest of the Aramaeans does not mean that their territories were incorporated into the kingdom of Israel. It is only that the tide had now turned. Just as Israel had once paid tribute to the Aramaeans, so now the Aramaeans must pay tribute to Israel.

The southern frontier of the Israelite sovereignty is generally referred to as "the steppe sea" (*yam haʻʻarabah,* "the sea of the Arabah — 2 K 14, 25), which is to say, the Dead Sea, although it is not clear whether this refers only to the northern end of the Dead Sea or is meant to include Moab as far as the southern end of the Sea. This means that, in the north and east, the frontiers of the Davidic-Solomonic empire were reestablished. In the Southern Kingdom, it was the energetic Azariah who overcame Edom and reopened the route to the harbor of Elath. David and Solomon had succeeded in uniting the two halves of the kingdom, which were never entirely harmonious in their politics, into a personal union. Now, however, the two halves of the kingdom had fallen into two autonomous kingdoms. For all that, the splendor of the ancient kingdom seemed to have burst into new blossom.

In the newly won territories "across the Jordan" (*'eber hayyarden*), Jeroboam II established governors in order to guarantee a consistent political and economic administration. If the settlement list in 1 Chronicles 5, 3-26 is actually meant to give a picture of the situation at Jeroboam's time, then it would follow that, together with his political expansion, he had also undertaken a strong colonizing movement. The tribe of Manasseh settled as far as Salkah, a southern spur of Mount Hermon, and the tribe of Reuben extended their raids, with flock and shepherd, as far as the Euphrates.

This great advance in foreign politics occasioned an unparalleled economic development at home. Passing along the newly opened trade routes, the riches of the Orient found their way to Samaria and Jerusalem. The Transjordanian possessions witnessed the rise of a class of newly rich large estate owners, who, in the time to follow, made their presence felt in domestic politics. In the Palestinian heartland itself, a great social regrouping was in slow but very determined progress. Side by side with the new rich, the poor class grew ever larger. Economic prosperity tended to blunt religious sensitivity. These were the years in which the prophet Amos made his appearance as guardian of the social conscience of his country, and the prophet Hosea, to preach fidelity to the covenant. Without some knowledge of the politico-social background the preaching of these two prophets is easily misunderstood.

b) Assyrian satellite states: "Whether Israel cared to admit it or not, this era of great prosperity and glory was owing to the descendancy of the Assyrian power. The half century after Adad-nirari (from approximately 800 to 750) was a time of bitter internal and foreign difficulties for Ashur. The many resettled populations did not readily fall into a political equilibrium. Only the energetic general Shanshilu was in a position to put down the great revolt of the year 763, which had been occasioned by a solar eclipse." [22] These problems were further aggravated by the occurrence of the pestilence which several times laid waste wide stretches of the country. In the north, in the kingdom of Urartu (Armenia), Assyria meets with a worthy opponent. It seemed for a time that Urartu was destined to take over the Assyrian heritage in northern Syria.

Despite her manifold weakness, Assyria was unwilling to renounce her claims to sovereignty in Syrian territory. The annals recount campaigns for the years 773, 765, and 755 against Syria.[23] They were not, however, productive of any lasting success. Instead of continuing their repeated attacks upon the city of Damascus, the Assyrians left the subjugation of this city to the newly formed satellite state of Hamath and Luash. Evidence of this fact is furnished by the politically and religiously important inscription on the Zakir pillar.[24]

The inscription records a time of siege, and a campaign of ten kings against Hazrah, the city of Zakir. They had already completed the investment wall, higher than the city's own fortifications; a line of investment trenches had already been completed, deeper than the defenses of the city itself. When the crisis was at its very climax, God's help was most clearly in evidence. The "God of heaven" (ba'al šemaim) spoke to the king through his seers (hāzîn) and diviners (?): "Do not be afraid. I will stand by your side and save you from all these kings who are undertaking siege against you" (lines 13-15).

From the remainder of the text it is clear that Zakir was not only liberated but also managed to defeat his enemies. As a memorial to

22. Schmökel, GAV 259. The solar eclipse here referred to is one of the most important dates for the establishment of the Assyrian chronology.
23. RLA II, 430.
24. Discovered in 1910 in the Arab village of Afi, some 30 mi S of Aleppo. Unfortunately only four fragments of the bottom part of the column survive, but they contain the valuable inscription. The top of the column, as in the case of the Melkart column, must have carried a representation of the god, but only the knees of the figure have survived. It is still possible to make out a piece of his richly fringed garment. The original column must have stood almost 7 feet high. DOT 242-250.

this victory, he erected the stone pillar with its inscription. On this memorial stone he refers to himself as "king of Hamath and Luash." He is conscious of having been chosen by the god of heaven. The ten allied kings who take the field against him are under the leadership of Bar-Hadad of Damascus. Once again we note the names of the petty Syrian states, from Cilicia to Damascus, who had united against Ashur in the battle at Qarqar. How are we to fit the evidence of this inscription into our larger knowledge of history?

Assyrian policy had succeeded in driving a wedge into the Aramaean league of states. Zakir was, apparently, an Assyrian, since he comes from the city of Anah on the Euphrates. It was perhaps with Assyrian aid that he had seized the kingship of Hazrah,[25] the capital city of the petty state of Luash.[26] Against this Assyrian satellite the neighboring states arose in unity. The "miraculous" relief of the besieged city could thus be ascribed to Assyrian aid. Established in its position, Zakir had then succeeded in subjecting Hamath, his neighbor to the south, and exerting pressure as far as Damascus. Damascus was thus bounded on the north by the double state of Hamath and Luash, just as it was bordered on the double kingdom of Israel-Judah in the south. Threatened on two fronts, Damascus ceased to present any real danger.

The Zakir inscription has cast a welcome light on a difficult area of Biblical history. Jeroboam's successes against the Aramaeans were possible only by the fact that Damascus was, at the same time, sorely pressed from the north. After the subjugation of Damascus, Jeroboam's sphere of influence reached "from the entrance of Hamath as far as the Sea of the Arabah" (2 K 14, 25) and thus bordered on the Assyrian satellite state of Zakir. The possibility of a subsequent confrontation between Zakir and Jeroboam would not be excluded. At all events, there is some evidence in the corrupt text of 2 K 14, 28: "And he recovered for Israel, Damascus and Hamath, which had belonged to Judah."

c) ECONOMIC MIRACLES IN JUDAH UNDER UZZIAH (791/90 — 740): When we speak of an economic miracle in Judah, we are not applying our modern concepts to an ancient text. Scrip-

25. In the Assyrian sources this is recorded as *Hatarikka,* situated in Northern Syria half-way between Arpad and Hamath. In the Bible, it is referred to in Zph 9, 1 and probably also in Nb 24, 7; Ez 47, 5.

26. Assyrian *Luhati;* the location is not certain, probably a large district S of Aleppo.

27. C. Gordon, *Historical Foundations of the OT,* 219, suggests the questionable state of *Ja'udi* (*Sam'al*) in Northern Syria, modern Turkey, in the Gulf of Iskenderun. But the text is too corrupt to yield any certain information.

ture itself to the reign of Uzziah as "a miracle" — "he was marvelously helped" [28] (2 Ch 26, 15). The miracle involved was, of course, the fact that Uzziah "grew strong" (*hāzaq*). His accession to the throne had not been accompanied by any very favorable auspices. The thistle of Judah had been trampled by the cedar of Israel; Jerusalem was plundered, her walls torn down, and the aged king Amaziah was retired from his throne. The young king of Judah, upon his accession to power, was, at first, only a vassal dependent on the favor of Israel. He has two names in Scripture: " *ᵃzar-yahu* and *'uzzi-yahu.*" Whether he assumed a new throne name when he became king we cannot determine. His name is, at all events, the program of his life: "Yahweh helps" or "Yahweh is my strength." No better name could have been chosen for a zealous reformer of the Yahweh religion.

Uzziah quickly hit upon a program for his reign. The situation was abundantly clear. At the first opportunity he set about rebuilding the broken section of the city wall. He further strengthened the fortifications by the erection of three towers, at the "Corner Gate and at the Valley Gate and at the Angle." The first two constructions belong to the western defenses; the "Angle Tower" was apparently situated somewhere in the eastern wall (Neh 3, 2). Next the army had to be reorganized, if the land, humbled on all sides by its enemies, was ever to rise again. The fundamental unit of the new army was not the ancient clan levy (*bêt-abôt* — "father-house"). The conscriptions were now rigidly carried out and the members were recorded by the royal scribe (*sôpher*). According to the usual translation, 2600 family heads were mustered, providing a levy of some 307,500 fighting men (2 Ch 26, 12). Such numbers are, in the history of the Ancient Near East, a sheer impossibility. The Roman Empire, at the time of its greatest extension, counted only 180,000 in its

---

28. EB II, 386 explains the Hebrew verb *hiphlî* (Hiphil from the root *pālâ'*) as "help was forthcoming to him" and thus abandons the fundamental meaning of "accomplish something extraordinary, miraculous." Cf. the substantive *pele'* "wonder, miracle." The word has a very wide range of meanings.

armies.[29] How was a dwarf state like Judah to bring more than 300,000 men into the field! The numbers become more probable if we once again translate the questionable word *'eleph,* not as "thousand," but in keeping with the ancient terminology of war, as "clan levy." [30] The text of 2 Chronicles 26, 12 must, according-ly, read: "The whole number of the heads of fathers' houses of mighty men of valor, for the clan levy (*ḥêl-'ᵃlaphîm*): six hun-dred." When the army was mustered out, it was primarily the sheikhs and clan heads who were counted, each of them providing a certain number of fighting men. According to the treasury lists of Mari, a clan represented between 10 and 20 men. For Judah, this would amount to a military strength of 6000 — 10,000 men Half of these, 300 *'eleph,* formed a standing army (*ḥêl-sābā*), while the other half was held in reserve (2 Ch 26, 13). The army was equipped with the most modern weapons. Particularly worthy of mention, in the eyes of our historian were the "machines" [31] with which arrows and large stones could be hurled into the hostile ranks from a fortified position (2 Ch 26, 15).

Hand in hand with the organization of the army, the new king devoted himself to strengthening the fortifications. It seems that the circle of defense fortresses, begun by Rehoboam and strengthened by Jehoshaphat, was renewed and enlarged. Parti-cular attention is centered on the watch towers in the wilderness of Judah (2 Ch 26, 10). Archaeological expeditions have dis-covered significant evidence of such towers in the southern terri-tory (Negeb).[32]

---

29. Cf. Vol. III, 264, note 92.
30. When Ben-Gurion suggested this interpretation (Radio Jerusalem, Hebrew broadcast June 10, 1960), there was almost a national crisis. The orthodox demanded public recantation in Parliament. But the popular reaction to this new interpretation does not affect its basic truth. The "thousands" should simply be taken out of our Bible translations, since they only serve to undermine the credibility of Scripture.
31. The newness of this military apparatus is evident in its very name. It was called simply "the invention" (*ḥiššabôn*).
32. W. Zimmerli, *Die landwirtschaftliche Bearbeitung im Negeb,* ZDPV 75 (1959), 151.

Thus equipped, Uzziah was in a position to take up battle with his hereditary enemies. Now was the time to settle accounts with the Philistines, who had seized the opportunity of Judah's weakness to make extensive inroads into the territory. Uzziah conquered the cities of Gath, Jabneel, and Ashdod, and had their city walls pulled down. He next directed his attention to the southern territory once held by Solomon, with its mines and the harbor at Elath. He succeeded in subjugating Edom, whom Amaziah had already conquered at Sela. This opened the door to the south country. From Elath the ships were free to make their way to Ophir; the mines furnished precious bronze for war and peace, and the great caravan routes once again gravitated towards Jerusalem.

The securing of the caravan routes involved a few highly successful campaigns against the Arabs, designed largely to intimidate and terrify, both in the territory of the Sinai peninsula as well as the territory of the royal road east of the Dead Sea.[33] Just as during David's reign, Ammon paid its tribute to Jerusalem (2 Ch 26, 8). The glorious days of great empire seemed actually to have returned.

Uzziah devoted particular attention to the rural economy. "He loved the soil" (*'ᵃdamah* — 2 Ch 26, 10). In this country, so little blessed with rain and springs, the water supply has always presented a serious problem. Uzziah had a series of cisterns dug, in which the precious rain water could be preserved for man and animal, as well as the irrigation of the fields. The great crown estates lay in the "Lowland" (*šᵉphelah*), the fertile plain between the Mediterranean and the foothills of Judah, and in the territory referred to simply as "plain" (*mîšôr*), an area which is to be located not in Transjordania, but to the south of

---

33. Cf. GTT, No. 1000: Instead of *Gur-ba al* we are to read Negeb, the southland extending as far as the Sinai Peninsula. The Me'unites mentioned in 2 Ch 26, 7 have their name from the city of *Ma'an*, even today one of the most important trade and administration centers in southern Jordania. Its importance is due, in both modern and ancient times, to its position along the great communications line between north and south, about 200 mi S of Amman and 65 mi N of Aqabah.

Judah.[34] In this capacity, he did real pioneer work and turned the wilderness into arable ground. The king was the most important, though not the only large estate owner in these newly acquired territories. It seems that the colonization of this new country led to hoarding of land holdings. These large-scale agricultural undertakings were a heavy pressure on the small peasant holdings in the Judaean mountain country. This explains the social inequities which were the constant objects of prophetic preaching. On the one hand we have the newly rich, devoid of all social conscience, and on the other hand, the throngs of the impoverished. There were two sides to the economic miracle that now took place in Judah.

In his religion, Uzziah followed in the footsteps of his father Amaziah. "And he too did what was right in the eyes of the Lord" (2 K 15, 3). This was true, however, only so long as Zechariah, of whom we have no further knowledge, was his mentor and advisor. After his death, Uzziah seems to have embarked upon a questionable religious policy. Not content with merely tolerating the cult of the high places, he also claimed priestly prerogatives and wanted to officiate at the incense offering himself. For this presumption he was stricken with leprosy. The reins of government were taken over by his son Jotham, acting as co-regent. He himself was forced to spend the last ten years of his life (751-740) in "a separate house"[35] (2 Ch 26, 16-21). The regnal years of Uzziah and his son Jotham thus overlap, a fact which must be noted in determining the chronology of

---

34. W. Zimmerli, *Die landwirtschaftliche Erschliessung des Negeb*, ZDPV 75 (1959), 151.

35. *bet-hahophšit* occurs only here. Variously interpreted: "hospital" (*haphaš* = to be weak), "house of repose" (cf. Ps 87/88, 6): "Among the dead is my repose," (*hopheš*) or "house of the separation," (*hophši* = free, for oneself). In the Ugaritic texts it occurs in the form *bt hptt*, as a reference to the subterranean dwelling of the God Baal. Was Uzziah isolated in a cave, or in a cellar chamber, or in some other form of burial chamber? Médebielle ClamB III, 748. — Possibly the enigmatic locution is simply a reference to the royal palace excavated in Ramath-Gilead S of Jerusalem, where Amaziah withdrew after taking ill. The excavation evidence points to this era.

this era.[36] Still, Uzziah, in the forty years of his reign (791/90 — 768 as co-regent with Amaziah, 767-751 as sole ruler), had done great things for the country.

After an initial period of tension, relations with Israel had improved. In terms of world history, both kingdoms, Israel and Judah, had reached a climax beyond which they could no longer advance. Surely it was tempting to believe that the "day of Yahweh" was imminent, and, together with it, the world dominion of Israel. It is, however, precisely in this politically and economically brilliant period that the harbingers of future storm are most in evidence. The prophets of this time, Amos and Hosea, are not deceived by the brilliant façade. They lay bare the inner rot and function as the inexorable prophets of eventual doom.

---

36. Chronology (cf. table in the appendix): After the failure of the feud between "the cedar and the thistle," Uzziah was co-regent with his father Amaziah (791/90 — 768). Whether Amaziah, now condemned to life as a private citizen, was not in sympathy with his son's politics and planned to attempt a *coup*, we do not know. At all events he fled from Jerusalem and was received in Lachish where he was murdered (2 K 14, 18). Hereupon Uzziah becomes sole ruler (768-751). When he took ill, his son Jotham took over the reins of government. Jotham was thus co-regent during his father's lifetime (751/750 — 740), and then sole ruler from 740-735. The 16 years of Jotham's reign (2 K 15, 5 and 15, 33) thus include the years as co-regent and the years of sole rule. The distinction is clear from various synchronisms.

CHAPTER VI

THE PROPHET AMOS, CHAMPION
OF RIGHT AND JUSTICE

1) "GO, FLEE AWAY TO THE LAND OF JUDAH" (Am 7, 12)

THE preaching of the shepherd Amos of Tekoa was more than painful to Amaziah, the high priest at the national sanctuary in Bethel. He considered it as absolutely dangerous to the state. What Amos was proclaiming was nothing less than the destruction of the royal house, laying waste of the countryside, and the expatriation of the people. Amaziah, accordingly, sent word to King Jeroboam II, informing him that Amos was planning a conspiracy. The country could no longer bear his ministry. He suggested to the prophet that he "go, flee away to the land of Judah, and eat bread there, and prophesy there" (7, 12).

Amos' answer is a surprising one. He told the angry priest: "I am no prophet, nor a prophet's son;[1] but I am a herdsman,

---

1. G. R. Driver, *Amos VII, 14*, ET 67 (1955), 91-92 takes Amos' answer not as a refusal but rather as a vehement affirmation: "What! I am not a prophet!?" — Similarly P. R. Ackroyd, ET 68 (1956), 94: "Am I not a prophet? Am I not the son of a prophet?" — that is, a genuine prophet, not a professional prophet but one called from God. E. Vogt, *Waw explicative in Amos VII, 14*, ET 68 (1957), 301 argues for the conventional interpretation: "I am not a prophet," that is, "not a

and a dresser of sycamore trees, and the Lord took me from following the flocks, and the Lord said to me, 'Go, prophesy to my people Israel' " (7, 14ff.). Amos was not a prophet by profession, a member of that monk-like community which lived on the charity of the faithful; he was a prophet in virtue of Yahweh's direct call. By vocation, he was a shepherd [2] in the Judaean steppe of Tekoa, and also a dresser of sycamores [3] He would thus have had sufficient income to live independently of the mendicant prophetic community. But he was driven on by an irresistible power to abandon herd and sycamore. Amos does not present any explicit description of the experience of his vocation. God must have one day seized upon him with an irresistible power. He described this experience with images and figures, which are

prophet in the sense of a professional prophet." Amos' consciousness of his divine call is explored in H. Junker, *Amos, der Mann, den Gott mit unwiderstehlicher Gewalt zum Propheten machte*, TTZ 65 (1956), 321-328.

2. In 7, 14 Amos calls himself *bôqēr*, "cattle-breeder," and in 1, 1 a *nôqēd*, a seldom used word for sheep-breeder. Arabic *maqqad* refers to a type of sheep with heavy wool. IntB VI, 777. — Since Mesha of Moab also calls himself a *nôqēd* (2 K 3, 4), Amos certainly need not be regarded as an impoverished shepherd; it is quite possible that he owned herds of both cattle and sheep. — More recently he has been presented as a hepatoscoper with an official position in the cult. The basic meaning of the root *nqd* is presented here as "to point, to mark out," which is not a reference to distinguishing one sheep from another, but rather marking out the liver for purposes of augury and auspices. In Ugarit the expression *rb khnm* "high priest" occurs as parallel to *rb nqdm* "chief of the shepherds." A. Murtonen, *The Prophet Amos — a Hepatoscoper?* VT 2 (1952), 170. Eissfeldt, EinlAT 483 rejects this interpretation as unjustified. In Ugarit the word shepherd is used in a metaphorical sense, whereas in Amos it has its original meaning. There is nothing in the entire book to suggest service in the liturgy or hepatoscopy.

3. Before the sycamores were edible, they had to be lightly channeled (before they were ripe) in order for the bitter sap to flow out. Since figs do not flourish in the high country near Tekoa, Amos must have owned some property of his own along the Coastal Plain or in the Jordan sink or he must have hired himself out for this tedious work.

a striking expression of the powerful constraint that binds cause and effect in his experience: "Do two walk together, unless they have made an appointment? Does a lion roar in the forest, when he has no prey? Does a young lion cry out from his den, if he has taken nothing? Does a bird fall in a snare on the earth, when there is no trap for it? Doeś a snare spring up from the ground, when it has taken nothing? Is a trumpet blown in the city, and the people are not afraid? Does evil befall a city, unless the Lord has done it? Surely the Lord God (*'ᵃdonay*) does nothing, without revealing his secret to his servants (*'ebed*) the prophets (*nabí*)" (3, 3-7). None can resist the word of God. Amos sums up the experience of his vocation in the telling brevity of this statement: "The lion has roared: who will not fear? The Lord God has spoken; who can but prophesy!" (3, 8).

2) "WE CAN NO LONGER KEEP SILENT"

Conditions in Israel are such that it would be a sin to keep from speaking out against them. Pfeiffer [4] and others maintain that the activity of the prophet Amos was confined to a few months' time, or even to a single festival day at Bethel. But the text makes it clear that Amos stirred up the whole country with his preaching (7, 10). He preached not only in Bethel, but also in Gilgal (4, 4), and primarily in the capital city of Samaria (3, 9-11; 4, 1-3; 6, 1-7). When did he break his silence? "Two years before the earthquake" (1, 1). Excavations [5] point to the existence of a great earthquake in the strata of the time of Jeroboam II. The precise year cannot be determined. Since the Assyrian peril plays no great role in the preaching of Amos (6, 2), his primary activity must have coincided with the climax of political and economic development of Israel under Jeroboam II. The period between 760 and 745 (before the rise of Tiglath-Pilesar!) would probably come closest to the facts. [6]

---

4. Introduction 577.
5. In Hazor, BA 20 (1857), 41; 21 (1958), 45.
6. Robert-Feuillet, IntrAT 490.

a) JUSTICE AND SOCIAL ORDER:[7] The pulsebeat of Ancient Near East life could be felt at the city gate (*ša'ar*). Not only great affairs of state, but even the complaints of its least citizen were all heard at the city gate. In the days of Amos, too, the city gate was the seat of justice (5, 10, 12, 15). But what kind of justice? The prophet unmasks the complete collapse of the judicial administration: "Do horses run upon rocks? Does one cloud the sea with oxen? But you have turned justice into poison and the fruit of righteousness into wormwood" (6, 12). The stipulations of the law were pliable. The preservation of justice presupposes, in principle, the will and intention of distinguishing between good and evil. It is this mentality and capacity and determination to distinguish good from evil that Amos refers to as "justice" (*sedaqah*). The expression of this justice in the life of the community is the judgment (*mišpat*). The two belong together. Amos mentions them in one and the same breath. Justice must produce proper judgment, and judgment must proceed from justice.[8] In whose hand was the administration of justice? As far as we can gather from the polemics of Amos, it was not the responsibility of one single court. Normally, the administration of justice lay in the hands of the citizens who enjoyed a certain authority either by their family position or by their possessions. When a case came up for judgment, these men would take their place at the city gate, where the accused was summoned for judgment.[9] The case of the man who was in the right, the "righteous" [10] (*saddîq*), had

---

7. V. Maag, *Text, Wortschatz und Briffswelt des Buches Amos*, 228-235. — L. Randeline, *Ricchi e poveri nel libro del propheta Amos*, FrancLA II (1951/52), 5-86. Explicit studies on the social conditions in the days of Amos. There are four classes of the wealthy: estate owners, aristocrats, merchants, judges. Amos' battle is not against the civilization as such, but only against misuse and decay. The oracles are not aimed at annihilation, but only conversion and salvation.

8. V. Maag, *ibid.*, 229.

9. *pāqad*, "visit, call to account" (3, 2, 14).

10. "Just" here refers not to the abiding quality of moral perfection, but to a threatened claim to justice; a man is *sadîq* if he is in the right but his right has to be fought for.

to be weighed against that of his adversary. Witnesses were also summoned in the decision. The guilty party was punished according to the law. According to what law? Obviously there were recorded norms which went back as far as the time of Moses. But together with these, there was a large body of unwritten tradition, a corpus of general principles which must be applied to the individual case. The law was thus interpreted by custom and the common estimation of the body politic — both of which elements were controlled by the ruling class. If, accordingly, the ruling class was without conscience, the administration of justice must necessarily suffer.

In addition to this community judiciary council, priests and kings had, from time immemorial, been concerned with the adminstration of justice. The king himself supplied a sort of court of last appeals (2 S 15, 1-6): certain civil ratifications (Lv 13, 1ff.) and particularly difficult and hard to resolve cases were, on the other hand, referred to the sanctuary, which was to render a decision by direct appeal to God's judgment (ordeal — Nb 5, 11-31). In the strict procedure of the courts, therefore, any man who had a grievance could obtain justice. The reality of the matter, however, was quite different. The administration of justice had fallen into the hands of the powerful and suffered violent abuse. There is a whole series of expressions in Amos for the oppression of justice: oppression (*'ašûqîm* 3, 9), terror (*mehûmôt* 3, 9), violence (*ḥamas* 3, 10), and robbery (*šôd* 3, 10). Then there are the references to men deprived of justice: needy (*'ebyônîm* 2, 6; 4, 1; 5, 12; 8, 4, 6), poor and afflicted (*dallîm* 2, 7; 4, 1; 5, 11; 8, 6), the poor who bow under their burden (*'anawîm* and *'aniyyîm* 2, 7; 8, 4). This is the first appearance in recorded history of an underprivileged social class which does not owe its misery to economic incompetence; their misery has a religious overtone. For these poor, oppressed, and wretched men are called just men (*saddiqîm*), in one and the same breath: they are men who have been deprived of their rights.

On the other side stand the powerful. For them, the adminstration of justice is simply a profitable business. Where justice is a matter of profit, the right of the individual always comes off second best. Inequities in the system of fines were closely related to this. We can no longer precisely determine the provisions set up in this matter by the arbitrary interpretation of the privileged, but Amos has much to say against the abuse. The taking of pledges was a simpler problem. In settlement for a claim it was customary to demand a pledge of the guilty party. The excesses to which this practice could lead are easily under- stood from the provisions of Deuteronomy (24, 6, 17), according to which a widow's handmill and clothing cannot be taken as a pledge. If a person has nothing else, even his coat and clothing could be demanded in pledge, but it must be returned that same evening, if it were the only covering and protection for his body (Ex 22, 25). The pledge of one's clothing is thus the desperate act of the very poor. The heartlessness of the creditor in Amos' day had reached a shameful point: those who had unjustly ex- torted property in pledge used it to pass their idle moments: "They lay themselves down beside every altar upon garments taken in pledge; and in the houses of their God they drink the wine of those who have been fined" (2, 8).

A further scourge upon the impoverished classes was the practice of debt slavery. If a debtor was unable to pay his creditor he could arrange to settle his debt by working as his slave. If, however, the creditor was not satisfied with his work, he could sell him in turn, as a stipulation of this contract, and thus eventually have some payment for the debt. This was a sore point in the economic miracle of Israel. Against the new large estate holders the small farmers were helpless. They sank deeper into debt, thus affording the new rich classes with a perfect opportunity to incorporate the property offered as pledge and to drive its former owners into slavery.[11] For the "great

---

11. A. Alt, *Der Anteil des Königtums an der sozialen Entwicklung in den Reichen Israel und Judah*, Kleine Texte III, 348-372. Since the Hebrews first occupied the land they observed the principle of inviolable heritage, thus achieving a compromise between poor and rich. The gradual growth of an unpropertied lower class is to be ascribed to the fact that hereditary property which had passed from its owner's

lords" such an opportunity, if desired, could easily be fabricated: "They sell the just man (*saddîq*) for money, the poor man (*'ebyôn*) for a pair of sandals; they prey upon the paltry holdings of the needy (*dal*) and pervert the right of the poor (*ᵃnawîm*)" (7, 6-7). In business dealings, deceit was the order of the day. Weights were increased, measures were diminished, and instead of good grain, only the inferior product was sold to the poor (8, 5). According to the example of the king himself, who built a summer palace and a winter palace and furnished it with ivory ornaments (3, 12), the wealthy class began to build their own luxury dwellings.

In this vast concert of injustice, oppression, and degradation, there was, as might be expected, no lack of dissolute women, whom the prophet bluntly calls "cows of Bashan." [12] "Hear this word, you cows of Bashan, who are in the mountain of Samaria, who oppress the poor, who crush the needy, who say to their husbands, 'Bring, that we may drink!' " (4, 1). Dissolute parties, to the accompaniment of music, seem to have been anything but rare (6, 4ff.).

b) RELIGION NONETHELESS: It could hardly be said, although we might have supposed it to be true, that this was an unreligious or godless era. Quite the contrary. The official cult flourished as never before. Pilgrimages to the national sanctuaries in Bethel (4, 4; 5, 5; 7, 10) and Dan (8, 14), where Yahweh was worshiped under the image of the bull, were a religious climax in the course of each year. Gilgal [13] seems to have enjoyed particular popularity

power (judgment for debt or dying out of his family) reverted to the status of royal property. In this manner the king became the first great land-owner in the kingdom. Then there were the newly acquired territories. The king drew upon both these sources to repay or reward his deserving officials, and they accordingly enlarged their holdings.

12. So called not only because the art of cattle husbandry flourished in the country of Bashan (= "fat"), but because it was precisely in this territory that the estates of the new rich class were located. Their estates were in Transjordania, but they enjoyed the life of the capital.

13. Gilgal, "on the eastern end of the border of Jericho" (Jos 4, 19), a

in this respect (4, 4; 5, 5). The cult festivals and feast days were kept most conscientiously, sacrifices of food and holocausts of fat animals were offered in abundant measure (5, 21), and the magnificent official cult was accompanied with songs and harp playing (5, 23). But the very presence of cult prostitution, for example, is ample evidence of the unholy purposes for which the sanctuary was now abused (2, 8).

Political success had made the country secure and economic development had made it fat. People were boasting of the victorious campaigns at Carnaim and Lodebar (6, 13) and looking to even greater triumphs. For the thinking of that age it went without saying that all this success was a gift from Yahweh, just as the Assyrians always ascribed their victories to the god Ashur or the Moabites to their god Chemosh. In the popular philosophy, the "day of Yahweh" (*yôm yahweh*) played a decisive role. This is "that day" (*hayyôm hahû'*), on which Yahweh will let his power shine forth in glory and magnificence. Accordingly, they looked to better times and a more promising future. The intelligent men of that day (*maskîl*) were, however, well aware of the fact that this situation could not last much longer. In opposition to the popular opinion of their day, they were convinced that "the times were evil." They held their peace, however, in the face of the general terror (15, 13). Such a silence the prophet could not share.

3) THE CALL TO PENANCE

Amos was a man to shake up consciences, to foretell doom; but he was also the herald of a new era. He is on the one hand

sacral point of focus for the confederation of the tribes since their entry into Palestine. Located somewhere in the Jordan sink. In *Hirbet al-Mefgir*, 1 mi N of Jericho, excavation has established the ruins of an early Israelite settlement, but according to the Talmud (4, 19) we must look in the East. — The investigation of the *Tulul en-Nitlah*, located east of Jericho, and apparently retaining something of the name Gilgul or Gilguliyeh, yielded only Byzantine and Arabian remains. — Others have sought Gilgal in the mountain country, either in the vicinity of Bethel or near Shechem. But a location in the Jordan sink seems more probable. GTT No. 464; Rinaldi, Amos 160; BRL 197.

a moral preacher, setting out to heal the grossness of contemporary morality; but the disquieting nucleus of his preaching is his firm faith in God. Since he is the herald of God in an era that has forgotten God, he naturally becomes a preacher of penance. The motives of his call to conversion develop naturally from his concept of God.

a) NATIONAL EXAMINATION OF CONSCIENCE: The call to penance is a call to individuals, but the prophet's first address is to the people as a whole; for the people, in their relationship to Yahweh, in election and in rejection, always appear as a unity, a composite personality. The individual is irrevocably bound up, for better or for worse, with the community. Despite these social bonds, he is not relieved of his personal responsibility. In his message to the people, the individual is always the object of address, and the commission and omission of the individual have their effect upon the people as a whole. History thus turns into a constant dialogue [14] between God and people. But this is not yet the true individuality of the prophet's preaching. The pagan peoples known to the culture of the Bible also shared the belief that the fate of a people depended upon its position in the face of their god; this went without saying. Amos, however, bursts the narrow boundaries of a purely political relationship between God and people; he makes both people and individual stand in the immediate presence of the Creator God, who, among the multitude of the nations, has called Israel to a particular vocation.

That is why Amos chooses the first motif for his penitential message from history itself. The beginning of Israel's way with God was a free election: "You only have I known (chosen)[15] of all the families of the earth" (3, 2). Yahweh led them out of Egypt, struck the Amorrites, and prepared a country for them. He called up prophets and Nazirites. But they would not listen to Yahweh's voice; they told the prophets: Do not prophesy! —

---

14. This is not simply a modern attitude forced upon ancient thought. One other example is the Mesha inscription in which Moab's fate is ascribed to the wrath or favor of their god Chemosh.

15. The verb *yāda‛*, literally "to know," has a much wider range of meaning than our English equivalent. It can mean also "to love, to choose."

and made the Nazirites drink wine (2, 9-12). Possessed of the land promised by Yahweh, they still kept running, in great numbers, to the sanctuaries of Bethel, Dan, and Gilgal, where they offered sacrifice. But Yahweh had no part in their pilgrimage and sacrifice. For Amos, the whole of their religious activity is not the service of God but rather an outcry (*pešaʿ*)[16] against Yahweh: "Come to Bethel and transgress; to Gilgal, and multiply transgressions" (4, 4). Where, then, is the place for Yahweh, if not in the sanctuaries of Israel? But Yahweh is no longer God of this people; the gods of Canaan have broken into the sanctuary itself.

Despite this large-scale defection, Yahweh was still in the midst of his people. One blow followed after another, to open their unbelieving eyes: famine and drought ate up the economic prosperity; pestilence and war rode violently through the land. Widespread destruction, like that of Sodom and Gomorrha, terrified the people,[17] but they could not find the path that led to Yahweh (4, 6-12).

That his people turned justice into injustice and good into evil wounded Yahweh in the depths of his being. Seeking God would mean simply "seeking good and not evil" (5, 14). The maladministration of justice, and its attendant social oppression, are not phenomena unrelated to God; they are a constant challenge to the eternal justice.

Amos was not preaching a new God. His call goes back to the earliest origins of Israel. Hence the constantly recurring plea: "Seek, hear, be converted, go back!" Up to this time, the answer of the people had been negative. Every honorable man necessarily had to admit that conditions could not continue — simply because Yahweh was Yahweh, simply because God is God. His very essence is holiness (2, 7; 4, 2). What would happen if this God were to walk among his people (5, 17)? Along the path of his feet judgment and destruction would gape and yawn.

b) PROPHET OF DOOM: The first blow Amos strikes is di-

---

16. *pešaʾ*, basic meaning "to rebel, to revolt," especially against God.
17. Probably a reminiscence of the crisis from Aramaea.

rected against the false belief in the day of Yahweh.[18] This is
not a day of light, but a day of gloom (5, 18). And its coming
is imminent. This is brought out, with progressive clarity, in the
series of five visions (7, 1-12; 9, 1-4). The first two plagues —
locusts and the fire mounting up from the deep — the prophet
was still able to turn aside by his prayer. But when he saw
Yahweh standing by the wall with a plumbline, he was forced
to admit that destruction could no longer be put off. Finally,
when he saw the harvest basket, there was no longer any doubt
but that the end had come.[19] The last vision made it only too
clear that God was already beginning his terrible punishment (9,
1).

The judgment now beginning goes far beyond the frontiers
of Israel. Yahweh is the God of all peoples. Every nation has
its own proper measure. When the measure is full, the judgment
begins. Eight times Amos insists upon the truth that "Yahweh can
no longer revoke his punishment" (1, 1-16). The peoples have
filled their measure to the brim with evildoing. Damascus threshed
the captives with threshing sledges of iron; Gaza and Tyre trafficked
in slavery with their prisoners of war; Edom knew only anger and
cast off all pity; Moab ripped open even pregnant women, Judah
forgot the laws of God, and there is no measure to the wickedness
of Israel. Amos shatters all the proud privileges of Israel upon
which they presumed to rest their confidence. Israel is no better
than the Philistine and the Aramaean, which were also called
by Yahweh (9, 7). In the face of his judgment there is no escape.
The man who escapes from the lion falls to the vengeance of the
bear; even if he reaches his house in safety, he is bitten by a
serpent there (5,9). Even if he makes his way into the netherworld,
the hand of God's judgment shall seize upon him there. And if
he rises up to heaven, God's hand shall drag him down. If he

---

18. Amos is the first Biblical author who deals with this eschatological
    imagery, but he is not its inventor or creator. Such images were
    common in the world of the prophets and made up a part of the
    popular eschatological views of the times. Amos simply enlarges the
    imagery to take on new meaning. V. Maag, Amos 246.
19. There is a word play here: *kelûb haqqayis* "harvest basket with ripe
    figs" and *qês* "end" (8, 1).

hides himself on the top of Carmel, even from there the Lord will search him out, and though he hide in the bottom of the sea, God will command the serpent and it will bite him (9, 2-3).

With inimitable clarity and persistence Amos announces: "The end is coming, the end is near." This preaching of the day of Yahweh can no longer be kept silent. The events of human history are subject to the inexorable judgment of God. Amos intones a dirge over Israel: "Fallen, no more to rise, is the virgin Israel!" (5, 1ff.).

The images and colors with which Amos paints the coming of this day are not essentially new. That Yahweh will darken the day into night (5, 8), sending earthquakes (2, 13; 9, 1), fire (1, 3ff.), and storm (1, 14), recalls the great theophanies on Sinai (Moses — Elijah). His throne is in the heavens, and from there he sends the rain (9, 6). He made the Pleiades and Orion and calls out evening and morning (5, 8). There is no place in the world which is not subject to his power. Yahweh is omnipresent and omnipotent, the creator of heaven and earth. Amos' picture of God is not a revolutionary concept. The above mentioned images all developed quite naturally from the traditional treasury of Israel's faith.[20] When, finally, the hymn-like expressions are concluded with the credal formula "Yahweh is his name" (4, 13; 5, 8; 9, 6), Amos is only taking his position on the fact of the Sinai revelation, where Yahweh became Israel's God. In behalf of Yahweh's sole divinity, Elijah had also worked zealously; for him too, Yahweh was the God of the consuming fire, who would tolerate no other god beside him. If Elijah's zeal had helped to promote the restoration of the first three commandments, which proclaimed the sole divinity of Yahweh, then Amos' energetic activity can be seen as a battle to restore the outraged moral imperative of the rest of the ten commandments.

4) THE FALLEN HOUSE OF DAVID — PROPHET OF SALVATION

We almost get the impression that after the Day of Yahweh

---

20. A. Feuillet, *L'Universalisme et l'Alliance dans la Religion d'Amos*, BiViChr 17 (1957), 17-19.

there will be no further time. The threats of destruction were not merely the product of imagination. A sober appraisal of the contemporary world situation could have prompted any thoughtful man to make a rather accurate conjecture as to the fact that ruin was about to befall his country Israel. Even in the midst of a peaceful era, when men were still boasting of their conquest of Carnaim and Lodebar, Amos was already proclaiming the ascendancy of a people who was destined to overthrow all Israel's glory, from Hamath to the Brook of the Arabah (6, 13-14). And indeed, when the Assyrian armies once again turned to the conquest of the western countries — Calneh could not resist, Hamath fell, and even Gath was overcome — it became more and more obvious that Amos was right. This great political reversal, already outlined on the far horizon, is, for the prophet, a concrete and historical event. Once again the war machinery of a mighty empire is destined to cut its path through Israel. Amos lays bare the ultimate impulse behind the course of contemporary events, and refers everything to the one ultimate fashioner of human history, Yahweh, who had chosen Israel as his firstborn (6, 1), but now takes the field against his own people. For it is Yahweh who stirs up the Assyrian as the instrument of his divine judgment.

If Yahweh has now become the principal enemy of his people, will his people ever manage to survive? Apparently not. And still Yahweh does point to a way out of the catastrophe. Yahweh's devastating blow will strike only the "sinful kingdom" (*mamlakah ḥatta'ah,* 9, 9). For Amos, the divided kingdom and the schism of the national faith were the first beginnings of destruction. He evaluates the national-religious catastrophe in the same light as the Books of the Kings, which constantly repeat, in tragic monotony, the stereotyped sentence of rejection for a series of individual kings: "He did what was evil in the sight of the Lord, and followed the sins of Jeroboam ben-Nebat, which he made Israel to sin" (2 K 13, 1 etc.). The annihilation of the sinful kingdom does not, however, mean the complete destruction of the people. A remnant will remain (5, 15).

Amos thus becomes the herald of another Israel, the holy

remnant, which will come out of the catastrophe purified. Obviously this concept of a holy remnant is not something entirely new for Amos.[21] Elijah was also familiar with it. There was only a very small group who did not bend their knee before Baal. Amos gives this concept of the holy remnant a much deeper significance, in terms of salvation history. Throughout this whole time of foreboding doom, nothing was more expressive of the impending catastrophe than the situation in Zion. There was still the divine promise of the abiding existence of the "booth of David." In the overall structure of the Book of Amos, accordingly, the promise of the restoration of the fallen "booth of David" is not an alien concept (9, 11ff.); it is an essential part.

After judgment comes salvation, and it will be manifest in three principal points: David's kingdom will be reestablished in its unity (9, 11), unprecedented fertility will blossom (9, 13) and the people will live in peaceful possession of their restored country (9, 15). It is Yahweh alone who brings near this day of salvation. He is the creator of the new era in which his kingship can work freely and without resistance. That a very definite Son of David is destined to play a particular role in this new phase of the divine rule is not expressly stated by Amos; it is, however, implicit in the image of the "booth of David."

The words and images with which Amos announces the ruin and salvation of Israel seem to be definitive, and yet they stand mid-way in the course of history. Their fullest understanding can be achieved only by a careful awareness of their prophetic perspectives. Beyond the conditioned course of human time, the prophet envisions the horizon of final judgment and ultimate salvation, some part of which is always being experienced in every individual area of human history.

Amos was thus the first to strike the great themes of classical prophecy, themes which his great successors were to enlarge upon and enrich, presenting them with greater depth. In every prophet's work, however, there is one leitmotiv in the foreground of his

---

21. V. Maag, Amos 200.

preaching. Amos saw the relationship between God and man exclusively, so to speak, *sub specie societatis* — in terms of human society. For him, the religious question is transformed into the social problem. It was his insight into the social crisis of his day that made ready his soul to accept the sowing of a prophetic mission.[22]

5) THE BOOK OF AMOS

We could hardly expect the Book of Amos, in its present state, to have been spared the vicissitudes of history. Amos had many prophetic predecessors, who made just as strong — and perhaps stronger — an impression on the course of history. And yet, these older prophets survive only in brief accounts of their activity. The actual words of their preaching have all been lost. Amos is the first prophet whose preaching has survived in a written text. How did it come to be written down? We can only conjecture the answer. Exiled from his country, and deprived of any further opportunity to preach the word of Yahweh, Amos might have decided, upon his return into Judah, to record his words and visions in writing. The Book of Amos would, accordingly, be a most eloquent witness from a man condemned to hold his peace.[23] There were many who would read his writing. In such times of oppression, the word of truth finds its way through closed doors and silent alleys more quickly than if it were spoken aloud.

The division of the text is obvious. The inscription (1, 1) combines the concepts which seem irreconcilable: "The words (*dabar*) of Amos, . . . which he saw" (*ḥazah*). How can we see words? An explanation is to be found in the fact that the Hebrew word *dabar* means both word and event, happening. Indeed. But perhaps this combination of words is deliberately chosen in order, from the very outset, to characterize a book which can, actually, be divided into two sections, "words and visions." [24]

---

22. V. Maag, Amos 226.
23. IntB VI, 771.
24. Sellin-Rost, Einleitung 124 divides the book into the record of a vision (7-9) and a collection of proverbs (1-6).

In the Book of Amos, the oldest of the written prophets, we find evidence of the three principal types of prophetic literature: a. collections of oracles (1-6), b. biographical details, narratives of the prophet's life, in the third person (7, 10-17), c. autobiographical vision narratives, testimony in the first person (7, 1-9; 8-9).

The book does not begin with a lengthy introduction on the prophet's vocation and fate in life. The person of the prophet is hidden behind his work. The "words" which are committed to writing are certainly not mere excerpts from his lengthy penitential preaching; they are small units, short and pithy, in the form of the ancient divine oracles. The collection of oracles (1-6) is, accordingly, not the product of one single outburst; it is a series of originally independent statements. Eissfeldt [25] claims to isolate 25 individual oracles. The sequence of these oracles is not entirely obvious. A division based on the areas of activity — threats against Samaria (1-4, 3), and then against the national sanctuary in Bethel (4, 4-6) — is not convincing. As in the case of other collections, it might well be a systematic and mnemotechnich (memory-helping) consideration that prevailed in the sequence. The collection begins with a series of threat oracles against the nations, all the more effective for the sheer monotony of their simple repetition (1, 3-7b). The next unit is the judgment against Israel (2, 7c-16); this is followed by five collections which begin with the introductory words "Hear" (3, 1; 4, 1; 5, 1) and "Woe" (5, 18; 6, 1) — these are also clearly recognizable as a unit.

The vision account (7-9) is obviously an independent unit, and it contains more than the story of Amos' visions. The first three visions (locust plague, fire from the great deep, and the plumbline) follow immediately upon each other. Then, however, the series is interrupted by the narrative account of Amos' flight from the sanctuary at Bethel (7, 10-17). The fourth (8, 1ff.) and also the fifth (9, 1ff.) visions are followed by words of threatening and repentance. The book comes to a close with the heralding of the restoration of the house of David and the beginning of the future era of salvation (9, 11-15).

What is the work of Amos' own pen and what is the work of a later hand? On this question there is diverse opinion. Almost unanimously, the following sections are regarded as later additions to the text: a. in the oracles on the nations, the strophes on Tyre (1, 9-10), Edom (1, 11-12), and Judah (2, 4-5), all of which can fit only into the political situation existing after the destruction of Jerusalem (586); b. the hymns (4, 13; 5, 8-9; 9, 5-6), which appear to have come into the text from the liturgy; c. the prophecy of salvation at the conclusion of

---

25. EinlAT 488.

the book (9, 11-15), which, it has been claimed, is irreconcilable with the threats expressed in the body of the text and could only have been added in an effort to provide a conciliatory final note to the entire book.[26]

The grounds on which these various sections have been rejected have, however, recently been assailed as inconclusive.[27] Both the hymns and the prophecy of salvation belong to the original content of Amos' prophecy. There is also a modern tendency to attribute a much greater age to the Book of Amos, in its final form, than was customary in earlier criticism.[28] If the collections on the prophets Elijah and Elisha were already completed a generation after their deaths, then a date for the final redaction of the Book of Amos could most probably be set towards the end of the eighth century. As distinguished from the collections of the earlier prophets, which contain only narratives about the masters, in the Book of Amos it is the prophet himself who speaks his own living word, stamped with the clear mark of his strong personality, and this in itself is further witness to its genuinity. The movement to enlist the written word in the service of prophecy may have originally begun with Amos. How much he himself recorded we do not know. But obviously, his disciples would preserve the words of their master, passing them down in writing from one generation to another.

Even if the final form of the book was not reached without a long series of tradition — and this is certainly true for every Old Testament book — still the Book of Amos does present a singular and very compact unity in language, style, and composition.[29] If St. Jerome [30] characterizes Amos as a man unskilled in speech (*imperitus sermone*), this does not mean that Amos has no power as a speaker. It is true that he was not a polished orator. His images came to him from the immediate experience of nature — for he was a man closely bound up with the world of nature — and his images are more convincing than any well turned periods. "Apart from Isaiah in his best passages, none of the later prophets can approach Amos in purity of language, classical simplicity of style, and

---

26. Cf. Eissfeldt 489, Weiser 198, Pfeiffer 580.

27. G. J. Botterweck, *Zur Authentizität des Buches Amos*, BZ, NF 2 (1958), 176-189. — J. D. W. Watts, *The Origin of the Book of Amos*, ET 66 (1953), 109-112 assigns the visions over a long course of time. The climax and turning point is the New Year's Festival, on the 15th day of the 7th month of the year 752. The concluding prophecy of salvation is assigned to the time of the destruction of Samaria (722).

28. Latest date suggested is after the Exile between 500 and 200 (Pfeiffer, IntrOT 583), middle view, in the Exile itself (Sellin-Rost, Einl. 126), earlier dating before the Exile (Botterwecke, 1, c.).

29. Robert-Feuillet, IntrAT 491, Unité de ton.

30. Jerome, *Preface to Amos*, Migne, PL 25, 990.

originality of image." [31] His life in Tekoa along the margin of the desert became a figure for his mission. As a shepherd he frequently had to ward off the attacks of lions. Two legs or a piece of the ear was all he could sometimes save (3, 12); he was constantly threatened by lions, bears, and serpents (3, 4, 8, 12; 5, 19). He observed the bird-snarer (3, 5), the fisher (4, 2), saw the heavy-laden harvest wagon make its way into the village (2, 13), experienced a plague of locusts (7, 1) and drought (7, 4), and knew how the mason sets his plumbline (7, 7). On the basis of this book, we might reconstruct a brief culture history of the people, great and small, of his day. Amos was a keen observer of the morals and the immorality of his time.

Amos enlisted his powerful oratory in the service of his vocation. He became the herald of destruction, tearing down the political and religious façades of his day and summoning both the individual and the people as a whole into the immediate presence of God, who is a God of justice and judgment. "The Lord roars from Zion, who will not be afraid?" But it would be one-sided to see Amos exclusively as a herald of doom. It is true that, in the depths of his dejection, he intones a dirge over the virgin Israel (5, 2ff.); but he also has a message to the remnant, the foundation of a new beginning. Amos has thus sounded the themes of classical prophecy, themes which are destined to be more and more developed in the further course of history.

---

31. Pfeiffer, IntrOT 583.

CHAPTER VII

THE PROPHET HOSEA, HERALD OF GRACE IN A GRACELESS AGE

HOSEA BEN-BEERI [1] was a younger contemporary of the prophet Amos. He too made his appearance at a time when Israel was flourishing under Jeroboam II; but his activity also extends into the years of confusion that followed upon the death of Jeroboam (754). According to the inscription of the book (1, 1), he was still living in the reign of King Hezekiah (728) and apparently even after the destruction of Samaria (722). Other authors tend to limit his activity to a briefer span, the decade between the appearance of Tiglath-Pilesar (745) and the Syro-Ephraimite war [2] (735). Even though his appearance cannot be dated to the precise year, it is still the imminent destruction of the Northern Kingdom that forms the historical background for activity. Hosea was the last prophet of the Northern Kingdom,

---

1. *Hôšēaʿ* is especially popular as a proper name in Ephraim. It is a shortened form, either derived from *Yeho-šûaʿ*, "Yahweh is salvation," or *Hôšaʿ-yah*, "Yahweh brings salvation." *EncMikr* II, 800. The interpretation of *Beʾērî* is uncertain. Probably it is also an abbreviated form: *beʾēr* "well," and the name of some god which has now dropped. *EncMikr* II, 8.

2. Pfeiffer, IntrOT 566.

spiritually related to the prophet Jeremiah who, a century later, was destined to herald the destruction of Judah.

It was not only by the word he preached, but even more forcefully it was by his personal fate that Hosea became the herald of a new age. In a graceless age, marked by lies and violence and infidelity, he became the preacher of destruction, but even more so the herald of grace. Approximately contemporary with him, the prophets Isaiah and Micah were at work in the kingdom of Judah. The times seemed to be out of joint, an unparalleled climax of prophetic activity. Since both Israel and Judah were fighting for their very existence, the deepest religious powers of the people once again came to life, saving what was to be saved for a new era. At this turning point in history stand the great prophets.[3]

1) MARRIAGE TRAGEDY AND BREACH OF COVENANT

Moral sensitivity is easily offended by the command that Hosea received from Yahweh. Not only the reader of today, but the prophet's own contemporaries shook their head at what the prophet did: "Go and take to yourself a wife of harlotry" (*'ešet zenûnîm*) (1, 2). What does a prophet have in common with sin? The prophet's behavior seems all the more questionable if we are correct in interpreting the meaning of his wife's name: "So he went and took Gomer, the daughter of Diblaim" (1, 3). Neither Gomer nor Diblaim can be proper names; they are rather "professional names." Gomer means "hot coal," Diblaim "two fig-cakes." [4] Together they mean a passionate and sensual woman, who could be had for the price of two fig-cakes.[5] She was abandoned to the spirit of immorality (4, 12; 5, 4). Hosea actually took this "hot coal" to wife. This marriage was destined

---

3. H. W. Wolff, *Hoseas geistige Heimat*, TLZ 81 (1956), 83-94. Hosea's spiritual milieu is presented as the levitical-prophetic opposition bloc of the last years of the Northern Kingdom.

4. *EncMikr* II, 525; cf. Prv 27, 29. F. Nötscher, EB II, 668 argues against this symbolic interpretation.

5. Compare this with the sorry figure of the poor girls who sold themselves to the occupation forces for a cup of chocolate; they were ironically referred to as "Chocolate girls."

to be a sign, a crying out against all Israel. It was no run-of-the-mill marriage. Israel herself was the "wife of harlotry" whom Yahweh had, nevertheless, taken to himself.

That such a marriage was a serious risk can easily be imagined. The three children whom Gomer bore were like the marriage itself, prophetic signs. All three have names synonymous with judgment.[6] The first son was named after the city of Jezreel, where Jehu had once, in a bloody massacre, extirpated the faithless dynasty of Ahab. But since the house of Jehu proved to be just as faithless, judgment was destined to fall upon it as well. In the year 754 catastrophe broke over the house of Jehu. Jeroboam II was still permitted to die, after a lengthy reign, in peace. His son and successor Zechariah reigned only six months, and was then murdered by Sallum, who was able to maintain his position for no longer than a month before he was put aside by Menahem. The name of Jezreel was a very pointed reference in the days of Hosea. The bloody beginnings and the bloody end of the dynasty of Jehu were all bound up with this word. Hosea was witness and herald to a political revolution.

The second child was a girl, "Not pitied" (without pity, lô-ruhamah), so named as an expression of her birth into a graceless age. Yahweh will not take back the threatening oracles spoken through his prophet Amos (1, 6). The third child, a boy, is called "Not my people" (lô-'ammî). The rejection of Israel had been once and for all determined. Are these last two names to be interpreted as evidence of the fact that Hosea's marriage had broken up and that the children born of Gomer were not his children? Was his wife guilty of adultery? Legal action and repudiation must be the immediate consequence.[7]

---

6. TUR-SINAI, *EncMikr* II, 803, interprets the name as a wish for good fortune, a solution that is admissible with little doctoring of the text. — F. S. North, *Solution of Hosea's Marital Problem by Critical Analysis*, JNES 16 (1957), 128-130, argues that a made-up episode in the life of Hosea was later given a symbolic interpretation during the exile. Gomer herself was blameless. But this solution sacrifices too much of the story's impact.

7. F. Nötscher, EB III, 675: "The question of whether Hosea's marriage is simply a vision of an allegorical poem has already been variously

Hosea repudiated his unfaithful wife. She was free to follow her lovers after her own pleasure [8] (2, 9). The pain and bitterness occasioned by this tragic marriage can be felt in every line of the prophet's story. But Hosea's love was greater than Gomer's infidelity. He turned to her again and took her back.[9] The fact that he had to buy her for fifteen shekels of silver and a homer and a letheth of barley [10] is not to be interpreted as a bride-price; it is exactly equivalent to the sum that must be paid to buy the freedom of a slave. This would seem to indicate that, after her separation from Hosea, Gomer had fallen into temple slavery

---

answered by the ancient Fathers, and the answer is still not satisfactory. But there is more and more evidence for regarding the marriage as an historical fact. There are also some serious moral and esthetic considerations against the solution of allegory or vision. Only a genuine marriage, not an allegorical one, could ever have aroused the necessary public attention." — Pfeiffer, IntrOT 568, thinks that the marriage was a happy and successful one, and that the symbolic names have nothing to do with the prophet's personal life. "The point of ch. 1 is not an imaginary domestic tragedy of Hosea but the moral and religious defection of Israel."

---

8. It is possible that Gomer was a qĕdēšah, a "sacred cult prostitute" (the word is related to qādôš = holy) and was thus obligated to devote some time to the cult of the Baal Temple. Her activity was then dictated by her pagan religious convictions, and she was thus in opposition both to her husband and his God, Yahweh.

9. For a brief examination of the interpretations of Hosea's marriage that have appeared over the last 30 years, cf. H. H. Rowley, *The Marriage of Hosea*, BJRL 39 (1956), 200-233. There are four possible solutions: — a. only one marriage, but reported in two different styles. Ch. 1 3rd person, ch. 3 1st person. R. Gordis, HUCA 25 (1954), 9-35. — b. After repudiating Gomer, Hosea undertook a marriage with a second wife who was of equally questionable reputation. G. Fohrer, *Umkehr und Erlosüng beim Propheten Hosea*, TZ 11 (1955), 161-185. — c. Hosea enjoyed an ideal marriage; the whole story is simply allegory and poetry. Pfeiffer, IntrOT 568. — d. Ch. 3 is a continuation of ch. 1, reconciliation with the repudiated wife.

10. *homer*, etymologically means an "ass's load," from *hamôr* "ass"; *lētek* occurs only in this passage and refers to a smaller unit of measure. R. de Vaux, *Les Institutions de l'AT*, I, 303. — The total price was about the worth of a slave (Ex 21, 32). EB III, 674.

working as a cult prostitute, a living parable, in her own person, of Israel's defection to the Baal cult.

Although the name Gomer does not appear in chapter three — and many have interpreted this as evidence of a new marriage with a different woman — today, on the basis of the Ugarit texts, we can consider it as definitely established that the reference is to the same marriage with Gomer, now reestablished.[11] It is understandable that, after everything that had happened between them, their relations were not immediately restored to their former condition. Hosea kept strict watch over his unfaithful wife, cut off all contact with her paramours, and avoided her himself. Only after she had suffered a change of heart did he restore her to his former fidelity and love (3, 1-5).

This marriage tragedy opened the prophet's eyes for a still greater tragedy, the serious consequences of which his contemporaries did not wish to face, the tragedy of God's relationship with his people Israel. That is why Hosea summons the children of Israel to a great marriage tribunal [12] against their mother, the people of Israel (2, 4ff.). With passionate dedication he harangues the people to finally remove the signs of harlotry from their face and breast.[13] This people, in its blindness, is running after its "lovers" (2, 6). These lovers are simply the gods of fertility, the be'alîm, to whom the people looked for the continued blessing of the fruits of the earth. And yet it is really Yahweh who gives his people grain and wine and oil, silver and gold and wool and

---

11. Hosea uses the not as yet adequately explained word wa'ekkeréha (root: ñakar) which has also been verified in the Epic of Keret in Ugarit. Soldiers on the way to war gave their wives over into some sort of safe-keeping and took them back upon their return home. The Ugaritic text is in C. H. Gordon, UM II (1955), 102, 191. English translation is ANET 144. The root nkr thus means "to remarry, to regain possession of one's lost wife." This is a theme of rather frequent occurrence in the literature of the Eastern Mediterranean. Cf. Menelaus and Helen, David and Michol, Krt and Hry. Gordon, UM III (1955), Glossary 1244.

12. The verb used here is rîb, "to lodge a complaint, to sue." (2, 4).

13. Consecrated temple prostitutes could be recognized by their clothing (veil), tatoo marks, amulets, and bright jewelry. EB III, 670.

flax (2, 10ff.). But they did not recognize him (2, 10), and this referred not only to intellectual recognition, but rather to the ready acceptance of God, in heart and mind and deed. Since there was no longer any room for Yahweh, Yahweh himself accepts the bitter consequences and, through the mouth of his prophet, declares the formal verdict of divorce: "She is no longer my wife" [14] (2, 2). Accordingly, the children are no longer his children. Their very names are a statement of judgment: "Not pitied, Not my people." The covenant is severed.

This could have been an end to the history of God's relationship with his people. God withdraws his providential care and abandons his faithless people to the impulses of their own corrupt hearts. But God does not think like a man and his love is not a man's love. That is why he makes such a violent inroad into the life and fate of his prophet, in order to reveal a new level of his own being. God can repudiate, but not forever; God can chastise, but only for human improvement. Eventually will come "that day" (2, 18, 23), the day on which Yahweh will renew the broken covenant (*berît* 2, 20) and reiterate the broken marriage vows, this time for ever. And I will say to "Not my people": "You are my people" (2, 23). They will be called sons of the living God and they will be as numerous as the sand of the seashore (2, 1). "Not pitied" will turn to "Pitied" and instead of the bloodied seed of Jezreel there will be a new seed of blessing. New Israel will address Yahweh in perfect truth as "My husband" and no longer as "My Baal" (idol consort) (2, 18). After harmony is reestablished with God, there will be harmony throughout the whole cosmos (2, 22).

After his eyes were opened by his own bitter experiences, Hosea became the interpreter of his confused age. Just like Amos, he is aware of the inexorable approach of God's judgment. It is true that Amos also looks beyond this judgment to a new era, which he also paints in figures reminiscent of paradise; Hosea goes even further. He develops the concept of "love" (*ḥesed*) proper to the theology of history. Yahweh is a God of justice,

---

14. This is the formula for repudiation used in Mesopotamia. EB III, 670.

but even more a God of love. The events of human history will make it clear precisely what hour has sounded in this two-fold relationship between God and people. The old covenant is shattered, the divorce is completed. But this does not mean an end to history. For it is God who works in history. It is he who chooses, rejects, and restores. The goal of human history is simply the love of God. In this role, Yahweh appears as sensitive and emotional as the prophet himself. We can speak here of a humanization of God.[15]

What unfolds before the eyes of Hosea is a future in which Israel is completely free of the Baal cult. Then she shall find her way back to God as the one source of all her gifts. The land will overflow with fertility. The destruction of the Baal cult will also spell the eventual disappearance of the faithless Northern Kingdom; the loyalties of the remnant to be spared will return to "David," the royal house of the kingdom of Judah (3, 5). In Hosea, too, we can speak of messianism in only the broadest and the most general terms. In the foreground we find the predominant element of faith in a God who rejects and restores, a God who introduces the new era of love — Hosea does not use the concept of "kingdom." God is the only agent. In the days of the new covenant, in keeping with this ideal relationship between God and humanity, an ideal ruler from the house of David, a son of David, will ascend the throne. But this idea in Hosea is still well in the background. It was his mission to announce that God is love.

2) AN EVIL AND ADULTEROUS GENERATION

By his own personal fate, Hosea was already a stirring source of prophecy. It was precisely these bitter personal experiences that sharpened his insight into the deeper significance of his era. His was not only the mute prophecy of signs and figures; he was an impassioned herald of the outraged, abandoned, and still indestructible love of Yahweh for his people. David had already characterized the driving force of human history as "the word and heart of Yahweh" (2 S 7, 21); Hosea seizes upon this idea

---

15. J. L. McKenzie, *Divine Passion in Osee*, CBQ 17 (1955), 167-179.

and brings it to such a full development that he deserves to be called simply the prophet of love. Whether he is storming out against his people in a holy anger, conjuring up the early days of Yahweh's love with Israel, proclaiming the impending judgment, weeping over his people's destruction, prophesying the future restoration and the new beginnings, it is always the love of Yahweh, everywhere at work, that permeates his thought. If Amos evaluates his generation in terms of its social irresponsibility, and can, accordingly, be called the herald of justice, Hosea sees everything in terms of divine love. The covenant on Sinai had made Israel Yahweh's betrothed wife. Whatever this people did or suffered in the subsequent course of its history, everything was henceforth determined in view of this bilateral relationship. This is the historical position from which Hosea undertakes a critque of Israel's history. In his day, the marriage relationship between Yahweh and Israel was faring poorly; but not only in his day. The "spirit of harlotry" (*rûaḥ zᵉnûmîm* 5, 4) was always manifest in his people. Their history seems to be one uninterrupted act of adultery against Yahweh.

a) SACRIFICIAL HEIGHTS AND PLACES OF PILGRIMAGE: Hosea took stock of the actual religious situation of his day and was forced to admit that there was hardly any room left for Yahweh. Israel was in the service of the gods of the earth. On sacred high places and groves they venerated the divine powers (*bᵉʿalîm*): "They sacrifice on the tops of the mountains, and make offerings upon the hills, under oak, poplar, and terebinth, because their shade is good. Therefore your daughters play the harlot, and your brides commit adultery" (4, 13). The fertility cult so firmly rooted in Canaan had enticed Israel into the aura of its sensuous appeal. The strongest hope of the Israelite farmer was fertility, God's blessing on his fields, his flocks, and his family. Instead, however, of approaching Yahweh directly as the final giver of all good gifts, the devotees of the Baal cult stopped at the preliminaries and paid their veneration to the mysterious forces of the earth. This conduct the prophet unmasked as adultery, and adultery in two senses: first, spiritual adultery, since Israel was forgetting her God, and as adultery in the flesh. For in the fertility groves it was the "sacred wedding" that was practiced in the belief that the performance of the reproductive act was essentially bound up with the divine powers of fertility. Hosea mocked these sacred groves with their proud trees dedicated to the idols. If Yahweh were to pass these sacred heights and groves, only thorns and thistles would flourish on the altars. But now the Israelites feel security on these sacrificial heights. The day will come, however, when they shall say to the mountains, "Cover us," and to the hills, "Fall upon us" (10, 8).

The many sacrificial high places and groves do, indeed, seem to testify to a believing and pious people. For Hosea, however, they are nothing more than open harlotry. This harsh judgment was applied with even greater severity to the many places of pilgrimage throughout the country. We are astounded at the many names which are mentioned in the proportionately brief book of Hosea, a review of religious practice. From the great number of pagan sanctuaries, a few were outstanding for their fame and popular appeal. They became places of pilgrimage, to which Israel paid religious visits. Those were not simply sanctuaries erected in the Israelite era; the Israelites, after taking possession of the country, began to conform to the Canaanite practices.

Already in the days of her first possession of the Promised Land, the sanctuary of Baal-Peor [16] had exercised a sort of magical power of attraction over Israel (9, 10). The first confrontation with the Canaanite fertility cult was Israel's first great defeat (Nb 25, 1ff.). The sanctuaries of Adama on the Jordan and in a city of Gilead enjoyed a well established fame. They are also way-stations in the story of Israel's defection and breach of covenant, although, apart from their mention in Hosea, we know no further details. Shechem had experienced a renewal of the cove-

---

16. Full name *Bêt-ba'al-pe'or*, "house (= temple) of the God of Peor." O. Henke, *Zur Lage von Beth-Peor*, ZDPV 75 (1960), 155-163. Opposed to the former identification with *ḥirbet es-seh-gayil*, he locates it on the tell of *ḥirbet 'ayun musa*, near the spring of Moses. The field exploration established the presence of an ancient Moabite settlement. A female figurine testifies to the fertility cult practiced there. The proximity of the spring invited early settlement.

nant under Joshua; but now, on the way to Shechem, there is a band of priests who commit murder (6, 9), probably a reference to child sacrifice and cultic immorality. With the same holy anger, Hosea rejects the activities at Mizpah and Mount Tabor [17] (5, 1).

The prophet's primary attack, however, is directed against the national sanctuaries at Bethel, Dan, and Samaria. What was going on here in the name of religion bordered on the grotesque: "Men kiss calves!" (13, 2). Whereas there is no explicit mention of the cultic image in the case of the other sanctuaries, the prophet says of Samaria: "The calf of Samaria shall be broken to pieces" 8, 5). Accordingly, even in Samaria, the capital of the Northern Kingdom, there was a bull cult. The sanctuaries of Bethel and Dan were well known and even notorious since the time of the political and religious division of the kingdom. For Hosea, however, the "place of God" (bêth-'El) is a "Place of delusion" (bêth-'awen 4, 15). In the same breath, Hosea mentions Bethel and the pilgrimage center of Gilgal (4, 15; 9, 15; 12, 12), where people went on pilgrimage not only from the Northern Kingdom, but also from Judah. What is the point of this attack upon Gilgal? Was it originally a sanctuary of Yahweh? Yahweh, after all, refers to Gilgal as "my house" (9, 15). But into this house the worship of idols had made its way. That is why Yahweh hates it. He will give them "a miscarrying womb and dry breasts" (9, 14) as their punishment. We conclude that the same fertility cult flourished in Gilgal as at Baal-Peor.

Summing up his judgment, Hosea comes to the verdict that Israel has "sinned from the day of Gibeah" (10, 9). The meaning of this passage is not entirely clear, although it appears to be a reference to the shameful activities at Gibeah (Jg 19-21). History itself must serve to warn the Israelites that the "abomination," that is, defection from Yahweh, which is running rampant throughout the country, can only call down war and devastation as its punishment. For Hosea, the history of Israel is not a closed book of the past. Times gone by are present to his preaching, as an

---

17. It is impossible to determine which Mizpah is meant here; probably the cult site from the days of Samuel, north of Jerusalem (1 S 7, 5).
   — There is no further information on a sanctuary on Tabor.

example and as a judgment. He thus becomes, for the Old Testament, the one great critic and theologian of history.

b) CRITIQUE OF HISTORY: "Hosea's critique begins with the patriarch Jacob-Israel (12, 3-7). It is not the honorable and patriarchal traits that he delineates, quite the contrary. Jacob is, for Hosea, the original type of deceit: "In the very womb he took his brother by the heel, in his manhood he strove with God." If their great ancestor was such a person, how could the posterity be different?[18]

Hosea's thoughts are fond of returning to the days of Israel's wandering in the desert, the days of the first love between Yahweh and his people: "When Israel was a child, I loved him, and out of Egypt I called my son" (11, 1). Tenderly, as only a mother can be tender, Yahweh cared for his young people. He taught them how to walk, and took them in his arms (11, 2). From the days of Egypt he was Israel's God and savior ($m\hat{o}\check{s}\hat{i}a^{\prime}$ 13, 4), striking a covenant with him ($b^e r\hat{i}t$ 2, 20; 8, 1; 10, 4) and entrusting him with his own law.

So far as we know, Hosea was the first to compare the Sinai covenant with the marriage contract, and develop all its negative and positive consequences. On the side of God, this covenant was a loving act of choosing and recognition: "It was I who knew you in the wilderness" (13, 5). This divine initiative on the part of God should have provoked an equally generous response in love from his chosen people. "My people are destroyed for lack of knowledge; because you have rejected knowledge, I reject you from being a priest to me" (4, 6). In Hebrew idiom, the expression "knowledge of God" ($da^{\prime}at$ $^{\prime}el\hat{o}h\hat{i}m$)[19] never means merely the sum total of religious knowledge of God. People and

---

18. M. Gertner, *An Attempt at an Interpretation of Hosea XII*, VT 10 (1960), 272-284, comes to the conclusion that chapter 12 is a compact unity of its own, an ancient historical midrash dating back to Hosea himself.

19. E. Baumann, *Wissen um Gott als Urform der Theologie*, EvT 15 (1955), 416-425. — H. W. Wolff, *Erkenntnis Gottes im AT*, EvT 15 (1955), 426-431. — J. L. McKenzie, *Knowledge of God in Hosea*, JBL 74 (1955), 22-27.

leaders alike were not without their necessary knowledge, but they forgot, they no longer recognized Yahweh; that is, they no longer wanted to know of Yahweh, since they had chosen other gods for themselves. Accordingly, the *da'at 'elohîm*, the loving recogniton of God, is one of the fundamental concepts of Hosea's theology of history. Understanding and heart alike, the whole person, are called upon to recognize God and to acknowledge him in every sphere of human life.

As a new concept in the theology of history, Hosea introduces the word *hesed* [20] a word which has no precise English equivalent. On the part of God, *hesed* is the love which chooses, the grace of the covenant; on the side of the people, it is a return of love, fidelity to the covenant: "I desire steadfast love (*hesed*) and not sacrifice, the knowledge of God, rather than burnt offerings" (6, 6). No matter how magnificent the divine service might be, it is meaningless if the covenant is broken. Expressed in figurative language, *hesed* is the flower which blossoms from the loving acknowledgment of God (*da'at*); the harmony which rises from the bond of love between God and his people, effecting a stable order (*'emet*) in every realm of human life.

Hosea is forced to admit that this fundamental relationship has been disturbed. As a consequence, all order and harmony have disappeared: "There is no faithfulness (*'emet*), no love (*hesed*), and no knowledge of God (*da'at 'elohîm*) in the land; there is swearing, lying, killing, stealing, and committing adultery; they break all bounds and murder follows murder. Therefore the land mourns" (4, 1-3). Falsehood and deceit are the basic condition of the faithless people (12, 1). In their retinue march violence and oppression. For where God has lost his right, man too is condemned to destruction. Political security can never supply this deep, interior loss. Even when they make their covenants, they are only lying to each other (10, 4). Any appeal to the world powers of Ashur or Egypt is meaningless (7, 11).

Hosea's critique of history makes it very clear that Israel is

---

20. G. Farr, *The Concept of Grace in the Book of Hosea*, ZAT 70 (1958), 98-107. The NT equivalent of *hesed* is *charis*, the unmerited and forgiving love of God.

a rebellious and adulterous generation. This statement is not, however, simply a statistical or non-partisan statement. For the prophet, the contemplation of history is also a "meeting for judgment with Yahweh" (2, 4; 12, 3). Hosea has assembled and delivered the case for the prosecution. His is the further duty of pronouncing sentence, and, in terms of the contemporary situation, this can only mean a condemnation. Like the trumpets of judgment, his powerful cry rings throughout the country: "Hear" (4, 1; 5, 1). On "that day" Yahweh will trample the high places and the sacred groves, strike off the horns of the altar and, once and for all, drive away the political machinations which lead to treaties with Ashur and Egypt. There will be no longer any king, any prince, any sacrifice, any stone pillars (*massebah*), any priestly garment (*'ephod*), by which to ascertain God's will, and there will be no household gods (*teraphîm* 3, 4).

Once again we have an end to the way of God with men, inaugurated so magnificently on Sinai, and it is an end in the abomination of the desolation (*šiqqûsîm* 9, 10).[21] The people must make its way to a new starting point, to a time of bondage in an Egypt and to a time of wandering through a desert (11, 5) before it can return, before there can be any remnant to survive.

3) CONVERSION AND NEW COVENANT

Hosea's picture of God is gloomy with the prospect of imminent judgment. This explains the comparison with predatory beasts: "Yahweh is a lion, a panther, a she-bear for Israel." Predatory animals lurk beside the way, falling upon their victim, tearing it to bits, and leaving whatever is left to the jackals (13, 7). Death and plagues and hell and pestilence are all to do their work.[22] These somber elements could well be multiplied. But if we concentrate too much attention upon this negative element, we present a completely wrong picture of the message that Hosea

---

21. Cf. Dan 9, 27.
22. "Death, where are your plagues? Sheol, where is your destruction?" (13, 14) has a negative meaning in the context. St. Paul (I Cor 15, 55) freely reworks the sentence and uses it in a positive context: as expression of the victory over the forces of hell.

preached. He is a caller to judgment, but he is also the herald of a new salvation.

Yahweh has no pleasure in destruction. The memory of the ruin of Sodom and Gomorrah and the other cities is very much alive in the prophet's spirit (11, 8b). Their existence is blotted out forever. Is this to be the case with Israel? The answer must be a strong and confident No. And why not? Because Yahweh has a heart (*lēb*): "My heart recoils within me, my compassion grows warm and tender" (11, 8c). The judgment must come because "Ephraim had no heart (*lēb*)" (7, 11). The Biblical concept of heart (*lēb, lēbāb*) is not a sentimental idea. Biblical psychology is much more closely bound up with the physical organs than our modern concepts. A man feels and thinks in his "liver," is moved in his "bowels," trembles in his "bones." It is worth noting that the head (*rō's*) has no part to play in this symbolic language. The function of the head, in the interior processes of activity, was attributed to the heart. For us, the heart is almost exclusively the seat of love; but the ancients thought, willed, decided, and loved with and in their heart. The heart is, accordingly, the organ in which human salvation or ruin is determined. The religious tragedy of this book lies in the fact that Israel's heart was divided (10, 2), fed to the full, lifted up (13, 6). Wine and new wine took away their understanding, and closed their heart to the call of God (4, 11). The dialogue between heart and heart, between God and the people, has grown dumb: "They do not cry for me from the heart" (7, 14). This is merely a different expression for what the prophet's tragic marriage experiences had already symbolically declared. The covenant of life is broken.

Hosea, however, also speaks of a time to come, a time in which "Yahweh will once again speak to her heart" (2, 16), where the divine-human dialogue will be resumed again. Meantime, however, must come the days of judgment and conversion. The prophetic appeal to penance is addressed to the heart of the people and to the heart of each individual. It is in the heart that conversion must take place.

In the midst of this judgment we hear the stirring cry: "Come, let us return to the Lord; for he has torn, that he may heal us.

He has stricken, and he will bind us up. After two days he will revive us; on the third day he will raise us up, that we may live before him" (6, 1-2). Apart from a few obscurities, this prayer of penance clearly expresses faith in the restoration of a torn and stricken people. The sequence of events involves a play on words: on the first day torn, on the second revived, on the third raised up.[23] The new era will culminate in the *da'at 'elohîm* (6, 3), which, once again, is not simply knowledge, but love and recognition of God. Knowledge and heart (*da'at* and *lēb*) always go together.

The raising of the people is the work of God; for it is Yahweh who tears and strikes, who binds and heals, who revives and raises up. He is the savior (*môšîa'*), beside whom there is none other (13, 4, 10; 14, 4). It seems to be a contradiction, but it is actually the very essence of the divine direction of human history, that salvation cannot come without human cooperation. It is within man's power to oppose his personal preferences to the plan of God. Conversion (*šûb*) is another leitmotiv in the preaching of Hosea; he uses it both for God and man: "Return to Yahweh" (*šûbû 'el yahweh* 14, 3) — is his word of conversion to a rebellious people. If it does not return to Yahweh, and if the evil is not converted (5, 4), they must return into the bondage and slavery of Egypt (8, 13; 9, 3). But if it resolutely decides to be converted, to go back to Yahweh (2, 9; 5, 15; 6, 1), then Yahweh's anger will turn from them as well (14, 5).

This conversion will follow upon the establishment of the new or renewed and eternal covenant (*berît*). Hosea uses the word *berît*, covenant, for political alliances with the world powers Assyria and Egypt (12, 2; 10, 4), but also for the covenant struck on Sinai and later broken (6, 7; 8, 1). Political alliances bring no assurance of salvation (14, 4). They only drive Israel to the

---

23. We can no longer determine whether this triadism was already a well developed proverbial formula, perhaps in the meaning of a short time, or a borrowing from the vocabulary of the fertility cult. The Baal cult celebrated the death and restoration of nature. It might be that Hosea has simply taken over this common conception, but filled it with new meaning. EB III, 681. — J. B. Bauer, *Drei Tage*, Bibl 39 (1958), 354-358.

brink of ruin. Salvation comes only from the renewal of the old covenant. It is not something completely new that is substituted, any more than Hosea married a second wife. Just as Yahweh remains always the same, so does his covenant. Only in the being of God we now see a new era, the witness of his eternal love, refusing to be conquered by defection and infidelity. "On that day" (2, 20) the love of God will triumph; for "that day" is the day of the new espousals between God and his people, an espousal destined to last for all time (le'ôlam).

Against the somber backdrop of his age, with its threat of impending ruin, Hosea sounds the clarion of a "new and everlasting covenant" (2, 19, 21). The timbers of the royal palace were already smoldering, like fire under the ashes (7, 6). It needed only to break out, and king and palace would be consumed. "After the death of Jeroboam II, fierce party conflicts broke out. None of the series of kings which rose and fell so quickly really enjoyed power; none of them created any permanent order. The Northern Kingdom was subjected to a sorry interlude of tyranny. The Assyrian had laid his paw upon the land, but not yet bared his claws." [24]

Hosea had been sent at a very definite crisis of history; his preaching was directed, primarily, to his contemporaries. The imminent destruction of Israel, as the political consequence of the Assyrian rise to world supremacy, could be predicted without benefit of prophecy. But Hosea is not speaking in terms of political analysis; it is only in virtue of his religious interpretation of contemporary history that he becomes a prophet, a champion for the rights of God in the midst of the national collapse. In the last analysis, this was a collapse only for Israel. For Assyria, the destruction of Israel was only another milestone along the road to world empire.

What was the possible hope and assurance in these days of impending doom? Political alliances prove to be deceitful. Taking stock of the religious situation revealed the complete collapse of the nation's faith. It is understandable that men of vision were

---

24. J. Wellhausen, *Geschichte*, 111.

seriously disturbed: the time was ripe for destruction. Nothing better had been deserved.

Hosea's greatest accomplishment consists in the fact that, without mitigating the fact of eventual destruction, he proclaimed the gospel of a new and eternal covenant, in the very midst of this national ruin. He spiritualized the ancient concept of covenant, giving it a universal and personal depth of meaning.[25] Greater than the justice of God, which must necessarily press for judgment, is the divine love. What is the prospect of this new era which opens before the intuition of our prophet? Gone are the gods with their cult, gone is the rebellious priesthood, gone are the princes and kings, while the people have been expatriated and the land become a desert. But from the very ruins will rise a new people, eternally dedicated to God in fidelity, love, and justice. The earth will once again be paradise (2, 23). Among the other blessings it enjoys (14, 6-9), the new people will find its way back to its "king David" (3, 5b). Messianism plays a quite subordinate role in Hosea. The idea is present, since the house of David as well as the new covenant were promised an eternal (l^e'ôlam) rule, but for the Northern Kingdom this promise is hardly carried out. For Hosea, messianism represents one part of the great hope in the future. It is the Book of Hosea, however, which already prepares the messianic material upon which the later prophets are to build further.[26]

4) THE BOOK OF HOSEA

"Hosea is, together with Jeremiah, the most subjective of all prophets, and, in this respect, he stands in sharpest contrast to his predecessor Amos." [27] It was his own personal suffering that matured him for his mission. "If Amos speaks of the divine necessity as with its own inner voice, Hosea is completely permeated with the word of Yahweh, in its most human conception. Even in externals, his speech is a departure from the prophetic style;

25. A. Feuillet, *L'Universalisme et l'alliance dans la religion d'Osée,* BiViChr 18 (1957), 2, 7-35.
26. E. H. Maly, *Messianism in Osee,* CBQ 19 (1957), 213-225.
27. J. Wellhausen, *Geschichte,* 111.

his words are almost monologues, the product of a soul that has been deeply moved by its own anguish and by a strong sense of compassion." [28]

This strong personality has also given a definitive stamp to its literary product. Hosea knows how to sing of Yahweh's love for his ungrateful people, with a tenderness and inimitable delicacy (6, 4; 11, 3), but he can also burst into the flames of passionate preaching and express the anger of an unrequited love (5, 14; 13, 7, 12ff.). He does not shrink from blunt expression in unmasking the perverted religious orgies (2, 2-13). Frequently, in the passion of his excitement, he interjects images and sentences that already led St. Jerome to the conclusion that Hosea is speaking in slogan-like sentences (*quasi per sententias loquens*).[29] Hosea was such a passionate personality that we might very well expect his literary work to betray the traits of his personality. Commentaries and introductions have been concerned with the effort of introducing some system into the fourteen chapters of his Book. The first three chapters can be isolated as an introduction. They are concerned with the marriage tragedy and the prophetic insight derived from this experience. But the remaining chapters, 4-14, are, according to Pfeiffer, arranged "in chaotic confusion." [30]

It is obvious that the Book of Hosea, like the Book of Amos, in the form we know today, was not written down as a single composition, in an hour of literary enlightenment. If we consider the fact that it represents only a small excerpt of a prophetic activity that extended over some twenty-five years, we have already outlined the literary problem involved. First comes the oral preaching, the word. It was from the abundance of available material that the prophet himself, and later his disciples, chose what was to be preserved for future times. In this work of composition, it was not the temporal sequence, but rather the affinity of subject matter which set the tone. Despite this "chaotic confusion," the text itself suggests a tripartite division:

a) ORACLES ON ISRAEL (4-11): chapter 4, 1 announces the theme of the collection. There is a trial (*rîb*) between Yahweh and Israel. 4, 1 and 5, 1 begin with the same words: "Hear the word of the Lord, oh

---

28. *Ibid.,* 112.
29. Pfeiffer, IntrOT 571.
30. *Ibid.,* 570.

people of Israel." Chapter 6 does not contain any explicit address to Israel, but it continues the thought expressed in 5, 14; 7, 1: "When I would heal Israel,...." 8, 8: "Israel is swallowed up." 9, 1: "Rejoice not, oh Israel." 10, 1: "Israel is a luxuriant vine." 11, 1: "When Israel was a child,..."

b) ORACLES AGAINST EPHRAIM (12-14, 1): 12, 1: "Ephraim multiplies falsehood...." Together with a further repetition of the leitmotiv: Yahweh's trial (*ríb*) of his people: 13, 1: "Ephraim was exalted in Israel." [31]

c) PROPHECY OF CONSOLATION (14, 2-9): Beginning with Israel (14, 2) and ending with Ephraim (14, 9).

This division is based upon a purely formal point of view, but still it gives at least a rudimentary insight into the development and growth of the text. At the beginning we have the smaller units [32] which were apparently collected during the lifetime of Hosea himself. According to Pfeiffer [33] chapters 1-3 were written before the year 744, that is, before the beginning of the Assyrian threat, since, in this time, the prophet was still hoping for Israel's continued existence. Chapters 4-14 would then date to the years 744-735, in which the ultimate destruction of Israel grew more and more obvious. The passages, however, which treat the glorious resurrection of the nation after its destruction and deportation, would be the product of a Judaic redactor from the post-exilic era. It is obvious that this final Judaic redactor must be credited with more than the mere title at the beginning (1, 1) and the wisdom oracle at the end of the Book (14, 10). The work of his hand, organizing and augmenting the text, is everywhere evident in the course of the Book. It is to his efforts [34] that we must assign the mention of Judah in 1, 7; 4, 15; 5, 5. The tendency to date every oracle about Judah and the salvation to come in the post-exilic era [35] is a result of the unproven hypothesis that Hosea was merely a herald of doom, without any hope.

The very fact of his tragic marital experience would militate against this negative interpretation. After rejection comes re-acceptance. And, in the last analysis, Hosea's mission and purpose was to lead rebellious Israel back to Yahweh, the God upon Zion.

---

31. E. Zolli, *Il significato di rd e rtt in Osea 12, 1 e 13, 1*, RSOr 32 (1957), 371.
32. Cassuto, *EncMikr* II, 14 units in ch 4-14.
33. IntrOT 569.
34. Robert-Feuillet, IntrAT, 494.
35. Pfeiffer, IntrOT 573.

Accordingly, it was quite impossible for him to exclude Judah and the Davidic dynasty from his theology of history. The promised restoration and unification of Israel, under Davidic leadership, is thus part and parcel of the original scope of Hosea's preaching.[36] It is quite certain that, in the Book of Hosea, we have a faithful witness to the preaching of the prophet Hosea, although the interpretation of individual passages is frequently obscure. "His brevity of speech, the pregnant depth of expression, and especially the often desperate condition of text forces us, despite every attempt at emendation, to be content with pure conjecture and to give up the prospect of definite explanation." [37]

---

36. R. Gordis, *Hosea's Marriage and Message; a New Approach,* HUCA 25 (1954), 9-35.

37. Nötscher, EB III, 7. — H. S. Nyberg, *Studien zum Hoseabuch,* Upsala (1935), defends primarily the importance of oral tradition here. In the Ancient Near East it was just as reliable a witness as written sources.

CHAPTER VIII

THE PROPHET ISAIAH, HERALD OF
THE HOLY IN AN UNHOLY ERA

IN the title to the Book of Isaiah, the activity of the prophet is
identified as falling within the reigns of Uzziah, Jotham, Ahaz,
and Hezekiah. This period outlines one of the most dramatic
epochs not only in Biblical mystery, but in the whole history of
the Ancient Near East. For the kingdoms of Israel and Judah,
the illusion of security, which the long and peaceful reigns of
Jeroboam II and Uzziah had apparently introduced, had finally
passed away. The banner of Ashur (5, 26) was once again
unfurled, and borne in victory against the kingdoms of the middle
country. "He will raise a signal for a nation afar off, and whistle
for it from the ends of the earth; and lo, swiftly, speedily it
comes! None is weary, none stumbles, none slumbers or sleeps,
not a waistcloth is loose, not a sandal-thong broken; their arrows
are sharp, all their bows bent, their hooves seem like flint, and
their wheels like the whirlwind. Their roaring is like a lion, like
young lions they roar; they growl and seize their prey, they
carry it off, and none can rescue. They will growl over it on that
day, like the roaring of the sea. And if one looked to the left hand,
behold, darkness and distress; and the light is darkened by its
clouds" (5, 26-30).

In Zion and in Samaria hardly anyone paid attention to the clouds gathering along the northern horizon. People still felt secure in the midst of the new economic prosperity. But Isaiah shattered the outward appearance of security, laid bare the inner rot and corruption, and became the herald of impending doom. The destroyer comes in the figure of Assyrian military power; but this is only a tool of the "Holy One of Israel." The fire of annihilation breaks out from God's own sanctuary. The God of Israel is a holy God. And that is why catastrophe must inevitably make its appearance.

When the Assyrian armies drew closer to the frontier, Israel and Judah hastened to seek political alliances. But this dream too is shattered by the preaching of Isaiah. He summons people and king alike before the immediacy of God himself. There is no survival apart from faith in God. Isaiah thus becomes a preacher of the holy God in an unholy age. The unholiness of his age is further evident in the fact that no one wanted to hear the words he spoke. Even if Isaiah withdrew, from time to time, and withheld his preaching, since he was speaking to deaf ears, a spirit of interior necessity and the consciousness of God's direct command always prompted him to return to public square and assembly, to the courts of the mighty politicans, to assert the prerogatives of the Holy One of Israel. His first preaching reaches its climax in the Syro-Ephraimitic war. Faced with incredulity and contempt, he withdrew to the circle of his disciples. But when the storm clouds once again gathered over the horizon of Jerusalem, he once again appeared in public, herald of destruction and prophet of salvation.

A) THE HOLY ONE OF ISRAEL

THE EARLY PREACHING OF THE PROPHET ISAIAH (740-735)

Isaiah was called to be a prophet in the year of King Uzziah's (Azariah's) death, that is, the year 740. This year had already been preceded by a full decade of confusion in the foreign and domestic politics of the Northern Kingdom. Jeroboam II was allowed to finish his glorious reign in peace, and to pass on his crown to his son Zechariah. Under his reign, however, the flame of revolution quickly broke out. The prophet Hosea compared the turbulent situation to an oven: "For like an oven their hearts burn with intrigue; all night their anger smoulders; in the morning it blazes like a flaming fire. All of them are hot as an oven, and they devour their rulers. All their kings have fallen; and none of them calls upon me" (7, 3-7). In their godlessness, there was no distinction between overthrower and overthrown.[1] Zechariah [2] reigned only six months during the year 754. Towards the end of the year, in autumn, he was murdered by Shallum who maintained the throne for only a single month. Then, upon the news of the *coup d'état* in Samaria, a certain Menahem ben-Gadi asserted his power in the ancient royal city of Tirzah, marched against Samaria, struck down Shallum, and himself seized the power. He crushed all resistance with brutal force. The city of Tiphsah, whose location remains unknown, closed its gates to him. He overran it and completely destroyed it (2 K 15, 8-16). Menahem succeeded in maintaining his power for some ten years [3] (753-743).

1) THE TERRIBLE SPLENDOR OF ASHUR

In the year 745 the young general Tiglath-Pilesar III (*Tukulti-apal-esara*, 745-727) achieved political control by a *coup d'état*. This move served as impetus to a thorough-going restructuring of the political balance of power throughout the Ancient Near

---

1. Nötscher, EB III, 684.
2. *Zekar-yahu* "Yahweh has remembered, he has given a son" (cf. the Song of Anna 1 S 1, 11). Accadian *zakâru* "call"; "you call my name," that is, to call into existence, to create. Compounds with *zakâru* are frequent, for example *Sin-izkur* "the moon god Sin remembered, he has created." *EncMikr* II, 923.
3. Chronology: The "ten years" (2 K 15, 17) are an express reference to the reign in Samaria, and thus must be counted only from 752. Those were preceded, however, by the reign in Tirzah; accordingly Menahem's rule goes from 753/752 to 743. This is not one of the cases described in the Appendix!

East.[4] It is true that in some inscriptions he calls himself son of Adad-nirari, but he must really have been a "son of nobody," a usurper. Having made his way upwards through the army, he based his political position on the strength of that same army. He made Assyria into an avowed military state. In order to secure his rule, he broke up the heretofore great provinces, whose administrators had constantly rebelled against the king, creating new and smaller administrative districts, which he entrusted to proven administrators. This policy made enemies of the former ruling class. He went even further, abrogating the tax indemnity for Assyria and Haran, a step which was not designed to win the friendship of the priestly class in the great temples. He had eyes only for his army. Accordingly, he undertook a series of technological improvements in the weaponry, thereby assuring a military superiority in the face of his enemies.[5]

The wheels on his war chariots were now equipped with eight spokes instead of the customary six. Together with the driver and the chariot fighter, he also supplied each chariot with a shield-bearer to ward off hostile missiles. This precautionary move emboldened him to do away with the relief horse, which had formerly run beside the two draft horses and frequently created considerable confusion. He thus achieved considerable maneuverability. The horsemen which made up his cavalry were equipped with scale-armor, a measure which afforded so much protection that the specialized auxiliary troops which were customarily supplied to receive hostile missiles, were now no longer needed. There were similar improvements in helmet, shield, bow, and lance. Particular attention was also focused on the mighty siege machines which were powerful enough to beat down even the strongest fortifications.

With all these reforms, which Tiglath-Pilesar seems not to have introduced too rapidly, he set the foundation for a policy of military extension unlike anything existing before his time. Even his policies towards the subjugated nations took on new

---

4. Cf. W. v. Soden, *Herrscher im Alten Orient*, (1954), 90-93: Tiglath-Pilesar organizes the Assyrian Empire.
5. M. A. Beek, *An Babels Strömen*, (1959), 95.

direction. It had been customary to retain conquered kings and princes in their administrative positions, obliging them only to the payment of tribute. But these princes generally took advantage of the first good opportunity to recover their independence. Accordingly, he generally did away with the conquered rulers, dismembering their kingdoms and creating new Assyrian provinces, which were then entrusted to Assyrian governors. In his policy of resettling entire populations, he went far beyond his predecessors. Hundreds of thousands of men were driven from their native land and resettled in foreign territory. As a result, large sections of the Assyrian empire were occupied by a very mixed population which soon forgot its native individualities in the midst of the new foreign environment. Since this resettlement process involved primarily Aramaean ethnic groups, the Aramaean language spread far and wide even in Assyria. Conquered in war, the Aramaeans, in their language and culture, both conquered and survived their conquerors. Tiglath-Pilesar III introduces the series of Assyrian military emperors,[6] who were destined to bend the ancient world to their own wills for more than a century.

The fact that these new rulers took the name of Tiglath-Pilesar, a name made glorious in the history of ancient Assyria, as their throne names, is in itself a statement of their official program. Tiglath-Pilesar I, appealing to the Accadian dream of world dominion, had set about world conquest in the name of the God Ashur, around the year 1100 B.C.[7] The third Tiglath-Pilesar found himself in a similar situation. The victorious winged sun of Assyria had, since the year 800, fallen more and more under the shadow of the rising kingdom of Urartu in Armenia, with its capital city Tušpa on the Van. Energetic rulers, such as Argisti I (c. 780) and particularly Sardur II, made the former Assyrian vassal states in Northern Syria subject to their own empire, and thus constantly pressed Assyria back to her original territories in Mesopotamia. The corridor to the western sea, which Assyria had won at such a price in the ninth century, was now

---

6. Schmökel, GAV 261.
7. A. Moortgat, *Geschichte Vorderasiens bis zum Hellenismus*, (1950), 397ff.

lost. The rise of Urartu created something of a balance of power in Asia Minor. Ashur and Urartu represented the two poles of the balance, and the smaller middle states, Aram of Damascus, Israel, and Judah, were free to pursue their own development. If Tiglath-Pilesar meant to reestablish the Assyrian world empire, his first objective must be a war with the kingdom of Urartu. An occasion for this attack was afforded by the "rebellious" Mati'ilu, king of the north Syrian city of Arpad in the country of Bet-Agusi. When Tiglath-Pilesar first marched towards the west, he was opposed by Sardur II, at the head of his Syrian allies. The confrontation took place in the territory of Kummuhi on the upper course of the Euphrates, and resulted in a complete victory for the Assyrians. In headlong panic Sardur fled back across the river into the protection of his own country, abandoning his assembled allies. The vengeance of the victor was now directed against the city of Arpad, whose three-year siege (743-740) and eventual conquest afforded the Assyrian general staff with an object lesson for future conquest.[8]

The appearance of a victorious Assyrian army in Northern Syria was a broad hint for the former Assyrian vassals. If Urartu could not resist, how could the smaller states stand before the terrible splendor of Ashur? They chose what was the wisest course, appearing with rich tribute in the camp of the new Assyrian overlord, and this they did as early as 743, at the beginning of the siege of Arpad. It must have been a most impressive panorama. Hittite kings from Asia Minor, Kue, Kummuh, Meliddu, Gurgum, and Phoenician cities of Gubla, Tyre, Resin of Damascus,[9] even the Arab queen Zabibe and many others brought: "gold, silver, lead, iron, elephant hides, ivory tusks, magnificent colored robes, linen cloth, violet and purple stuffs, ebony, beech wood, sheep whose fleece was colored with bright purple, etc."[10] The long row of tribute-bearers included *Me-nu-hi-im-me* (*al*) *Sa-me-ri-na-a,* that is, Menahem, from the city of Samaria. This is a

---

8. Schmökel, GAV 262.
9. In the Assyrian texts under the form *ra-hi-a-nu,* Aramaic *ra'yan,* Hebrew *hasyon* and *resin.* BA23 (1960), 49.
10. AOT 346; DOT 54; ANET 283 a.

confirmation of the Biblical narrative (2 K 15, 19ff.), according to which Menahem had to pay one thousand silver talents as the price of his continued reign. In order to raise this incredible sum, more than two million dollars in gold,[11] Menahem was forced to tax his more prosperous subjects 50 shekels each. The Assyrian king was thus party to a sarcastic mockery: 50 shekels was the customary price of a slave.[12] Shortly after his return from this expedition of homage, Menahem died. His son Pekahiah (742-741) assumed royal power under the most unfavorable auspices (2 K 15, 23). It was his office primarily to collect the tribute. The popular reaction was understandably bitter. The anti-Assyrian elements formed a coalition, murdered Pekahiah, and raised Pekah (740-731) to the throne (2 K 15, 27)). The new king embarked upon an anti-Assyrian policy.[13]

What was Judah's position in the face of these new political configurations? Tiglath-Pilesar, in his annals,[14] makes explicit mention of a certain *Az-ri-ya-au* (*mat*) *Ya-u-da-ai,* a certain Azriau from the land of Judah. The text is, unfortunately, preserved only in fragments, and there have been various interpretations. Since the original translation of Rost was, in my opinion, incorrect, some quite impossible historical reconstructions were based on this text. Azriau, who was supposed to have been king

11. IntB III, 269.
12. D. J. Wiseman, *Iraq 15* (1953), 153.
13. Chronology: Menahem's tribute is generally dated in the year 738 (M. Noth, GeschIsr 1956, 233; Robert-Feuillet, IntrAT 459 etc.), and this date is supposed to belong to the "proven" Biblical-Assyrian synchronisms. But W. W. Hallo BA 23 (1960), 47, note 69, says "The widely accepted date 738 for the Menahem passage in the Annals may be considered definitely unproven." Accordingly, this date must finally be abandoned. It is based on the text of Azriau (cf. below note 17), which has been, I feel, the basis of false conclusions. Menahem's homage before Tiglath-Pilesar coincides with the beginning of the siege of Arpad in 743. Y. Yadin, *Scripta Hierosolymitana* 3, (1960), 1-17 dates the potsherds of Samaria in the last two years of Menahem, a position which I regard as highly questionable. Cf. above page 135, note 10.
14. Assyrian text and German translation in P. Rost, *Die Keilschrifttexte Tiglat-Pilesar* III, I (1893).

of the Aramaean state of Yaudi in Northern Syria, was explained as the force behind the opposition [15] to Tiglath-Pilesar. There was even more discussion of a Northern Judah, which was supposed to have arisen under the influence of King Uzziah of Judah.[16] But a new examination of the text in the Assyrian annals makes it clear [17] that this Azriau is really identical with Uzziah, king of Judah. He was not the soul of the resistance against Ashur, but rather, just like the other middle kingdoms, had been forced to pay his tribute to the Assyrian conqueror who appeared in the north. He remained largely true to his pro-Assyrian policy, although Israel and the Philistines had gradually defected into the

15. Noth, GeschIsr 233, Anm. 3.
16. W. Thomas, DOT 53.
17. Chronology: I have recently made a new translation and detailed commentary of the text of Azriau in my article "Textkritische Bemerkungen zu den Synchronismen der Könige von Israel und Judah," VT 12 (1962), 88-119. The following are the most important points made: a. Condition of the text: our knowledge of Azriau is based on the annals of Tiglath-Pilesar, as published by P. Rost, *Die Keilschrifttexte Tiglat-Pilesars* III, I (1893). The excerpts published by Gressmann (AOT 345) and Pritchard (ANET 282) are misleading, since they suggest the presence of a compact text, and this is not the case. Only fragments have survived. The decisive line 131 does not describe Azriau's revolt against Ashur, but should be translated instead: "the cities along the coast of the Western Sea which they violently tore away from him in sin and contempt against (for) Azriau." — b. Historical situation around 743: The ascendancy of Tiglath-Pilesar and his victories in Armenia forced the middle powers to adjust to the new balance of world power. In this new situation, Azriau-Asaryah-Uzziah and his co-regent Jotham adopted a neutral if not pro-Assyrian position. Then the allies attacked his territory, probably as early as 744. Under the pressure of the Assyrian march upon Arpad they were forced to let the occupied territories go. We find the same situation as in the Syro-Ephraimite war, although it is better known there. The problem of Azriau is dealt with most thoroughly in H. Tadmor, *Azriyau of Jaudi. Scripta Hierosolymitana* 8 (1961), 232-271. His material is used extensively in this account. But since the original Assyrian text was read in the established manner, Tadmor's results are different from mine. In my opinion, Azriau was at all events not the head of an anti-Assyrian coalition that was defeated around 738. What is needed here is further investigation and perhaps some new evidence.

anti-Assyrian camp. This policy earned him the enmity of his neighbors, who took the opportunity to occupy some of his cities by force. In the year of the tribute payment, 743, Uzziah shared the throne of Judah with his co-regent Jotham. It was Uzziah, however, who had already embarked upon the pro-Assyrian policy which his successors Jotham, Ahaz, and, to some extent, even Hezekiah were to follow, despite the hostile reaction of their neighbors.

In the year 740 the besieged city of Arpad fell into Assyrian hands. Bar-Sur, king of the north Syrian state of Sam'al, was put to death and his son Panammu II was raised to the throne, with no other choice than to embark upon a pro-Assyrian policy. In an effort to discourage further rebellion, Tiglath-Pilesar completely destroyed the current political structure of the country, replacing it with an Assyrian province administered from Kullani.[18] The native population was deported, while other conquered foreign peoples were resettled in their place, a first example of the mighty population resettlements that were to follow. In Israel, however, this same year saw the accession to power of King Pekah ben-Remaliah (740), and the first beginnings of the anti-Assyrian policy that was to lead to the eventual destruction of the Northern Kingdom (2 K 15, 25).

In that same year, 740, King Uzziah died in Jerusalem, old and feeble after 52 years of rule, the last 10 of which had been spent in isolation because of his leprosy. It was in this very same year, the year of Uzziah's death (Azariah, Is 6, 1), that the prophet Isaiah was called by God, a pivotal and climactic point in the history of the Ancient Near East. The entire world was trembling before the awesome splendor and power of the god Ashur. The conquest of the Assyrian armies was not only a military phenomenon; it was a time of religious crisis. The king sent the first news of his military successes to his god Ashur.[19] With the fall of the lesser kingdoms, their gods were also considered vanquished. The ascendancy of Tiglath-Pilesar, fighting in the name of his god Ashur, also spelled a twilight for the gods of the con-

---

18. ANET 283.
19. W. v. Soden, *Herrscher im Alten Orient*, 96.

quered territories. This is the most stirring ingredient in Isaiah's vocation. Yahweh, the God of a tiny state which hardly has a single voice in the world politics, refuses to tremble before the awesome splendor of the god Ashur. Quite the contrary; he reveals himself as God of the world, whose glory fills heaven and earth, a god to whom all peoples of the earth, even Ashur, are ultimately subject.

2) THE THRICE-HOLY GOD

"In the year that King Uzziah died I saw the Lord sitting upon a throne, high and lifted up; and his train [20] filled the temple. Above him stood the seraphim;[21] each had six wings: with two he covered his face, and with two he covered his feet, and with two he flew. And one called to another and said: 'Holy, holy, holy is the Lord of Hosts; the whole earth is full of his glory' " [22] (Is 6, 1-3).

With this first-person account, Isaiah records the experience of his call from God. In spirit or in reality, he was standing in the temple of Jerusalem, close to the threshold leading to the sanctuary. His eyes were suddenly open and he saw the throne of God. Earth and heaven met. Both were filled with "his glory." [23] The individual elements of the vision are nothing new. Long before Isaiah the God of Israel was called "God of hosts" (*Yahweh sebā'ôt*); there had been other experiences of his exalted holiness, inexorably jealous and suffering no other god beside himself. Micah had also seen Yahweh on the lofty throne, surrounded by the hosts of heaven (*seba-haššāmáyim*) (1 K 22, 19);

---

20. *šûl* is the lower seam of a garment.
21. Not "over him," but cf. Gn 18, 2, 8: "to stand before someone, prepared to serve."
22. Thus the Vulgate: according to MT, literally, "the fullness of the whole earth is his glory."
23. The cultic school ties the vision with the festival of Yahweh's enthronement at the New Year festival. Isaiah is supposed to have experienced Yahweh's coming to his people in the ritual of the festival. But since the existence of such a festival is still very questionable, any conclusions based on its existence cannot have much weight. IntB V (1956), 208.

we are dealing here with the form of expression common to the religious concepts of that day. The new and exciting element is the tremendously compact experience of God's holiness. "Here we touch upon something that expresses the deepest and most intimate essence of the God of the Old Testament. This is not simply one divine attribute from among many others, but rather his most intimate and essential property, bound up most fully with his life and spirituality." [24] With the vision of Isaiah, the gospel of a holy God flares up like a fire of judgment, but the course it follows is also a source of consolation and new life. We are reminded of the fire of Elijah the prophet.

The throne of Yahweh is surrounded by creatures of fire. Only in Isaiah are these heavenly creatures called seraphim. In the vocation vision of Ezekiel it is cherubim which bear the divine chariot. Even though the scientific derivation of the word seraphim is not completely clear, it is at least a phonetic echo of the root *sāraph,* "to burn, to glow." The presence of creatures of fire before the throne of God should certainly occasion no great surprise. But since a book of Scripture must be interpreted primarily on the basis of its own contents, there are passages in Isaiah which lend some clarification to the concept of seraphim. Isaiah 14, 29 presents a dramatic climax to the threat of judgment against the Philistines: "From the serpent's root will come forth an adder, and its fruit will be a flying serpent" (*sāraph me'ôphē-ph*).[25] Isaiah 30, 6 proclaims a threat against the southland which it describes as "a land of lions, vipers, and flying serpents" (*sāraph me'ôphēph*). The Book of Isaiah itself presents the concept of flying serpents and dragons. Whereas in the two passages just quoted the seraphim are threatening in character and portrayed as dangerous creatures, in Isaiah 6, 2 they are heavenly creatures before the throne of God.[26] Has Isaiah simply taken over a mythological concept? The yardsticks of human judgment

---

24. Sellin, *Theologie des AT,* (1936), 19.
25. The very same word *śārāph* is used to refer to the poisonous serpents of Nb 21, 6-9 and Dt 8, 15.
26. Sellin, l.c. 47, interprets them as dragon-like priests in the temple of the heavens.

are inadequate when we have passed through the gate of God's kingdom. Only in image and parable can we grasp the world beyond our senses. It is only understandable that Isaiah too should employ current conceptions of other-worldly creatures. But when he borrows the conceptions of mythology, they turn into something new.[27]

The seraphim are no longer simply winged serpents or dragons, the expression of human anxiety and insecurity; they are spiritual beings, standing before God's throne, and thus good creatures, ever waiting upon the commands of God. In assigning six wings to them, Isaiah describes the position of creatures in the face of God in much more penetrating and immediate form than a scientific treatise could hope to accomplish. With two wings they cover their face, because the abundance of God's light is so immense that their creaturely eyes would necessarily be blinded. No one can contemplate God without being blinded.[28] With two wings they cover their feet; no one can ever escape the presence of God. He dwells at the ends of the world, at the fountain of the great primordial streams.[29] And still every creature, be he man or angel, is drawn up with an irresistible power of attraction towards the throne of God, his one destined abode and repose. That is why they have their other two wings spread out in constant flight towards God. God is the *tremendum mysterium,* in whose presence every creature trembles and conceals himself; but he is also the *mysterium fascinosum* towards which every creature is inevitably drawn with an elemental and primordial force.

These suprasensory creatures which are contemplated in sense images as mixed creatures, continually acclaim the thrice-holy. The foundations of the threshold shook at their voice and the house was filled with smoke. It would be only logical to expect that the prophet's soul would overflow with an un-

27. R. Guardini, *Die religiöse Sprache.* In the collection of "Die Sprache" published by the Bavarian Academy of Fine Arts, (1959), 11-31.
28. Moses too (Ex 3, 6) and Elijah (1 K 19, 13) cover their faces when God appears.
29. R. Follet, *El in alveo duarum abyssorum,* VD 34 (1956), 280ff.

expected blessedness. But quite the contrary. He cries out "Woe is me! I am lost!" (6, 4). Whence this contradiction? In this contemplation of the thrice holy, his own unholiness is laid bare in the most devastating manner. Judgment and destruction can be the only consequence. What is the holiness before which he shrinks? What is the fundamental meaning of the angels' acclamation?

Qādôš, qādôš, qādôš yahweh sebā'ôt
māle'ah kol-hāāres kebôdô.

Holy, holy, holy is Yahweh of hosts,
filled is all the earth with his glory (6, 3).

Linguistic research has provided some very important background here. The root *qdš* seems to imply some such basic meaning as "separate, seclude, remove from normal usage." [30] The holy (*qādôš*) would accordingly be something separated or secluded, something to be surrounded with religious awe. The opposite of *qādôš* would be *hol* "untied, loose, profane." [31] In this manner, places, objects, and persons too can all be removed from profane usage, that is, declared "holy" and "bound up" (*re-ligio*). While such linguistic investigations are quite useful, they by no means exhaust the Biblical concept of holiness. [32] On the basis of linguistics and usage we can prove only that the Old Testament, in its concept of holiness, was indebted to the common background of Ancient Near Eastern religion. [33] It is in terms of the concept of divinity that the corresponding concept of holiness must necessarily develop. In the religions outside Israel the predicate holy was reserved for objects, rituals, and persons involved in the official cult, but only in the most exceptional cases is it used for the divinity himself. The Old Testament, on the contrary, characterizes God himself in the first position as the holy one. "There is no doubt that a personal element has thus been given prevalence in the conception of holiness, an element which elevates it from the sphere of nature's wondrous powers and a cult involving places

---

30. From a root *qdd*, "cut." Cf. the Greek *temenos*, from *temnein* "cut"; Latin *sanctus* from *sancire*, "to bound"; Polynesian *tabu* from *tapa*, "to mark out and thus to distinguish, to separate." — Others take it as coming from a root *qd'*, "to be pure, bright," a root also found in Arabic and Ethiopic. Eichrodt, *Theologie des AT*, 176-177.
31. Sellin, *Théologie des AT*, 20.
32. E. Jacob, *Théologie de l'AT*, 68.
33. Eichrodt, l.c. 177.

and things, onto a higher and spiritual stage." [34] Moses had already proclaimed faith in a personal and holy God whose imperious will is manifest
in his commandments. Elijah followed Moses' lead. Amos is the
champion of justice, and Hosea is the champion of fidelity to the
covenant; for Isaiah, God's perfection culminates in his holiness: hence
the threefold repetition of the angels' acclamation.

The thrice-holy is also an expression of God's essence. The seraphim,
by their acclamation, acknowledge God as he is: thrice holy. This holiness
is far above the mere blind conglomeration of life-giving forces.[35] According
to the categories of the Bible, Israel's God is, from the beginning, a
God who speaks, a person, a God who undertakes dialogue with his
human creatures. Man, as a person capable of free self-determination, can
accept or reject God's call. It is from this personal dimension that holiness
develops. "Holy" is, accordingly, a concept bound up not only with
things, but primarily with a person. God's holiness exists in a threefold,
that is, infinite abundance, since he was the first to speak the word
(Gn 1) and has thus stamped his law upon all creatures, especially on
man. Man is holy when he directs his conduct according to the will of
God, made known in creation (Gn 1) and Law (Sinai). This is the
exciting element in the vision: the holy will of God is destined for fulfillment not only in the court of the heavenly hosts; his majesty (kābôd)
fills the entire earth (6, 3c.). Here, once again, kābôd is not merely the
expression of some impersonal power, a reference, as it were, to the
awe-inspiring apparitions of the wholly other God of holiness,[36] but
rather the expression of his personal majesty. This is the whole point
and difference in Isaiah's concept of God. He does not proclaim God as "a
wholly different God" — if God were "wholly different," what relationship
would he have with man? Rather, he proclaims him as the God present,
in a most personal and intimate way, both to his world and to his creature
man. Man is holy when he directs his conduct according to the will of
God's and man's essence is really visible. Man, created in God's image
and likeness, must appear, in the brilliant light of God's holiness, as like
unto God, as holy. And it is immediately obvious that he does not
submit to the appeal of the divine king (mélek 6, 5c.).

This, for humankind, is a fundamental catastrophe. The
thrice-holy God and his unholy people! In the vocational vision,
accordingly, it is only the recognition of God's kingly dominion

---

34. *Ibid.*
35. *La Sainteté est la force vivificante.* E. Jacob, *Théologie de l'AT*, 71.
36. *Ibid.*: Le kabod a un aspect plutôt negativ, il est la puissance qui
    écrase, il est parfois mis en relation avec les manifestations terrificantes
    dans la nature . . . .

(*malkut*) that is involved. Isaiah has a vision of God on the throne of heaven; the seraphim recognize his kingship by their thrice-holy. The prophet himself refers to God expressly as king (*mélek*), but can only recognize the woe upon his people who have made no place for God's glory and dominion.

The ceremony which now follows is simply a ritual of consecration through which Isaiah is empowered to undertake a new establishment of God's royal dominion. One of the seraphim takes a glowing coal [73] from the altar with a pair of tongs, touching it to the prophet's lips and making them pure. When God the king asks: "Whom shall I send, and who will go for us?" Isaiah answers boldly and directly: "Here am I! Send me!" (6, 8). He thereby becomes the bearer and herald of the divine king's claim to dominion upon earth. But he must also realize that he will be dealing with a people whose ears are deaf, whose eyes are blinded, and whose heart is fat. He must realize that they are stiff-necked and unwilling to accept the kingship of their God. God holds out little prospect of success. None the less, he sends him as the last offer of his unwearied mercy. The word of Isaiah is not destined to effect the hardness of the people's hearts, only to lay bare a condition that already existed. This is the sarcastic point of the frequently mistranslated sentence (6, 10): "Make the heart of this people fat, and their ears heavy and shut their eyes; lest they see with their eyes, and hear with their ears, and understand with their hearts, and turn and be healed." [38] The prophet must, of sheer necessity, stand forth as a herald of eventual destruction. If God is the thrice-holy, it must necessarily follow that everything unholy will be burned away. From this catastrophe there will remain only the root and stock of a new era, "a holy seed" [39] (*zera' qodeš* 6, 13).

---

37. *rispah* is one of the flint stones upon which the fire was laid.
38. Same meaning in Mt 13, 14 and parallel texts.
39. F. Hvidberg, *The Masseba and the Holy Seed*, NorTT 56 (1955), 97, refers the sacred seed to the cult of Adnois which was supposed to be rooted out. The textual emendations required to support this view are not convincing.

3) THE UNHOLY PEOPLE

In the days of Isaiah's early career, that is, the years from the time of his vocation in the year of Uzziah's death, 740, to the beginning of the Syro-Ephraimite war in 735, we can assign the following texts with a reasonable degree of accuracy: 2, 6-22; 3, 1-15; 3, 16 to 4, 1; 5, 8-24; 10, 1-4; 9, 7-20 and 5, 25-30. We shall concentrate only on the principal motifs.

a) THE TERRIBLE SPLENDOR OF YAHWEH (*pahad Yahweh* 2, 6-22): Leaving his vision of heaven and returning to the realities of earth, Isaiah is conscious of a terrible contrast. In heaven the fiery creatures were proclaiming: "The whole earth is full of his glory" (6, 3); but the prophet himself must cry out: "The land is filled with diviners and soothsayers, . . . the land is full of silver and gold, . . . the land is full of horses and chariots, . . . the land is full of idols" (2, 6-8). Such a condition can only provoke God's judgment of rejection. Yahweh is ready to reject the house of Jacob (2, 6). God has arisen to strike his terror into the land filled with unholiness (2, 19b). For the Lord God of hosts has set a day of reckoning upon everything that is proud and lofty, upon all the cedars and oaks, mountains and hills, walls and towers, and the mighty ships of Tarshish. Before the terror of Yahweh's glory the idols, in all their vanity, disappear. They are cast out to the bats and rodents. Only the majesty of the thrice-holy remains exalted. In this proclamation of the terrible day of Yahweh, Isaiah follows the preaching of the prophets Amos and Hosea. Politically, Israel is threatened by the terrible splendor of Ashur; more threatening still is the awesome power of Yahweh.

b) COLLAPSE AND ANARCHY (3, 1-15): If God withdraws his hand, all the securities of human ordering collapse. The human leaders who are active in the sphere of political, military, and religious life are pushed aside. Immature and unseasoned youngsters accede to power. There is no longer any authority and no respect. In the general collapse of the body politic, there is no one to take a leading hand. There is none left to produce order:

all the essential elements of society are gone. The man who has a little food and clothing left will be approached and asked to take over the government: "You have a mantle; you shall be our leader, and this heap of ruin shall be under your rule," but in that day he will speak out saying: "I will not be a healer; you shall not make me leader of the people." [40] Isaiah paints a grotesque picture of political collapse. At the time he made these grim statements, the state was still secure. Jotham, following in the footsteps of Uzziah, had fortified the kingdom in the political, military, and economic sphere. The traveler to Jerusalem in these days would have found everything in perfect order. But for the prophet all this is a mere façade; within everything is rotten and ripe to fall. This is why Yahweh is about to enter into judgment with "the elders and the princes of his people" (3, 13).

c) FASHIONS, COSTUME, PERFUME, WOMEN (3, 14—4, 1): If fashion is the yardstick of economic prosperity, the citizens of Jerusalem must have had it not only good, but very good. Isaiah was a sharp observer of the life about him. His critical judgment spares not even the proud daughters of Zion. [41] He sees them as they mince daintily along, playing the coquette, their necks outstretched, their hair in curls. Only the best suffices for their clothing. The finest underclothing, outer clothing, robes and cloaks, veils, precious sashes, — there is no end to their finery. Little bells tinkle from their ankles at every step; bands of gold and silver flash from their arms. There is an abundance of rings for finger and ear alike and — as we note even today among the Beduins — rings for the nose. Their necklaces are adorned with little suns and moons and amulets. [42] They carry perfume boxes. But the prophet takes no delight in this highly civilized society. Men's fashions seem to have been equally luxurious.

The whole thing must have struck the prophet like a night-

---

40. J. Ziegler, EB III, 24.
41. The details of this fashion parade (3, 16-23) cannot always be exactly interpreted since they involve technical expressions not clearly understood.
42. Literally: bātê-hannépheš, "little soul houses."

mare. Even in the midst of all this prosperity he saw the seeds of ultimate destruction. Instead of perfume there would be rottenness, instead of well-set hair there would be only baldness, instead of a rich robe there would be a girding of sackcloth. To make the misery complete, on that terrible day there would no longer be enough men. They would all have fallen in battle or been sold into slavery. On that day seven, that is, very many, women will take hold of one man. If only they are permitted to bear his name, they are willing to clothe and feed him from their own substance, provided only they no longer have to face the shame of being no man's wife (4, 1). All this will come to pass because, in the midst of all the external culture, the cultivation of the soul has been abandoned. The level of feminine fashion and morality is a perfect index of moral decay.[43]

d) THE SEVEN-FOLD WOE (5, 8-24 and 10, 1-4): In this seven-fold woe, the prophet enters into judgment with the ruling classes. The large estate owners could not get enough money. Oppression of the peasant class was a daily reality. The wealthy owners joined field to field, vineyard to vineyard, house to house. Their bad conscience was assuaged with wine and strong drink, and by the wild music of the lyre and harp, timbrel and flute. The courts no longer assure justice, they only condone profit. The caricature of the satiated mocker, who claims to be above good and evil, sets the tone of public morality. It is no wonder that such a society fills the prophet with horror. When the Holy One of Israel (5, 19) makes his appearance, surely he will burn this unholy people like stubble in the field. They are drawing judgment upon them with strong cords and with cart ropes.

e) THE AVENGING HAND OF GOD (9, 7-20 and 5, 25-30): Like the trumpet call of judgment sounds the mighty refrain, repeated four times: "For all this his anger is not turned away and his hand is stretched out still" (9, 11b, 16b, 20b; 5, 25; 10, 4). Isaiah was sent as God's herald not only to Jerusalem and

---

43. EB III, 27.

Judah; the evils of the kingdom of Israel do not escape his prophetic sentence. This section is a clear presentiment of the immediate destruction from within and from without. But nobody would believe destruction was coming: in their arrogance they were saying: "The bricks have fallen, but we will build with dressed stones" (9, 9). And yet the enemy, in the east and in the west, had already arisen to devour Israel. The threat from without was heightened by disintegration within. The leaders are godless seducers (9, 15). The warring parties are devouring each other (9, 19). In Isaiah's eyes, this was no mere phenomenon of a social revolution; God had a clear hand in everything. But the people could not see this, and in their blindness they turned away from the one road to salvation.

Isaiah's introductory proclamation is not essentially different from those of the prophets Amos and Hosea. He too is a herald of judgment, proclaiming the nearness of the "day of Yahweh." Whereas Amos based the judgment to come on his insight into God's justice, and Hosea refers to God's love and fidelity to his covenant, Isaiah sees everything from the point of view of God's holiness. Even the concept of the small remnant, destined to survive as a holy seed for a new era, is common to all three. In the later preaching of Isaiah there is a clearer picture of the idea of a ruler from the house of David. This, too, was present already in his predecessors; but from this time onward it becomes the leitmotif of future history.

B) "SIGNS AND PORTENTS" (8, 18)

PREACHING IN THE TIME OF THE SYRO-EPHRAIMITE WAR

The great vassal procession in Northern Syria in the year 743 may have given the impression that the western countries had bowed before the terrible splendor of Ashur. Friends by force, however, are not true friends. In following up his policy of securing his conquests, Tiglath-Pilesar had to continue his war with the kingdom of Urartu and bring it to a successful conclusion. His first attack had succeeded in breaking Urartu's predominance over the north Syrian states. In the year 753 he carried the battle into the land of Urartu itself, where he conquered Sardur III in a pitched battle, then laid siege to the capital city of Tušpa on the Van. The siege was unsuccessful. He had to be content with erecting a victory column for the city walls. At all events, the enemy in the north had been brought down — a dubious success for Ashur, since the victory had also destroyed the bulwark against the equestrian hordes pressing down from the north. Still, after this victory Tiglath-Pilesar was free to concentrate on the destruction of the Syro-Palestinian alliance.

As we have already seen, in Samaria an anti-Syrian policy had won the upper hand. Pekah-Remaliah [1] with the support of the large estate owners in Gilead, had succeeded in removing the pro-Assyrian Pekahiah (2 K 15, 23) and had joined the first beginnings of the anti-Assyrian coalition. The movement gained further impetus from Rezin king of Damascus. Members of the alliance were: the Phoenican cities of Tyre and Sidon, the Philistine territory with Gaza, the Edomites, and even the Arab queen Zabibe, together with the western countries which had formerly paid homage to Tiglath-Pilesar. Egypt was also in sympathy with the coalition. There was only one neuralgic point in the whole bloc, the pro-Assyrian policy of Judah.

Jotham (740-735 as sole ruler), following in the footsteps of his father Uzziah, had promoted the development of rural economy, had improved the fortifications (he strengthened the Ophel wall in Jerusalem), and cleared the way to the South Sea. He even succeeded in making Ammon a tributary for three years (2 K 15, 32-38). In his external policy, he remained faithful to the pro-Assyrian commitments entered into under Uzziah. He was much too clever a politician to succumb to the charm of a campaign against Assyria. This won him the enmity of his neighbors. In the Biblical account of Jotham's reign we read: "In those days the Lord began to send Rezin the king of Syria and Pekah the son of Remaliah against Judah" (2 K

---

1. On the basis of the Dead Sea scrolls the name would be *rûm-la-yahu*, "May Yahweh prove himself exalted," Bibl 33 (1953), 162.

15, 37). When Jotham died in 735, the allies believed that the
time had come to intervene in the internal politics of Judah. In
the overall strategy of their war against Assyria, they could not
tolerate a pro-Assyrian bloc in their rear. Accordingly, they
meant to take advantage of the empty throne in Jerusalem by
installing their own candidate, a certain ben-Tab'el [2] (7, 6) instead
of Ahaz the descendant of king David.[3] On the basis of a contemporary Assyrian letter [4] it is clear that Tab'el (ta-ab-i-la-ya)
refers to a district in Transjordania north of Ammon, the full
name being Bet-Tab'el. The "son of Tab'el" [5] is thus not a personal name; the word simply refers to the Transjordanian Aramaean, from the district of Bet-Tab'el, through whose accession
to the throne to come from Transjordania. Shallum, Menahem, and
effectively controlled.[6] He would not have been the only pretender
to the throne to come from Transjordania. Sallum, Menahem, and
Pekahiah also came from the newly colonized east.

---

2. Jotam, *EncMikr* II, 622-624.

3. Abbreviated form for *Jeho'ahaz*, "Yahweh has seized upon"; in
   Assyrian documents it is *Jauhazi*. The signet ring of a "servant"
   (*'ebed*) of Ahaz has been discovered. *EncMikr* I, 297.

4. In 1952 a letter was found in Nimrud which casts important light
   on the Assyrian messenger service of that era. The letter dates from
   732-722. The writer was a certain *Qurdi-Assur* (*-lâmur*), probably the
   governor of Upper Galilee under Assyrian occupation. One day a messenger came from the land of Tab'el and brought him a written
   account of an attack upon a Moabite city. The governor then composed the letter which he sent by return messenger to Nimrud, where
   it has been preserved until our own day. E. Vogt, "Filius Tab'el,"
   Bibl 37 (1956), 263-264. Text H. W. F. Saggs, *Iraq 17* (1955), 131-
   133, interpretation: W. F. Albright, BASOR 140 (1955), 9-11.

5. The name is Aramaean and means "good is God," but the Hebrew
   version is differently pointed to produce the form *tob'al*, i.e., "not
   good."

6. J. Bright, *A History of Israel*, (1960), 256 argues that Tab'el was
   the son of a princess from Bet-Tab'el who had been married at
   the court of Jerusalem, and was thus stepbrother to King Ahaz. It
   could be expected that a prince of Aramaean extraction would decide
   in favor of an alliance with Aramaea. But the solution is not really
   convincing.

The young Ahaz, twenty years old [7] (2 K 16, 2) found himself in a most precarious position. Edom had defected from the empire and occupied the harbor city of Elath (2 K 16, 6); Ammon was refusing tribute, and the west was threatened by the Philistines who had destroyed Beth-shemesh and occupied a portion of the southern territory. The greatest peril, however, threatened from the north. Israel and Aram had united in their effort to control the policy of Judah. In this crisis, in which the very existence of the Davidic dynasty was at stake, the prophet Isaiah appeared before the king with an oracle from God.

---

7. Chronology: The regnal years of King Ahaz have been dealt with in some detail in my article: *Textkritische Bemerkungen zu den Synchronismen der Könige von Israel und Judah*, VT 12 (1962), 88-119. These are the most important points: Ahaz' reign is introduced in 2 K 16, 1 as follows: "In the seventeenth year of Pekah son of Remaliah, Ahaz the son of Jotham, king of Judah, began to reign. Ahaz was twenty years old when he began to reign, and he reigned sixteen years in Jerusalem." These figures destroy the outlines of the accepted chronology. If they are correct, then the synchronism between Hezekiah and Hosea (2 K 18, 1, 9, 10) must be wrong, and this is hardly likely. It seems to me that the riddle can be solved by recognizing a miswriting of the tens. In the immediate context of the passage there are four such miswritings: a. Hezekiah could not possibly have been 25 years old when he came to the throne, because his father Ahaz was only 36 years old; read instead of (2) 5 only 5 years old (2 K 18, 2). — b. Ahaz' first year is synchronous with the (1) 7 year of Pekah (2 K 16, 1). — c. Ahaz reigned only (1) 6 years (2 K 16, 2). — d. Pekah reigned not 20 but only 10 years. — The miswriting can be explained on the basis of palaeography, '*srm* for '*srh*. This is the only textual emendation I have found it necessary to introduce into the Biblical numbers. It is justified by the fact that it makes the other synchronisms for this era achieve a perfect harmony. The numbers of years, I think, have been faithfully handed down. Accordingly, Albright's suggestion that Rehoboam ruled 8 instead of 17 years, Omri 8 instead of 12, Ahab 20 instead of 22, etc., are not the fruit of sober textual criticism, but brilliant and unwarranted conjecture. Cf. E. R. Thiele, *A Comparison of the Chronological Data of Israel and Judah*, VT 4 (1954), 187. The year of Ahaz' accession to power is thus synchronous with the year of Jotham's death, the year in which the Syro-Ephraimite war broke out. Ahaz' reign is thus to be dated 735/734—728 (6 years).

1) "A REMNANT SHALL RETURN" (*še'ar yāšûb* 7, 9)

Judah, suddenly attacked from all quarters, was not equal
to the hostile storm. In a military encounter north of Jerusalem
Ahaz was dealt a decisive defeat. Not only his warriors, but
also women and children were carried off to Samaria and Damascus. In Samaria there were enough reasonable people to recognize
this civil war as an outrage to their common national allegiance,
and thus to protest against the introduction of prisoners of war
from Judah. It was primarily the intervention of the prophet Oded
that guaranteed the humane treatment of the prisoners of war
in Samaria. They were given food and drink, and then shipped
off to Jericho where they were set free (2 Ch 28, 5-15).

After this military defeat, Ahaz had no further alternative
than to return to the fortress of Jerusalem and hold out against
the advent of some possible relief. The only report was that
Rezin of Damascus and Pekah ben-Remaliah of Israel were
marching towards the siege of Jerusalem — they were already
camping in Ephraim — "His heart and the heart of his people
shook as the trees of the forest shake before the wind" (7, 2).
Ahaz went out to inspect the most vulnerable part of his fortifications, north of the city, "At the end of the conduit of the upper
pool on the highway to the Fuller's Field" [8] (7, 3). There he was
met by the prophet Isaiah, leading his son *še'ar-yašûb*, "A remnant
shall return," by the hand. Ahaz looked for an oracle of victory.
The prophet's very name *yeša-yahu* "Yahweh saves," was already
a solution to his crisis. But the prophet does not have a word
from God: "Take heed, be quiet, do not fear, and do not let
your heart be faint because of these two smouldering stumps of
firebrands . . . . It shall not stand, and it shall not come to pass"
(7, 4-7). In such a desperate situation, certainly the most com-
forting assurance could be the knowledge that the enemy will
not conquer. But the prophet makes the nation's salvation dependent upon its faith in Yahweh: "If you will not believe, surely
you shall not be established" [9] (7, 9). The only security for the

---

8. J. Simons, *Jerusalem in the Old Testament Times*, (1952), 192.
9. Hebrew pun: *'im lô ta'amînû, ki lô tē'āmēnû*, from the stem *'amēn*,

future existence of the nation (*'āmēn*) is dependent upon faith in Yahweh. If the king refuses this test of his faith, then the name of the child "a remnant shall return" or "a remnant remains" becomes an oracle of threat.

2) IMMANUEL, "GOD WITH US" (7, 10-25)

From the wording of the text, "and Yahweh spoke to Ahaz" (7, 10) it is not clear whether the scene has shifted, perhaps to the royal palace, or whether this conversation too took place outside the city walls. Since the proclamation of the "sign" is intimately bound up with the narrative of the preceding dialogue, it would certainly appear that the scene has not shifted.

Isaiah was proclaiming salvation from the hostile crisis in the name of Yahweh. He could feel that Ahaz, in his heart, was not in sympathy with the prophet's words. In order to convince him, he offers him a sign from God (*'ôt*). The choice is left to the king, whether the sign should come from heaven on high or the depths of Sheol. The king's answer was predictable: "I will not ask, and I will not put Yahweh to the test." It was among Israel's special prerogatives that she could call upon (*šā'al*) Yahweh in times of doubt or crisis and demand a sign. For David and the other faithful kings it was a normal practice to call upon Yahweh in times of personal crisis, before undertaking military campaigns, and at any important moment.[10] When Ahaz refuses to ask, he is admitting that he has begun to look to more powerful gods who would save Jerusalem. He has already reckoned on the assistance of Assyria in his plans and aspirations. What is the point of bothering Yahweh for a sign? In his own

---

"to be fast, trustworthy." *Hiphil* (causative form) *he'emîn,* "to let be secure, to believe"; *Niphal* (passive) *ne'eman,* "to be secured, to remain steadfast."

---

10. At Saul's anointing as king (1 S 10, 22); during war, to inquire the advisability of attack (1 S 14, 37); David inquired into Yahweh's will on his gli flight (1 S 22, 10); on the battle of Qe'ilah (1 S 23, 2), etc. The examples could easily be multiplied by consulting a concordance.

mind, the decision is already made. Accordingly, he rejects the proffered sign.

The Hebrew word *'ôt*, just like the English word "sign," has a variety of meanings. It can refer to a military standard in war (Ps 73/74, 9), a heap of stones erected as a monument (Jos 4, 6), the stars as heavenly signs to mark the change of time (Gn 1, 4), the rainbow as a sign of peace (Gn 9, 12), the phylacteries as a sign of membership in the people of God (Dt 11, 18), and many others. Generally, however, it is used as a sign confirming the word of God. This does not always imply a miracle in the proper sense of the word. The fortuitous coincidence of several individual phenomena could pass for a sign from God.[11] Nor did the sign have to follow immediately upon the divine oracle; considerable time could elapse between the two. That God had spoken to Moses in the burning bush, Moses realized only through the sign of the Exodus (Ex 3, 12). The fact that Eli's sons were to fall in battle was to be a sign that Samuel had spoken the truth (1 S 2, 34). The course of history as such thus becomes a prophetic sign. Most of the time, however, the word *'ôt* is used for miracle signs, especially for the plagues of Egypt and the miracles of the Exodus (Ex 4, 8, etc.). Generally, too, we find the phrase *'ôt u-môphet,* "signs and portents." [12]

When, accordingly, Isaiah offers the king his choice of a divine sign, this does not necessarily involve a wonder or portent visible to the senses. He is merely guaranteeing, in the name of God, that some event will occur by which he can with certainty recognize the truth of what the prophet has spoken. The king was free to determine his own sign; but he declined. Accordingly Isaiah proclaims a sign in spite of the king, and in view of his frivolous refusal it can only be interpreted as a portent of punishment.

The common translation of the portent oracle is as follows: "Therefore the Lord himself will give you a sign (*'ôt*): Behold, a young woman shall conceive and bear a son and shall call his name Immanuel" (7, 14). This sentence is not an isolated statement. The context is clearly explained by the prophet himself in the words that follow. What is he describing? Obviously, the catastrophe which is about to break over the land. God is whistling

---

11. 1 S 10, 7: Saul, departing from Samuel, meets with a band of prophets.
12. Explicit discussion of the words in: M. Brunec, *De sensu "signi" in Jes 7, 14,* VD 33 (1955), 257-266; 321-330, 34 (1956), 16-29.

to the fly along the Nile and the bee which is in the land of Ashur, and they shall come in huge swarms and settle upon all the steep ravines and in the clefts of the rock, and on all the thorn bushes and on all the pasture land (7, 18). These are simply the images of an imminent invasion which will lead the land to the brink of disaster. In that day the Lord will shave with a razor that has been hired beyond the River the hair of the head, and of the "feet" (euphemism for pubic hair), and the hair of the beard. Where formerly a thousand vines were growing there will now be thistles and thorns. They will seek out the vineyards no longer to harvest the grape, but to hunt with bow and arrows. Over what was once finely cultivated fields they will now run cattle and sheep. Happy the man who has kept alive a young cow or two sheep. He will at least have the bare essentials for life, a little milk and butter (7, 18-25).

The child Immanuel, whose birth is now expected, is a very obvious and recognizable sign for the coming of these terrible catastrophes. The child will have to grow up on the nourishment which reflects the land's disaster: butter and honey,[13] even before he reaches the use of reason. "For before the child knows how to refuse the evil and choose the good, the land before whose two kings you are in dread will be deserted" (7, 16), that is, within three or four years at the most, the enemies of Judah will be annihilated by the invasion of the Assyrian hordes. Jerusalem will have respite, without looking to help from any other source than Yahweh: the very name of the child is guarantee of the fact that God, despite all the imminent crisis, is still "with us." Hence the warning against an alliance with Assyria: "Take heed, be quiet, do not fear" (7, 4).

---

13. The interpretation of "milk and honey" as the food of paradise might apply to other passages, but in this context it is merely the food of the impoverished populace after the military catastrophes. There is a regression to primitive conditions. Hence the dual interpretability of the expression; the food of primeval times is either the food of paradise or the food of time of crisis. A poor Turkish peasant, living in the middle of Anatolia, served me dinner on Nov. 6, 1958, consisting of a dish of thick milk, a piece of a fresh honeycomb, and a few pieces of bread.

This, in itself, is a sufficient explanation of the Immanuel prophecy. Isaiah has clothed his prophetic message not only in transitory words, but, so to speak, in flesh and blood. He confesses, speaking of himself: "I and the children whom the Lord has given me are signs and portents in Israel" (8, 18). Breaking the statement down, we might say that the "word" has become fresh in Israel and his children: the word of judgment is children "a remnant shall return" and "hasten to the booty," and the word is salvation in his own name "Yahweh saves." Along these terms, it might be logical to suppose that Immanuel too is the child of the prophet.[14] There is, however, considerable evidence to the contrary. The birth in question clearly involves a "maiden." But the prophet's wife has already had several children. Who, then, is this mysterious mother of the Immanuel?

First we must face a more fundamental question: whether the word used in the original text, " '*almah*," is properly translated as virgin (LXX *parthenos*, Vg *virgo*). A close examination of the evidence presents the following picture. Not only the Greek translations by Aquila, Symmachus, and Theodotion,[15] but many manuscripts of the Septuagint, and based on the Septuagint many early Christian authors, all use the neutral expression νεανίς (*adulescentula, juvencula*):[16] that is, a young, marriageable maiden, who, after her marriage, would conceive and give birth in the normal manner. Was this word chosen deliberately to play down the sense of miracle? Given the anti-Christian tendencies of the three Greek translators (A, S, Th), this conclusion must not be excluded. For, if the word *parthenos* is taken in its strict sense, conception and birth could only proceed from a miracle. The ultimate answer comes, however, not from the translators, however deserving of reverence, but from the original Hebrew text and the related Semitic languages.

'*almah* appears in the Old Testament nine times. Two of the occur-

---

14. The view of Joseppus, *Liber memorialis*, Migne, PG CVI, 89, 92. J. Coppens, *Une Interpretation originale du Fils de la 'Almah*, ETL 33 (1957), 509-510. — Attacked by N. K. Gottwald, *Immanuel as the Prophet's Son*, VT 8 (1958), 36-47. — J. Stamm, *Die Immanuelweissagung*, VT 4 (1954), 20-33.
15. Cf. the apparatus in the Göttingen LXX. J. Ziegler, *Isaias*, (1936), 147.
16. After the Septuagint had become the Bible of the early Church, the three above named authors each set about establishing a critical text for the synagogue. It cannot be denied that they exhibit a certain anti-Christian tendency.

rences, referring to musical directions which are no longer understood (Ps 45/46, 1; 1 Ch 15, 20) are obviously excluded. The seven remaining passages will give the underlying sense "marriageable maiden" (*puella nubilis, virgo matura*).[17] For the wisdom poet, the "way of a man with a maiden" (*'almah*) (Prv 30, 19) is one of nature's unsolved riddles. Eleazar wants to recognize the "maiden who draws water" (*'almah*) as the destined bride of his master (Gn 24, 43). Maidens (*'almah*) form the retinue of the bride in the Song of Songs (1, 3; 6, 8). It is they who dance upon the news of a victory (Ps 67/68, 26). Finally, Moses' sister is also called *'almah*, when she speaks to the Egyptian princess along the Nile about the child in the basket of reeds (Ex 2, 8). Accordingly, it would seem that in the Old Testament the word *'almah* never means a married woman, but always a young, marriageable maiden. It was presupposed that such a maiden would soon marry and share the expected blessing of childbirth. Any contemporary listener who heard the prophet's oracle: "Behold, a young woman shall conceive and bear a son," would hardly think in terms of a miraculous conception and birth.

This interpretation has recently been confirmed by the discovery of texts from Ugarit. In the Kuriti epic we hear of the expedition of the kingdom of King Kuriti against Udum, to fight for the hand of the maiden (*galmat*) Huraia, who was to bear him the desired heir to his throne. Upon his return he hears a blessing oracle from the god El:

"The woman (*att*) thou tak'st, O Keret, The woman thou tak'st into thy house, The maid (*glmt*) thou tak'st into thy court, Shall bear seven sons unto thee; Yea, eight she shall produce for thee." [18]

The oracle is similar to Isaiah's words: "Behold, the *'almah* will conceive and bear...." The Ugaritic *galmat* corresponds to the Hebrew *'almah*.[19] Moreover, there is an almost perfect literal correspondence in the narrative of the marriage between Yaris and Nikkal: "Behold, the *galmat* will bear you a son" (*hl glnt tld bn*).[20] Thus, quite unexpectedly, we have new light on the language of Isaiah. *'almah* clearly refers to a young maiden, on the threshold of marriage, a maiden for whom the rich blessing of children is prophesied and hoped.[21] Since the Ugaritic

---

17. Lisowsky, *Konkordanz zum hebräischen AT*, (1958), 1072.
18. C. H. Gordon, UM II, Text 128, lines 21-25. — A. Jirku, *Die Ausgrabungen in Palästina-Syrien*, (1956), 54. — English ANET 146.
19. C. H. Gordon, UM III, Glossary Nr. 1483.
20. Gordon, UM II, Text 77, line 7. Cf. Robert-Feuillet, IntrAT 509.
21. The fact that in the epic of *'Anat Ba'al* a goddess who is already the mother of two sons is referred to as *galmat* does nothing to change the above mentioned manner of speech. In myth, virginity is simply the symbol of everlasting vital force and fertility. The Greek Aphrodite boasts of herself as Parthenos, although she has enjoyed many gods as consorts. Cf. Gordon, UM II, Text 51, Fragment 7, line 54.

texts quoted above refer to a marriage which has been definitely planned and will soon take place, we might capture the connotations of the word 'almah by translating "bride." Who is the bride or "young maiden" of whom the prophet speaks?

There are many answers. Only the most important can be examined here. L. Köhler believes that the "virgin" and her child are not persons, but merely types. In their joy over the newly dawning era of salvation, all the young brides in Israel will give their newborn sons the name which echoes this salvation, Immanuel, "God with us." [22] Stamm is opposed to this collective interpretation.[23] After the new discoveries in the area of cult, scholars believed that they had discovered the new understanding for the Immanuel prophecy. It was explained as the *heiros logos,* the sacred word of cult which accompanied the *hieros gamos,* the "ritual marriage" on the feast of the new year, where the king and the divine bride, by performing the sex act, were supposed to call down the blessing of the fertility gods on land, herd, and the human community, somewhat after the manner of analogical magic.[24] We have had to make constant reference to the inroads of these pagan cults into the Yahweh religion, throughout the whole course of Israel's history. There is, however, no sufficient proof for the practice of a new year celebration with ritual drama and ritual marriage.[25] From such questionable presuppositions, only questionable conclusions can be drawn. L. G. Ringnell abandons the cultic interpretation and sees 'almah as a symbolic figure for the people of Israel as such, destined, in the labor and travail of the imminent catastrophe, to give birth to a "son," the new Israel, the holy remnant.[26] N. K. Gottwald [27] presents a rather capricious solution suggesting that 'almah refers to the temple music. The term would, accordingly, refer to choirs of young maidens, and even when one of the choir maidens ('almah) married, she would continue to bear the title 'almah; accordingly, the

---

22. On Is 7, 14, ZAW 67 (1955), 48-50. — G. Fohrer, *Zu Jes 7, 14 analyzed with Is 7, 10-22,* ZAW 68 (1956), 46-54.

23. J. J. Stamm, *Neuere Arbeiten zum Immanuelproblem,* ZAW 68 (1956), 46-54.

24. F. Hammershaimb, *The Immanuel Sign,* Studia Theologica 1951. — Critical discussion J. J. Stamm, *Die Immanuelweissagung, ein Gespräch mit Hammershaimb,* VT 4 (1954), 20-33.

25. W. Fischer, *La Prophétie d'Emmanuel et la Féte Royale de Sion,* Étude Theol. et Rel., Montpellier 3 (1954), 55-97 maintains an indirect influence of the Canaanite royal ritual.

26. L. G. Ringnell, *Das Immanuelzeichen,* ST 11 (1957), 99-119.

27. *Immanuel as the Prophet's Son,* VT 8 (1958), 36-47. 'almah has the specific meaning of "female temple musician." Even after marriage, she would have continued to hold the title "virgin" as a cult singer and dancer.

prophet's own wife, even though she had been a mother several times, is still the *'almah* of the prophecy.

Against all these precarious attempts at interpretation, all of them opposed to the properly messianic sense of the prophecy, J. Coppens defends the traditional point of view.[28] The Immanuel prophecy is, in his eyes, a directly messianic prophecy, and, moreover, in the literal sense of the word. By way of proof, he presents a conspectus of the various interpretations which have been argued since the Middle Ages, most of them clearly in favor of the direct messianic literal sense. On the other hand, the older authors, who represented the indirect messianic (i.e. typological) interpretation of the Immanuel prophecy, have all but disappeared.[29] According to them, Immanuel was simply Hezekiah, Ahaz' son, and the *'almah* would be the queen. The most serious objection against this interpretation — apart from the interpretation of *'almah* as a young maiden — was based on chronology, since Hezekiah must already have been born during the prophet's earlier career (2 K 18, 9-10; 18, 13; 16, 2). On the basis of our chronology, this objection no longer applies. Thus, a new door has been opened to a deeper, chronologically oriented understanding of the Immanuel prophecy.

Let us return once again to the context of the Immanuel prophecy. Not only Jerusalem, but David's dynasty as such was threatened with destruction. The enemy was already on the march against Jerusalem, bound and determined to topple Ahaz from his throne and substitute an Aramaean as king. The prophet Isaiah confronted the young king with an oracle from God. Though the enemy is bent upon the annihilation of David's house, Yahweh has established David's house for all time. The Immanuel prophecy is simply a new actualization of Nathan's prophecy.[30] What Yah-

---

28. *La Prophétie de la 'almah,* EphThLov 28 (1952), 648-678.

29. Robert-Feuillet, IntrAT 510. Among the ancient authors we must mention Justin Martyr and the Rabbis of the time of St. Jerome. Pius VI has condemned only those scholars who see the passage as neither directly nor typically messianic.

30. E. Wurthwein, *Jesaijah 7, 1-9. Ein Beitrag zum Thema: Prophetie und Politik, Theologie als Glaubenswagnis,* (1954), 47-63. The Immanuel prophecy is to be interpreted in terms not only of the Assyrian peril, but even more so the Nathan prophecy and the covenant. — W. Vischer, *Die Immanuelbotschaft im Rahmen des königlichen Zionsfestes,* TSt 45 (1955), 5-54. Isaiah is the executor for the Nathan prophecy. The terminology is supposed to be taken from the official and cultic

weh had once sworn to David he will now substantiate in this
hour of crisis. The whole point of the Immanuel prophecy is centered on the promise that the house of David will never be annihilated, even though the heart of the king and the heart of his
people is shaking like the saplings in the woods, in the face of
the approaching army. The prophet has offered a divine guarantee
in the form of any sign Ahaz might choose. The king refuses
his choice.

Nonetheless, the prophet proclaims the divine oracle: "Behold, the young woman will be pregnant and will bear a son! And
YOU [31] will call his name Immanuel."

Even before the child has reached the age of reason, those
who were bent upon the destruction of the house of David will
be annihilated. The birth and life of this child will make it clear
that "God was with them." It is especially Ahaz the doubter, who
has refused to choose a sign from God, "deep as Sheol or high
as heaven" who must recognize Yahweh as his savior, by naming
his child "God with us" (Immanuel).

Upon the occasion of his accession to the throne, in the year
735, Ahaz was exactly twenty years old (2 K 16, 2), and thus
of a marriageable age. Probably he had already begun to "look

texts for the succession to the throne and the festival of Zion. But,
given the uncertainty of such a festival's existence, the argument must
remain questionable.

31. The material for the textual criticism of this passage is presented and
evaluated in L. Dequeker, VT 12 (1962), 331-335. It is clear that there
is one unified textual tradition. The Greek and Latin translations present a confusing variety: "You will, he or she will, you (pl.) will,
they will." If the Hebrew consonants qr't are translated "she will
call," this involves violence to the grammar of the passage. Instead of
postulating the irregular form qara't (3 pers. fem. pl.), it is a more
obvious solution to interpret the consonants as the regular form of
the 2nd. pers. masc., thus: qara'ta "you will call." In form and
content the announcement of Immanuel's birth is most closely reminiscent of the birth of Isaac: "God said (to Abraham): Sarah, your
wife, will bear you a son, and YOU will call his name Isaac" (Gn
17, 19).

about for a wife to bring into his house, or a maiden (*'almah*) to take into his palace, so that she might present him with an heir to the throne." [32] In keeping with the Ugaritic idiom, the Hebrew *'almah* is simply the young bride-consort of King Ahaz. In the court of Judah, the queen mother occupied a position of special honor.[33] Accordingly, every king of Judah also bears his mother's name. Hezekiah's mother was Abi, daughter of Zechariah (2 K 18, 2). She was thus the *'almah,* the royal bride and young mother of the heir to David's throne, Hezekiah. Since Hezekiah was only five years old when he succeeded to the throne in 728,[34] his birth would fall in the year 734/33, which would correspond perfectly with dating the Immanuel prophecy in the year 735/34. Thus, the mother of Hezekiah is perfectly borne out by chronology. It follows that Isaiah did not understand the word *'almah* in its New Testament sense.

The New Testament authors do not quote the Old Testament in keeping with the canons of historical criticism. In their interpretation of Scripture, they are the children of their times.[35] The history of the past has little interest for them; they read the books of antiquity from the fullness of their own era. But it is the historian's objective to chart the actual development of salvation, to establish time and place wherever something new is visible. There ought, accordingly, be no wonder that the messianic picture of the prophets is different from the picture of Christ proper to the Evangelists.[36] And yet the two pictures are coherent in terms of a higher unity. On the basis of the newly experienced facts of salvation, the Evangelists suddenly saw the prophets' words in a new light. Matthew, for example (1, 23), could witness to Christ's virgin birth as a fact. Proof for this actual occurrence was sug-

---

32. Cf. above quotations from the Ugaritic texts, p. 216.

33. Cf. above on *gebirah*, p. 17.

34. Cf. above note 17.

35. The peculiarities of OT quotations in the NT are examined by R. G. Bratcher, *A Study of Is 7, 14,* BiTrans 9 (1958), 97-126.

36. F. L. Moriatry, *The Emmanuel Prophecies,* CBQ 19 (1957), 226-233 explains the "process of revelation" from Isaiah to Matthew. The Evangelist is giving a legitimate explanation of what the prophet has seen only in indistinct division.

gested by the Immanuel prophecy. The Greek Bible had already translated *'almah* as *parthenos,* and thus prepared for its interpretation as "virgin" in the proper sense of the word. In technical terms, accordingly, we must say that the Immanuel prophecy was indirectly messianic, since it referred directly to Hezekiah who is a type of Christ. In like manner, the Virgin Mary is only indirectly referred to in the figure of the *'almah.* Such a distinction, however, creates too great a gulf between prophet and Evangelist, as if the prophet's word had been fulfilled only in the distant future and not already in the circumstances of his own time. Now, since the prophecy of Nathan, every king was the bearer of the whole promise which could not take form in the future without being a bodily reality in the present time.[37] The covenant which Yahweh had struck with David was valid in all its particulars for each and every legitimate successor to the throne. With each new king, there was a reawakening of the hope that this new bearer of the royal blood would realize the ideals so dear to the heart of Yahweh. The bitter reality, however, forced the expectancy of the ideal into the more and more distant future. It was the prophet Isaiah who first painted the image of the ideal ruler to come, in clearer and clearer terms. His consciousness that faith in the everlasting glory of the Davidic dynasty grows into a faith in a personal Messiah, king of the future. In the perspective of prophecy, present and distant future are joined. But the future cannot be reality without the contemporary descendant of David bearing the sacred burdens of God and passing them down from generation to generation until the day of final fulfillment. It is asking more of the Old Testament than it is prepared or allowed to give [38] if we expect to find the miracle of the virgin birth in the fullest sense of the word already clearly expressed in the Immanuel prophecy. The miracle lay in the course of history. The house of David did not fail, because Yahweh remained faithful

---

37. R. de Vaux, *Les Institutions de l'AT,* 173: "... ce texte de l'adoption de toute la dynastie davidique, car cette adoption devait évidemment devenir effective pour chaque souverain."
38. Separating the passage from its historical context destroys its value as a dogmatic proof!

to his word, proclaiming through his prophet that he had even greater plans for the future.

3) "THE SPOIL SPEEDS, THE PREY HASTES" (8, 1, 23a)

Dismissed by the king, Isaiah did not seek refuge in silence. In order to present an even more compelling picture of the judgment to come, he resorted to symbolic activity. He called witnesses, among them Uriah, the high priest, to represent the crown, took a large tablet, and wrote upon it in "common characters":[39] "Belonging to the Spoil Speeds, the Prey Hastes" (*maher-šālal-haš-baz*).[40] The tablet was probably displayed in the temple court, where everyone could see it and wonder. Isaiah then went into his wife, who is here called a prophetess, and properly so: she conceived and bore a son who was destined to be a sign in Israel. Just as in the case of the Immanuel prophecy, Isaiah makes an explanation for his strange conduct: "Before the child knows how to cry 'my father' or 'my mother,' the wealth of Damascus and the spoil of Samaria will be carried away before the king of Assyria" (8, 4). For "this people" — by this he meant the king and the people of Judah — have refused the gently flowing water of Shiloah, and therefore the mighty floods of the Euphrates will rage over them, until the water reaches to their neck (8, 5-8).

Meantime, Ahaz had not been idle. He had gathered together all the gold and silver which was to be found in the temple and in the palace treasury; this he sent to Tiglath-Pilesar with this message: "I am your servant and your son.[41] Come up, and

---

39. That is, in the common script that everyone could read. By way of contrast, apparently, to the sacred script (hieroglyph or cuneiform) that only the priests and scholars could read. Cf. Hab 2, 2. J. Ziegler, EB III, 41.

40. A. Jirku, *Zu "Eilebeute" in Jes 8, 1, 3*, ThZ 74 (1949), 118, presents a new interpretation. The word *mahēr* is not an imperative "hasten!" but, on the basis of Ugaritic parallels, a noun with the meaning of "warrior." The name of the boy thus means "warrior of the booty, hastening to prey." Cf. Gordon, UM, Glossary on *mhr*, no. 1075.

41. Note the use of the word "son" to express the relationship of dependence. Vassal kings are "sons" of the chief kings.

rescue me from the hand of the king of Syria and from the hand of the king of Israel, who are attacking me" (2 K 16, 7-9). This afforded the Assyrian a most welcome opportunity to invade the west. The kingdom of Urartu had been destroyed. Tiglath-Pilesar was thus free to devote his undivided energies to the problems of Syria and Palestine. In three successive campaigns, in the years 734, 733, and 732, he completely reshaped the politics of the western countries.

It is witness to Tiglath-Pilesar's military and diplomatic adroitness that he did not begin his campaign with a frontal attack against Damascus, the bulwark of the allied forces; his goal was rather to defeat the allies one by one. On the basis of new text finds,[42] from the northwest palace in Calah (Nimrud), the course of the campaign in the year 734 can be reconstructed as follows. After the pacification of Urartu (735), Tiglath-Pilesar appeared on the northern Phoenician coast with a powerful army: ". . . and that city in the midst of the sea, I cast her down. His heart was throbbing; he put on sackcloth." [43] This is a reference to the city Arvad [44] which, just like Tyre, had been built on a fortified island along the coast, from which vantage point it had established its land and sea supremacy. In keeping with the new policy, the conquered territories were grouped together into an Assyrian province with its capital city at Simirra, opposite Arvad on the coast.

The Assyrian army made its way through Tyre and Sidon towards the south. The badly mutilated text only suggests the conjecture that there was an open confrontation "on the border,"

---

42. A. Alt, *Tiglat-Pilesars III, erster Feldzug nach Palästina*, Kleine Texte II, 150-156.

43. *Ibid.*, 152.

44. Today the isle of Ruad, about a mile from the coast. 2500 x 1550 ft. Owing to its favorable location, it was a point of support that was hotly contested in every era of history. To visit the still preserved crusaders' citadel one requires a special permission, since currently there is a Syrian garrison in residence. The top of the citadel affords a splendid panorama, northwards to the Semitic Olympus, the Safon or Mountain of the North, and southwards deep into Lebanon. It can be reached by motorboat from Tartus. Visited on Dec. 1, 1958.

"in the territory of the house of Omri (Israel)," in which Israel and probably the Aramaean allies were defeated. "I filled the field with the corpses of her warriors as with grass." [45] The scene of this battle must have been either the Plain of Acco or the Plain of Sharon which stretches southward from Carmel.

Nothing suggests the possibility that Tiglath-Pilesar, despite this victory, had changed the direction of his campaign. In the eponym lists for the year 734 [46] we note this entry: "*a-na-mât-Pi-liš-ta* — into the land of the Philistines." Surprised by these sudden tactics, the Philistine cities offered no further resistance. Even Hanunu of Gaza,[47] a perpetual agitator against the Assyrians, fled before the approach of the Assyrian armies into Egypt, leaving his city to the victor. As a sign of Assyrian supremacy, the victor had the "images of the great gods and the image of his kingship raised in gold" over the conquered city.[48] Even the fugitive Hanunu was generously treated; he returned and reassumed his throne, but only by the grace of Assyria. Tiglath-Pilesar was not content with the conquest of Gaza. In order to provide a buffer against Egyptian penetration, he sent a division as far as the "Brook of Egypt" (*nahal musur*). Here too, he erected "the image of his kingship" as a sign of Assyrian supremacy. He entrusted the Arabian sheikh Idibi-ilu [49] with the defense of the frontier. The conquered territories along the Palestinian coast were grouped into the Assyrian province of Du'ru, named after the city located on the sea. Tiglath-Pilesar had reason to be satisfied with the results of his campaign. The Mediterranean coast, along its whole eastern extent, was completely in his control, the gate to Egypt had been barred, and the hostile alliance had been destroyed. Aram of Damascus and Israel must surely be destined to fall of their own weight.

---

45. Alt, l.c. 155.
46. RLA II, 431.
47. ANET 283b.
48. *sa-lam šarru-ti-ia.* The word used here, *salmu*, Hebrew *selem*, is discussed in the treatment of Gn 1, 26. Created man is an "image" that is, a bearer of God's dignity in creation.
49. ANET 283b, 284a. — DOT 55 (c).

On the basis of the extant Biblical and Assyrian sources, the events of the campaigns in the year 733 and 732 cannot be clearly distinguished. At all events, Tiglath-Pilesar was free to devote all his energy to the conquest of his two principal opponents. For each of these two years we find the same entry in the eponymous annals: "*a-na-mât di-maš-qa*, — into the land of Damascus." [50] The inscription in the annals [51] presents a grotesque picture of the battle against Rezin of Damascus: "His warriors I took captive, . . . their weapons I shattered, . . . their battle array I disbanded. He (Rezin) fled all alone, for his life. . . . Like a young fawn (mouse?) he ran into the gate of his city. His princes I impaled alive and displayed them throughout the land. . . . I shut him up like a bird in a cage . . . . His orchards I cut down and left nothing behind." This is followed by the sad list of prisoners and booty. The narrative makes it clear that Rezin was defeated in an open battle and forced to withdraw into the fortress of Damascus. For a year he withstood the enemy siege.

Meantime the Assyrian hordes were free to swoop down upon Israel. They invaded from the north, across the territory of the Jordan sources. "In the days of Pekah of Israel, Tiglath-Pilesar king of Assyria came and captured Ijon, Abel-beth-Maacah, Janoah, Kedesh, and Hazor, (the territories of) Gilead, Galilee, and the land of Naphtali; and he carried the people captive to Assyria" (2 K 15, 29). According to Assyrian sources as well,[52] the invasion took place from the north, from the territory around the Jordan sources. Mute witness to the magnitude of the catastrophe which now broke over Israel are the ruin and devastation visible in the strata excavated at Hazor.[53]

The destruction of Damascus in 732 was an open sign for the Jordan sources. Mute witness to the magnitude of the catastrophe which now broke over Israel are the ruin and devastation to the terrible splendor of Ashur. A palace inscription from Nimrud

50. RAL II, 431.
51. TGI 51; AOT 346; ANET 283.
52. DOT 55, 57: "The city of Abilakka (apparently Abel-beth-Maacah) in the territory of Bit-Humria I took."
53. Y. Yadin, *Excavations at Hazor*, BA 19 (1956), 6.

enumerates princes from Asia Minor as far as the Brook of Egypt; among them is *Ya-u-ha-zi ya-u-da-a-a,* i.e., Ahaz of Judah, and, standing peacefully at his side, his bitter adversaries Edom, Ammon, and the Philistines from Ashkelon and Gaza. When, according to 2 Kings 16, 10-16, Ahaz, from Damascus, sent the high priest Uriah, in Jerusalem, the model of an Assyrian altar with instructions to erect a similar structure in the Temple; this was the bitter price he was forced to pay for his "deliverance." Assyrian marriage symbols, royal insignia and images, statues of the gods with altars — from Tushpa in Armenia as far as Gaza and the Brook of Egypt, as we have already seen, and now even in Jerusalem proclaimed the conquest of the god Ashur and his king. This would have meant the final destruction of the Yahweh cult in Jerusalem, if Yahweh had been like the gods of the other nations. It remains a riddle just how the high priest of Yahweh bowed to the command of the king, and erected an Assyrian altar in the Temple. Was he perhaps merely yielding to the inevitable, in the quiet hope that times would change? The prophet Isaiah, however, would not bend; it is now that he begins his most earnest proclamation of Yahweh's terrible judgment which is destined to break over Ashur. Under this Assyrian pressure, the Canaanite Baal cult was also free to revive its ancient practices. Ahaz led the way with his "good" example. He sacrificed and burned incense on the high places, "and on the hills, and under every green tree" (2 K 16, 4). On one occasion, the circumstances of which are not clear, he "even burned his son as an offering" (2 K 16, 3; 2 Ch 28, 3); that is, he sacrificed him to the pagan gods.[54]

Ahaz could well be content with the success of his policies.

---

54. The sacrifice of a son here has been compared with the incident in the threatened attack upon Jerusalem during the Syro-Ephraimite war, where Ahaz, like Mesha, was forced by the extremity of the crisis to this desperate expedient. This argument, however, not only contradicts the chronology, but is utterly without foundation in the text. The Greek translation of 2 K 16, 3 and 2 Ch 28, 3, read plural, *bana(y)w* "his sons," thus justifying the general conclusion that Ahaz tolerated human sacrifice in his kingdom and allowed "the sons (of Israel) to pass through the fire."

By his call for Assyrian assistance, he was not only liberated from the pressure of his enemies, but was also in a position to concentrate on revenging himself against his enemies. Damascus was completely subjected, and the kingdom of Israel had been reduced to the territory in the mountain country around Samaria. In Isaiah's opinion, Ahaz could have achieved the same results much more cheaply, simply by neutrality and trust in Yahweh. He had preferred, however, to appeal to Assyrian help, and had thereby delivered his land, in spirit and in substance, to the foreign rule.

That Tiglath-Pilesar did not make an Assyrian province of the remnant state of Samaria is probably the result of a *coup d'état* which had meantime occurred. He himself had a hand in the game; this is his boast: "Pe-ka-ha (Pekah), their king, they overthrew, and I set A-u-si (Hoshea) as king over them." [55] This must have taken place towards the end of 731 or the beginning of 730. In the same manner, the Assyrian had been involved in the internal politics in the city of Ashkelon, dethroning Mitinti, who had "broken his oath," and raising his son Rukibtu to the throne.[56] The new king Hoshea had to pay a heavy tribute simply to remain a free and independent vassal of Ashur. The Palestinian territories which had been occupied by the Kingdom of Israel were annexed to the province of Magidu (Megiddo) while the Transjordanian territories were joined to the province of Gilead.

4) "TO US A CHILD IS BORN" (9, 1-6)

In these days of extreme humiliation Isaiah was the comforter of his people. He proclaimed that, despite the present catastrophe, Yahweh is Lord of the world and Lord of all peoples, that Yahweh continues to plan for his people. Even the present catastrophe was part of his will. The catastrophe must come because he is the Holy One of Israel and as such he must become "a stone of offense, and a rock of stumbling to both houses of Israel" (8, 14). All that is unholy must be burnt away in judgment. History is only the judgment of God in its inevitable fulfillment; the prophets are

---

55. AOT 348; ANET 284; DOT 55.
56. ANET 283.

but the heralds of divine judgment. Evidence of this is the judgment oracle of burdens against Damascus and Ephraim (17, 1-
11).

The Holy One of Israel, who is consuming fire, surrounded
by creatures of fire, does not want merely to annihilate, but rather
to introduce a new era of salvation. At a time in which everything
has grown dark, Isaiah proclaims: "The people who walked in
darkness have seen a great light" (9, 2). This light has shone particularly upon those territories which had suffered most under the
fury of Ashur, "the way of the sea, the land beyond the Jordan,
Galilee of the nations" [57] (9, 1). The day of victory will dawn,
glorious like the day of Midian.[58] The rod of the oppressor, which
lay heavy on the shoulders of the war prisoners and expatriates,
the brutal boots of the soldier, the officers' robes "rolled in
blood" — all this will pass away. People will rejoice as at harvest
time, or when the booty is divided.[59]

What is the cause of all this jubilation in the midst of disaster?
It is simply the knowledge of the "birth," that is, the accession to
the throne [60] of a new ruler: "For to us a child is born, to us
a son is given; and the government will be upon his shoulder, and
his name will be called 'Wonderful Counsellor, Mighty God,
Everlasting Father, Prince of Peace.' Of the increase of his government and of peace there will be no end, upon the throne of David

---

57. A. Alt, Jes 8, 23-9, 6: *Befreiungsnacht und Krönungstag. Fs. A.
    Bertholet* (1950), 29-49 examines the political situation between 732
    and 722. Israel had lost its border territories: Transjordania, Galilee,
    and the Coastal Plains (Highway along the Sea). It is to these cut
    off branches that the prophet announces the night of liberation through
    the birth of the descendant of David (i.e., his accession to power).
58. Gideon's victory over the Midianite Robber bands (Jg 7; Ps 82/83,
    10).
59. Is 9, 2 is wrongly translated in the Vulgate. Instead of "multiplicasti
    gentem et non multiplicasti laetitiam" (You have increased the people,
    but you have not increased their joy), we should read: "You have
    increased the jubilation, indeed you have made grow the joy." The
    error arose by improperly dividing the words: instead of *haggoylo'*
    (the people, not), we must read *haggilah* (jubilation).
60. The accession to the throne is symbolically called the hour of the
    new ruler's birth. Cf. Ps 2, 7b; 109/110, 3c.

and over his kingdom, to establish it and to uphold it with righteousness from this time forth and forever more. The zeal of the
Lord of Hosts will do this" (9, 5-6).

Since the Immanuel prophecy had been made before the
threatened walls of Jerusalem, the messianic image of the prophet
had grown more profound. What he had threatened had come to
pass. "The two smouldering stumps of firebrands" (7, 4), who
meant to destroy the house of David, had themselves been destroyed. At this crisis of his people's history, where once again
all human plans had availed nothing — the cities destroyed,
the long columns of prisoners of war and expatriates — Isaiah
proclaims a new beginning from God. For it is not man who introduces a new era. The only agency that is really at work in the
sentence "to us a child is born, to us a son is given," is not the
unqualified third person of historical necessity; the impersonal
passive form of the verb is, rather, an even more forceful expression of the personal activity of God. In the Immanuel prophecy
the figure of the Messiah is still clouded by the dark storms of
judgment; but here everything is light, victory, the end of suffering, and eternal peace. Immanuel was only a symbolic name.
Now the prophet returns to his task, and with a whole series
of new names, attempts to describe the essence of this ideal
ruler.

The Vulgate, reads six names, *Admirabilis, consiliarius, deus fortis,
pater futuri saeculi, princeps pacis* (Wonderful, Counselor, God, Hero,
Father of the World to Come, Prince of Peace).[61] The Hebrew text,
however, would suggest grouping the first four names into two, "Wonderful Counselor, Hero God"; there are, accordingly, a total of four messianic
names. It is not impossible that Isaiah, in composing his song for the
accession to the throne, took the Egyptian royal titles [62] for his model.

----

61. The Greek and Old Latin translations read this as one single name:
"*Magni consilii angelus,* angel of the great council." The other names
are grouped into a declaratory sentence: "I will bring peace upon the
princes, and bring him peace and prosperity."

62. The Pharaonic titulature has undergone a long development, ending
in the formation of five throne names: 1. Horus-title, the Pharaoh
as the incarnate God Horus; 2. Nebti "he who belongs to the two
goddesses," the falcon goddess of El-Kab (Upper Egypt) and the
Uraeus serpent of Buto (Lower Egypt); 3. *nesut-bit* "he who to

This would not be the only detail in which the royal court of Israel was indebted to the example of the Pharaohs. There is, at all events, no direct borrowing.

The various names are an attempt to delineate the various spheres of activity upon which the new ruler will embark. The first name, "Wonderful Counselor" (*pele' yo'es*) describes his diplomatic and political objectives. In a chaotic world without counsel, he will be a source of counsel and a creator of order. This goes far beyond human power; hence his name "Wonderful Counselor." The second name describes his warrior and military capacities. *'el-gibbôr*, literally, God-Hero; in terms of Hebrew idiom, this does not necessarily predicate divine attributes of the new ruler. David's heroes are called *gibbôrîm* and accomplished extraordinary deeds of heroism. The Messiah, however, is simply the *"Hero"* without further specification. Similar intensifications of a concept are expressed by the addition of the word *'el* (God); e.g., "The mountains of God," which means simply "the very high mountains." A "God of a hero" is, accordingly, a superior type of military hero. It is only when we look backward from the messianic fullness of meaning that we can see the divine character of the Messiah Jesus foretold in these words, and thus recognize them as a form of speech which goes beyond the common idiom.

The third name, "Everlasting Father" (*'abi-'ad*) is concerned with the sphere of administration.[63] "Father" (abbot) is a title from the category of high court officials (22, 21). The new ruler will be father of the house, steward of the house for his whole life. The fourth title "Prince of Peace" (*sar-šalôm*) signifies the crowning of his whole work.

Just as the Immanuel prophecy proceeds from an historical situation which can be precisely determined, this throne song

---

whom the rush-reed (Upper Egypt) and the bee (Lower Egypt) belong"; 4. the current throne name; 5. *sa-Re'* "son of the sun god Re." Drioton-Vandier, *L'Egypte* (Clio) (1952), 139, 144, 175. — A. Scharff, *Geschichte Ägypten*, (1960), 62, bound up with the place names that they cannot be simply borrowed. The only point of similarity thus remains the number five. If we read the beginning of verse 6 as "increaser of dominion, kingdom," instead of "great is his dominion," the Hebrew text also contains five titles. The Egyptian titulature may have been prepared for foreign adaptation by their incorporation into the court style of the Phoenicians and the Amorrites, and thus made their way into Israel. Cf. G. Lanckowski, *Beeinflussung des Christentums durch ägyptische Vorstellungen*, ZRelGg 8 (1956), 14-32.

---

63. Often wrongly translated: "Father of the prey."

must also have had a very definite *Sitz im Leben*. When Ahaz
died in the year 728, he was followed by Hezekiah on the throne,
who was then a child of five.[64] This was, in my opinion, the occasion for Isaiah, seized by the spirit, to compose his prophetic
song for the accession to the throne. It was not, accordingly,
directed primarily towards a distant and indefinite future; it
was composed rather for a very definite day and for a very
definite hour. The content of the song is nothing essentially new.
Isaiah portrays himself as the guardian of the great prophecies
of the future given to the house of David through the prophet
Nathan. The house of David was not some imaginary grandeur
of the distant future; it was a fact of flesh and blood in the prophet's
own presence. What was once destined to become reality in the
future must already strike its roots in the present. If the great
ruler was actually to be born some day, it must be from the flesh
and blood of David's line who were now upon the throne. If the
prophet, in this song for the accession to the throne, already un-
furls the splendid banner of an ideal ruler, he also charges him
with the whole holy burden of the future. Whether this fullness
is destined to become reality in this child or only in some future
day is hidden from his eyes. At all events, Hezekiah will be the
bearer of the salvation to come. Precisely in these days in which
darkness lay over the entire land Zion and the house of David were
destined to become a rock of hope for the sorely tried people.

Both prophecies, the birthday song (Immanuel) and the
coronation song, are thus directed primarily to King Hezekiah.
It is precisely in this concrete objectivity that the incarnation of
the word is most strikingly evident. The fragile vessel of Hezekiah
was incapable of grasping the entire fullness of this prophecy. In
what must have been a very deep sense of disillusion, the prophet
might well have begun to turn away from Hezekiah, while his
searching eye focused upon the great ruler of the future who
was destined to come. The prophet, too, is subject to the law
of faith; his is not always the way of vision.

---

64. Cf. Appendix on chronology.

C) DECLINE OF THE KINGDOM OF ISRAEL

1) KING PHUL OF BABEL

After the victorious conquest of the western lands, Tiglath-Pilesar set his sights upon the restless Babylonians. Around 730 Babylon witnessed a political chaos that was without parallel, and which must have served as a powerful incentive for the newly strengthened Assyrian attack. It is true that the Babylonian kingdom was still in the hands of a native king. Nabu-nasir (747-735) was still exercising a shadow of rule. The real power, however, lay in the hands of the Aramaean sheikhs, constantly growing in power; their greedy eyes were fixed upon the crown of Babel. Nabunasir's son and successor Nabunadinzer fell, after only two years, under the hand of a rebellious governor named Nabušumu-kin. He himself, however, after only two months, was murdered in central Babylonia by the Aramaean prince Ukinzêr of Bit Amukkani, who thereupon seized the throne for himself.

For Tiglath-Pilesar, this was an invitation to attack Babylonia. Just as in his western campaigns, he laid waste the country-side, destroyed the cities, and settled their inhabitants in foreign lands. The capital city of Babylon offered a bitter resistance. Upon its conquest in the year 729, Tiglath-Pilesar resolved upon a most extraordinary step. He refused to enter into the holy city as victor and enemy; he espoused the role of Marduk and made himself king of Babylon under the name Pulu (in the Bible Phul). Accordingly, he won the priesthood for himself and favored the humbled country with an appearance of self-determination. From now on he bore the glorious title "King of the whole, King of Assyria, King of Babel, King of Sumer and Accad, King of the four ends of the earth." [1]

The deposition of Ukinzêr meant the "pacification" of the Aramaean border states. Among these, even Marduk-Apal-Id-dina, prince of Bit-Yakini, who later became one of Ashur's chief opponents, followed the ascendant victor.

---

1. Schmökel, GAV 264.

Tiglath-Pilesar had succeeded beyond what any of his predecessors on the Assyrian throne had ever managed to accomplish.
Under the scepter of the Assyrian dragon the whole of the Ancient
Near East was actually united. When Tiglath-Pilesar died in 727,
he left his son a mighty empire of which he could proudly say that
it reached "from the bitter sea of Bit-Yakini (on the Persian
Gulf) to the mountains of the north, from the rising sun to the sea
of the setting sun, as far as Egypt," with a population whose individual elements had been rendered powerless by the full-scale
repopulation policy, which had also transformed them into something of a proletariate, and a strict central organization which controlled the whole. It needed, no doubt, an iron hand to hold the
monstrous construction together.[2] What, in this political picture,
was the role of Israel and Judah? That of a humiliated province,
without political significance. But it was precisely by this heavy
millstone of history that the precious wheat of revelation was
ground fine.

2) THE YEAR OF KING AHAZ' DEATH (728)

Serpents, adders, flying dragons, smoke from out the north,
diplomatic messengers from all nations .... This is how Isaiah
characterizes the political situation in the year of King Ahaz' death
(14, 28-32). The world was once again in a state of confusion,
but not because of the death of the unimportant King Ahaz. One
year after him (727) the mighty Tiglath-Pilesar ended his career.
His kingdom, forced with sword and blood, seemed ready to
collapse. The subjugated peoples hoped for liberation. But the
clear-seeing prophet had this proclamation to make: "From the
serpent's root will come forth an adder, and its fruit will be a
flying serpent" (14, 29).

Tiglath-Pilesar was dead indeed, but his son and successor
Shalmaneser V (726-722) proved equally energetic in controlling
the reins of world dominion. The Assyrian sources for his reign
are sparse. In the eponymous annals [3] for the year 726, we know

---

2. *Ibid.*, 265.
3. RLA II, 432.

the entry: "*šulmanu-ašarêd* took his place upon the throne";
for the later years of his reign only one word has been preserved,
the preposition "*a-na* — against." The names of the lands or
cities against which his campaign was directed have been destroyed
in the text. Following his father's example, he also identified
himself with Bel of Babel, and as king of Babylon, bore the
throne name Ululai. From an Aramaean document we learn that
he carried off prisoners from Bit-Adini in Northern Syria.[4]

On the basis of the Biblical narrative, the death of Tiglath-Pilesar was the sign for a general uprising in the western countries.
In Palestine, the Philistines also made a powerful bid for freedom. Apparently it was once again Hanunu of Gaza who led the
defection and, accordingly, sent his agitators even to Jerusalem.
Here, because of the influence of the prophet Isaiah, the news was
coolly received. The answer given to the ambassadors was the
expression of a genuine Isaian faith: "The Lord has founded
Zion" (14, 32b). In Israel, however, King Hoshea believed the
time had come to shake off the Assyrian yoke.

3) "WOE TO THE PROUD CROWN, AND TO THE FADING FLOWER . . ." (28, 1)

Isaiah regarded Ephraim's recolt against Ashur as sheer mad-
ness. Only a hopeless drunkard could undertake such an ill-fated
policy. Ruin was destined to take its course. Like a hailstorm,
like a destroying tempest, like a storm of overflowing waters it
will thunder upon the country. The proud crowns of the drunkards
of Ephraim will be trampled in the dust. Like the first ripe
figs before the summer it will be greedily devoured (28, 1-4).

Hoshea had ascended the throne in the year 731/30 with
Assyrian help. After Shalmaneser's accession to the Assyrian
throne, he continued to play the role of *'ebed,* i.e., slave and
subject, and continued to pay his tribute (2 K 17, 3). The day
finally came, however, when he refused further payment, a sign
that he had crossed into the anti-Assyrian camp. This was a defection he could not have dared alone. According to Flavius Jo-

---

4. Schmökel, GAV 265.

sephus,[5] Tyre also had defected. The Philistines, under the leadership of Hanunu of Gaza, certainly must have had a part in the rebellion. The Books of the Kings show that the greatest hope was centered upon Egypt, upon Sô (or Sewe), King of Misraim [6] (17, 4). This hope proved deceitful. So it was no longer supported by the old Egyptian empire. He was only the prince of a small kingdom in the territory of the delta.

Thus the Assyrian tempest broke over the western countries, just as Isaiah had prophesied. In the seventh year of Hoshea, the fourth year of Hezekiah, that is in the year 727, Shalmaneser marched against Samaria and besieged the city. For three years the northern capital withstood the attack. In the ninth year of Hoshea, the sixth year of Hezekiah, in late summer or early fall of the year 722, the city capitulated in the face of superior power.[7] The victor did not treat the conquered people gently. In keeping with the military practices of that day, the captured Hoshea, who had formed the soul of the resistance, was put into a cage (*bêt-kele'*) and probably executed (2 K 17, 4). The scheduled deportation of the populace was checked almost in the beginning by the death of Shalmaneser in December of that same year, 722. The remnant of Israel thus enjoyed two years' grace before Sargon set the final seal upon its doom.

For the Biblical theologian of history, the destruction of Samaria represents a critical and pivotal point in the history of salvation and rejection. He was not so concerned with evaluating the political causes and movements behind the destruction. Then too, together with Israel the other smaller states had all passed under Assyrian sway. What could Israel possibly have hoped to accomplish against the gigantic strength of the Assyrian empire? In 2 Kings 17, 7-18 the stages of her religious decline are once again enumerated: defection to the foreign gods, erection of sacrificial high places with massebot and asherot sacrifices to the pagan

---

5. R. de Vaux, *Rois*, 187 (JerB).

6. S. Yeivin, *Who was Sô', the King of Egypt?* VT 2 (1952), 164-68.
   Sô' is not a personal name, but the title of the Egyptian wazzier.

7. H. Tadmor, *The Campaigns of Sargon II, of Assur*, JCS 12 (1958), 37.

idols and abominations, contempt for the prophetic call to repentance. The covenant struck with Yahweh had long since been
broken. The invisible and imageless god of the covenant had
been honored in the form of a bull; instead of the creator, they
worshipped the host of heaven. They had chosen Baal for their
supreme god, sacrificing their sons and daughters to him, and
falling into sorcery and magic. There was no longer any room in
Israel for Yahweh. That is why the end was inevitable. The
political development of these times can explain the political decline of the kingdom of Israel; but to see this whole sorry catastrophe, in the last analysis, as the story of Israel and her God —
this is the unique contribution of the Bible. This idea is expressed
in the prophet Isaiah (ch. 28) more clearly than in 2 Kings 17,
7-18. The proud crown of the drunkards of Ephraim has been
taken away, trampled underfoot; but God's history has not come
to its end. As so often before in the earlier history of salvation
and rejection, the nadir of judgment and despair is also the beginning of a new salvation. Isaiah rivets his attention upon "that day"
(28, 5), the day on which Yahweh of hosts will himself become
the crown of the holy remnant that survives. Does this mean that
the prophet had fled from the unholy realities of his time into a
dream world of a better future? Are we to understand his opposition to political solutions simply as a retreat to a happier
position above the attack of the world powers?

It is true that Isaiah hoped to see a blessed day in which God
would be all in all. He is, however, not a dreamer; he is God's
herald in a concrete time. What has actually survived from David's
mighty kingdom? Only a remnant. And this remnant is now gathered around Jerusalem and the kingdom of Judah. But what
are the prospects here? Is Yahweh really the supreme God in every
sphere of life? Not at all. The prophet paints a picture of the
abominable situations in Jerusalem (28, 7ff.). It seems that the
departure of the Assyrian troops from Samaria and the news
of Shalmaneser's death was celebrated in Jerusalem by the most
dissolute revelry. "These also" (28, 7), the men of Judah, priests
and prophets too, reel with strong drink, and the tables are full
of vomit. With stammering tongues they mock the unwelcome

prophet.[8] "Precept upon precept, precept upon precept, line upon a line, line upon a line." They feel secure because they have made a covenant with death and devil; but all this is falsehood and delusion (28, 15). Even though Yahweh is disgusted with Jerusalem, he has not abandoned his plan. If he cannot work with his people, he will still accomplish his masterplan of history despite them. "For in Zion he has established his cornerstone, a foundation for the future, a testing stone, a cornerstone" (28, 16), against which the mighty, overflowing waters will break (28, 2). This foundation is simply faith: "He who believes will not hesitate" (28, 16). And thus once again Isaiah's leit-motiv shows through. The existence of the people can be guaranteed only by their faith. All other guarantees are nothing. From the transitory appearance of an earthly, political kingdom gradually rises the imperishable kingdom of faith and believers. In terms of theology history, the political kingdom of Israel must necessarily fall, so that the interior structure of the kingdom of faith appears. After the destruction of Samaria, the whole hope of the surviving remnant centers upon Zion.

4) DEPORTATION AND REPOPULATION IN THE NORTHERN KINGDOM OF ISRAEL

Shortly after the conquest of Samaria, in December of 722, Shalmaneser V died. The succession to the Assyrian throne involved a real revolution in domestic politics. It was not the son of the deceased king who succeeded to the throne; it was a general who seized the power for himself. As a protest against the former regime, he called himself Sargon, that is, "true, real king" (*šarruukin*). Tiglath-Pilesar had, in his day, broken the power of the great princes and the temple, creating smaller administrative districts. The disposed princes had long been waiting for their vengeance. Shalmaneser's death was their opportunity. With their

---

8. Is 28, 10: *saw, lasaw, saw lasaw, qaw laqaw, qaw laqaw* — an imitation of the slurred speech of the drunkards who made mockery of the prophet for preaching only commandments (*saw*) and plumbline (*qaw*) (guideline for conduct). The above translation is from M. Buber, *Bucher der Kundung*, 88.

support, Sargon II (721-705) succeeded in his coup. In gratitude for their help, he restored the ancient tax indemnities for Ashur and Harran, and patronized the temples. In his foreign policy he followed the footsteps of his predecessors. His campaigns and acta are the object of frequent, and often contradictory accounts, which, in their totality, present a very clear picture of that era.[9]

In the first year of his reign Sargon was occupied with domestic politics, the reorganization of his kingdom. Accordingly, it was impossible for him to have concluded the siege of Samaria in the year 721, as was formerly believed. Our more precise knowledge of the sequence of events is owing to the discovery of the Nimrud Prism.[10] This makes it possible to correct the ascription of the conquest of Samaria to the first year of Sargon's reign, as it is reported in the annals. The annals are, in their literary genre, glorified accounts of the mighty deeds of the Assyrian rulers. In order to fill up the first, otherwise uneventful year of Sargon's reign, the court historian simply substituted the conquest of Samaria which had already taken place under Shalmaneser.

Only after he had secured his throne did Sargon turn his energetic attention to the subjugation of the rebellious small states in the west. The soul of this resistance in Syria was Ja'ubidi of Hamath, described in the Assyrian accounts as "a commoner" (ḫubšu), who had seized the throne and incited open rebellion in the cities of Arvad and Simirra, along the sea coast, as well as Damascus and Syria. He was defeated at Qarqar and taken captive. As a terrible deterrent for the other rebellious princes, Sargon had him flayed. Throughout the whole territory the victor

---

9. We might point, among others, to the Chorsabad Annals, victory inscriptions and records of the ruler's glory in the palace of Chorsabad, which present a sequential account of history in terms of years. Opposed to this style are the eponym canons, which present only the most important events of a given year in short and telling entries. There is also the "Babylonian Chronicle," which originally presented a complete history of the years 747-539. Large sections of it are still extant, and combined with other sources, they form the most important foundation for OT chronology. There are also the prism and ostraca inscriptions.

10. C. J. Gadd, *Iraq 16* (1954), 173-201.

reestablished "peace and order." Part of the conquered army, 200 chariots and 600 horsemen, he incorporated into the Assyrian army.[11]

After the conquest of the north, Sargon moved along the sea coast, and, inland, towards the south. Damascus was forced to subjection. Along the Phoenician coast he captured Tyre, which had been under siege since Shalmaneser's time. The most inveterate agitator against his power was still at work in Gaza. Hanunu had won the Egyptian commander Sib'e to his cause.[12] The decisive confrontation occurred along the Egyptian frontier at Rapihu. Sib'e fled like a shepherd whose flocks had been stolen; Hanunu was captured and carried off to Ashur in chains.[13]

It was this same campaign that witnessed the final disposition of Samaria. On the Nimrud Prism [14] the course of events is described as follows: "The men of Samaria, together with their king, my enemy, conspired against me not to serve me and not to pay tribute, and they began to war against me. In the power of my great gods, my lords, I fought with them and I counted 7280 men, together with their chariots and the gods of their trusting, as booty. 200 chariots I took from their midst for my royal watch. The rest I settled in the middle of Assyria. The city of Samaria I rebuilt and made it greater than before. I settled it with inhabitants from the territories subject to my power. I set an official as governor over them and counted them among the inhabitants (subjects) of Assyria." The annals give the number of deportees as 27,290.[15] Part of them was settled in the territory of Halalu in the Habur River, and part in the cities of the Medes

---

11. ANET 285; lines 33-37.
12. Probably to be identified with Sô, the Egyptian king named in the account of 2 K 17, 4. In the Assyrian sources he is called simply *turtan*, the official who occupied the most important position after the king, something like a commander-in-chief. "A high military and administrative official, second in rank only to the king," ANET 285a, Anm 4.
13. Annals, ANET 284-285.
14. E. Vogt, *Samaria a. 722 et 720 ab Assyriis capta*, Bibl 33 (1958), 535-541.
15. ANET 285a.

(2 K 17, 6). Israel's deportation formed only a small part of the repopulation project so brutally undertaken by the Assyrians. The resettled elements were probably quickly absorbed by the majority of the foreign population surrounding them; they have left no trace behind them. A potsherd from Nimrud, written in Aramaic, has cast a new and unexpected light upon this dark era. It contains good Hebrew names, such as Menahem, Hanan'el, Zekar'el, Haggai, etc., and is apparently a register of deported Israelites.[16] The number of deportees, approximately 30,000 men, is proportionately rather small. Obviously this was not a population exchange; it was simply the resettlement of the dangerous elements, among them the intellectual and military class.

Their place was taken by immigrants from all the districts of the vast empire, a colorful conglomeration of uprooted ethnic elements. 2 Kings 17, 24 mentions people from Babylon, Cuthaa, Avva, as well as the Aramaean section of Syria, the cities of Hamath and Sepharvaim. The Assyrian annals [17] also refer to Arab tribes in Samaria: "The tribes of Tamud, Ibadidi, Marsimanu and Haiapa, the Arabs, who live far into the desert and recognize no overseers or officials and have paid no royal tribute — I deported the survivors and settled them in Samaria." The resettlement of the Arab tribes was possible only after the military campaign in the seventh year of Sargon (715/14). Accordingly, the resettlement of new ethnic elements involved a considerable span of time.

This huge melting-pot policy also had its religious overtones. The new settlers brought their native gods with them (2 K 17, 29-33). The countryside, devastated by long wars and now only thinly populated, was reclaimed by wild animals. Particularly it was the lions who formed an immediate peril. In order to remedy the plague, no attempt was made to examine the natural causes; the fault must lie in the fact that the new arrivals did not recognize the God of the country, and could not show him proper reverence. By royal grant, one of the expatriated Israelite priests

---

16. W. F. Albright, *An Ostracon from Calah and the Northern-Israelite Diaspora*, BASOR 149 (1958), 33-36.

17. ANET 286a (120-125).

was allowed to return home. Significantly, he settled in Bethel, the center of the Yahweh-bull cult and "taught them how they should fear the Lord" (2 K 17, 25-28). This, however, could hardly have produced any far-reaching changes in the basic philosophies of the pagan population. They continued to venerate their ancient gods, adding the name of Yahweh only because he seemed to have authority in their new locale. But still the stage was set for a monotheistic permeation of this newly forming population of Samaria. In the further development of its history, Yahweh proved himself stronger than all the pagan gods.

5) HEZEKIAH'S RELIGIOUS REFORMS IN JERUSALEM

According to the judgment of 2 Kings 18, 3 and 2 Chronicles 29, 2, Hezekiah closely approached the ideal of his father David; this he accomplished primarily by reforming the cult, just as David had done, and taking a stand against the inroads of the Canaanite and Assyrian paganism, for which Ahaz had opened wide the door. It is impossible to determine the year in which this reform was initiated.[18] The external impulse was apparently given by the destruction of the Northern Kingdom. Even though a great part of the population remained cold to the religious dimensions of the tragedy, the deeper thinkers were thoroughly shaken. The events of history appear to be indifferent, in themselves. The prophet Isaiah, however, stood boldly at the pivotal juncture of his era and proclaimed that the decline of Israel was not a political event but a religious one. Its most fundamental cause lay in the breach of the covenant. If Jerusalem and Judah were to escape a like fate, they could do so only by a renewal of the covenant. We are certainly not wrong in seeing Isaiah as the spiritual author of the reform movement, although his name is not expressly mentioned in connection with the cult reform.

Under Ahaz, the Yahweh cult in the Temple seemed to have come to a complete collapse. The Temple was closed, the perpetual light extinguished, the incense offerings and holocausts discon-

---

18. The dating of 2 Ch 29, 3, "In the first year," is not certain on the basis of textual criticism. LXX has the general statement: "When he was in command."

tinued (2 Ch 29, 7). Then, one day, King Hezekiah, now fully grown, summoned the priests and ordered them to reopen the cult. First of all the Temple had to be purified from its desecration. All the instruments of pagan cult were carried to the Kidron Valley and burned (2 Ch 29, 16); even the brazen serpent of Moses was destroyed, because it had become the object of a pagan cult (2 K 18, 4). Then the priests offered three-fold sacrifice, to purify the royal house, the house of God, and the people of Judah. After these purificatory rites, the official cult could be resumed in all its ancient solemnity. The number of sacrifices offered is overwhelming. The service of the priests and Levites at the Temple, as well as their revenues, were regulated by new legislation (2 Ch 31, 2-19).

After the reforms had been accomplished in the capital city, they spread throughout the country. The sacred high places were destroyed (2 K 18, 4), and the covenant with Yahweh was renewed. Since the Northern Kingdom had lost its political autonomy, Hezekiah attempted to salvage what he could of its religious destiny. By sheer necessity, Jerusalem had become the only hope of the surviving remnant. The idea of a religious union with the remnant-Israel was certainly not without its political overtones, since David's descendant must obviously recognize his position as legitimate authority for the northern tribes who had fallen under foreign control. The king decided to celebrate the Pesach in a most extraordinary manner. It was not to be celebrated, as formerly, by the individual families in their villages and cities, but by the entire people united in Jerusalem.[19] The royal messengers hastened with Hezekiah's Easter letter throughout the country, from Dan to Beersheba (2 Ch 30, 5). They went from city to city, through the territory of the tribes of Ephraim and Manasseh, as far as Zebulon (2 Ch 30, 10). Although they were laughed to scorn and mocked, there were still a goodly number of sober-minded people who heeded the call of the king and came to Jerusalem for the Easter festival. In order to conciliate the separated brethren, Hezekiah had set the date for Easter

---

19. M. Rehm, EB II (1956), 392.

according to the Israelite calendar rather than the Judaic observance. This follows from the note in 2 Chronicles 30, 2, according to which the king, after due consultation with "his princes and all the assembly in Jerusalem," had deferred the celebration of the Pesach until the second Judaic month, which corresponded to the first month in Israel.[20] The throngs were so huge that the seven days of the Easter festival were not sufficient to accommodate all the sacrifices required, and seven more days had to be added. This Easter festival in Jerusalem, together with the renewal of the covenant with Yahweh, forms a strong counterpoint to the destruction of Samaria, the capital of the Northern Kingdom, whose destruction was owing precisely to its breach of the Yahweh covenant.

D) THE BROKEN REED EGYPT

Sargon could indeed point with pride to the subjugation of the western countries and the conquest of Samaria for the year 720, but in Babylonia he was denied success. Here the Aramaean princes, still loyal to Tiglath-Pilesar III, were certainly not inclined to accept Sargon's illegal accession to power as a *fait accompli*. The most powerful among them, Marduk-apal-iddina (Merodach-Baladan) from Bit Yakini, had immediately occupied the throne in Babylon and won the support of Elam who was once again beginning to stir. When Sargon directed his military power against him, he was beaten back. Merodach-Baladan managed to maintain his control over Babylonia for ten years [1] (720-710). Quite understandably, he did everything in his power to undermine Assyria's power. Throughout this decade, Babylon becomes the center of the anti-Assyrian policy. Even Jerusalem was drawn into this diplomatic tug-of-war. At the same time, Egypt too came under the control of a new "hard master" (Is 19, 4).

1. THE HARD MASTER OF EGYPT

Sargon was faced with a second threat on the part of Egypt which

---

20. S. Talmon, *Divergences in Calendar-Reckoning in Ephraim and Judah*, VT 8 (1958), 48-74.

---

1. Schmökel, GAV 268.

had recovered its strength.[2] At the beginning of the divided kingdom of Israel-Judah, Pharaoh Shishak had exercised considerable influence in the fate of Palestine. Despite its overwhelming success, his invasion of Palestine, which was more or less a marauding expedition, had no real after-affects. It was only the flaming sign of the rise of the new dynasty of Libyans. The rule of the so-called 22nd dynasty was contemporary with the split kingdoms of Israel and Judah. The influence of Egyptian politics, however, is visible only at the beginning and at the end of the divided kingdoms. Why is there no sign of it in the interval between? The answer is connected with the Libyan interpretation of their power. Earlier, during the migrations of the sea peoples, the Libyans had pounded on the gates of Egypt,[3] but had been turned away by military force. What they could not accomplish by their armies, they achieved in a peaceful way. From Libya as a center, they made their way into the kingdom of the Pharaohs. Libyan warriors were highly sought after. The Pharaoh rewarded their military service with gifts of land and garrison quarters. Gradually, Libyan military colonies began to rise throughout the country. At the head of these individual settlements stood the "great chieftain of Ma."[4] At a favorable moment, Shishak, "the great chieftain of Ma," operating from Heracleopolis, seized the rule for himself around 950 and thus founded the dynasty of the Libyans.

The knowledge of this period of history is very sketchy, since hardly any inscriptions have been preserved. This could hardly be an accident; it is much rather proof of the fact that the Libyan Pharaohs were not in a position to undertake any great community projects, since they lacked the solidarity of power. They had changed little in the internal structure of the kingdom. About forty percent of the arable land had remained in the possession of the great temples. When Shishak established his son as high priest in the temple of Amon at Thebes, this was equivalent to a divided kingdom. The Thebaid formed a church and temple state all its own. In the other districts of the empire, the Pharaoh was only *primus inter pares,* first among his peers. Towards the end of this period two dynasties are officially counted (22, 23); actually the kingdom had dissolved into its various administrative districts, and energetic local administrators had begun to claim the title of king. Around 730 four such kings could be counted: Osorkon IV of Bubastis, Inpur of Tentremon, Pephnephdubast of Heracleopolis, and Nemrod of Hermopolis. We must also count Tephnach, prince of Sais, who succeeded in stirring up

2. Cf. the corresponding section in A. Scharff, *Geschichte Ägyptens, die Athiopenzeit,* 175-180. — N. Drioton-J. Vandier, *Les peuples de l'Orient Méditerranéen,* II, *L'Égypte,* (1952[3]), 522-555.
3. In Egyptian texts the form is *Msws, Meswes,* or *Masawas.* Apparently they belong to the Berber peoples.
4. *Ma* is an abbreviation for *Masawas.*

considerable agitation.[5] This is the picture of Egypt as mirrored in the Greek historian Herodotus: it was a land whose character had been set by the caste-system. Military service was hereditary among the Libyan families; the control of the temples was equally inviolable, and formed the various castes of priests. Kingship and priesthood appeared to guarantee the permanence of this situation. But they were both seriously hampered by a basic incompetence.[6]

The impulse for a restructuing of Egyptian politics proceeded from two quite opposite poles: first, Tephnach (730-720), the "prince of the northern district" (district five) with its capital at Sais on the Nile Delta, thus, the extreme north of the kingdom; second, the no less energetic Kashta, king of the country of Cush in the extreme south. Tephnach immediately won the recognition of the princes in the Nile delta; he then took the ancient capital of Memphis. Thus, just as in olden times, Lower Egypt was once again united under his hand. But Tephnach was not content: he was seized with the dream of a united Egypt. Accordingly, he made his way against Middle Egypt. The king of Hermopolis capitulated, while the king of Heracleopolis offered resistance. These exploits had an alarming effect upon the Theban priesthood, who now deliberately awakened the sleeping lion of Cush.

Cush, or Nubia,[7] had, since the beginning of the New Kingdom, formed the southern buffer state for Egypt, and had been administrated by a "prince of Cush." Around the year 1,000, when the power of the Pharaohs had sunk to its lowest point, this prince made himself autonomous and established the tiny kingdom of Cush, with its capital at Napata in the vicinity of the fourth cataract. Although it was politically independent, it was under considerable religious influence from the Amon cult at Thebes. Huge temples were erected on Mount Barkal in honor of the Theban god Amon. The real occasion for the entrance of Cush into the politics of Egypt is beyond our present knowledge. At all events, King Kashta of Cush invaded Upper Egypt, apparently in an effort to control the great treasures of the Amun temple. These treasures were under the control of a high priestess, the so-called "divine wife of Amun." The Cushite arranged for the adoption of the then divine wife as his daughter and successor to his throne. By this means, the treasures of the temple made their way indirectly into his possession. His residence remained the city of Napata, and not Thebes. He seems, accordingly, not to have been too strongly involved in Egyptian affairs, but rather to have been content with a sort of suzerainty.

---

5. Drioton, l.c. 526-527.
6. *Ibid.*, 539.
7. The Greeks called it Ethiopia. (It has nothing to do with modern Ethiopia-Abyssinia). The Cushite dynasty has also been called the Ethiopian dynasty.

More precise knowledge about the kingdom of Cush is available only for the time since the reign of King Pianchi [8] (751-716) who recorded his military exploits on a huge stone pillar in the temple of Amun at Napata as an impressive, in fact stunning testimony to posterity.[9] In the 21st year of his reign occurs the famous confrontation with Egypt. The occasion for the attack was presented by the victorious campaign of Tephnach against Thebes. Pianchi at first sent only his general with a small detachment. He was successful in a first battle along the Nile. The enemy ships were destroyed. Many captives remained in his hands. Thereupon the Cushite army marched downstream along the Nile. In the district of Heracleopolis, on the left bank of the *bahr Yussuf,* the decisive battle was fought on land, a second defeat for the Egyptians. Instead of pursuing his retreating enemy further, the Cushite army turned around and laid siege to the city of Hermopolis in its rear.

When this news reached Pianchi, he was extremely dissatisfied. The tactics had allowed the retreating enemy time to recoup his strength and gather new forces. Pianchi now undertook the generalship himself. Hermopolis was invested with a huge earthen wall. Special mention is made of the fact that he erected a huge tower from whose heights the archers could direct their arrows straight into the city. In this desperate situation, the besieged general Nemrod sent his wife to the besieging army in front of the city to make arrangements for the surrender. It was owing to her influence that the besieging army showed some measure of mercy to the captive city. Pianchi seems to have been a great lover of horses; when he finally took the city he was most concerned about the horses, who had not enough fodder.[10] After the conquest of Hermopolis, Pianchi continued his campaign further towards the north. Pepachnephdebast of Heracleopolis welcomed him as liberator. Crocodilopolis and Aphroditopolis, however, refused to pay him homage. Pianchi ignored the two cities for the moment and concentrated his attack upon the city of Memphis. His ultimatum, which demanded immediate surrender, was refused. The Egyptian attempt to breakthrough the circle of besieging forces was unsuccessful. All that remained was a total siege, a prospect which offered little promise for the attacker. Memphis, the city of the white walls, had strong fortifications and walls. The open side was protected by the river, which was now at flood depth. The attack was anticipated from every quarter excepting from the river. Tephnach had prepared the city for total defense and had then escaped from the besieged city by night, to enlist a second army. Before he could accomplish this move, however, Memphis had fallen. Pianchi had led the attack from

---

8. *Pi-anchi* "he who is of life, i.e., the living one."

9. Scharff, *Ägypten,* 177.

10. Drioton, *L'Égypte,* 541.

the side exposed to the river. The city, overcome with surprise, was taken and given over to plunder, excepting for the temples which were spared upon the express command of Pianchi.

After the fall of Memphis, the various dynasties were quick to pay homage to the victor. Among them was Osorkon IV, the last Pharaoh of the 23rd dynasty. Tephnach had withdrawn, with what was left of his troops, into the marshy and inaccessible territory of the delta. Completely abandoned, he decided to negotiate with the victor. Pianchi was content with the formal recognition of his suzerainty, and did not demand the surrender of Tephnach's hereditary princeship in Sais.

Pianchi could point with pride to his unheard of success. He had, so to speak, overnight become the master of a giant empire, extending from the 4th cataract of the Nile to the Mediterranean Sea. While he managed to accomplish the construction of a kingdom by his brilliant military tactics, he was unequal to the task of maintaining it. After accepting the homage of the nations, he withdrew, to everyone's surprise, back into the Cushite capital of Napata in the extreme south, abandoning ancient Egypt to her own fate. Tephnach reasserted his power and reduced at least the delta territory as far as Memphis to a state of subjection. His son Bocchoris (720-715) is considered the founder and sole representative of the 24th dynasty; among the Greeks he is considered one of the six great lawgivers.[11]

Bocchoris' accession to power, in the year 720, took place in an extremely agitated era. As we have already seen, that same year saw the rebellion of the western countries, beginning with Hamath as far as the Brook of Egypt, in an attempt to shake off the yoke of Assyria. Assyrian sources testify to the fact that Egypt too was drawn into this battle. Egypt's immediate neighbor, Hanunu of Gaza, was the most active agitator against Assyria. We do not, however, have any accurate knowledge as to which Pharaoh sent the Egyptian banner into the field under the generalship of Sib'e. We cannot exclude the possibility that it was Bocchoris to whom this campaign against Assyria was entrusted. But it might equally well have been true that the Pharaoh of Bubaste or Tanis, perhaps Osorkon IV, sent the relief army. At all events, it was not the ancient, fabled full power of Egypt that was defeated at Rapihu, but only the levies of an Egyptian prince, who was no stronger than any of the petty kings in Palestine-Syria. After the defeat, the Egyptian had to accept the payment of tribute to Assyria. On a badly mutilated Prism inscription [12] Sargon boasts that Silkani, the king of Musri,[13] sent him

---

11. *Ibid.*, 544.

12. ANET 286c.

13. Assyrian texts distinguish clearly between Musri, Egypt proper, and Cush, which occupied Egypt.

twelve fine horses which had no equal throughout the country. It is possible that Silkani is identical with Osorkon IV, the last ruler of the 23rd dynasty.[14]

The change of ruler which took place in 716 in Cush was followed by a mighty change in Egyptian politics. Pianchi's successor, Sabaka (716-701) immediately transferred his residence from remote Napata to Thebes, thereby asserting his claim to sovereignty over Egypt. Just like his father, he too must have subjugated Egypt as far as the delta, in a victorious campaign. There are, however, no reliable accounts. He is supposed to have captured and exiled Bocchoris. This second conquest of Egypt by the Cushites took place in the year 715.[15] Unlike his father Pianchi, Sabaka considered himself as an Egyptian Pharaoh, and is thus generally accepted as the true founder of the Ethiopian dynasty (715-663). He too changed little in the feudal structure of the kingdom, contenting himself with the subjugation of the district princes. In the Assyrian sources we frequently find the double title: "The kings of Musri (Egypt) and the king of Meluhha (Cush)." [16]

The prophet Isaiah viewed the upheaval in Egypt with warm interest. Even though his burden oracles against the nations are difficult to date, it would seem that chs. 19, 1-15 are an echo of the Cushite conquest of Egypt. Egypt is in a state of absolute confusion: Egyptian is fighting against Egyptian, kingdom against kingdom, city against city. "The spirit of the Egyptians within them will be emptied out" (19, 3). The princes of Soan (Tanis) and Memphis, the old cities of the Pharaohs, have been made to stagger (19, 14). The Nile is dried up, the fishermen lament, poverty stalks the land (19, 5-10). "The hard master, the fierce king" (19, 4) who is oppressing Egypt is none other than Sabaka, the Cushite conqueror from the south.[17]

This united kingdom of Egypt and Cush, administered by a powerful hand, now forms the hope of all those who tremble in the face of Assyria's terrible splendor. The ascendancy of the Ethiopian dynasty also changed the course of politics in Jerusalem. "They take refuge in the protection of Pharaoh, and seek shelter in the shadow of Egypt" (30, 2).

---

14. W. F. Albright, BASOR 141 (1956), 23-26.

15. On chronological problems, see Drioton, *L'Égypte*, 572, *Die Regierungszeit der Kuschitenkönige ist noch nicht gesichert.* — W. F. Albright, BASOR 130 (1953), 4-11.

16. ANET 287.

17. Most interpreters take this "strict master" as an Assyrian king like Sargon, Sanherib, or Asarhaddon. As a result, Isaian authorship is called into question. The argument seems to be unfounded, since the chapter can be easily understood in reference to the contemporary history.

2) HEZEKIAH'S FIRST REVOLT (714-711)

2 Kings 20, 1-11 and Isaiah 38, 1-22 tell the story of Hezekiah's critical illness and its miraculous cure. The prophet Isaiah, speaking in the name of Yahweh, could assure the king fifteen more years of life (2 K 20, 6). Since Hezekiah ruled 29 years, this event must have taken place in the 14th year of his reign, that is, 714. It was precisely in this time that the politics of Jerusalem witnessed a powerful tug-of-war. Since the days of Uzziah, Judah had remained loyal to its anti-Assyrian policy. Now, however, the world situation had changed. Egypt had found a "strong master"; in Babylonia Marduk-apal-iddina (Merodach-Baladan) had succeeded in achieving independence. It certainly seemed that Judah's hour had also come to shake off the Assyrian yoke.

The embassy from Merodach-Baladan (2 K 20, 12-19; Is 39, 1-8) was well disguised as an official visit of state. The ambassadors from Babylonia did not, however, come simply to express their congratulations upon the king's recovery; they were to bring Hezekiah over to the anti-Assyrian camp. When Hezekiah showed them all his treasury, he did so primarily in order to demonstrate his strength as a potential ally in the likely event of a war against Assur. And thus the fall of Assur was accomplished on the plane of diplomacy.

It was not only Babylonian ambassadors who made their way to Jerusalem in these days. Along the coastal plain, Azuri, King of the Philistine city of Ashdod, had undertaken a lively campaign against Assyria. Not only in the Assyrian annals, but also in the royal inscriptions [18] Sargon reproaches him for "having sent ambassadors to the neighboring kings full of enmity towards Ashur." In the Prism inscription [19] these are expressly named as the kings of the Philistine country (*Pi-liš-te*) of Judah (*Ya-u-di*), Edom and Moab. There is further mention of the Pharaoh (*Pir'u*) of Musru (Egypt). "With countless foul lies" they stirred up

---

18. ANET 286.
19. ANET 287.

rebellion against Ashur. When the western countries refused to pay further tribute, Sargon was forced to attack, unless he meant to abandon his interests in the west.

This time the rebellion was full of promise. In the year 714 Sargon was held fast in Urartu. He actually had to reconquer his hereditary kingdom. Babylonia was as good as lost since 720. We have already described the first triumphal campaign against Palestine in the year 720, which ended with the second conquest of Samaria. In Northern Syria, however, the city of Carchemish held out as a final outpost of resistance. King Pisiris sought support from his allies. He spun his web as far as Asia Minor and won the allegiance of Mita (Midas), the fabled king of the Phrygian Muski. The subjugated kingdom of Urartu also joined with him. In the year 717 Sargon forced Carchemish to its knees. The help from Phrygia was not forthcoming. The next blow was directed against Urartu. After a long mountain warfare he succeeded where Tiglath-Pilesar had failed: the capital city of Tushpa on the Van was taken. In desperation, King Rusa took his own life, and countless booty streamed from this highly civilized and well administered state into the coffers of Assyria. Sargon had not only defeated a strong opponent; he had also annihilated the powerful bulwark against the Cimmerians who were pushing towards the south — and in the future course of Assur's history this proved to be a fateful error.[20]

After these successes, Sargon was free to direct his victorious standards against the new focus of unrest in Palestine. The annals date this campaign in the 11th year of Sargon, that is the year 711.[21] Sargon first directed his attention to the turmoil of internal politics in Ashdod. Azuri was deposed and replaced by his brother Ahimiti, who, understandably enough, was forced into a pro-Assyrian policy and the payment of tribute. He was soon opposed by a Greek mercenary captain, who is called simply *Ya-ma-ni,* the Ionian, the Greek, or Yadna, who established himself upon the

---

20. Schmökel, GAV 267.
21. There are three accounts of this campaign: The Annals of Sargon, the great inscription, and Prism A. ANET 286-287.

throne. This was a sign of open rebellion and could only mean war.

The royal inscription [22] creates the impression that Sargon did not command a very large army, but that he had merely sent a division to subdue the city of Ashdod, while *Ya-ma-ni,* hearing of the approach of the Assyrian army, had fled towards Egypt. According to the Prism inscription,[23] however, the expedition was a large-scale undertaking. Sargon boasts that he crossed the Tigris and the Euphrates at flood stage, as if they were a paved road. The approach of the Assyrian army spread such terror that all resistance collapsed. The allies preferred to continue paying tribute, rather than to resist. The Prism inscription lists the following tributaries: the kings of Philistia, Judah, Edom, and Moab. The royal inscription also shows that the king of Cush entered into diplomatic relations with Sargon: "He sent ambassadors to treat of peace." Actually, he was forced to bow before the pressure of Assyia and deliver Ya-ma-ni who had fled to Egypt. Sargon could boast of a mighty success. From Armenia as far as Egypt, all the country was trembling before the terrible splendor of Ashur. On an inscription found in Nimrud [24] Sargon proudly refers to himself as "subjugator of the land of Judah" (*mu-šak-miš mat Ya-u-du*). Let us now look to the Biblical sources for some indication of this decisive event in Judah's history.

One obvious source is Isaiah 20, which clearly refers to the campaign against Ashdod. The prophet's symbolic actions, on this occasion, are more powerful than any verbal message. His people had set all their hope upon the help of the newly awakened kingdom of Egypt. But this hope proved to be illusory. For three years Isaiah went "naked and barefoot," clad only in a leather girdle, "as a sign and portent against Egypt and Cush." Sargon, king of Ashur, will lead the captives of Egypt off to Ashur in precisely the same condition, "barefoot and naked." The military

---

22. ANET 286 (90-112).
23. ANET 287 (8).
24. *Ibid.*

penetration of the Cushite general Sabaka was definitely checked by the terrible splendor of Ashur. All who hoped in him were confounded.

The evidence from the Assyrian sources, according to which Judah paid tribute to Sargon, is confirmed in 2 Kings 18, 13-16. On the occasion of Sargon's approach, Hezekiah sent messengers into the Assyrian camp with this message: "I have done wrong; withdraw from me; whatever you impose on me I will bear." Thereupon the "king of Assyria," that is, Sargon,[25] demanded 300 talents of silver and 30 talents of gold. In order to raise this sum, the gold had to be stripped from the very doors of the temple. Sargon could in very truth refer to himself as "conqueror of Judah." There is no other historical event which could possibly justify this title. Accordingly, Hezekiah's first rebellion, which began in the 14th year of his reign, came to a sorry end after only three years. These are the three years in which the prophet Isaiah went about barefoot and naked. Hezekiah's first rebellion can be dated, accordingly, from 714-711.

3) ORACLES AGAINST THE NATIONS (Is 13-23)

Isaiah took a position not only against the politics of Judah; he incorporated the whole of contemporary history into his proph-

---

25. Chronology: There is a thorough investigation of the account of two revolts of Hezekiah (711 & 701) in my article, "Textkritische Bemerkungen zu den Synchronismen der Könige von Israel und Judah," VT 12 (1962), 88-119; Bright, HistIsr 282-287 devotes a whole chapter to the problem. The crux of the problem is whether 2 K 18, 13-19, 37 (parallel to Is 36ff.) describes one or two campaigns. On the basis of the Egyptian chronology, Albright (BASOR 1952, 163) decides for two campaigns in the years 701 and 688. In our dating, a second campaign in the year 688 is quite impossible since Hezekiah died already in 698. There are two campaigns but they fall in the years 711 and 701. The account of the first is to be found in 2 K 18, 13-16 (Sargon's campaign against the western countries). This section was not taken over by the editor of Isaiah, because he probably still knew that it was describing a different campaign. When the two accounts were fused into one (Sargon and Sanherib) in the Book of Kings, the names Sanherib and Lachish worked their way into the first account, and must thus be eliminated.

etic preaching. The contemporary Assyrian sources form the best commentary for his "burden oracles." The very nations which had been bowed under the terrible splendor of Assyria are now, under Isaiah, forced to bow to the burden of Yahweh's judgment. This is the prophet's clear argument that it is not the triumphant god of Ashur who makes history, but the one true God Yahweh in Zion.

Sargon humiliated the Phoenician cities of Tyre and Sidon, subjugated Philistia, Edom, and Moab, and was the first Assyrian ruler to bend the Arab tribes to his will.[26] All these political events have found their monument in the partially poetic "burden oracles" of chs. 13-23. These oracles are named from the word *massā*, by which they are all introduced. The term is also translated as "threat oracle," but its original meaning is closer to the concept of "burden." The word of the prophet is at the same time the proclamation of judgment. The sentence is passed upon individuals and nations as "the burden of God's judgment." For example, the burden oracles against Baal (13, 1), Moab (15, 1), Damascus (17, 1), Egypt (19, 1), Edom (21, 11), Arabia (21, 13), Jerusalem (22, 1), Tyre and Sidon (23, 1). Whether all these oracles are the work of Isaiah himself is a matter of some dispute.[27] It is primarily the oracles against Babel (ch. 13; 14 and 21) which are ascribed to a different author. It is, however, very strange that the name of Babel should be missing from the ranks of burden oracles against the foreign nations, since Babel had played such a decisive role, under King Merodach-Baladan, in the campaign against Assyria. The cry: "Fallen, fallen is Babel" (21, 9) twice sounded in the days of Isaiah. Surely the collapse of Merodach-Baladan in the years 709 and 703, especially since Jerusalem had rested such great hopes upon him, must have awakened a powerful echo. Isaiah was, *a priori*, opposed to a covenant with Babel. This accounts for the song of mockery (*māšal*) directed against the King of Babel (14, 4-21), which belongs to the most magnificent creations of Hebrew poetry.[28] This is not the work of some un-

---

26. DBS IV, 661 accordingly includes the oracles against Moab, Edom, and the Arabs in the war-filled era around the year 715.

27. Cf. Eissfeldt, EinlAT 375ff.

28. *Ibid.*, 385.

known poet; it must be ascribed to the prophetic and poetic genius of the great Isaiah himself.[29] "How are you fallen from heaven, O Day Star, son of Dawn!" [30] (14, 12) Even the shades in hell (šᵉol) stretched out when he was cast forth into their midst, and a bed was prepared for him on maggots and worms.

After his defeat, Merodach-Baladan fled towards Elam. The small Aramaean principalities in southern Babylon were quickly overcome by Sargon. Mass resettlements of the population were designed to guarantee the impossibility of any future rise to power. Sargon did not refer to himself as "King of Babel," but took only the modest title "administrator of Babel." He regarded himself as the liberator from the foreign hegemony of the Aramaeans, venerated the gods — an expression of this policy is to be found in the triad of divinities, frequently mentioned from this time forward, Ashur, Nebo, and Marduk — and attempted to win the sympathies of the Babylonian population in every conceivable manner.[31]

After the liberation of the four corners of the earth, Sargon officially marked the beginning of the new world era by the construction of a new world capital. He abandoned Nineveh and built a new city some ten miles up the Tigris, "Near the sources at the foot of the mountains of Musri," calling the new capital Sargon City (Dur Sharukin) after his own name.[32] The present heap of ruins still testifies to the immense proportions of this enterprise. In the ninth year of his reign (713) he acquired the territory of Magganubba. Sixteen years of building activity produced the new residence in almost geometric dimensions. The city plan is practically a square (some 11,000 x 10,000 ft.). The city wall, 77 ft. thick, was provided with 156 towers. The palace was erected in

---

29. *EncMikr* III, 917: Since Babel was conquered several times, it is quite possible that the ancient Isaian song was given a new interpretation and transformed in keeping with the new circumstances and thus eventually turned into a sort of allegory of all tyrants hostile to God.

30. In the Vulgate it is translated as *lucifer*, "light-bearer." In Tradition it has been typically interpreted with reference to the fall of Satan. Originally it is a clear reference to the goddess Istar, who bore the epithet "the shining one" (Hebr. *helel*, Accadian: *ellu, ellitu*), i.e., the morning and evening star. P. Grelot, VT 6 (1956), 303.

31. Schmökel, GAV 268.

32. RLA II, 249-252.

the northern corner, upon a terrace some 16 ft. in height. It was a complex of rooms grouped about two large and several smaller courtyards. Beside the temple arose the step-tower, with its temples. The external façade of the palace was adorned with bull colossi in stone, while the interior walls were covered with relief work. The pictures, in rich abundance, describe the military and private life of the king. Brief inscriptions cast some light upon the events portrayed. On the surfaces, containing two friezes, there is a middle panel filled with annal-type inscriptions, which are among the most important historical sources of this era.[33]

Sargon had no time left to enjoy this new magnificence. On a military campaign far from his fatherland — where and in battle against whom we can no longer determine — he finally fell. His death severely shook the kingdom he had built up with sword and blood from the island of Cyprus in the Mediterranean to the island of Tilmun in the Persian Gulf, from the borders of Egypt to the Caucasus, from Cilicia as far as Media.

4) HEZEKIAH'S SECOND REBELLION (704-701)

Just like ten years before, upon the death of Sargon in the year 705, the entire anti-Assyrian coalition revolted to a man. Merodach-Baladan, whom Sargon had driven from Babel, now succeeded in reestablishing his claim to the throne for a brief period. It is more than likely that, on this occasion too, anti-Assyrian emissaries from Babel made their way into the friendly courts. In Palestine it was Hezekiah himself who this time assumed leadership

---

33. On the eve of the military revolt in Mossul, Dec. 19, 1958, I was still able to visit the ruins at Chorsabad. The Tigris bridge in Mossul had already been occupied by the military, and the main streets out of the city looked like a camp. Only with a special travel pass, issued from the city commissariate, was I able to leave Mossul for Chorsabad, where I could sit quietly and commune with antiquity among the ruins and excavations. The mountains of Kurdistan shone a vivid redbrown on the horizon. The city of Sargon had once been surrounded on all sides by a fertile plain. This time I saw an Iraqi peasant, working with a primitive pointed plow. It was drawn by an ass and a camel working in peaceful harmony, and he was tearing up the earth more than he was plowing it. A picture of unforgettable melancholy at the foot of the pride and glory of Sargon's citadel!

of the rebellion. In order to protect his rear, he sent secret messengers "to a people feared near and far, the nation mighty and conquering, whose land the rivers divide" (Is 18, 2), that is, to Egypt, to the courts of Hanes and So'an [34] (30, 4). He meant to win not only the Cushite suzerains, but also the princes of ancient Egypt to his cause.

Isaiah took a forceful position against this policy. Once again he had recourse to symbolic activity. He took a tablet and ceremoniously wrote these words: "*rahab hāmāh wešābat* — the monster, it roars and — lies idle" [35] (30, 7-8). The great sea monster Rahab, which has been compared to Egypt, does indeed make a most ferocious roar; in reality, however, it is only a sluggish crocodile, which growls and then simply lies motionless. What the prophet meant is that no help would be forthcoming from Egypt. Just as in the Syro-Ephraimite war, once again Isaiah represents a policy of confident calm. "In returning and rest you shall be saved; in quietness and in trust shall be your strength" (30, 15). Once again, however, the state policy was not his to determine.

Hezekiah embarked upon a feverish preparation for the inevitable confrontation with Ashur. First of all, Jerusalem must be made capable of withstanding a siege. His first move was to strengthen the existing fortifications: "He set to work resolutely [36] and built up all the wall that was broken down, and raised towers upon it, and outside it he built another wall; and he strengthened the Millo in the city of David. He also made weapons and shields in abundance. And he set combat commanders over the people" (2 Ch 32, 5-6). Hezekiah did not rest with restoring and strengthening the existing works; since the city had grown too big for its former walls, he also began surrounding the "new city" (*mišneh*) with a protective wall.[37] This work was completed

---

34. Ḥanes like Heracleopolis, which has already been mentioned as a royal city. Cf. above, 245ff.
35. According to the translation of M. Buber, *Bücher der Kündung,* 94.
36. *yithazzaq,* "he showed himself strong," a word play with the name *hizqi-yahu.*
37. Simons, *Jerusalem in the OT Times,* 156, 291f., 332f.

only under his successor Manasseh, since Hezekiah himself was overcome by the Assyrian peril. In the event of siege, the most important factor and the chief necessity for life was the water supply. In order to secure this vital provision, Hezekiah undertook what was for his time and circumstances a truly stupendous project. The abundant stream of the waters of Gihon in the Kidron Valley lay outside the city walls. Hezekiah had a tunnel carried through the city hill called Ophel, and thus brought the water into the walled section of the city. The outside entrance to this spring was filled with rubble (2 K 20, 20; 2 Ch 32, 3, 30). The tunnel, over 1700 ft. in length, is further remarkable for the fact that it runs not in a straight line but in an S-curve. This fact has been explained by various conjectures. It can hardly be explained by lack of technical expertise. It is possible that the engineers chose this route as a detour to avoid violating the royal burial sites. The excavation was begun from both sides of the mountain at the same time. At the point where the workers met in the middle there was an inscription carved into the rock wall, one of the oldest monuments of the Hebrew language.[38] Hezekiah's preparations for war were not confined to the city itself. Although it is not specifically recorded, the other Judaean fortresses must also have been put into a state of military preparedness.

In this great chain of anti-Assyrian coalition stretching from the Phoenician coast all the way to Egypt, there was one missing link: Padi, the King of Ekron, would have no part of the alliance. This prompted Hezekiah to undertake a summary expedition into the country of the Philistines (2 K 18, 8), a move which is also recorded in the annals of Sanherib: [39] "The officials, the patricians,

---

38. Hebrew text in Galling, TGI 59; Translation in ANET 321. The inscription was discovered in 1880, when the completely buried tunnel was excavated. The piece of stone containing the inscription was cut out and taken to the museum at Stamboul, since Palestine then belonged to the Turkish Empire. Despite highly placed recommendations I was unable to see the inscription at Stamboul in November of 1958, since the section of the museum which houses it was closed for repairs. I made my way through the tunnel in July of 1951, on my knees in some places.

39. ANET 287; TGI 57.

and the people of Ekron — who had thrown Padi, their king, into fetters because he was loyal to his solemn oath by the God Ashur and handed him over to Hezekiah the Jew (*Ha-za-ki-au amel Ya-u-da-ai*) —and he held him in prison unlawfully — had become afraid and had called for help." With the elimination of King Padi, the unified front against Ashur was completed. The resistance had every prospect of success. On Hezekiah's side he could count not only the Phoenician and Philistine cities, Edom, Moab, and Ammon, but also the newly risen kingdom of the Ethiopians in Egypt.[40]

When Sanherib (*Sin-ahhe-riba*) ascended the Assyrian throne on the 12th of the month Abu [41] (705-681), he had to reconquer his kingdom, just as his predecessors had done. His first years were occupied by the unsettled conditions in Babylon. He had neglected — most likely out of deliberate contempt towards Babel — to "seize the hands of Marduk" during the new year festival, and thereby claim symbolic and actual rule in Babel. Since the Babylonian throne was thus officially unoccupied, Marduk-zakir-šumi (703), "son of a slave," seized the sovereignty. He was quickly put down by the old Assyrian enemy Merodach-Baladan (703). Sanherib now had recourse to armed intervention. He defeated the Elamite auxiliaries, conquered the city Kuta and finally Babel, whose inhabitants were repopulated into Israel, banished Merodak-Baladan [42] for a second time, and raised the pro-Assyrian Belibni (702-700) to the throne of Babel. The Babylonian question was thus temporarily solved.[43] Sanherib was now free to turn to the west.

In the year 701 he attacked the "land of Hatti," the Assyrian name for the western countries. He followed the ancient campaign routes along the Phoenician coast towards the south.[44] His first

---

40. *Ibid.*
41. Eponym canon, RLA II 435.
42. In order to completely obliterate his memory (*deletio memoriae*), the victor went so far as to remove Merodak's name in the corner-stones and replace it with his own. R. Follet, *Une nouvelle inscription de Merodak-Baladan,* Bibl 35 (1954), 413-28.
43. Schmökel, GAV 272.
44. There is an explicit account of the Palestinian campaign of Sanherib

move was to break the resistance of the Phoenician coastal
cities. At the news of his approach, Luli, King of Sidon, fled across
the sea to Cyprus, where he died. In his place, Sanherib installed
Tuba'alu as king. The other Phoenician cities, beginning with
Arvad in the north and extending to Acco in the south, bowed
before the terrible splendor of Assur and paid their tribute.
Obstinate resistance was encountered only in the land of the
Philistines. "Since these cities did not quickly enough cast themselves before my feet, I laid siege to them and overcame them and
bore off their spoil." [45] Sanherib seems to have located his first
principal camp in the vicinity of Joppa. From this stronghold he
overran the neighboring cities of Bene-Barqa, Beth-Dagon, and
Azuru. One expeditionary force ravaged the coastland as far
as Ashkelon. Since King Sidqia would not bow to the Assyrian
yoke, he was besieged. After the capture of the city, Sidqia, together with his wife, his sons, his daughters, and his gods, was
carried captive into Assyria, while Sarru-Ludari was installed as
king in his place. The city of Ashkelon was quick to bow before
the yoke of Assur.[46]

Meantime the Egyptian relief troops under "Tirhakah" [47]
were rapidly approaching (2 K 19, 9). The confrontation took
place in the vicinity of Eltekeh (*Al-ta-ku-u*).[48] "The king of the
land of Musri, the archers, chariots, and horse of the king of the

---

on the so-called Taylor Prism. Text: ANET 287; DOT 66; TGI 56;
an outline of the campaign in B. Mazar, *EncMikr* I, 727. The sequence
of events taken from this source.

---

45. TGI 56, line 67.
46. *Ibid.*, 58-64.
47. In 701 Tirhakah was not yet king. He reigned probably from 689-
663. Either the name Tirhahak was added later as a gloss to the
indefinite expression "King of Cush," or it was actually Tirhakah, as
crown prince, who commanded the campaign. Macadam, however,
has argued that Tirhakah was not born until 708 and thus could
not possibly have led a campaign in 701. This position is not so well
founded as it might at first appear. There is a thorough treatment
of the chronological problems involved in Drioton-Vandier, *L'Égypte*,
548, note 1. — W. F. Albright, BASOR 130 (1953), 4-11.
48. The position of Eltekeh is contested. GTT #336.

land of Meluhha (Cush), armed forces without number allied themselves and came to his help . . . . Placing my trust upon Ashur, my master, I fought with them and dealt them a severe defeat. The leader of the chariots and the sons of the king of the land of Musri, together with the leader of the chariots of the king of Meluhha I took prisoner." [49]

After thus warding off the Egyptian attack, Sanherib was free to devote his full attention to the conquest of Judah. The city of Ekron was the first to feel his wrath. Hezekiah had conquered the city and carried off its king, Padi, in chains to Jerusalem. After the conquest of Ekron, Sanherib dealt most severely with the pro-Judah factions. He had them put to death and hanged on pikes all around the city. Padi, whose release from Jerusalem he was able to force, was once again installed as king in Ekron.

After these successes, it was time for the general attack upon Judah. In his inscriptions, Sanherib claims to have conquered 46 cities of Hezekiah.[50] This action involved the entire Assyrian military machinery. This is most likely the subject represented on the reliefs in the royal palace at Nineveh, which represent the battle at Lachish in a series of tableaux.[51] He further claims that he captured 200,150 people, young and old, woman and child, horses, mules, and asses, cattle and flocks beyond number, and counted them as his booty from the conquered cities.[52] The number is almost certainly placed too high,[53] but whatever the actual figure, it is clear indication of the absolute catastrophe which befell the kingdom of Judah. The Prism inscription makes specific reference neither to Lachish nor Libnah. The siege of both cities is, however, recorded in 2 Kings 18, 17 and 19, 8.

While Sanherib was still besieging Lachish, he sent a detachment against Jerusalem to force the surrender of the city. The importance he assigned to this undertaking can be assessed by the fact that he insisted upon sending his most highly placed offi-

---

49. TGI 57, lines 74-82.
50. *Ibid.*, 13.
51. Lakišrelief, ANET Nr. 371-374.
52. Galling, TGI 58.
53. *Ibid.*, note b, probably only 2150.

cial, the Tartan, the Rab-saris and the Rab-saqeh. According to the Vulgate interpretation it would appear that these are personal names;[54] actually, however, they are the titles of highly placed court officials. Sanherib sent his "commander in chief in the field, his chief steward, and his cupbearer" [55] to Jerusalem — men who were in a position to follow up his demands with appropriate force. The story of the official confrontation before the walls of Jerusalem (2 K 18, 17-9, 7) is unparalleled for its vivacity and its clearness and minuteness of detail. The Assyrian messengers had taken their place by the conduit of the upper pool, on the highway to the Fuller's Field. They shouted up to the city walls, demanding that the king send a representative to treat with them. Hezekiah, on his side, dispatched a committee of three: Eliakim ('al-hab-bayit) who was (over the household), the "secretary of state" (sôphēr) Shebnah, and the "recorder" (mazkîr) Joah.[56] The Assyrians proclaimed their message to the city walls in Hebrew, so that everyone could understand. This policy was obviously dictated by motives of propaganda. The interpretation of this use of the Hebrew language as stemming from religious motives— the gods of the other peoples had not been able to withstand the power of Assur, and how could Yahweh succeed — is not simply a later, pious embellishment of the narrative, especially since even the Assyrian military records are often composed as preliminary reports to the god Assur.[57] This long propagandizing

---

54. Vulgate translation: "Misit autem rex Assyriorum Thartan et Rab-saris et Rabsacen."

55. *Tartan*, literally "the second," hence representative; generally used in a military sense, "commander-in-chief, captain," but also used to mean "crown prince." H. Cazelles, VT 8 (1958), 103-106. — *Rab-saris* is a loan word that has made its way into the Hebrew. *Saris* develops from *ša-reši* (*šarru*), "he who stands at the head (of the king)," the man charged with ceremonial functions at court. One of his primary charges was the king's harem. Thus the name is also used for eunuch. *Rab-saris* is thus equivalent to "chief court steward." *Rab-šaqeh*, either from *šaqu*, Pl. *šaqe*, "chief," or from *šaqu* Pl. *šaqe*, from the root "to drink," and thus "chief steward."

56. On the court officials cf. Vol. III, p. 222 and also R. de Vaux, *Les institutions de l'AT* I, 199-203.

57. Schmökel, GAV 266.

speech was followed by absolute silence from the city walls. The king had demanded: "Do not answer him" (2 K 18, 36).

When Hezekiah heard the message he rent his clothing, covered himself with sackcloth, and went into the temple. He sent his three ambassadors, also clad in sackcloth, to see the Prophet Isaiah (2 K 19, 1ff.). In this terrible hour, when Yahweh was being openly blasphemed, who could better prophesy the fate of the threatened city than the prophet of Yahweh! In purely human terms, Isaiah must have derived some satisfaction from the fact that, in this hour of peril, the king was forced to turn to him; it was Isaiah, after all, who, from the very beginning, had been opposed to the treaty and the rebellion. In this decisive moment, however, he did not advise submission; as the mouthpiece of Yahweh, he was actually in a position to prophesy the liberation of the city and the annihilation of the Assyrian army. This he could proclaim only in his absolute faith in the unicity and living power of Yahweh. The gods of the other cities were dead and non-existent and thus they could perish. But the god of Israel is a living God, before whom even the triumphant Assur must eventually bow.

The embassy had been dismissed and returned to the Assyrian camp. Meantime Lachish had fallen.[58] Sanherib stood before the gates of Libnah (2 K 19, 8). From this point he sent a second embassy to Jerusalem, repeating his demand for the surrender of the city, this time in written form.[59] This time, too, Isaiah displayed his faith in the invincibility of Yahweh, "The Holy One of Israel" (19, 22). Jerusalem would not bow. The prophet made bold to proclaim that not a single Assyrian arrow would find its way into the holy city. It is rather Yahweh who

---

58. The excavations still attest to the dimensions of the destruction. One such discovery was a mass grave with 1500 skeletons piled in all directions. G. E. Wright, *Judaean Lachish*, BA 18 (1955), 9-17. D. Diringer, *Sennacherib's Attack on Lachish. New Epigraphical Evidence*, VT 1 (1951), 134-36.

59. R. de Vaux, JerB, *Rois* argues that the narrative in 19, 9b-35 is not a literary doublet to 18, 17-19a, on the basis of both narratives being similarly constructed. The evidence presented there seems unconvincing.

will "put a hook into the nose" of the proud conqueror and drive him back on the road along which he had advanced (19, 28).

Sanherib does indeed claim, in his annals,[60] that he laid siege to Jerusalem: "The king himself, like a bird in his cage, I shut up within his royal city Jerusalem. I cast up bulwarks around the city walls and those who dared to set foot beyond her gates I punished for their presumption." But this is not the true course of events. The text is a masterpiece of concealing the facts. He did indeed shut up Hezekiah like a bird in a cage, within his city of Jerusalem; that is, he completely isolated him within his capital. The text does not, however, necessarily imply a siege of Jerusalem. The fact that Sanherib "heaped up fortifications against him," [61] can refer to the 46 besieged cities of Judah instead of Jerusalem itself. The text in the annals is, accordingly, not sufficient evidence to prove that Jerusalem was actually besieged; the text would appear to indicate such a siege, but this is not actually the fact. Sanherib's fate caught him up short. We read in 2 Kings 19, 36: "And that night the angel of the Lord went forth and slew a hundred and eighty-five thousand in the camp of the Assyrians; and when the men arose early in the morning, behold, these were all dead bodies. Then Sennacherib king of Assyria departed, and went home, and dwelt at Nineveh." What we have here, at all events, is a religious interpretation of the catastrophe that befell the Assyrians. This story is, understandably enough, passed over in silence by the Assyrian records. Still, the annals do contain one brief sentence: "And annihilation ensued," [62] — a statement that the Assyrian reader would probably understand as a reference to the annihilation of the enemy. There is one legendary echo of this event in the Greek historian Herodotus, who ascribes the destruction of the Assyrian army to a plague caused by rats, recording that all the leather clothing and equipment was completely devoured.[63] Since rats are universally recognized as bearers of the plague, it was probably an outbreak

---

60. TGI 58, lines 20-23.
61. *Ibid.*, 21.
62. *Ibid.*, 33.
63. Drioton-Vandier, *L'Égypte,* 549.

of the pestilence that forced Sanherib to undertake this speedy departure.

He was, nonetheless, able to point to a certain success. The resistance of the western countries had been broken. Even though Jerusalem itself had not been conquered, Judah had been seriously humiliated. The western districts of Judah were entrusted to the pro-Assyrian kings of Ashdod, Ekron, and Gaza. Hezekiah himself was forced to purchase the remnants of freedom he still enjoyed by the regular payment of tribute. His hope in the broken reed of Egypt had proved illusory. The reed was broken and had only pierced the hand of the man who sought to lean upon it.

5) SPIRITUAL RULER AND KINGDOM OF PEACE

It was precisely in this era in which Jerusalem was faced with imminent destruction that Isaiah raised his voice for the last time. Had his activity not been a singular insuccess? Who, after all, had listened to him? At the very beginning of his prophetic activity he had warned against a covenant with Ashur. But Ahaz had only shrugged his shoulders: "I will not bother your God" — and had called the Assyrians into the country. Even in the case of Hezekiah towards whom the Book of Kings and Chronicles exhibit a friendly attitude for his restoration of the official cult, the prophetic word was not destined to fall upon fruitful ground. Despite the warnings against an alliance with Babel and Egypt, Hezekiah twice let himself become embroiled in a rebellion against Ashur and thus brought his entire kingdom to the very brink of destruction. The "rulers of Sodom and people of Gomorrah" (1, 10) were equally disinclined to listen to the unpopular prophet. Seen in purely human terms, Isaiah was bound to turn aside from this people. He did not, however, withdraw into a secluded corner, like a disillusioned and embittered man; just as passionately as in the days of his early vocation he is still fighting, in the days of his old age, "the argument of Yahweh with his people" (1, 18). Yahweh himself is not less passionately interested in the course of events. Precisely because he is the "Holy One of Israel," the threatened catastrophe must not break upon the people who have abandoned his covenant. "The ox knows its owner, and the ass its master's crib;[64] but Israel does not know, my people does not understand" (1, 3).

The economic, military, and political reconstruction accomplished by the always very able Hezekiah thus ended with a total collapse within and without. "And the daughter of Zion is left like a booth in a vineyard, like a lodge in a cucumber field, like a besieged city. If the Lord of Hosts had not left us a few survivors, we should have been like Sodom, and become like Gomorrah" (1, 8). But the prophet's confidence in the one Yahweh is never broken: Yahweh dwells in Zion and has chosen the house of David. This twofold inheritance — faith in the God of Zion and the son of David — is Isaiah's gift, in his final prophecies, to all the generations to come. The boundaries of the long awaited kingdom are, in his prophetic vision, no longer identical with the political boundaries of the states of Israel and Judah, no more identical with the people of Israel as such; the boundary assumes broader and less well defined proportions; the boundary is to be found wherever man makes a decision for or against the Holy One of Israel. Only a remnant shall survive, but it will be the foundation of the future.

a) THE SPIRITUAL RULER (11, 1-5): Faith in the mission of the house of David is one of the pillars upon which Isaiah constructs his preaching. This faith would have been in a position to determine also the political fate of the kingdom. But even in the royal house it would seem that this message was not taken seriously. In open opposition to the general opinion, Isaiah had proclaimed the birth song for the son of the 'almah (7, 14) and later the song that celebrated his accession to the throne (9, 1ff.). His prophecy had always been aroused by a definite historical occurrence.

Even the messianic promises destined to be completely fulfilled only in the distant future must be directed towards the contemporary ruler from the house of David. The distinction between direct and indirect messianic prophecy does not accurately

---

64. On the basis of this text, the ox and the ass have found their way into the crib scene.

describe the true situation. It introduces too stark a distinction between the historical events of the present time and the salvation-
history promises of the future. The future salvation can become
reality only by virtue of the fact that it is already present, in
seed or root, in the contemporary, and sometimes unworthy,
bearer of the promises first made to David. Only in its further
development was it possible to recognize the fact that the future
bearer of salvation did not perfectly fit the expected and envisioned figure. Since every king of Judah was an anointed, that
is, a *mašᵃḥ*, a "messiah," the promises could all be made to
apply with direct reference to the contemporary king from the
line of David; indirectly they pointed far beyond the present time,
to a future in which the ideal was destined to be perfectly and
completely fulfilled.[65]

What survived Sanherib's campaign? That proud tree, the
wealth of Hezekiah, had been cruelly cut down. Evidence of
this are the 46 destroyed cities in Judah, the occupied territories,
and the extreme distress rampant in the country. Only the "stump"
(11, 1ff.) remained. But it was precisely this stump of Jesse [66]
according to the prophecy of Isaiah, that was destined to sprout
again, bringing forth a blossom more splendid than before. Isaiah
does not paint the figure of the king of the future in terms of
entirely new concepts or imagery. He draws upon the contemporary
fund of faith and conviction, which he brings one step forward.
It is endowment of the spirit that made kings and judges [67] stand
out from the common multitude and made them capable of
fulfilling their mission. The promised bringer of salvation is
distinguished from his predecessors only by the fact that the
spirit does not merely lay hold of him in a transitory manner for
one particular act; it is the fullness of the spirit that rests upon
him in an abiding manner: "The Spirit of the Lord shall rest

---

65. Cf. above p. 221, note 37.
66. Cf. the Christmas carol, "Lo, how a rose e'er blooming," particularly
   in its German original, "Es ist ein Reis entsprungen." The reference is
   to the shoot upon the root of Jesse, and the song has a tragic side, the
   utter bankruptcy of the human condition at the time of Christ's birth.
67. Cf. Gedeon (Jg 6, 34) and Saul (1 S 11, 6), etc.

upon him, the spirit of wisdom and understanding, the spirit of counsel and might, the spirit of knowledge and the fear of the Lord" (11, 1ff.). The Biblical word $r\hat{u}^a\dot{h}$ [68] ("spirit") refers to that power (*dynamis*) which emanates from God and produces wonderful things throughout the world. The man who is seized by the "spirit" is lifted up into the divine sphere of activity. What he then accomplishes is not an activity of his own; he and the spirit form one single community of action. In the case of the judges, the endowment of the spirit was evident in individual extraordinary acts of heroism. The Messiah, however, will bear the fullness of the spirit. Accordingly, the work which he accomplishes will not be something transitory; it will be fulfillment and perfection.

The fullness of spirit proper to the Messiah is further explored in the three paired attributes which refer to the three great missions of this ideal ruler. The first pair "wisdom and understanding" (*hokmah û-bînah*) bear upon his personal qualifications. These two gifts can best be illustrated in the ideal figure of Solomon. The gift of understanding qualified him for a profound insight into the essential continuity of existence, so that he recognized all plants and animals by their name and could catalogue them in an ordered system.[69] Wisdom is the gift of the ruler par excellence. It enables him to assign everything to its proper place, to distinguish between good and evil, and to find the correct decision in matters of judgment.[70] This personal endowment with the ruler's gifts of "wisdom and understanding" is a prerequisite for fulfilling the ruler's mission in the political and religious spheres. The second pair of gifts refer to the Messiah in his capacity as political king and religious priest. When all human diplomacy, despite all human craft and cunning, have become involved in an inextricable confusion, the Messiah, the "wonderful counsellor," will find a solution, simply because the "Spirit of counsel" (*'essah*) rests upon him. His counsel, however, will not be simply a weak recommendation without any power or resolution. The "spirit of might" (*gebûrah*) also rests upon him, and in the strength of this spirit he will accomplish all the plans of Yahweh, in the face of every resistance, acting as "the hero of God" (*'el-gibbôr*). "He shall smite the earth with the rod of his mouth, and with the breath (*ruah*)

---

68. R. Koch, *Geist und Messias*, (1960), 72ff.
69. Cf. the Solomonic sapiential poetry, Vol. III, 420ff.
70. 1 K 3, 16: Solomon's judgment.

of his lips he shall slay the wicked" (11, 4b). In the era of Israel's heroes, in the age of the judges (*šôpheṭim*), individual men, acting in the powerful spirit of Yahweh, accomplished the judgment of God. There are two elements involved here: expulsion of the national enemy and, as the happy consequence of this victory, the liberation and salvation of the oppressed people. The Messiah will be characterized by a similar "judging" (*šāphat*) in the definitive sense of the word: "With righteousness he will judge (*šāphat*) the poor" (11, 4). He is "judge," that is, liberator, savior, and redeemer, since, through his endowment with the spirit, he is possessed of ways and means to establish the rule of God despite the opposition of helpless human diplomacy, which is a counterpoint to the spirit of counsel, and brutal military power, which is the abuse of the gift of strength.

The ideal ruler's ability to accomplish his religious mission in an ideal way is guaranteed by his endowment with the "spirit of knowledge and the fear of the Lord" (*da'at we-yir'at Yahweh*). This, at all events, is the normal translation of the third pair of gifts. The scope of the Hebrew word *da'at* is not, however, adequately rendered by the English word "knowledge." Knowledge is a term unilaterally restricted to the intellectual knowing of a thing; the Hebrew, however, thought more with his heart than with his head and reason. He thinks, feels, decides, "knows," that is, loves, all with his heart. There is a subconscious principle in operation here: a man can know properly and fully only when he loves. The gift of knowledge, accordingly, refers simply to that absolute surrender to Yahweh's call, and thus the equally absolute recognition of his dominion. When Hoshea compares the relationship of Yahweh to his people in terms of marriage, he is already referring to this gift of "knowledge," the capacity to answer yes to God's offer of love. The human person is drawn and carried along into the mystery of divine love (*mysterium fascinosum*). But despite the fact that he is raised up into the level of divine love, the human person cannot abandon his creaturely existence. No man can look upon God without dying — that was the universal conviction. Accordingly, the gift of "fear of the Lord" reminds man, no matter how lofty his mission and endowment, to abide within the limitations of his creaturely existence, to bow in reverence to his mission before God (*mysterium tremendum*).

As we have said above, Isaiah is not painting the picture of the spiritual ruler to come in new or different colors. All of his contemporaries could understand what the words meant. If all these prophecies were actually to be accomplished, then indeed would begin the era of God's wonders, since "spirit" is equivalent with "wonder." According to the prophetic conception of things, the Messiah himself is thus the greatest of God's wonders. The spirit seizes upon him not only in a transitory manner, but rather rests upon him in an abiding way (*nāḥah*).

It has been customary to speak of the seven gifts of the Holy Spirit. As we have just demonstrated, the Hebrew text describes three matched pairs of spiritual gifts, a total of only six gifts. By counting the expression "spirit of Yahweh" which is common to all six as a separate gift, we have the number seven. This number can be compared with the seven-branched lampstand: with the principal branch (spirit of Yahweh) and the three sets of secondary branches.[71] The common number seven is, however, not based upon the Hebrew text, but rather upon the ancient Greek and Latin translations, which translate the Hebrew word *yir'at Yahweh* (11, 2d, 3a), in its two occurrences, with two different words. In 2d it is translated *eusebeia, pietas,* that is, "piety," and in 3a it is translated *phobos theou, timor domini,* "fear of the Lord."

b) THE KINGDOM OF PEACE (11, 6-16; 2, 1-5): Isaiah's picture of a spiritual ruler to come in no way involves an eschatological or supra-historical framework. He is hoping for the ideal ruler, who will be completely and permanently filled with the spirit of God. Since he will proceed from the "stump of Jesse," his ideal picture is a reflection of David, to whom the mighty promises were first given. Just as the expectancy of the descendants of David is thoroughly within the framework of human history, so is the expectation of his kingdom. The animal idyll is not to be understood as an actual restoration of the dream of paradise, but rather as a mighty allegory. Animals do not change their nature. A lion will never eat hay, and a bear will always be a bear. But one thing will be different. The threat that wild animals will present to humankind will cease to exist; the flocks will be able to graze in peace, and the shepherd will no longer fear the attacks of robbers. The mother need no longer fear that her child, as he plays, will be bitten by an adder. The great peace will make its appearance simply because there is no more evil throughout the land. Just as the sea is full of water, the whole land will be full of knowledge, that is, recognition, adoration, and love of God. The ultimate reason behind this kingdom of peace, is, accordingly, Yahweh, who makes his throne upon Zion and who has endowed the

---

71. EB III, 53; DBS IV (1949), 764. — M. Knepper, BiKi 10 (1956), 40-52 applies the three pairs of gifts to the three fundamental human activities of knowing, willing, and accomplishing.

son of David with the fullness of the spirit. The kingdom of peace is thus the kingdom of God, and the Messiah is the mediator of Yahweh's sovereignty.[72] As such, the son of David shall be raised up "as an ensign to the people" (11, 10). The remnant [73] scattered from Egypt to Assyria, will see this ensign and assemble under it. For the remnant of the people, left by Ashur, there will be a highway, and they shall make their way home, as they once returned home from out of Egypt. The prophet has a very concrete image of the rally and return of the broken people. After the Assyrian storm under Sanherib, this promise must have been indeed a consolation for the defeated nation. Isaiah directed their eyes towards the splendid future planned by Yahweh. The fact that he looked to the fulfillment of this expectation within the course of human history is obvious from the terms of his prophecy: in those days the fraternal strife between Israel and Judah will be buried, and the ancient hereditary enemies, the Philistines in the west, Moab, Edom, Ammon, and the desert tribes in the east, will all be subject to the new ruler. Only then will the

---

72. Eissfeldt, EinLAT 384 argues that "here there are some colors that we do not generally find on Isaiah's palette, although we know them from many paintings of the glories of the end-time that are of later composition." Against this position we might well argue that the ideal kingdom necessarily belongs to the concept of an ideal ruler. "The presentation of the wondrous gifts of the Messiah must be recognized as Isaiah's work without further ado." But why not the concept of a kingdom of peace as well? We must leave open the possibility that this concept took on a new actuality in later eras. — H. S. Gehman, *The Ruler of the Universe. The Theology of the First Isaiah,* Interpr. 11 (1957), 269-281. — H. Junker, *Ursprung und Grundzüge des Messiasbildes bei Isajas,* TTZ 4 (1957), 193-207.

73. This is true already for the time of the prophet Isaiah and not only for the Babylonian Exile as is frequently argued. In the year 732 the first resettlement of the Northern Tribes took place, and in 722-720 the second. On the occasion of Sanherib's campaign in 701 large parts of the Judaean populace were also deported. Thus, even in Isaiah's day, the dispersion of Israel and Judah among the gentiles was a *fait accompli.* Mention of this diaspora does not, in my opinion, demand any later dating, in the Exile or the post-Exilic era. There is, once again, the possibility that Isaiah's original thought was re-interpreted in the light of later historical events.

great kingdom of peace begin. "His dwelling shall be glorious" [74] (11, 10). Zion will be the focal point, not only for the remnant saved from Israel, but for all the world.

Thus did Isaiah sing his swan song, the high song of Zion (2, 1-5). These lines must stand as the climax of his prophetic preaching.[75] It may be that primordial conceptions of the "mountain of God" are operative here;[76] the Babylonian terraced towers were conceived of as "mountains of the gods" and, at the same time, the foundations of heaven and earth. It may be that the prophet employs this conception in the service of his faith. Just as Yahweh, the living God, stands far above all the other gods who are mere nothingness, so the mountain of his dwelling place surpasses all other mountains. In the prophetic vision, the earthly, geographical restrictions have ceased to be. The land of Judah becomes a mighty plateau, and Jerusalem shall rise up in its midst as a lofty-walled city, with the mountain of the temple rising high above all other mountains. This mountain of God will be the goal of every nation and tribe. "They shall beat their swords into plowshares, and their spears into pruning hooks. Na-

---

74. In the Vulgate *menûḥa*, "peace," is translated as *sepulchrum* "grave." Accordingly, the banner raised among the nations is interpreted as the cross.

75. Of the 150 Zion passages in the OT 45 are found in Isaiah, and 38 in the Psalms. — H. Wildberger, *Die Völkerwallfahrt zum Sion, Jes 2, 1-5*, VT 7 (1957), 62-81. This victorious faith in the "God of Jerusalem" has recently been confirmed by the discovery of a graffito in an excavated site at Lachish. Most scholars agree that it is the work of a man who fled there in the year 701 to escape the threat of Assyrian invasion: "Yahweh is the god of the whole earth; the mountains of Zion belong to him, the God of Jerusalem!" N. Lohfink, *Wandkritzeleien aus der Israelitischen Königszeit*, StZ 170 (1961/62), 390-392.

76. The same prophecy is to be found almost literally in Micah 4, 1-5. Eissfeldt, EinlAT 383 argues that a concept of universalism extending to the whole world is not the work of either Isaiah or Micah, but comes from post-exilic days. We must point out, however, that universalistic thinking, a world empire, was not foreign to the time of Isaiah. What he does is to assert Yahweh's claim to world sovereignty in the face of the universalistic claims to power advanced by the God Ashur.

tion shall not lift sword against nation, neither shall they learn war any more" (2, 4). What Isaiah foretold of the spirit ruler, that is, that he will be a judge (*šāphat*), is here proclaimed of Yahweh himself. This is not evidence of a plurality of sources; it is much rather the expression of one and the same prophetic theology. The Messiah stands in the light of the spirit's divine power; but it is God himself who produces all this new creation acting through his Messiah.[77]

Thus ends the activity of the prophet Isaiah. At least forty years — from the time of his first call in the year of Uzziah's death (740) to the campaigns of Sanherib (701) — he stood in the crossfire of contemporary history. He was a voice crying in the wilderness, little heard, misunderstood and attacked; but he was nonetheless the architect of the future, the herald of judgment and even more so of salvation — a mission already evident from his very name: Yahweh is salvation. The date of his death remains unknown. The legendary "Martyrdom and ascension of Isaiah"[78] tells this story: under the pressure of persecution from the faithless king Manasseh he fled with his disciples to a solitary mountain in the wilderness, where he was captured by the king's minions and sawed in two with a grafting-saw.

E) THE BOOK OF ISAIAH

The literary problem represented by the Book of Isaiah has been characterized by R. H. Pfeiffer in the following terms: "A miniature library rather than a book. Isaiah is not essentially different from the Book of the Minor Prophets, and could nearly be regarded, like Psalms and Proverbs, as an anthology or rather a collection of collections."[1] This presupposes the fact that the Book of Isaiah, as we have it today, was

---

77. The NT Christology continues this same aspect: in the liturgy we still have the formula, *"per Christum . . . ."*

78. Eissfeldt, EinlAT 752-754. Literature and texts. The part which concerns the martyrdom is said to be of Jewish origin and dates from the first century B.C., an era in which many martyrdom legends were in vogue as the result of the Maccabean persecutions. Hb 11, 37 alludes to the legend. The same story is found in the Talmud, Jebamot 69, 2.

---

1. IntOT 448. The same point is made by G. Hölscher, ThLZ 77 (1952),

not composed by one single writer, as we would expect a modern literary work to be. In terms of the more than forty years of Isaiah's prophetic activity, this can be easily enough understood. His book is not a collection of memoirs, recorded in the peace of his old age, looking back upon days gone by and recording his life's work in orderly fashion. Isaiah, as prophet, was primarily the herald of God's word. He turned to writing only in an attempt to substantiate the spoken word. There is an obvious comparison with the formation of our Gospels. At the beginning we have the preaching of Jesus; the recording of his words took place only in the second generation. The Gospels are the precious gift of Jesus' disciples. In like manner, we owe these prophetic writings of Isaiah mostly to his disciples who received and kept their master's words and preserved them in writing for the times to come. The master himself may, in fact, have written a few of these words himself, but the book as such is the work of his disciples. This interpretation is a necessary key to the proper understanding of the prophetic literature as such and the Book of Isaiah in particular.

1) THE WRITTEN WORD IN THE SERVICE OF PROPHECY

There are some indications that Isaiah enlisted the written word in the service of his preaching: for example, in proclaiming the birth of "the spoil speeds, the prey hastes." "Yahweh said to me, 'take a large tablet and write upon it in common characters.'" [2] "Belonging to Maher-shalal-hash-baz" (8-1). Isaiah got some reliable witnesses and did as Yahweh had instructed. If plunder and rapine came over the country, everyone could think of the threatening name recorded on this tablet and recognize that the prophet had foretold the truth. In the days in which Isaiah was active against the Egyptian alliance, he had another slogan: "Rahab growls and sits still" (30, 7). He wrote it on a tablet to be a witness for all time to everyone who could understand. "And now, go write it before them on a tablet, and inscribe it in a book, that it may be for the time to come as a witness forever" (30, 8).

It would appear that Isaiah did not confine his efforts with the recording of prophetic slogans. After his repulse by Ahaz, he turned to his disciples in an effort to preserve the words he preached at least within their smaller circle. The prophetic teaching did not consist primarily in long penitential sermons which were then handed down in their entirety by the attentive audience. They are closer to the impressive tone of poetry than to the sermon style. Words of this kind, with their

---

2. $be\underset{.}{h}eret\ 'en\hat{o}\check{s}$ "with the stylus-stroke customary to the people" (M. Buber), i.e., with the normal form of handwriting that everyone could read, and not in hieroglyphs or cuneiform which only the scholars could read.

rhythm, assonance, and alliteration are simply not the product of everyday speech. We catch a glimpse of the poet's genius, chiseling and polishing his words. Once composed, it preserved its final form. These prophetic poems, which by their very nature were destined for public presentation, Isaiah entrusted to his disciples. This might be the meaning of the rather difficult verse 8, 16: "Bind up the testimony, seal the teaching among my disciples";[3] that is, the prophet's word is to be recorded on a scroll, which is then to be rolled up, bound, and sealed.

This scroll or volume may well have been composed of the events narrated in the first person in ch. 6 (the inaugural vision and vocation) and 8 (threat oracles delivered during the Syro-Ephraimitic war). Chapter 7, lying between these two, is written in the 3rd person. Since narratives frequently pass from 1st to 3rd person,[4] it is possible that chapter 7 also belongs to this first recording. The first scroll, would, accordingly, comprise the essential elements of Isaiah's early preaching. It does not seem, however, that he could have composed and recorded the rest of his preaching in any regular manner, since otherwise he would not have required a specific order from Yahweh to write down the oracle against Egypt (30, 8). The recording of the rest of the prophetic words is, most likely, owing to the enthusiasm of the prophet's disciples.

2) COLLECTIONS

When we inquire into the motivation behind this work of collection and recording, it was certainly not simply the literary interests in the poetic creations of the great master. Neither was it an attempt to create a complete life story, especially since elements that belong in the same temporal succession are parcelled among various sections of the book. The only purpose was their faith that the prophet's words were the product of divine inspiration and had thus not died together with the prophet's death. They would continue to preserve their message for every age. This explains why the organization of the material is along thematic rather than chronological points of view.

Elements that are temporally quite distinct but perfectly coherent in terms of content are thus quite logically grouped together to form a literary unit. The oracles of threat and judgment are generally coupled with prophecies of consolation, in imitation of Isaiah himself who was not simply a somber herald of repentance, but even more so a herald of salvation. Accordingly, these smaller units of his book combine the call to penance and the proclamation of future salvation. The present literary content of the book suggests the following outline for the first part of Isaiah's Book:

---

3. Translation of M. Buber, *Bücher der Kündung*, 31.
4. *EncMikr* III, 925.

1. *First collection*: chapters 1-10: Words and Visions against Jerusalem and Judah.

   Consolation: Ch. 11: Messiah and Kingdom of Peace.
   Ch. 12: Thanksgiving Song of the Redeemed.

2. *Second Collection*: Chs. 13-23: Threat Oracles Against the nations.
   Consolation: "The great Isaian Apocalypse."
   Ch. 24: World Judgment.
   Ch. 25: The New Kingdom of God Upon Zion.
   Ch. 26: Songs of Praise and Thanksgiving.

3. *Third Collection*: Chs. 28-33: The Book of Woes or the Assyrian Cycle.
   Consolation: "The Smaller Isaian Apocalypse."
   Chs. 34-35: Annihilation of Edom and Redemption of Zion.

   Appendix: Chs. 36-39: Narrative of Sanherib's Campaign. Hezekiah's sickness, etc.

These collections were probably originally written on separate scrolls. Their combination into one single book represents only the final stage in a long process of collection. How long this process lasted cannot be accurately determined. But at all events, the three above-mentioned collections had a long history before them. Within the individual collections, modern criticism has identified a: Material written by the prophet himself, b: controversial material, c: material which is definitely not from Isaiah. "A completely illuminating and absolutely convincing analysis can probably never be arrived at," [5] since the criteria employed are too diverse.

a) *The Immanuel-Cycle* (6-9, 6):

The nucleus of the first collection is formed by the Book of Immanuel (6-9, 6), which probably existed as an independent unit. This explains why the inaugural vision appears in ch. 6 and not in ch. 1. The three chapters present words and events from the time of the Syro-Ephraimite war and the years immediately following, that is, from the years between 735 and 730. This nucleus was quickly expanded by two other rings: ch. 1-2, 5 (threat oracles against Jerusalem) and 10, 5-11, 16 (Ashur's

---

5. Eissfeldt, EinlAT 369-370, *Hier auch eine genaue Aufgliederung der einzelnen Abschnitte*, 371-398. — L. J. Liebreich, *The Composition of the Book of Isaiah*, JQR 46 (1956), 259-277. The present form of the book was consciously composed as a unity by the final redactor, and the individual sections were adapted to fit the harmony of the whole. D. Jones, *The Tradition of the Oracles of Isaiah of Jerusalem*, ZAW 67 (1955), 226-246.

pride and the spiritual ruler), which date only from the end of Isaiah's career, the days of the Assyrian threat (704-701). This leads to the surprising conclusion that the latter part of Isaiah's preaching comes first in the order of his book. Texts from his earlier career (740-735) lie in between (2, 6–5, 30; 9, 7–10, 4). Some of these are obviously compact unities: the song of the vineyard (5, 1-7), the seven woes (5, 8-24 and 10, 1-4), and the song of the outstretched hand (9, 7–10, 4). The thanksgiving song in ch. 12 was added after the collection was complete.

b) "Burden" Oracles and the Great Apocalypse:

The nine burden oracles against the nations — so called from their opening words *massa'* (burden) — are an echo of the political and religious activity of Isaiah from the years 715-701, when Judah was taken in tow by the politics of Egypt and defected from Assyrian influence, in an alliance with her neighbors. They furnish testimony for the universal orientation of the prophet, who subordinates the day-by-day of political activity to the ultimate sentence of God the judge. Taken as a whole, they are a testimony to Isaiah's belief in a world judgment. What the individual does and what the nations as a whole do — everything is subject to God's final judgment. Isaiah's concept of God clearly manifests universalistic characteristics. Yahweh is certainly not simply the national god of Israel, who is destined to triumph over the other gods. For judgment is not accomplished in terms of one's belonging or not belonging to the community of Israel; it is rather a question of ethical principles, justice and truth.

The nine burden oracles are followed, as a "consolation," by the so-called great apocalypse of Isaiah (chs. 24-26), which form a clear break with the tenor of the burden oracles and are thus almost unanimously attributed to a different author. This is, however, "a judgment which does not begin to approach its religious content, since the critic must . . . simply get used to the idea that words like this have a value in themselves, quite apart from the consideration by whom they are spoken and from what era they date." [6] What are the grounds for arguing that this apocalypse is not the work of Isaiah himself? First we must consider an argument based on style. The apocalypse exhibits a style quite different from those parts of the book which are clearly the work of Isaiah. This

---

6. Eissfeldt, EinlAT 383. From the Catholic point of view it must be added only that inspiration and authorship need to be strictly separated. Even texts whose authorship is contested or wholly unknown can be inspired, and a part of Scripture. Authorship is a problem of textual, literary, and historical criticism and must be approached on that plane alone.

can better be appreciated from reading the Hebrew original text,[7] but even in translation the difference in style can be appreciated by the careful reader. The apocalypse is full of strange words and uncommon forms of expression which Isaiah does not otherwise use. The style stands out for its accumulation of words and frequent repetition. This is characteristic of a later era, the time of Ezekiel, who describes his prophetic vision with magnificent formality, as precisely as possible (descriptive style), and still fails to grasp the essential concept. Isaiah's style, on the other hand, is concise, brief, striking, and sparing in words.

These stylistic considerations are further supported by the even more convincing argument from content. The burden oracles are always addressed to one definite nation, city, or even a definite individual person (*Shebna*). In the apocalypse, on the other hand, the horizon is expanded to include the world as a whole. Judgment is threatened no longer upon a definite people, but upon the entire world. Yahweh will annihilate the entire world. Those in power, those in lofty positions, the kings of this earth — they will all be bound in chains and cast into prison to await the final judgment that is to come. Upon Zion, however, Yahweh will enter into his kingly power and prepare a great banquet for all the nations; he will dry every tear, make an end to hatred, annihilate the rulers of this world, and gather together the dispersed members of his kingdom (24, 1-3, 13, 17-23; 25, 6-8; 27, 1, 12-13).

In the midst of these prophecies several songs have been incorporated. Departed is the birth (24, 4-6), departed are wine and happy song (24, 7-9), departed is the city of chaos [8] (24, 10-12). Despite considerable effort, it is not possible to determine precisely which city is here described as being destroyed.[9] It may be that the identification was deliberately left unspecified; it may be a description of the city hostile to God as such, which is a universal type and can never be exhausted by one particular identification. The temporal sequence of these sections, despite the individual character of the description, remains a matter of some difficulty. Every century from the Exile to the end of the Old Testament has been suggested as the time of composition. We cannot even determine that the songs are older than the prophecies. At all events, both have been combined to achieve a sort of compact tapestry of the end-time. So scholars have conjectured that this is a prophetic liturgy, that is, a series of texts which have been composed primarily for divine service.[10]

---

7. *EncMikr* III, 920 presents Hebrew examples.

8. *tohu*, cf. Gn 1, 2: "chaos, hell."

9. Proposals have included: Babel destroyed in 331 by Alexander and in 485 by Artaxerxes; Carthage destroyed in 146 by the Romans, and Samaria destroyed in 110 by Alexander Hyrkanus.

10. Eissfeldt, EinlAT 391.

This would make for a later composition, an era in which the great prophecies had all been recorded and were now freely employed in the
composition of liturgical texts.

Eissfeldt [11] has suggested three arguments for dating these selections
from the era after the Exile; but his argument no longer seems conclusive.
What he says is this: "To determine the time of composition we must
consider the existence of a large Jewish diaspora (27, 12-13), the existence
of a well developed anthology, and the first beginnings of a faith in
the resurrection." A really developed angelology, however, is hardly to
be found in the apocalypse. "On that day the Lord will punish the host
of heaven, in heaven" (24, 21) — this can be simply a reference to the
stars, sun, moon, and constellations, that is, the principal gods of the
Babylonian pantheon, whom Yahweh will annihilate together with the
kings who gave them homage. No more convincing is the allusion to the
Jewish diaspora. Even in Isaiah's day the sons of Israel had been scattered
"from the Brook of Egypt as far as the Euphrates." From that same era
we note the beginning of a hope in the future gathering and return of
the expatriates. As far as any reference to a faith in the resurrection is
concerned, the text in Isaiah makes no significant advance beyond the
content of Ezekiel's vision of the field of dried bones (Ez 37). All three
bases for proof are, accordingly, far too unsubstantial to authorize a
particularly late dating of the apocalypse. There is only one final conclusion: the basic theme of a world judgment and the salvation of
Zion is a genuine element in the thought of Isaiah himself, although it
was subsequently developed by his disciples into a universal picture
and then cast into the literary garb of a subsequent era. Since the return
of the expatriates was still being awaited, the apocalypse might well owe
its origin to the same circle of disciples living in exile to whom we are
indebted for the "Book of consolation," the so-called Deutero-Isaiah. The
apocalypse, too, is an effort to preach the gospel of consolation in a
godless world and era.

c) *The Assyrian Cycle and the Little Apocalypse* (28-33):

The third collection, the Book of Woes, also called the Assyrian cycle
(chs. 28-33), is made up, with a few exceptions,[12] of genuine Isaian
elements, either composed by the prophet himself or his immediate disciples. It is the precipitate of Isaiah's battle against the political alliances
of the years 715-701. This cycle is concluded, by way of a consolation,
by the little apocalypse (chs. 34-35). It treats of the annihilation of

---

11. *Ibid.*, 392.
12. Post-exilic additions have been argued in the case of 29, 17-24; 30,
    18-26; 32, 1-8. Ch. 33 could be a prophetic liturgy. Robert-Feuillet,
    IntrAT 505.

Edom and the redemption of Zion. Edom, however, is no longer an unknown people, but rather the type of God's enemies as such. The little apocalypse no doubt owes its origin to the same circle of disciples as the great apocalypse.

d) *The Historical Appendix* (ch. 36-39):

In an effort to present the available historical material on the career of the prophet Isaiah in a compact collection, the earlier edition of the originally independent collections under the title of "collection of the sayings of the prophet Isaiah" was further amplified by the historical material from the Second Book of Kings (18, 13-17; 20, 12-19). Only the Song of Isaiah is the genuine work of the prophet. All the available material on the prophet Isaiah was thus collected into a single volume. The precise era in which this collection was completed can no longer be accurately determined, since this is a question which is intimately bound up with the problems of the so-called Deutero-Isaiah, the great "book of consolation," which extends from chs. 40-66.

e) *Proto-Isaiah and Deutero-Isaiah*:

The Pontifical Biblical Commission [13] in its decision of June 29, 1908, proclaims that the objections which had been raised up to that time against the unity of the Book of Isaiah are not sufficient to seriously threaten the traditional point of view. The Biblical Commission claims that the prophet composed the second part of his book (chs. 40-66) at the end of his career, a time at which he had transposed himself, in spirit, to the distant future of his people. Since 1908, however, there have been several critical examinations on Isaiah 40-66;[14] these investigations present ample proof

---

13. *Enchiridion Biblicum* 1956[3], Nos. 291-295.
14. Ziegler, EB II, 15; DBS IV 696. — Even conservative authors, who believe that the traditional opinion must be defended at all costs, are coming to realize that Deutero-Isaiah is the work of an inspired scholar writing after the death of the prophet and that the content of the book was enlarged by additions down to the fifth century. Seraphin Gozzo, O.F.M., *De catholicorum sententia circa authenticitatem Is 40-66 inde ab anno 1908*, Antonianum 32 (1957), 369-410. — C. Lattery, S.J., *The Book of Isaiah the Prophet*, Scripture 5 (1952), 2-7. The traditional conception of the unity of the book does receive some attention in the above presentation insofar as the content of Deutero- and Trito-Isaiah are presented, not as something merely appended to the prophet's writings, but rather as a genuine development of what is quite properly his own thought and argument. In terms of canonical parlance, we might go so far as to say that Deutero- and Trito-Isaiah represent the authentic and official inter-

that the second half of the book cannot possibly have been written by the prophet Isaiah himself in the eighth century. The position taken by the Biblical Commission was dictated by dogmatic considerations; it was enunciated in a rationalistic era which argued for the absolute impossibility of any prophetic reference to the future. Today the position is much clearer, since the argumentation is no longer based on rationalistic prejudices, but rather on textual, literary, and historical criteria.[15] No Christian exegete could possibly doubt that a prophet can communicate God's revelation directed towards even the most distant future. It is precisely because he believed in God's revelation in the course of salvation history that the exegete must clearly examine into the historical circumstances of this phenomenon. In so doing he in no wise loses sight of the revealed word; actually he gains considerably since he cannot possibly be indifferent to the problem of what time and circumstance and era God has chosen to speak to mankind.

The fact that the Book of Isaiah has been the subject of such tremendous accretion is evidence of more than the fertility of the truths proclaimed by the prophet. His prophecy was not mere paper and ink recorded in dust-filled scrolls; it was the daily bread of the Church of the Old Testament, in a time of crisis. Proceeding from faith, it developed to a still greater faith. "The fact that the Book of Isaiah has been so richly developed by the additions of other eras is proof of the fact that this book was in everyone's hand and came to be recognized and appreciated in its true significance." [16]

F) THE BOOK OF MICAH

The name of the prophet Micah is, in itself, a profession of faith. It is the abbreviated form for *mi-ke-yah,* which means "who

---

pretation of Proto-Isaiah's message. The interpretation was the work of the same Holy Spirit's inspiration as was the original prophecy. Literary history does not destroy inspiration; it makes it more profound.

---

15. A. Vaccari, *La Sacra Bibbia,* Rom VI (1958), 19 continues to warn that we court great danger of error (*pericolo di errore*) if, despite the witness of tradition, we ascribe such large portions of the book to someone other than the prophet himself. By way of answer we must say that not everything can be proved by tradition. And furthermore, the traditional view of the unity of the book is being more and more substantiated by the new results of our investigations into authorship. All that results is a deeper and fuller appreciation of the book, not an error in interpretation.

16. A. Weiser, *Einleitung* 1957[4], 159.

is like Yahweh?" The first seven chapters of the Book of Micah are so full of this profession of faith that the earthly fate of the prophet has completely disappeared as something unimportant into the background, — a true witness of genuine prophecy. It is not the human person who is important, not even the prophet with his message, but only Yahweh and the word he speaks.

I) *Home and Origin*

In the inscription to his book, the prophet is introduced as *Mîkah hammorašti,* Micah from the city of Moresheth (1, 1) and in 1, 14 the city is referred to by its full name of Moresheth-Gath. The precise location is not definitely known,[1] but at all events it must be located somewhere in the border district of Judah along the frontier of the low country (*šephelah*). Since the word *môrašah* means "property," the city might well have been a foreign property, that is, a colony, of the city of Gath.

Micah, accordingly, comes from the frontier country and has experienced the bitter fate of this condition in his own body. The events of his lifetime left a deep impression upon the fate of this territory. In the inscription to the book, Micah's activity, just like Isaiah's career, is described as taking place within the reigns of kings Jotham, Ahaz, and Hezekiah. Whereas, in Isaiah, most of the events can be dated, Micah's prophecies are recorded without mention of date. They must speak for themselves. It is not, however, particularly difficult to recognize the traces of the catastrophe that struck that era. The imminent destruction of the Northern Kingdom made a profound impression upon him (6, 1ff.). In lamentation, barefoot, and naked he made his way, similar to Isaiah in his symbolic representation of the catastrophe (1, 8). Accordingly, his vocation, the time at which he was seized "with the power, with the Spirit of the Lord, and with justice and might" (3, 8), must have taken place before the year 722, and, as we might expect, in his native city, since he refers to himself simply as *Morašti,* the prophet from Moresheth.

The devastations of the frontier territory — whether this took

---

1. Generally identified with *tell el-gudeideh,* 1 mi NO of Beth Gubrin.

place during the first or second rebellion of Hezekiah is uncertain — find their echo in 1, 10-16. The places mentioned here,
although their geographical location cannot be determined in
each individual case,[2] are all located in the western part of the
frontier territory, the native country of Micah. It is possible
that, upon the approach of the Assyrians, the prophet made
his way to Jerusalem and there for the first time, his vision particularly sharpened by the crisis, was able to unmask the corrupt
life of the ruling classes.

II) *Micah's Message*

Micah followed the footsteps of his great predecessors. He
has been compared with Amos, who also comes from the country,
from following his herds, to take up the call of prophet. Blunt,
powerful, and clear language both have in common, as well
as the passion for right and justice. Even Hosea's leitmotif, fidelity
to Yahweh's covenant (*hesed*), continues to be operative in
Micah (6, 8b). Together with his contemporary Isaiah he fought
side by side against the destruction of the people. All the prophets
share the dual message of destruction and salvation that Yahweh
brings to pass in human history. Micah sums up the preaching
of his three predecessors in the catechism-like [3] brevity of his
three-fold message: "To do justice, and to love kindness, and to
walk humbly with your God" (6, 8). He too turns primarily to
history to illustrate the most realistic motives for repentance:
"O my people, what have I done to you" (6, 3) — a cry to repentance which still echoes in the liturgy for Good Friday.

1) HERALD OF DESTRUCTION

"It was an era of political unrest, which upset the nation in
its deepest roots and had thus brought the dregs of their lower
instincts to the surface." [4] Micah, just like Amos, turns to the
rich land owners: "They covet fields and seize them; and houses,

---

2. GTT #1529-1538.
3. Weiser, EinlAT 207.
4. *Ibid.,* 204 .

and take them away; they oppress a man and his house, a man and his inheritance" (2, 4). But the enemy will come and take away their ill-gotten property. In his blunt language, Micah goes on to say that they will tear the skin from these people and cut their flesh from their bones (3, 3).[5] A condition of general insecurity was the consequence of this political unrest. No one could be trusted, not even a man's wife or father or son. Careful silence was the counsel of the hour (7, 1-6). A prophet who would have been willing to join their wild revels would have been most welcome to the people. But it was Micah's duty to proclaim that judgment was already on its way, a judgment that was being represented not by any human insistence, but by Yahweh himself. Simply because God is God, the destruction of this godless generation could not fail to come to pass. "Evil (— destruction) has come down from Yahweh" (1, 12). It emanates from the very sanctuary of the temple, and treads upon the high places of the earth (1, 2). Even Jerusalem will be reduced to ruins (3, 12; cf. Jer 26, 18). These threat oracles are to be found in the first three chapters (excepting for 2, 12 — 13) and in 6 — 7, 7 which most critics agree are genuine.

2) PROPHET OF SALVATION

In contrast to his message of destruction, the prophet Micah's message of salvation is regarded as not part of the original corpus: most critics regard it as not genuine or at least as suspect.[6] It is, however, quite certain that the Book of Micah in its present form was not written by the prophet himself. Just as in the Book of Isaiah, it is the combined zeal of the prophet's disciples that have produced the Book of Micah. It was they who gathered the oracles and preaching of the great masters, from religious rather than literary motives. These were words of life and as such they necessarily made their way into the treasury of faith of the Old Testament Church. There is of course the possibility that these words

---

5. In an earthy way we might say that they make a goulash out of the people and devour them down.
6. Eissfeldt, EinlAT 500-505.

of the earlier prophets could be drawn from this treasury of the faith (*thesaurus fidei*) by men of later times, equally enlightened, to take on a new life and a fuller message. The degrees to which these later additions can be identified is a matter of the most painstaking scholarship. At all events the principle of criticism in terms of which only the oracles of destruction are considered the genuine work of the prophet himself must be rejected on the basis of methodology. It is true that the oracles of destruction have been handed down in a far greater proportion; but this can be interpreted simply as an effort to make the message of salvation stand out in sharper contrast.

a) *Yahweh, Shepherd and Bell-wether*:

The stamp of "non-genuinity" has been applied first of all to the prophecy of the return and reassembling of the remnant of Israel (2, 12-13), since this is a problem which actually occurs only after the destruction of Jerusalem (586). In my opinion, however, it was precisely in the days of Micah that the question of the fate of the expatriates and prisoners was a matter of the most pressing concern. In the year 732, Upper Galilee had already been resettled, and in the year 722-720 the mountain country of Samaria. Sanherib boasts that he destroyed 46 cities in Judah and carried away 200,105 prisoners as his booty. The number is obviously far too high, but it does clearly indicate that already around the year 700 a great diaspora had taken place, that is, a great scattering of the tribes of Israel and Judah. The question of what fate these homeless prisoners could expect was a burning issue for every thinking person of that era which had been forced to witness the resettling of vast populations and the dissolution of many family ties. Who could give an answer, who could point to a solution if not the prophet of Yahweh? The image of the herd and shepherd is an ancient Israelite manner of expression. Yahweh himself is the shepherd of his people, even when they are scattered. Micah compares him to the bell-wether whose task it is to prepare the way for the scattered sheep to follow. The rallying point is Yahweh in Zion. The form of expression and

the religious content of these verses all make for the genuinity
of this section. The same is true of 4, 6-7, which also promise a
time of gathering and restoration.   •

b) *Crisis From the Enemy — Kingdom of Peace* (ch. 4)

On the subject of 4, 1-5, 8, Eissfeldt [7] after answering many
objections, has this statement to make: "The critic is, accordingly,
forced, although with some reservation, to declare for the non-
genuinity of this section." The arguments he alleges, however, do
not seem sufficiently convincing for the scholar to necessarily ascribe these verses to some other source. The fact that the subject
refers to the gathering of the expatriate (4, 6-7), does not in
itself argue for a later time of composition; quite the contrary. As
we have just shown, the question of the fate of these prisoners
of war and expatriates was one of the most painful problems facing
the contemporaries of the prophet Micah. Verses 9-14 speak
of a war crisis, the siege of Jerusalem, and its unexpected liberation. Could this not be seen as a reference to the Assyrian peril
under Sanherib in the year 701? Tired of this everlasting war and
devastation, everyone was hoping for peace. The proclamation of
this kingdom of peace, an era in which the weapons of war
would be melted down and beaten into agricultural tools, is a
verbal echo of Isaiah 2, 2-4. It cannot be determined, however,
which prophet had done the borrowing. The Assyrian embassy
had blasphemed Yahweh. The gods of the other peoples had not
been able to help. How was Yahweh now to survive in the face
of Ashur's terrible splendor. This was the hour that witnessed the
heroic faith of Yahweh upon Zion, Zion the center of a new
world order of peace (4, 2d). The two sections, crisis from the
enemy and kingdom of peace, are meant to illustrate each other:
together they present a correct and contemporary picture of that
perilous year 701.

c) *"You Bethlehem"* (ch. 5)

---

7. EinlAT 502.

Despite the doubts expressed by many authors [8] I am inclined to list this section among the genuine preaching of the prophet because of its very ancient theological content. It takes up the prophecy of Nathan, a theme which was so popular with Isaiah, but it goes back beyond this prophecy to Jacob's blessing upon the tribe of Judah (Gn 49, 8-12): "The scepter will not depart from Judah . . ." (Gn 49, 10). What Micah says is this: "But you, O Bethlehem Ephrathah, who are little to be among the clans of Judah, from you shall come forth for me one who is to be ruler (*môšel*) in Israel" (5, 1). Ephrathah [9] refers to the whole territory, while Bethlehem is a reference to its most important city; it may also be an ancient term for the whole mountain country of Judah. Micah ties up the patriarchal prophecies of the great ruler to come from Judah with the concrete prophecy of Nathan about the ruler to come from the house of David. Zion and David are the focal points of the prophet Micah's hope for the future. Just like Isaiah, he fixes his attention upon the mother of the ruler who is to come: "Until the time when she who is in travail has brought forth" (5, 2a). In the Books of the Kings, the name of the queen mother, in the case of the kings of Judah, is always individually mentioned, since she enjoyed a position of special honor. The mother of the future ruler of this kingdom of peace will have a dignity far surpassing that of all other royal ladies (*gᵉbîrah*). The reference to the mother of the king as "she who is in travail" is thus quite in keeping with the historical practices of the Era of the Kings. The woman "who is in travail" was the hope of the future. As such, the prophecy of the woman who is in travail forms a counterpoint to the *"virgin-'almah"* prophecy of Isaiah, and could thus very well date back to the same historical circumstances, the Syro-Ephraimite war.

In the Patriarchal Blessings (Gn 49, 9), as well as the oracle of Bileam, Judah is compared to a lion. Taking up this image, verses 5, 6-8 describe the remnant of Jacob as a victorious line among the peoples. Verses 5, 9-14 might also be a reference to

---

8. *Ibid.*, 502.
9. Vol. III, 93.

the reforms of Hezekiah, since they refer to the destruction of the worship on the high places.

d) *"The Ephraimite Book of Consolation"* (7, 7-20)

The last chapter of Micah contains four separate units: 7, 7-10; 11-13; 14-17; 18-20. Many authors, such as Weiser, who are otherwise inclined to deny Micah's authorship for only a very few sections of this book, have explained this as a post-exilic proclamation of salvation for Zion, a message which presupposes the destruction of Jerusalem and the exile.[10] Even Robert-Feuillet [11] sees this as a post-exilic liturgy, that is, a text which has been composed from the common treasury of tradition and actually used for the divine services of the synagogue. On the other hand, according to Eissfeldt [12] "The composition of the poem in 7, 7-20 by Micah himself must be seriously considered." He refers to it as "the Ephraimite book of consolation," a spiritual message addressed to the sorry remnant which still survived the Northern Kingdom of Israel after the repopulation of the years 732 and 722. The question "Where is the Lord your God?" (7, 10) is raised not only by the pagans in their mockery, but also as a battle cry by the faithful remnant. The question is answered by the prophet. The enemies who are now making mockery will indeed trample everything underfoot; but the prisoners and expatriates will all return home, from Ashur to the Brook of Egypt. The country was laid desolate because of the sins of the people (11-13); but Yahweh will wash away their sin and sink it in the depths of the sea (19) and once again, with his staff, pasture the flock of his chosen people (14).

The Book of Micah is, accordingly, a faithful witness to the preaching of the prophet Micah. In consideration of the long prophetic activity, the chapters which survive are only a small remnant whose very existence we owe to the corporate zeal of his disciples. The words have been arranged according to their content and not the time of composition. The key to the actual order of the book might well be its use as a text for

---

10. Eissfeldt, EinlAT 503.
11. IntrAT 500.
12. EinlAT 504.

divine service. This would also explain the alternation of texts threatening destruction and texts promising salvation: 1-3: threat of destruction; 4-5: promise of salvation; 6—7, 6: destruction; 7, 7-20: salvation.

The fundamental position of this book is certainly not apocalyptic.[13] Arguing simply on the basis of historical background, we are certainly not justified in dating the composition as late as 200 B.C. We can no longer determine precisely when the book took on its present form. Some hundred years after Micah, at the time of the great prophet Jeremiah, the words of Micah were quoted as an argument against Jeremiah (Jer 26, 18). While this does not necessarily prove the literary existence of the Book of Micah, it does present a very strong argument. The words quoted are so in keeping with the personal character of our author that they alone can argue for the genuinity of the traditional text. Just as Isaiah, Micah himself or his disciples acting for him, may have made a written record of words designed primarily for oral delivery, in an effort to preserve the prophet's message for the days to come. The fact that the hand of the final redactor is everywhere in evidence can prove only that the words of the prophet, as they pass down through the generations, were guarded not as dead literature, but as a living tradition of faith.

---

13. Pfeiffer, IntrOT 589.

CHAPTER IX

PAX ASSYRIACA -- THE ASSYRIAN PEACE

UNDER the three energetic rulers, Sanherib, Esarhaddon, and Ashur-bani-pal, the winged sun [1] of Assyria attained its greatest prominence. They constructed a world empire such as had never been seen before. Even Egypt was forced to bow before the terrible splendor of Ashur. The four corners of the earth all lay in peace at the feet of the "great dragon" (*ušum-gal*). Whereas, in earlier years, it had been a marked exception for the great king to remain in "his country," that is, in Assyria, and not lead his soldiers into the field, the 60 years of the so-called three rulers, apart from a few unimportant expeditions, contain only three wars.[2] We can thus actually speak of a time of world peace under the reign of Assyria. This world peace, however, was not a time for the nations to relax. It was a peace maintained by force under threat of the terrible splendor of the great dragon. The smouldering fire was not without its occasional burst of flame.

---

1. The winged sun is the symbol of the Assyrian Empire, frequently found on relief sculptures. ANEP, 534-536.
2. BA 23 (1960), 57 adds: Sanherib's campaign against Judah (701), the conquest of Sidon by Esarhaddon (677), and the war against Egypt in the decade 673-663.

1) "SANHERIB (705-681), A VERSATILE MAN EVEN IN THE FIELD OF TECHNOLOGY, COMES TO RUIN FOR WANT OF MODERATION" [3]

a) *Babel in Constant Revolution Until It is Destroyed*

After the western countries had been settled in peace by the victorious campaigns of 701, the Babylonian question was still open.[4] The ancient metropolis of the Babylonian culture was overcome without resistance. At the same time Babylon had become an outpost for foreign powers. Elamites and Aramaeans were constantly trying to attack Ashur through Babel. Before his westward campaign, Sanherib had turned to Babel, where he expelled Merodach-Baladan who was attempting to secure the throne, and installed the pro-Assyrian Bel-ibni (702-700) as king. This did not secure peace. Bel-ibni sooner or later came under the spell of the nationalist agitation of Merodach-Baladan, who was still politically active, together with the prince of Chaldees Musizib-Marduk, and their Elamite supporters. Even though he had been supported by Sanherib, Bel-ibni embarked upon a hopeless insurrection. Predictably enough he was quickly overcome. Sanherib brought him and his entire court to Assur in chains. In order to establish peace once and for all, he made his own son Ashur-nadin-šumi King of Babel (699-694). This did indeed secure a few years of tranquility.

But Ashur's enemies were not at rest. The fire of rebellion was mounting in Elam. In the year 694 Sanherib decided to eliminate this hotbed of rebellion. The preparations for the campaign against Elam are beyond all proportion, even for Sanherib. He has ships built in Nineveh on the Tigris, and in Til-Barsip on the Euphrates, had them manned with Phoenician and Ionian sailors, and ordered them to sail to the Persian Gulf. With this

---

3. W. v. Soden, *Herrscher im Alten Orient*, (1954), 105-118.
4. Our precise knowledge of the course of events is owing to the Babylonian Chronicle with its year-by-year entries of the most important dates. ANET 301ff. Cf. Schmökel, GAV 272-274; "Assyria" in RLA I, 300.

fleet he attacked Elam from the sea, defeated the hostile army, destroyed many cities, and returned home laden with booty. Hardly had he departed when the Elamites launched a counter-offensive. Hallusu, king of Elam, fell upon Babylon, massacred the members of the pro-Assyrian party, made a prisoner of Sanherib's son Ashur-nadin-šumi, carried him off to Elam and in his place raised Nergal-ušezib to the throne of Babel (693). The revenge was no less terrible. Sanherib made his way to the southernmost part of the country, as far as the city of Uruk, a holy city from time immemorial, which he overcame, carrying off inhabitants and gods alike. In Babel Nergal-ušezib fell into his hands. He had him locked in a cage and placed before the city gates of Nineveh.

Babel, despite these disasters, would not rest in peace. The Chaldaean sheikh Mušezib-Marduk now laid claim to the throne (692-689). The united anti-Assyrian powers were successful in overthrowing Sanherib in a battle which proved costly to both sides. Sanherib, however, would not give up his claim to Babel. In the year 689 he won his final victory. It was then that he gave his wrath full course. Babel was destroyed, the statue of Marduk was brought to Ashur, the entire population was massacred, not a single temple was spared, and the "holy earth" was taken by boat to the island of Tilmun where it was strewn on the ground or else transported into the new year festival house at Ashur. Sanherib then diverted the stream into the ruins of Babel, in an effort to eradicate all traces of this hated city. Babylonia was thus reduced to "peace," although in reality it had become a cemetery. For twenty years Babel lay deserted. This is perhaps the desolation described in the oracle of Isaiah: "Hyenas will cry in its towers, and jackals in the pleasant palaces" (Is 13, 19ff.).

b) *Nineveh, The Great City*

Despite the confused situation created by his many military activities, Sanherib, shortly after his accession to the throne, began to build the city of his choice, Nineveh, into a new imperial capital. The prisoners of war supplied the slave labor. The residents of

Dur-Sarruken, which had been built by his predecessor, he abandoned, almost new, to his own demise. He surrounded Nineveh [5]
with a double wall 28 feet high with 15 city gates. "Streets and
public squares were widened, and a royal promenade was developed with a stone bridge — and this is the first record of such
a construction — across the palace moat. On both sides of the
city the king created parks with exotic fruit trees. The city and
gardens were abundantly supplied with water by a new series
of canals, laid out and constructed with considerable technical
skill. Sanherib next began the construction of a palace of unheard
of magnificence. The building stood in the western part of the
city, upon a tract of land that had been cleared of older buildings,
by drainage operations, and by re-routing the canal system. It
stood upon a lofty stone terrace. Cedarwood, marble, copper,
ivory, and every conceivable kind of treasure from the most remote provinces and vassal states were all heaped together, the
façades were built in the form of *bit-ḥilani* (vestibules with
columns), and decorated with stone or bronze colossi in the form
of lions or bulls; the interior rooms and the throne hall boasted
a mural decoration of hundreds of reliefs. Their restoration supplies us with considerable information regarding the military life
of that time. A botanical garden with artificial irrigation and an
adjoining zoological park provided additional charm. A new
arsenal was also established, on an equally prodigal scale. Ashur is
also said to have boasted the sensational 'new year's festival house'
with its magnificent gardens, whose trees were planted in beds

---

5. The ruins of Nineveh cannot be missed. The city gates, even today,
   rising like a gigantic earthworks, trace the outline of the city's ex-
   panse (664 hectares). Large parts of the city territory are empty fields
   today. On the Eastern ruin mound stands the Iraqi village of Nebi-
   Juni, named after the prophet Jonah. In 1846 the French vice-consul
   of Mossul P. E. Botta began excavating the mound at Kujundshik,
   but with no particular success. The first great excavation was con-
   ducted by A. H. Layard, 1849-53, who thus initiated the discovery
   of a whole lost culture. The material from Nineveh which pertains
   to the Biblical accounts is to be found in A. Parrot, *Ninivé et l'AT*,
   Neuchatel (1953). — City plan *Haag*, BibLex 1211; Galling, BRL
   396.

of soil artificially sunken into the bedrock and watered by a system of subterranean irrigation — further witness to Sanherib's originality and the magnificence of his designs. Everything necessarily had to be different, better, and more splendid than it had been in Duršarrukin." [6]

6. The description is from Schmökel, GAV 270-271. Sources listed there. — In my ten days' stay in Mossul (Dec. 14-24, 1958), I wanted to become thoroughly familiar with the ruins of Nineveh. From my quarters, Nineveh could be reached in fifteen minutes by foot, just across the Tigris, but only in peaceful times. At the time there was a state of revolution and the city was occupied by the military who had hermetically sealed off all access and exit from the city. Only from the roof terrace was I at first able to make out the clearly recognizable city 'wall and study the pointed minaret of Nebi-Juni. On Dec. 16, I decided to try a brief excursion, come what may. A paper from the police at Bagdad was my only defense. I was able to make my way across the Tigris bridge, despite its guard of soldiers, and the guardposts on the other bank as well, without incident. In good spirits I climbed up the hill of Kujundshik, which contains the palace of Sanherib. Along the sunny heights, the women of the village were spreading the freshly shorn wool to dry. I made my way, well covered, through the collapsed excavation ditches that had been abandoned. But when I once again appeared on top, I was immediately surrounded by soldiers. A cross-examination quickly ensued. With my primitive Arabic I was just barely able to make myself understood by these primitive people who spoke only the Iraqi dialect. The fact that I was Austrian, *nemsawi*, apparently stood me in good stead, since the days of Maria Theresa. I lost my interest in whatever further excursion might have been possible. I returned along the outside of the ancient city walls, but was not quite willing to give up the fight. I made my way boldly enough into the village of Nebi-Juni, under whose houses there are still ruins of Assyrian palaces. The streets are so narrow that a man could touch the buildings on both sides if he stretched out both arms. The houses are built of simple clay, as in ancient times. The attitude of the villagers was decidedly hostile. The only thing missing was actual physical violence: they would probably have stoned me if there had been any stones available in that clay village. Upon crossing the bridge back across the Tigris, I breathed freely again; but I was still proud to have set foot upon the soil of ancient Nineveh.

7. W. v. Soden, *Herrscher im Alten Orient*, 118-126; RLA I, 301; Schmökel, GAV 274.

2) "ESARHADDON'S (681-669) ARROGANCE AND ANXIETY" [7]

Esarhaddon's accession to the throne was accompanied by some quite mysterious circumstances whose precise explanation is still not understood today. According to 2 Kings 19, 36-37 and Isaiah 37, 38, Sanherib was murdered in the temple of his god Nisrok by his sons Adram-melek and Sar'eser. The murderers fled into the land of Ararat (Urartu). The next king was Esarhaddon. This account would appear to be the official version of the facts. The Babylonian chronicle,[8] on the other hand, tells a quite different story: "In the month of Tebitu, on the 20th day, Sanherib was killed by his own son in the course of a rebellion. From the 20th of Tebitu to the 18th of Addaru, there was open revolution in Assyria. Then Esarhaddon established himself upon the throne." In the Prism inscription [9] Esarhaddon describes the course of his accession to the throne in a narrative of considerable length, which is designed to conceal more than it reveals. He claims that, even though he was the youngest of his brothers, his father had destined him for his successor. He even went so far as to confirm this arrangement by a solemn oath on the occasion of an imperial assembly. The brothers, who had been passed over, appear to have effected an alteration of their father's will. Thereupon Esarhaddon fled to an unnamed place, from which he began his march against the capital city in which his brothers had seized the reins of government. He made his victorious way into Nineveh and annihilated his opposition. There is not a single word regarding his father's death. The naive reader is supposed to believe that the wicked brothers had been the murderers of their father. Still, it is hard to avoid the impression that Esarhaddon and his influential mother Nakiya shared the guilt of Sanherib's murder. It seems that throughout the entire length of his reign, Esarhaddon could not salve his bad conscience.[10] As a matter of fact,

---

8. ANET 302.

9. ANET 289-290.

10. It was only his successor who seems to have taken steps against those who were involved in the regicide. Assurbanipal remarks that he had his grandfather's murderers cut into pieces and thrown to the

Esarhaddon embarked upon a policy directly opposed to the course espoused by his late father. This extreme difference in political point of view could hardly have been a phenomenon dating only from the time of his formal accession to the throne. This is perhaps the key to Sanherib's tragic demise. This man had destroyed Babel and diverted the waters of the Euphrates into the city as a sign of its everlasting destruction. Esarhaddon, however, immediately upon his succession to power, gave official orders for the reconstruction of Babel and its temples. In an effort to spare the feelings of humiliated Babylon, he called himself not king, but only governor of Babel. After several successful campaigns he succeeded in creating peace with ever-restless Elam, so that there was no longer any peril from that quarter. Babylon, despite its many trials and travails, began gradually to recover, and to enjoy the *Pax Assyriaca.*

In the west, in the year 677, Esarhaddon once again had to follow the military example of his predecessors. The center of unrest lay this time in Sidon. "Without respect for my majesty, Abdimilkutte, King of Sidon, shook off the yoke of the god Ashur." [11] Sidon was no match for the Assyrian assault. Abdimilkutte fled into the open sea, where he was taken like a fish and beheaded. His proud victor boasts that 22 kings from the land of Hatti, that is, the eastern country, paid him homage. Among them were Ba'lu of Tyre, Manasseh (*Me-na-si-i*) of Judah (*Ya-u-di*), as well as those of Edom and Moab. Even Carthage (Qarti-hadasti — New city) is mentioned. As master of the Phoenician coastal cities, Esarhaddon considered himself ruler of the distant islands as far as Tarshish. Addressing the inhabitants of this country he offers them this mocking proverb as advice: "Where shall the fox flee in the face of the sun?"

Sidon could never have dared to undertake such a rebellion unless she had relied upon the strength of Egypt under the Ethio-

---

vultures and the fish. It would appear that he did this in an effort to turn aside the pestilence which had broken out in consequence of an unexpiated crime. ANET 288.

11. Account on Prism A and B, ANET 290, 291.

pian Pharaoh Taharkah (*Tarqu*). Just as in the case of Jerusalem, here too the help of Egypt proved illusory. As a result, the next step in the Assyrian policy, in order to establish peace throughout the west, must necessarily be the conquest of Egypt. Perhaps even the energetic Sanherib had formulated a plan to wage war upon Egypt, to be rid of the everlasting source of unrest. In the years 674/73 the first Assyrian army crossed the Egyptian frontier. The attack was, however, quickly repulsed. Apparently the reinforcements failed. Better equipped and manned, Esarhaddon made a second attempt two years later (671). This time he prevailed upon the Beduins to serve as experienced guides through the wilderness. He describes this campaign in the annals [12] (14, 12) in romantic terms. They made their way through a wilderness which was inhabited by two-headed serpents, "But I trod them underfoot and marched on . . . . Then there were no brooks. Water had to be drawn from a great depth, with lines and chains and buckets." The Assyrians probably made their way into Egypt through the Wadi Tumilat, the ancient land of Goshen. "Daily without interruption, I met Tirhakah, accursed he of all the great gods, in mighty battles. Five times I struck him with the points of my arrows and inflicted many wounds upon him, which will never again heal. His capital city Memphis (*me-im-pi*) I besieged. In only half a day I conquered it with mines, breaches, and assault ladders. I destroyed it, tore down its walls, and burnt it. The queen, the women of his palace, his 'heir apparent,' his other children, his possessions, cattle, large and small beyond counting, I carried off to Ashur." [13] This exaggerated and pompous narrative of his victory must have made his readers stop to think what a hero this Esarhaddon must have been to have accomplished such mighty exploits.

The sober reality behind this campaign consists simply in the fact that Egypt changed masters. Instead of the Cushite Taharkah, the Assyrian Esarhaddon now ruled over the land along the Nile. After driving out the Cushite troops, he established 22

---

12. ANET 292b.
13. Sengirle-Stele, ANET 293a.

district administrators, in the "liberated" country, following the ancient Egyptian pattern. For the sake of security, these administrators were each provided with an Assyrian "counsel," to assist in the fulfillment of the imposed duties. These successes on the distant frontier seem to have made little impression in Nineveh itself; the king, however, was extremely enthusiastic. On a victory column in Sengirli [14] Esarhaddon is depicted greater than life size. Before him kneel the proportionally tiny figures of the Cushite Taharkah and King Ba'lu of Tyre, begging for grace. Both have halters through their noses, and the great king is holding the ropes in his hand. This is a monument of deceitful arrogance, since neither of these two rulers ever fell into the power of the victor. The same type and images are displayed in an inscription on the brick wall at Dog River (*Nahr el-kelb*),[15] a point along the Phoenician coastal road at which the Pharaohs and kings of Mesopotamia before him had also perpetuated the memory of their mighty accomplishments.

Throughout the entire reign of Esarhaddon, the northern part of the kingdom had been threatened by a growing cloud. Tiglath-Pilesar III of Sargon, in defeating their one enemy, the kingdom of Urartu, had only succeeded in opening the door to an even greater threat, the hordes of Cimmerians rushing across the Caucasus from the northern plains. Shortly after 700, part of this tribe was making its way into western Iran spreading terror on all sides; in 690 a second horde annihilated the kingdom of Phrygia in Asia Minor. The Assyrians began to fear that these newcomers would make an alliance with the established mountain peoples and turn their combined forces against the cultivated land. Ashur was too weak for a counter-offensive. The peril seemed to be alleviated for a short time when Esarhaddon made an alliance with the Scythians who were also pushing down across the Caucasus behind the Cimmerians; he sent his own daughter to the king of the Scythians as wife and pledge of his alliance. The Cimmerians were thus held in check from the north by the

---

14. Illustration: W. v. Soden, *Herrscher im Alten Orient*, 121.
15. 9 mi N. of Beirut, situated directly on the coast. Illustration AOB 147.

Scythians and from the south by the Assyrians. The *Pax Assyriaca* had been secured for a brief time.

Under the pressure of these many crises, Esarhaddon took refuge in sorcery of every kind. By sacrifice, augury, and oracles he sought to learn the will of the gods, in order to turn away the threatening peril from himself and from his kingdom. The year 671 was particularly fraught with disaster. The court astronomers had calculated two total lunar eclipses, on July 2 and December 27. According to the astrological records, this could only mean disaster for the king. To escape this, the king recalled a ritual which had been carried out once before, around 1800 B.C. For the time of the threatened disaster, a substitute king was installed; he was to bring the disaster upon himself and thus fend it off from the real king. In the city of Akkad, on the basis of an oracle, the son of a minor official was chosen as substitute king and then installed as "King" for a period of 100 days. Esarhaddon was called simply "peasant" during this time. In the letters dating from these days he is addressed as "sir peasant." Esarhaddon survived this time of misfortune. The unfortunate substitute king died — obviously not without assistance — and was buried like a true king. It appears that his wife was forced to follow him to the grave.[16]

Despite the sacrifice of the substitute king, Esarhaddon was destined to rule for only a short time. Rebellion broke out in Egypt. The 22 district administrators appointed by the king preferred collaboration with their former ruler Taharkah to the Assyrian yoke. Esarhaddon sent an army under his general Ša-Nabu-šu and, since he considered the campaign of prime importance, later decided to march himself. In this enterprise he made too great a demand upon his body already weakened by age and disease. He took ill in the course of the campaign and died somewhere in Syria-Palestine.[17]

---

16. W. v. Soden, *Herrscher im Alten Orient*, 124.
17. *Ibid.*, 126.

3) "ASHUR-BANI-PAL (669-630?) CONDUCTS THE KINGDOM TO ITS FINAL MOMENT OF GLORY" [18]

"We know this last great ruler of Assyria, a most able general and energetic politician, and enthusiastic hunter, art collector, and passionate student of antiquity, on the basis of a considerable body of dedicatory and building inscriptions — there are no annals. These inscriptions, composed with extraordinary clarity, cast an excellent, although obviously one-sided, light upon the ruler's career. The information they provide is fittingly amplified by 26 letters which have been preserved and the many relief illustrations yielded by the northern palace in Nineveh — their magnificent animal representations are justly famous throughout the world. His library, 20,000 cuneiform tablets which Rassa discovered in Kujundschik in 1854, included the principal works of the whole Akkadian literature and we know that the king's archaeological interests requested ancient texts or copies from all the temple libraries in his country in order to complete his collection. It is owing to the literary activity of Ashur-bani-pal and the unexpected good fortune that the rediscovery of his library coincided with the very beginning of Assyriological investigation that we now possess a comprehensive knowledge of the previously all but unknown literature of the Sumerians and Akkadians." [19] Only the most important events of this long and fruitful reign can be mentioned here.

a) *No-Amon, Which Lay Along the River* (Neh 3, 8)

Esarhaddon's death had brought the expedition against Egypt to a standstill. Tirhakah (Taharkah) was allowed to reoccupy Memphis, driving the Assyrian soldiers and their administrative officials out of the country. For the year 666 we read that one of the sacred bulls of Apis died and was solemnly buried. In that same year, Ashur-bani-pal set out upon the conquest of the Nile country. The course of this campaign is described in a

---

18. *Ibid.*, 127-138.
19. Schmökel, GAV 278-279.

lengthy narrative from the Rassam cylinder.[20] Ashur-bani-pal marched not only with an Assyrian army, but also with the auxiliary troops he forceably collected from 22 kings along his route through the western countries. "Upon a trust oracle by Ashur, Bel, Nebo, the great gods, my lords, who march at my side, I defeated the battle soldiers of his army in a great open battle. Tirhakah . . . was blinded by the dazzle of my glory. He abandoned Memphis and fled to Ni' (Thebes)." There are some texts which would suggest the possibility that Ashur-bani-pal sent a detachment south up the Nile, and that after 40 days of sailing they burnt and plundered the surrounding territory but were not able to take the city of Thebes itself.

In Memphis, meantime, Ashur-bani-pal completely reorganized the city. The Assyrian garrisons were strengthened, and the expelled officials were reinstalled. The rebellious administrators he brought back to Nineveh. Fully aware that he could not rule over conquered Egypt without the assistance of the native ruling class, he not only spared Neho, district administrator of Sais, but also restored him to his lost kingship. He had him dressed in magnificent robes, adorned him with the golden chain symbolic of kingship, put golden rings on his hand, and presented him with a ceremonial dagger upon which he had inscribed his name. He then supplied him with war chariots, horses and pack animals, more than he had previously possessed, and sent him back to Egypt. Surely he could hope that a man so honored and provided would represent Ashur's interests.

A dream — and dreams played an important role in ancient Egypt — collapsed this newly established Assyrian hegemony like a house of cards. Tirkahah, Ashur's fierce enemy, had died in 664. His successor Tanutamon had dreamt that two snakes had raised their heads, one on his right and the other on his left. The dream was interpreted as a pressage of a glorious rule and the final expulsion of the Assyrian forces. The young king immediately made his way to Napata where he was enthroned in his native land of Cush. From there he proceeded up the

---

20. Found in the ruins of Kujundshik. Text: ANET 294.

Nile. In Thebes he was accorded a triumphant reception. "The sons of rebellion" that is, the princes who had previously bowed before the pressure of Assyrian influence, now joined forces with him. The rest of the journey to Memphis was like a triumphal procession. In his arrogance he boasts that he looked for a hostile army in the delta district but could not find one. His enemies had all retreated before him. He was thus able to establish a united kingdom of Upper and Lower Egypt, and the dream of the two serpents had been fulfilled. At this point, unfortunately, there is a break in the proud narrative of the dream stele.[21] What follows would have been a supreme indignity to record in Egyptian words. It is the story of Egypt's most bitter shame.

Upon the arrival of the Assyrian army, the balance turned once again. The dynasties which had espoused the Cushite cause now to turned to the Assyrian, fully aware that there was nothing else they could do, and kissed Ashur-bani-pal's feet. Tanutamon was forced to quite Memphis and withdrew up the Nile. The Assyrian army followed hot on his heels. The conquest and destruction of Thebes spread throughout the known world like lightning. In Judah, the prophet Nahum pointed to the fate of No-Amon [22] and proclaimed the threatening message that proud Nineveh would meet a like end: "Are you better than No-Amon, that sat by the Nile, with water around her, her rampart a sea, and water her wall? Ethiopia was her strength, Egypt too, and that without limit; Put and the Libyans were her helpers. Yet she was carried away, and went into captivity; her little ones were dashed in pieces at the head of every street; for her honored men lots were cast, and all her great men were bound in chains" (Nah 3, 8-10).

Ashur-bani-pal returned to Nineveh with all his accumulated booty, including two huge obelisks. "I carried off from Thebes heavy booty, beyond counting. I made Musur (Egypt) and Nubia

---

21. Drioton-Vandier, *L'Égypte,* 554.
22. Egyptian abbreviated name for Thebes: *No'* (Hebrew) or *Nywt* (Egyptian); the full form is *Nywt 'Imn* "city of (the god Amun)," or *Nywt rst* "city of the south."

feel my weapons bitterly and celebrated my triumph. With full hands and safely I returned to Nineveh, the city of my rule." [23]

Tanutamon, the man primarily responsible for this disaster, had escaped to Napata. In the south, the ancient Ethiopian dynasty maintained itself for a few more centuries. Instead of Napata, Meroe became the capital. The alliance with Egypt was finally dissolved. The kingdom of Meroe was set up as an African state with its own language and even its own script, the so-called Meroitic script. Thus the Cushites, the object of so many hopes in the days of Isaiah, had completely departed from the concert of Ancient Near Eastern politics.

The Assyrian dominion over Egypt did not last a decade. With the aid of Carian and Ionian mercenaries, Psammetich, the son of Neho who had been so singularly honored by Ashur-bani-pal, won freedom for his country in the year 655, thereby establishing the 26th and last Egyptian dynasty, which was destined to be dissolved by the Persians after the battle of Pelusium.

b) *Civil War* (652-648)

The succession to the throne was regulated in such a way that Ashur-bani-pal succeeded to the rule of Assyria while his older brother Šamaš-šumu-kin was ruler in Babylon. This well-meaning division of power was in reality fraught with danger. Probably it was the influence of his grandmother Nakiya, who was still quite energetic, that succeeded in maintaining a state of peace between the two brothers for more than a decade. But the anti-Assyrian forces were reawakening in Babel. Šamaš-šumu-kin set himself at the head of a powerful confederation, which, as in the days of Merodach-Baladan, gathered together all the dissatisfied elements, Aramaeans and Elamites in the east and the Syro-Phoenican states in the west. The four years of civil war (652-648) were marked by extremely bitter fighting. Upon the capture of Babel in the year 648, the "traitorous brother" found his death in the flames of the palace. In the annals, from this time on, a certain Kandalanu appears as king of Babel.[24]

---

23. ANET 295b.
24. Kandalanu is not the Babylonian throne name of Ashur-bani-pal, as Phul

Not content with this success, Ashur-bani-pal prepared for a decisive battle with that constant hotbed of discontent Elam. In the year 639 he destroyed the Elamite capital city of Susa, laid waste to the countryside far and near. Since that time there is simply no further Elamite history. A great enemy of Ashur had been annihilated, only to make place for a greater, the Persians who were advancing in their stead.

4) THE GODS OF ASHUR IN JERUSALEM

What was the position of tiny Judah in the midst of this Assyrian world empire? Hezekiah's attempt to kick against the goad was doomed to failure. It was only his phenomenal good fortune that prevented Jerusalem from being completely destroyed, and allowed the dwarf state of Judah to continue its existence, dependent upon the good will of Ashur. Manasseh (698-642) had to bow, willy-nilly, to the Assyrian yoke. Among the 22 kings of the country of Hatti, Manasseh (*Me-na-si-i*)[25] is mentioned alongside the kings of Tyre, Byblos, Edom, Moab, Ammon, Gaza, Ashkelon, Ekron, etc. All of them together were commanded to supply building materials for the king of the world, despite the extreme difficulties involved in transporting them to Nineveh. On the occasion of the Egyptian campaign Palestine lay along the route of the soldiers. Judah, like the other satellite states, had to supply a military levy.[26] The time for pursuing an independent policy had long passed. Nonetheless, seizing an opportunity which can no longer be accurately identified, although it was probably in connection with the civil war in Babylon, Manasseh allowed himself to be drawn into a rebellion against the Assyrian overlords. A most hopeless undertaking! He was taken prisoner, carried off to Babylon at the end of a rope and with a ring in his nose;[27] but then, in circumstances similar to those described in the

---

is for Tiglath-Pilesar (W. v. Soden, *Herrscher im Alten Orient*, 130): he was really a Babylonian governor, by the grace of Assur. This follows from inscriptions found in Harran in 1956, Bibl 40 (1959), 96.

---

25. ANET 291a.
26. ANET 294a.
27. Since the Chronicle is otherwise a faithful witness, the account of

case of the Egyptian administrator Neho, he was reestablished
as king, obviously not until he had sworn an appropriate oath
of fidelity (2 Ch 33, 11-13).

According to the judgment of the Biblical historian, Manasseh
is one of the very worst kings that ever sat upon the throne of
David, precisely because he made it possible for the gods of
Ashur and Canaan to find a place within its kingdom (2 K 21;
2 Ch 33). But in order to do him justice in terms of the historical
picture, we must recognize the fact that, as an Assyrian satellite,
he did not have a free hand even in matters of religion. Thus
the old cult of the high places with its Messeboth and Asheroth
broke out once again. In the very temple itself he was forced to
allow the erection of altars to the high Assyrian gods, that is,
to provide altars "for the entire host of heaven." Not only black
magic, sorcery, spell-casting, and conjuring of the dead became
prevalent, but Baal once again demanded his human sacrifices.
Manasseh even allowed his own son to be burned (2 K 21, 6).
This invasion of paganism was opposed by many brave prophets.
Manasseh simply silenced these unwelcome voices with the necessary force. He spilled innocent blood (2 K 21, 16).

Although the figure of Manasseh is written only in black
letters in the Books of the Kings, the Book of Chronicles presents
an entirely different side of this "evil" king (2 Ch 33, 14). After
his "humiliation," he completely reestablished the cult of Yahweh.
Is this simply evidence of his interior conversion? Or is it perhaps to
be taken as evidence of the fact that the winged sun of Ashur
was close to setting. The neglected fortifications of Jerusalem were
not only restored, but Manasseh also erected a new city wall,
which encompassed the newer sections of the city (2 Ch 33, 14).
Outside Jerusalem as well he restored and renovated the fortifications. Manasseh was a ruler who, under the pressure of circumstances, gave more ground than can be defended; but when
the pressure was removed he seized the opportunity to promote
the restoration of the threatened ideal, as soon as the time was

---

a deportation to Babel (2 Ch 33, 11) instead of Nineveh, as one might
have supposed, is hardly to be doubted. This would argue for a date
during the time of the civil war in Babylon.

ripe. His is a character hard to assess properly in the dim light of history.

At all events, Manasseh's reign represents a low point but also a turning point in the history of salvation and rejection that runs through the Old Testament. The terrible splendor of Ashur passed lightly over Jerusalem. The "great dragon" had displayed its power and the impotence of the other "gods." Yahweh, the god of Jerusalem, proved himself the stronger. It was precisely in the reign of Manasseh that the Assyrian twilight of the gods, long since envisioned by the prophets Nahum and Zephaniah, was becoming more and more evident on the horizon of history

UNDER THE HAMMER OF BABYLON

"You are my hammer and weapon of war:
With you I break nations in pieces;
With you I destroy kingdoms;
With you I break in pieces the horse and his rider;
With you I break in pieces the chariot and the
charioteer;
With you I break in pieces man and woman;
With you I break in pieces the old man and the youth;
With you I break in pieces the young man and the
maiden;
With you I break in pieces the shepherd and his
flocks;
With you I break in pieces the farmer and his team;
With you I break in pieces governors and
commanders." (Jer 51, 20-23)

CHAPTER X

THE ASSYRIAN TWILIGHT
OF THE GODS

THE decline of the Assyrian empire meant at the same time the decline of its gods. Ashur-bani-pal's world conquest had exhausted the strength of his kingdom. Egypt lay under his rule for hardly a decade until becoming independent under Psammetich in 655. Along the northern frontier, new peoples were forcing their way into the empire: Scythians, Cimmerians, Medes, and Persians. It was now only a question of time; how long could the bow stand the tension. There was a serious internal rift between Ashur and Babel. In the civil war Babel had been trodden underfoot; but downtrodden nations never become friends. It was precisely from this point of Assyrian triumph that the Assyrian twilight really begins. The downtrodden dragon of Babylon reared its head under the standard of Aramaea and Chaldea, and threatened to devour the kingdom and the gods of Ashur.

The last chapters of Assyrian history are partially hidden in the shadow of time. The countless text discoveries that cast such a clear light on the preceding glorious epochs are in strange proportion to the pitiful few that describe the final decades. There was nothing to record but the collapse and decline of the empire.

The primary source for this era is the new Babylonian chronicle.[1] In terms of literary genre, this chronicle is essentially different from the blood-thirsty and proudly victorious annals of Assyria. In the most objective manner, the important events are registered year by year. The history of war and military campaigns is not the predominant element. The five tables of the new Babylonian chronicle extant today deal with the years 626-622, 616-609, 608-605, 605-594, 557-556 B.C. Despite some lacunae, this chronicle affords some valuable insights into the development, triumph, and demise of the new Babylonian kingdom, and thus, indirectly, sheds considerable light upon the Biblical narratives.

1) THE SCYTHIAN STORM

The year of Ashur-bani-pal's death is not known.[2] This is no mere chance; an awe-inspiring storm of barbarians, the Scythian storm, suddenly fell upon the entire east. Although the records are not clear on this point,[3] these wild hordes seem to have overrun Syria and Palestine as far as the Egyptian border and put a definitive end to the already weakened Assyrian hegemony. Assyria herself managed to protect her native territory and Mesopotamia from this terrible flood of invasion.[4]

---

1. Complete text, with translation and historical introduction in D. J. Wiseman, *Chronicles of Chaldean Kings (1626-556) in the British Museum,* London (1956). This incorporates the earlier findings of C. J. Gadd, *The Newly Discovered Babylonian Chronicle, No. 21, 901 in the British Museum,* London (1923). Further texts ANET 301ff. — The discovery of the new chronicle has led to various scholarly studies: P. Nötscher, *"Neue" babylonische Chroniken und Altes Testament,* BZ NF 1 (1957), 110-114; H. Tadmor, *Chronology of the Last Kings of Judah,* JNES 15 (1956), 226-230; D. N. Freedman, *The Babylonian Chronicle,* BA 19 (1956), 50-60; E. R. Thiele, *New Evidence on the Chronology of the Last Kings of Judah,* BASOR 143 (1956), 22-27.

2. For the year 631 there is a dated business tablet from Nippur to Assurbanipal. M. Falkner, AFO 16 (1953), 309. — Probably died in 630/29.

3. The account of the Scythians is based on Herodotus, I, 104-106. Bright, HistIsr 293 argues that this information must be used with caution.

4. W. v. Soden, *Herrscher im Alten Orient,* 138.

It was during these uncertain years that the Medes, under their king Phraortes, thought the opportunity ripe to sweep down from their mountains and make themselves masters of Assyrian territory. The Assyrian army was, this time, still strong enough to drive them back into the mountains. Ashur had been granted one final breathing space. Ashur-bani-pal's son Sin-šar-iškun (c. 629-612), ,who bore the throne name Ashur-etil-ilani,[5] was the last to succeed to the Assyrian imperial throne.[6] Energetic like his father, he assumed the proud title "king of the universe," but his role in history was a tragic one. He was destined to meet his death in a bitter struggle against the inroads of the barbarian hordes.

2) NABOPOLASSAR, NEW LORD OF BABEL (626-605)

After the civil war (648), Ashur-bani-pal had installed a certain Kandalanu as Assyrian overlord in Babylon. This regent seized upon the confusion following the death of Ashur-bani-pal as an opportunity to shake off the Assyrian rule. Following this attempted coup, Assyrian troops were brought into the city, and this outrage provoked a national rebellion. It appears that Kandalanu fell in the battles that followed (627), for the following year is listed as a "kingless" year.[7] The Babylonian throne was once again without an occupant. It was at this time that the Chaldaeans seized the opportunity to assert themselves, as they had in the days of Merodach-Baladan. In October of 626 Nabopolassar defeated the Assyrian army not far from Babylon. He then grasped the hand of Bel and thus became master of Babel. He thus laid the foundation for the new Babylonian kingdom. The Aramaean Chaldaeans, who had been living there for many years, already

---

5. The current conception, that there were two different rulers who could be properly fitted into the historical scheme of things only with difficulty, has now been proven false thanks to the inscriptions discovered at Eski-Harran. E. Vogt, Bibl 40 (1959), 96.

6. The year of accession is not definitely known. Wiseman, *Chronicles* 90: *The Accession Year of Sin-šar-iškun*. — M. Falkner, *Neue Inschriften aus der Zeit Sin-šar-iškun*, AFO 16 (1952/53), 305-310.

7. Wiseman, *Chronicles*, 89-90.

considered themselves Babylonians. The kingdom they represent thus embodies many ancient Babylonian traditions.

W. v. Soden [8] gives this character sketch of the new ruler, who introduced a new style into the politics of the Ancient Near East: "Concerning the personality of Nabopolassar there is not much we can say. The few extant inscriptions, apart from some very brief references to the destruction of Assyria, describe only building projects. Their style manifests a deliberate identification with the ancient Babylonian kings, especially Hammurabi, and in some respects to the rulers of Akkad. Nabopolassar makes no attempt to disguise his humble beginnings. He calls himself 'son of a nobody' and 'a miserable nobody.' He attributes all his successes simply to the assistance of the god Marduk of Babylon and the other gods. His titulature remains surprisingly modest. It would seem that his piety was genuine. Departing from the traditional manner, he generally concludes his inscriptions with a prayer."

3) "THE MEDO-BABYLONIAN AXIS" [9]

After Babylonia had succeeded in shaking off the Assyrian yoke, the Medes renewed their violent attack upon Ashur. The intervening assimilation of the Cimmerians had tremendously increased the strength of the Medes.[10] They were no longer, as they had been 50 years ago, a loose confederation of numerous but largely powerless city princes; they were a people united under a powerful hand, marshalled under the powerful direction of a king, Umakistar (Cyaxares).[11] The Medes and Babylonians now begin to form the axis about which the history of Asia Minor turns. The invasion of the Medes upon Nineveh in the year 616 was once again repulsed, this time with Scythian assistance. But neither Cyaxares nor Nabopolassar were the kind of men to be dissuaded from their goal, the destruction of Assyria, simply by

---

8. W. v. Soden, *Herrscher im Alten Orient,* (1954), 139.
9. Bright, HistIsr 294.
10. Schmökel, GAV 282.
11. RLA I, 303.

an initial setback. The full course of this gigantic struggle is best described in the Babylonian chronicle.

4) THE LAST DAYS OF NINEVEH [12]

In his 10th year (616/15), in the month of Ajar (April/May) Nabopolassar made his way up the Euphrates in the territory of Assyria. Along the middle Euphrates he encountered no resistance. The people of Suhu and Hindanu offered him rich tribute and homage. It was only in the district of the city Qablinu that resistance was encountered. In the month of Ab (July/August) there was a twelve-day battle for the city. The Assyrians suffered a severe defeat; the city was taken and plundered. Nabopolassar, who now, in keeping with the ancient traditions, assumed the name "king of Akkad," followed this victory by a series of expeditions into the Assyrian territory designed to show his strength and intimidate his adversary. He returned to Babylon laden with booty. There is mention only, as it were, in passing of the fact that he brought the gods of the conquered nation with him. His victory was at the same time a victory of the Babylonian Bel over the gods of the subjected cities and nations.

Nabopolassar's victory had an alarming effect upon Egypt. The Pharaoh Psammetich quickly changed from his former hostility and played the role of Ashur's faithful ally. The political situation had done a complete *volte-face*. Ashur no longer represented any danger. What faced Egypt now was a new threat from the united forces of the Medes and Babylonians who were already preparing to assert their claim to the rich heritage of the collapsing Assyrian empire. It was no selfless sympathy with the ailing man in Nineveh that decided Psammetich upon a course of active military support. The continued existence of Assyria, no matter how weakened, as a buffer state between the world powers in this new configuration could only be an object of supreme desire. His sphere of influence in this new balance

---

12. In the following, we are basing the presentation on the Babylonian chronicle. Cf. Wiseman, *Chronicles,* Historische Einführung 4ff.; Text 44ff. — ANET 303-305. — TGI 59-63.

of power would be, as it had been in the glorious days of ancient Egypt, the territories of Syria and Palestine. The Egyptian troops were apparently embarked upon ships for Phoenicia, from where they marched to the Euphrates. In that same year 616 the united Assyrian-Egyptian army launched a counter-offensive against the lost city of Qablini. The military initiative, however, had already escaped them. Nabopolassar refused to commit himself on the Euphrates front. In the month of Adar (February 615) he met an Assyrian army in the territory of Araphu near the city of Madanu and drove it back to the Zab River.

In the 11th year of his reign (615/14) Nabopolassar began to carry the offensive into the Assyrian heartland. In the month of Ajar (April/May) he laid siege to the ancient metropolis of Ashur on the Tigris. On this occasion he was not successful. He was defeated and had to fight his way home. The resistance concentrated on the siege of the citadel of Takritain. For 10 days the tide of battle went back and forth. Finally, thanks to a desperate surprise attack, Nabopolassar succeeded in breaking through the besieging forces. Thereupon both armies returned to their camps, the one to Nineveh and the other to Babel.

In autumn of 615 in the month of Aharsammu (September/October), the Medes made their attack. They streamed down from the mountains and occupied the district of Araphu. In the 12th year (614/13), in the month of Ab (July/August) they succeeded in accomplishing what Nabopolassar had failed to do; Cyaxares conquered the all but impregnable fortress of Ashur — the city was built on a triangular rock promontory which dropped steeply into the Tigris. Nabopolassar marched immediately to offer his support. He came too late for the assault on the city. "Upon the ruins of the conquered city the king of Akkad and Cyaxares met. They swore mutual friendship and alliance."

The 13th year (613/12) can be considered the year of mighty preparations for the decisive encounter. There is mention of some "pacification expeditions" into the restless territory on the middle Euphrates. On that occasion Nabopolassar, fighting against the city of Anatu, is reported to have built huge siege machines and directed them against the city walls.

In the 14th year (612/11), the Medes and Babylonians joined forces for a decisive battle. They made their way up the Tigris and enclosed the city of Nineveh. The Assyrian forces defended themselves with the courage born of despair. For three months, from the third to the fifth month (June-August), the siege dragged on. Three major battles were fought. "On the ——— (the date can no longer be read), in the month of Ab (August/September), the city was captured.... The plunder of the city, a huge sum which cannot be reckoned they carried off as booty. The city itself they turned into a heap of ruins and debris." The Assyrian king Sin-šar-iškun perished in these battles. On the 20th of Elul, the following month, Cyaxares and his troops withdrew into their own country. Nabopolassar, however, was not content with the conquest of Nineveh; he marched upon Nisibis and carried off prisoners and spoils of war. In what remained of Assyria, with its new center at Harran, Ashur-uballit (612-606) was raised to the throne. With the aid of Egyptian support he sought to preserve what could still be preserved.

In autumn of 610, with the help of the Medes, Nabopolassar managed to conquer Harran. Ashur-uballit fled across the Euphrates into Syria. From there, supported by the additional strength of an Egyptian army which had been received by the king of Judaea, Josiah, upon its march through Palestine, he attempted to recapture Harran in the summer of 609. This decisive battle must have been fought with the most extreme bitterness and cruelty on both sides. The chronicle relates that three battles were fought in the course of as many months. Assyrians and Egyptians were thrown back across the Euphrates. And thus the "terrible splendor of the great dragon" was once and for all destroyed. The removal of Ashur-uballit in the year 606 was the final entry in the two-thousand year history of Assyria. Three mighty powers now occupied the field: Egypt, Babylon, and Media. The political balance of power was far from secure. The Assyrian dragon was dead, but the Babylonian dragon was beginning to rear his head. And the mountain peoples who had shared in the victory were not likely to rest content with their mountain territory. No matter which world power asserted the stronger hand, the fate of Judah was like a juggler's ball in her hand. At the battle of Megiddo, Judah's attempt to enter into the field of world politics, this fate had suffered a severe setback.

These were eventful years, determining the whole course of the future. That is why the writer of our chronicle concludes his narrative with these words: "He who loves Nabu and Marduk, let him preserve this and never let it out of his hands."

CHAPTER XI

THE PROPHETS NAHUM, ZEPHANIAH, HABAKKUK, AND JONAH

QUITE different from the objective style of narrative found in the Babylonian chronicle, presenting only the external skeleton of world history, are the prophetic texts in which the same world-shaking events have found a clear echo. They are passionately inspired accounts, passionate simply because they are fighting to represent the rights of a God Yahweh, who is passionately and jealously involved in the history of this world. The mighty God amid the great disturbances of human history is the master theme of their preaching. Religious interests are so predominant that it will be difficult to determine the precise historical events that kindled this prophetic zeal on each individual occasion. Nahum, Zephaniah, and Habakkuk fly their course like birds before a storm, a prophetic presage of Nineveh's destruction. In the Book of Jonah the fate of Nineveh, the "great city," has awakened an equally deep and powerful religious echo.

1) THE PROPHET NAHUM

Nahum's personal fate is completely hidden behind his prophetic activity. We know nothing more about him than his name, which proclaims the "consolation" of Yahweh.[2] The place of his birth, Elqos, is, likewise, not properly identified.[3] Pfeiffer[4] refers to Nahum as the last of the classical Hebrew poets. The power of his speech approaches that of the song of Deborah (Jg 5) and David's elegy upon Saul's death (2 S 1, 19ff.). The liveliness of his imagery is unsurpassed. His description of the breathtaking battle for Nineveh is so gripping, so thrilling, and so lively that the reader, swept along by the force of the language, can actually see and hear the struggle. What is more, this mighty poet, of whose work only three chapters have been preserved, is a prophet of Yahweh. His words are all aglow with the fire of the God whose prerogatives he is fighting for in human history.

a) "His Way is in Whirlwind and Storm" (1, 1 — 2, 4)

Nahum owes his allegiance to the god of Moses, who revealed himself on Sinai as 'el qannô, "the jealous god" (Ex 20, 5). This leitmotiv stands at the beginning of the book, explaining Yahweh's involvement in human history. It can not be a matter of indifference for Yahweh that his chosen people has been handed over to violence and oppression. In the alphabetic song (1, 1-8) which has been preserved intact only as far as the letter Kaph, the

---

1. A. George, DBS VI (1958), 291-301, Article *Nahum*, with the latest literature. In Qumran Scroll IV there is a fragment of *Nahum* with an interpretation, RB (1956), 60-62.

2. *Nahum* is probably the abbreviated form of *Nahumiah*, which Jerome translates as *consolator*, "consoler" (PL XXV, 1131). Similar formations are: Menahem and Nehemiah, simply developments of the idea that "Yahweh comforts."

3. According to Pseudoepiphanius (PG XLIII, 409), "across the Jordan near Begabara in the Tribe of Simeon," a contradictory identification, since Simeon settled in Southern Palestine. Perhaps it is Beth-Gubrin. According to Jerome (PL XXV, 1132), it is situated in Galilee. A grave of Nahum has been venerated, at El Qos 30 mi N of Mossul only since the 16th century.

4. Pfeiffer, IntrAT 595.

passionate character of God's interests is portrayed in equally passionate and, we might say, mythological imagery. "His way is in whirlwind and storm, and the clouds are the dust of his feet. He rebukes the sea and makes it dry, he dries up all the rivers." When he strides over the mountains the earth quakes. Who can endure the heat of his anger; with an overflowing flood he will make a full end of his adversaries. Like entangled thorns they are consumed and like dry stubble.

This triumphant image of God is not recorded without a deeper purpose. The contrast of eventual redemption is all the more powerful for this awesome prologue. "Behold, on the mountains the feet of him who brings good tidings, who proclaims peace" (2, 1). It is only because God is so powerful that he can annihilate the enemy and restore the "majesty of Jacob" (2, 3).

This is the overture for the song of Nineveh's destruction.

b) *"Wasted is Nineveh"* (2, 4—3, 19)

"Woe to bloody city, all full of lies and booty — no end to the plunder! The crack of whip, and rumble of wheel, galloping horse and bounding chariot! Horesemen charging, flashing sword and glittering spear, hosts of slain, heaps of corpses, dead bodies without end . . . ." The officers stumble as they go, and hasten to the wall. The river gates are opened and the palace is in dismay. Its mistress is carried off, while her maidens lament. "Plunder the silver, plunder the gold! There is no end of treasure, or wealth of every precious thing" (2, 9). "Wasted is Nineveh; who will bemoan her?" (3, 7). Desolate, desolation and ruin (2, 11) — this is her end.

Words like this do not need a commentary.[5] They are sufficient all by themselves. No mere poetaster could have produced them. The ruin of Nineveh is God's judgment. "All who hear the news of you clap their hands over you. For upon whom has not come your unceasing evil?" (3, 19).

---

5. H. Brunner, *Ein assyrisches Relief mit einer ägyptischen Festung*, AFO 16 (1952), 253-263. From the Northern Palace of Assurbanipal, a striking illustration for Nahum 3, 8-10: Representation of the conquest of an Egyptian fortress.

c) *Chronological Outline of the Book of Nahum*:

The three brief chapters of the Book of Nahum were not all spoken or recorded at the same time. Nahum's prophetic activity must have stretched over a rather long interval of time, how long cannot be determined. The oracle against No-Amon, that is, Thebes [6] (3, 8-10), presupposes the existence of a strong Assyrian kingdom, although it is already beginning to come apart at the seams. We surely cannot be too far wrong in dating this group of oracles towards the end of Ashurbani-pal's rule, approximately 640-630. The oracles against Nineveh are a prophetic threat, and must therefore be dated before the fall of the city, in the final years of the great collapse of the empire.[7] The Book of Nahum as we have it today is, like the books of the other prophets, the work of disciples who preserved their master's words and wrote this title over the final collection: "Oracle against Nineveh; the book of the vision of Nahum of Elkosh" (1, 1).

Only very little has been preserved from what was at least two or three decades of prophetic activity. What little is preserved, however, is such a powerful statement that the ideas expressed here have continued to work their influence upon the centuries that followed. Deutero-Isaiah (52, 7), seized upon the figure of *mebassēr*, the "herald of peace" [8] (2, 1). In a later era, in a time of extreme crisis, the victorious imagery of this book was reawakened to bear a deeper message. The monks of Qumran, for example, regarded this book, not as the witness of history past, but rather as a message destined for their own time. They interpreted it in terms of the struggle between the Jewish priest and king Alexander Jannaeus and the Seleucid Demetrius III, in the year 88 B.C.[9] Thus, the Book of Nahum, despite its original involvement with the final years of the Assyrian kingdom, displays a character that transcends mere time; it is contemporary to every age. "It is a most singular cry of faith and hope, always in the present." [10]

---

6. Cf. above: Assyrian conquest of Thebes, 303.

7. DBS VI (1958), 297. — Some exegetes take the book as a prophetic liturgy, composed for the festival in thanks for the fall of Nineveh. Robert-Feuillet, Introduction 516 finds this untenable; the book does not give the impression of being "composed," but rather appears as a product of intensely personal stamp.

8. For further discussion of Nahum's *Fortleben,* cf. DBS VI (1958), 299.

9. Qumran Scroll IV contains fragments of Nahum together with a *pešer,* i.e., an exegetical commentary, RB (1956), 60, 62. — Bibl (1956), 530-531.

10. "... son livre est-il resté au cours des âges un cri de foi et d'espoir toujours actuel," DBS VI (1958), 300.

2) THE PROPHET ZEPHANIAH (*Sophonias*)

Zephaniah has been called an epigone,[11] a poor descendant of the great prophets Amos and Isaiah. The word epigone, however, has a derogatory sound. Zephaniah is not simply a weak and unworthy scion of the great men of old; he is rather the worthy descendant of those great pathfinders whose spiritual heritage he claims and to whose message he adds a new and resolute strength for his own era. According to the book's inscription, his career is dated "in the days of King Josiah" (640-609), more precisely in the decade from 640-630. In the person of Zephaniah, the prophetic message which had been silenced in terror and blood during the rule of Manasseh, once again asserts itself. His genealogy is traced to a certain Hezekiah. It is not impossible that this is a reference to the great Hezekiah, king and reformer. At all events, Zephaniah is a genuine descendant, if not in the body, at least in the spirit, of that great champion of the faith in Yahweh who lived at the end of the eighth century. Zephaniah is among those who prepare the way for the reforms initiated by King Josiah. Nothing more is known about his background. It is possible, but not demonstrable, that his sermon on judgment was occasioned by the storm of Scythian invaders [12] rushing into Palestine in the year 630-625: there is an echo of this in his *Dies irae*.

a) *Dies Irae Dies Illa*

As suceessor to the prophet Amos, Isaiah takes up the message of the "day of Yahweh" that is to come. This day will not be light for Jerusalem; it will be darkness and gloom. Throughout the holy city there is no longer any place for Yahweh. The pagan gods have replaced him. Upon the rooftops they worship the "host of heaven" (1, 5a) and swear by Milcom,[13] the god of the Ammonites (1, 5c). They leap over the thresholds in their

---

11. Robert-Feuillet, IntrAT 515.
12. Cf. above, page 310.
13. Solomon had already erected a sanctuary for Milkom (1 K 11, 5, 33).

superstition [14] (1, 9). But they have no interest in the God of justice and conscience. The princes are like roaring lions, and the judges are like wolves; her prophets are wanton and faithless men, and her priests profane what is sacred (3, 4). The lord Yahweh will search through Jerusalem with a lamp [15] (1, 12) and bring every evil to light.

Judgment is standing directly before the gate. The day of Yahweh is "a day of wrath,[16] a day of distress and anguish, a day of ruin and devastation" (1, 15). "I will bring distress on men, so that they shall walk like the blind, because they have sinned against the Lord" (1, 17). Zephaniah is, like his great predecessors, primarily a preacher of repentance. The most powerful motive for penance and conversion is the message of the judgment to come. But his message looks to a time beyond this judgment, the herald of a new salvation. The bearers of salvation are the *'anwē-haares,* the humble of the land (2, 3), the poor and humbled people (*'am'anî wā-dāl* 3, 12).

The prophet Hosea had as his leitmotiv the concept of *hesed,* fidelity to the covenant and love; Isaiah fought for the rights of the *qᵉdôš-yisra'ēl,* the holy one of Israel; Zephaniah is the preacher of *'ᵃnāwah,* humility (2, 3b). This is the same theme that Christ chose for his program when he proclaimed: "Blessed are the poor in spirit, for theirs is the kingdom of heaven."

Zephaniah has a second heritage from his great predecessors. He too proclaims God's judgment upon the nations, in a form that corresponds to the new political situation (2, 4-15). Philistines, Moab, Ammon, Egypt, and Ashur are, just like Jerusalem itself, doomed to judgment. The book concludes with a vision of the future time of salvation (3, 16-20). Jerusalem is filled with joy; the daughter of Zion rejoices and exults; the powerful enemies are gone; Yahweh dwells in their midst, a warrior who gives victory and salvation (*gibbôr yošîa'* 3, 17).

---

14. Perhaps out of superstitious fear of the demons who lurked on the threshold.

15. In art Zephaniah is represented with a lamp.

16. From this passage the hymn *Dies Irae* takes its inspiration.

b) *The Literary Genre of the Book of Zephaniah*:

These three brief chapters are not a literary unit. Even this tiny book has a life history of its own. The prophet's own work [17] must obviously be identified in the great call to judgment and conversion (1, 2–2, 3; 3, 1-13). The oracles against the nations (2, 4-15) are, on the other hand, subject to some doubt, particularly because they are part of the standard vocabulary of prophetic judgment material and can be said to exhibit no traits characteristic of Zephaniah and his era.[18] Since individual songs and poems have been incorporated into other Biblical texts, the psalm-like section 3, 14-18a might well have found its way into the conclusion of the book from some liturgical text. The present state of the book dates to post-exilic times.[19]

3) THE PROPHET HABAKKUK

The Book of Habakkuk belongs to that same period of political reconstruction as the Books of Nahum and Zephaniah. Habakkuk proclaims the imminent destruction of the Assyrian dragon, but he must also cry "Violence!" (1, 2-4). He can envision the rise of the stronger adversary, the Chaldean, who will be a scourge in God's hand to strike down Ashur: "Lo, I am rousing the Chaldeans (*kasdîm*), that bitter and hasty nation . . . . Their horses are swifter than leopards, more fierce than the evening wolves . . . . They fly like an eagle swift to devour" (1, 5-10).

It was Habakkuk who, in the crisis of his time, first coined the phrase which the Apostle Paul, in a new and deeper insight turned into a foundation for his own gospel. It is generally translated: "The just man lives by faith" (Rm 1, 17). The Hebrew original says: *Saddîk be'emûnatô yihyeh*: "the righteous shall live by his faith (in God?) (2, 4). For Habakkuk it was a question not only of the terrible splendor of the great dragon, but also the problem of God's ordering of the universe. God himself, who is present from all time, and whose very essence is

---

17. U. a. Eissfeldt, EinlAT 519-523; Robert-Feuillet, IntrAT 514; Pfeiffer, IntrOT 600-601.
18. Eissfeldt 521.
19. Robert-Feuillet, 515. Generally opposed to a late dating of the book, around 200 B.C. as a pseudepigraph. Eissfeldt 520.

holiness (1, 12), was being called into question here. How was it possible for Yahweh to look in silence while the godless man (*rāšaʿ*) devoured the just (*saddîk*)? (1, 13).[20] Was there any justification for being "faithful" to Yahweh, while it was the dragon who was triumphant? [21] Habakkuk discovers the ultimate solution, "to take his stand and watch, to look forth to see what he will say." Yahweh's answer he is ordered to write as a witness to every generation to come (2, 1ff.). Illuminated by God, the prophet sees through the events of time and recognizes that the godless enjoy a brief span of time until judgment is fulfilled. In this judgment, however, it is the just who will prevail in ultimate victory, since they have held constant to the faith in Yahweh. Habakkuk strikes the same note as Isaiah: "If you do not believe, you will not abide" (Is 7, 9). It is faith alone that can promise ultimate survival in this time of universal collapse. The Hebrew word *ʾemûnah* means fundamentally "fidelity." It is applied to God himself: "From generation to generation his faithfulness endures" (*ʾemûnātô*, Ps 99/100, 5). Just as God does not withdraw his Yes, his Amen once spoken to man, so man achieves salvation only when he remains steadfast in his yes, in the amen he says to God. The "yes of God" in human form was, however, the Messiah Jesus (2 Cor 1, 19). St. Paul has, accordingly, reinterpreted an ancient prophetic heritage in a Christocentric context. Christianity is simply faith and fidelity to the God of history, who directs all the world of time to its ultimate goal.

The newly developing order of things Habakkuk proclaims in his woes against avarice (2, 6-8), against luxury and exploitation (2, 9-14), against tyranny and cynicism (2, 15-17), and finally against false gods (2, 18-20). In grandiose imagery, in chapter 3,

---

20. E. Nielsen, *The Righteous and the Wicked in Habakkuk,* Studia Theologica, Lund (1952), 54-78, attempts to elaborate a concrete, historical situation. The "just man" (ruler) is Jehoahaz, while the "godless one" is Jehoiakim installed as king by the Egyptians. Not convincing.

21. M. Stenzel, Bibl 33 (1952), 505-510, the sentiments are from the forensic sphere. A reworking of the older theme of Yahweh coming as judge. In Hosea Yahweh judges his own people; here he judges the nations.

he depicts Yahweh's coming to judgment, in images that are reminiscent of the exodus from Egypt and the great theophany on Sinai.[22] Yahweh comes from Teman, from Paran, from the desert of the south, as in the days of Exodus. The earth quakes, the nations tremble; he comes as a warrior with bow and arrows; his arrows flash forth light, and his lance is like lightning; in his wrath he tramples the nations. This is a song of victorious faith in the God of the world and history. No wonder that the monks of Qumran found an echo of their own time in these magnificent verses, and interpreted even the individual images as bearing upon their own life experience.[23]

The Book of Habakkuk is variously dated,[24] according to the interpretation of the Kasdim in 1, 6. Many editors prefer to read Kittaeans, that is, Greeks, and thus date the Book as late as the era of Alexander the Great. Similarly, the prophecies in chapters 1-2 and the hymn in chapter 3 are assigned to various dates and various authors. The grounds adduced for the distinctions are not convincing. The claim that Habakkuk was a cult prophet is also subject to considerable question.[25] The personal fate of the prophet is entirely hidden behind the force of his words; but these three chapters do represent a unity in language, style, and continuity of thought, a unity whose proper interpretation is possible only if they are examined against the background of the Assyrian twilight (626-612). There is a prophet Habakkuk mentioned in the Midrash-like narrative in the Book of Daniel 14, 33ff.; the historical prophet has nothing in common with this figure excepting his name.

4) THE PROPHET JONAH

The four brief chapters of the Book of Jonah form essentially three distinct scenes. First scene (1, 1—2, 11): Jonah ("dove")

---

22. M. Delcor, *La geste de Yahve au temps de l'Exode et l'espérance du psalmiste en Habakuk III*, Misc. Bibl. Ubach (1953), 257-302.
23. On the Habakkuk Commentary found in the caves along the Dead Sea, cf. Eissfeldt, EinlAT 813.
24. Eissfeldt, EinlAT 510ff.; Pfeiffer, IntrOT 597ff.
25. S. Mowinkel, *Zum Psalm Habakuk*, TZ 9 (1953), 1-23 considers Habakkuk as a cult prophet, and claims that he has worked prophetic and lyrical (cult-lyrical) "ideas of the autumn and new year's festival into his psalm." This is a typical position for the Nordic school with its one-sided cultic orientation.

receives a command from Yahweh to go to Nineveh and preach repentance. He refuses, flees to Joppe, where he takes a ship to Tarshish, generally identified with Tarshish in Spain, that is, the end of the world. A mighty storm arises on the high sea. The ship threatens to founder. Jonah is asleep in the the hold. The sailors cast lots to determine who is responsible for the storm. The lot falls upon Jonah. He confesses that he is fleeing from God; but he is ready to be cast into the sea in atonement. No sooner do the waves close over his body than a huge sea monster swallows him. In the belly of this monster he sings a moving psalm. After three days he is vomited out upon the land.

Second scene (3, 1-10): Jonah, now very docile, goes to Nineveh and preaches repentance. King, citizen, and beast alike fast and do penance. The threatened doom is averted.

Third scene (4, 1-11): Jonah goes off disconsolate, because he cannot understand that God should spare the great city. He is taught the proper answer by an *argumentum ad hominem*. He was enjoying the shade of a castor oil plant. A worm began to gnaw at the heart of the plant and made it wither. The sun beat down mercilessly upon Jonah's head. Jonah felt sorry for the plant. The book ends with the question: "Should not Yahweh pity Nineveh, the great city?"

a) *History and Legend* [26]

There was a prophet named Jonah ben-Amittai from Gath-Hepher [27] in the days of King Jeroboam II. He proclaimed the restoration of the frontiers of the kingdom of Israel "from the entrance of Hamath as far as the Sea of the Arabah (2 K 14, 25). This is all we know about him. If the Jonah of this present book is to be identified with the above-mentioned prophet, then he belonged to the beginning of classical prophecy, in the eighth century, and would have been a contemporary of the prophets

---

26. For a fuller discussion of the problem cf. A. Feuillet, DBS IV (1949), 1104-1131. — *Les sources du livre de Jonas*, RB (1947), 161ff. For a position against the too one-sided literary derivation, cf. B. Trépanier, CBQ 13 (1951), 9-16. — *EncMikr* III (1958), 608-613.
27. In the District of the Tribe of Zebulun, in Galilee (Jos 19, 13).

Amos and Hosea. But the Book of Jonah is quite different from the writings of the other two prophets. In Amos and Hosea we have a collection of prophetic messages, and the personal fate of the prophet is quite in the background; in the Book of Jonah, however, we have only the story of the prophet himself. Serious arguments can be brought to bear against a date in the eighth century. During the reign of Jeroboam II, Nineveh was only on the threshold of her mighty empire. According to Jonah 3, 3, however, Nineveh was already a great city. His description of the city takes on a colossal proportion, not in keeping with the historical evidence. "Nineveh was an exceedingly great city, three days' journey in breadth" [28] (3, 3). The phrase "three days" is only a popular image used to describe a gigantic city. The population is described in equally exaggerated manner. Counting children alone, who were still too young to know their right from their left hand, there were 12 ten thousands (120,000) (4, 11) — suggesting a total population of almost 1,000,000. This is, historically, highly improbable. Our narrator is speaking of Nineveh as a long since departed grandeur. Nineveh was so completely destroyed in 612 that only rubble and debris were left, and these ruins were quickly covered by a shroud of oblivion. Later centuries could not even identify the site upon which Nineveh stood, until the excavations of the last century rediscovered the ruins.

In addition to these historical improbabilites, there is the argument from language. Whoever wrote this book knew how to tell a story. His language is simple and gripping. The many Aramaisms do, however, point to an era in which Hebrew was subject more and more to foreign influences, and thus almost certainly to a time after the destruction of Jerusalem (586). There have indeed been attempts to explain Jonah's activity on the basis of Assyrian sources.[29] Esarhaddon, for example, faced by the imminent approach of the peril from the north — the inroads of the mountain peoples — might have proclaimed a hundred

---

28. Excavation has established a city perimeter of some 7 mi.
29. J. B. Schaumberger, *Das Bussedikt des Königs von Nineve in keilschriftlicher Beleuchtung*, Misc. Bibl. 2 (1934), 123ff.

days of prayer and penance. In itself, it is not entirely impossible that the king and people of Nineveh should have listened to a foreign preacher's call to penance. But when all is said and done, it is impossible to escape the fact that the Book of Jonah presents us, not with an historical narrative, but a work of religious poetry.[30] In terms of literary genre, it would be called a midrash, a literary form that was common in the last days of Old Testament literature. Well known Biblical names formed the nucleus of a cycle of legends which could be drawn upon to serve a new idea. The historical Jonah of the Book of Kings has given the hero of the Book of Jonah no more than his name. The theme of flight in the face of Yahweh's divine mission and command is clearly expressed in the prophet Jeremiah (1, 6). Whether or not a similar attitude was commonly ascribed to the earlier Jonah is a question we can no longer answer.[31]

b) *The Message of the Book of Jonah*

A world-wide universalism and a tolerant spirit of humanity give this little book a very sympathetic character.[32] It is because of this unreserved openness of view that the Book of Jonah has been considered one of the pearls of Old Testament literature.[33] Yahweh is not only the God of Israel. He has mercy upon all the nations and wills their salvation. It is, after all, the pagans who seek and find God in this book. The sailors recognize the power of Yahweh (1, 16), and wicked Nineveh repents and is converted. Only the prophet himself is represented as narrow-minded, incapable of grasping the thoughts of God. This book opens the gate to the pagans. Such a concept is indeed an ancient prophetic message, but it must certainly have taken on new

---

30. A. Feuillet, DBS IV (1949), 1119: "Ainsi le plus sage est d'abandonner complètment la thèse de l'historicité." — F. Spadafora, EncCatt IV (1951), 142, after weighing the various alternatives, comes to the conclusion that this is didactic rather than historical prose.

31. E. Haller, *Die Erzählung von dem Propheten Jona*, Theol. Existenz heute 65 (1958), 5-54 calls the book an "edifying story cast in the form of a life of the prophet."

32. Eissfeldt, EinlAT 495.

33. Fr. Noetscher, EB III, 746.

and very pressing significance after the return from exile, an era in which the Jewish culture and religion was beginning to adopt a more closed attitude to the pagan world about it. This would suggest the period between 500 and 300 B.C. as a probable date of composition.

This awakening to a recognition of God's world-wide dominion is, accordingly, the basic idea of this tiny book. It is a mistake to waste time and energy in an attempt to prove the possibility or historicity of the miracles described. The miraculous element in the Book of Jonah is only a medium of expression made to serve the purposes of religious truth. The theme of man being swallowed by a sea monster and then vomited up unharmed on land is a familiar theme in many, even primitive literatures. The author of the Book of Jonah simply made this popular motiv the vehicle of his religious message. The fact that the Gospels (Mt 12, 39-42; 16, 4; Lk 11, 29-32) refer to the miracle in Jonah as a prophecy of Christ's burial and resurrection is still quite justifiable, even though the point of comparison is no longer viewed as historical fact, but rather as symbolic poetry. Christ himself uses anecdotes, like the story of the merciful Samaritan or Lazarus the poor man, as the basis of his new moral preaching. It is from this point of view that we shall find the easiest key to a book that is certainly much in discussion today. "This tiny book has a thoroughly evangelical stamp; it lays the foundation for our Lord's most magnificent parables on the subject of God's mercy to all sinful men." [34] The fact that this idea is first expressed in terms of Nineveh and the great Assyrian empire, before whose terrible splendor all Israel was made to tremble, makes it all the more powerful a message. Even the mortal enemies of the chosen people of God can look to divine guidance and mercy.

---

34. A. Feuillet, DBS IV (1949), 1130.

CHAPTER XII

THE REFORMS OF KING JOSIAH

UNDER King Josiah, the kingdom of Judah enjoyed its final glory. This was possible only because the terrible splendor of Ashur was visibly on the decline, and the newly powerful dragon of Babylon had not yet stretched his claws towards the western countries. In this brief breathing spell of history Judah was free, shortly before its ultimate destruction, to once again develop its national and religious powers. The figure of King Josiah has been recorded in history like a second David. His work of reconstruction is the happier side of the decline of the Assyrian world empire. The more Ashur collapsed, the greater the success of the national and religious reform in the kingdom of Judah.

1) REGICIDE IN JERUSALEM

The long reign of King Manasseh (698-643) was completely dominated, religiously and politically, by the pressure exerted from Ashur. It was during his rule that the gods of Ashur invaded the city of Jerusalem. The fact that he was able to restore the frontier fortresses of Judah, even after his brief involvement with the politics of Babel, was not simply the result of disinterested sympathy on the part of the Assyrian overlords. Assyria was equally concerned with maintaining the frontier as a buffer state against the new strength of Egypt. Manasseh's son and successor Amon (643/42 — 640)[1] followed his father's policies. After a reign of two years, however, he met his death in a palace revolution. The force behind this conspiracy remains unknown. Perhaps the conspirators were hoping for a political change of course. Around 641-639 the western countries were in a state of political upset. Ashur-bani-pal had to undertake punitive expeditions not only against the Arabs of the desert, but also against the coastal cities of Acco in Philistia and Oso in the neighborhood of Tyre.[2] The coup in Jerusalem may well have been connected with this general unrest. The conspirators could not maintain their position because the ruling class of the "people of the country" (*'am haares*) were not on their side. They turned instead to the eight-year-old boy Josiah, whom they raised to the throne after taking terrible vengeance upon the murderers of their king. In the years that followed up to the death of Ashur-bani-pal, Judah was once again a vassal of the Assyrian empire.

2) THE THREE STAGES OF REFORM

As we have already mentioned, the national and religious reawakening of Judah under the rule of King Josiah is most intimately connected with the decline of the Assyrian empire. There are two accounts of the reforms. The first, 2 Kgs 22-33, concentrates everything on the 18th year of Josiah. In reading this account we get the impression that the reform was a very sudden and rapid development. The events are compressed to the briefest possible interval of time. The gradual stages of the reform movement are better appreciated on the basis of the second account in 2

---

1. Derivation of the name uncertain. Egyptian (God Amun) and Assyrian (star goddess Kamanu) have been proposed as roots. The Hebrew would have heard an echo of the word for "to be faithful." *EncMikr* I, 422.

2. *EncMikr* III, 417. — A. Malamat, *The Historical Background of the Assassination of Amon, King of Judah,* IEJ 3 (1953), 26-29. In connection with the Anti-Assyrian revolt between the Euphrates and the Mediterranean.

Chronicles 34-35. It was a slow and deliberate process. We can distinguish three separate stages which, in their own way, are a reflection of the major events in the world politics of that time.

a) *The Eighth Year of Josiah* (632)

This is the year in which Ashur-bani-pal died. The destruction of the Assyrian empire was under way. The border provinces were the first to attempt to shake off the Assyrian yoke. In Judah too there was a fresh new atmosphere of growing liberty. This situation is described in the brief note of 2 Chronicles 34, 3: "In the 8th year of his reign, while he was yet a boy, he began to seek the God of David his father." It was time to look once again to the national history.

b) *The Twelfth Year of Josiah* (628)

Around the year 630 the storm of the Scythian invasion broke over the western countries, sweeping away the final remnants of the Assyrian sovereignty. From the east the Babylonians and Medes caught Assyria in a pincer movement. For Judah this was an opportunity to blot out every trace of the foreign rule. Since politics as a whole in the Ancient Near East had a religious orientation, it is no wonder that the national restoration would begin with a religious reform: "In the 12th year he began to purge Judah and Jerusalem of the high places, the asherim, and the graven and molten images" (2 Ch 34, 3). The first wave of reform spread through the tribal territory of the kingdom of Judah, "from Gebah[3] as far as Beer-sheba" (2 K 23, 8).

The first victim of the reform movement was the Assyrian high places. These had been the scene of various forms of astral cult.[4] There were burnt offerings to Baal, to the sun, to the moon, and the whole zodiac (2 K 35, 5). The external symbol of the sun worship were the horses of the sun kept in the temple (2 K 23, 11). The second object of attack was the older Canaanite

---

3. Not Geba' Benjamin, but et-Tell located 20 mi N of Jerusalem. MAZAR, *EncMikr* III, 420.
4. E. Weidner, *Ein astrologischer Sammeltext aus der Sargonidenzeit*, AFO 19 (1959/60), 105-113.

paganism which had been more deeply rooted in the country and had flourished unopposed under Assyrian protection. Josiah did away with the worship of the high places throughout the country, tore down the altars, broke the incense stands, and destroyed the graven and molten images. Whatever could be burned he put to the torch. The ashes were strewn over the graves of those who had sacrificed, as a sign of perpetual desecration. He burned the bones of the rebellious priests on their own altars and scattered their ashes. The brief mention of the fact that Josiah returned to Jerusalem after purifying the country (2 Ch 34, 7) presupposes his having passed through the country with a division of soldiers, adding the strength of military support to his reform program. In Jerusalem itself he faced a herculean task. The two altars which Manasseh had erected in the outer court of the temple were beaten to powder and their dust was strewn in the Kidron Valley. A similar fate awaited the altars on the high places all around Jerusalem, an abomination which dated back to the days of Solomon (2 K 23, 12ff.). Two specifically Canaanite religious peculiarities, child sacrifice and sacred prostitution, had also made their way into Jerusalem. The houses of *qedēšîm,* "sacred cult prostitutes," in the neighborhood of the temple district — they were also occupied with weaving "veils" for the *asherah*,[5] — were all torn down (2 K 23, 7), and these "holy women" were driven out. The sites of child sacrifice in the Hinnom Valley, where "they sacrificed their boys and girls in fire in honor of Molek," [6] were also destroyed and desecrated.

c) *The Eighteenth Year of Josiah* (622)

The reform movement was gradually approaching its climax, which was nothing other than the complete restoration of the temple. The fact that the temple stood in need of considerable repair (2 K 22, 5) is some indication of the deplorable condition to which the house of Yahweh had been allowed to deteriorate. The necessary money was raised by contributions. All the

---

5. *EncMikr* II, 261.
6. Hebrew form of the Ammonite deity *malek* "he who reigns," i.e., the god king, G. C. O'Cellaigh, VT 12 (1962), 186ff.

people who came into the temple deposited their offering before the gate-keepers. Josiah simply sent his recorder Saphan to the high priest Hilkiah with orders to deliver the accumulated funds for the restoration of the temple. Without making any accounting ("for they deal honestly"), the money was simply delivered to the workmen who were repairing the house of the Lord and they in turn paid the carpenters and builders and masons, and bought the necessary timber and quarried stone for the project.

In the work of reconstruction, the high priest Hilkiah discovered the "Book of the Law" (*sēpher hattorah*) in the temple. He had the king informed. After briefly reading part of the book, the king was so disturbed that he sent a messenger to the prophetess Huldah who was living in the new city, to ask her if all the threatened disaster was really going to strike Jerusalem. The answer from God, which Huldah was forced to give the king, was inexorably harsh. The threatened calamity would indeed break over city and population alike. Only because Josiah had a receptive heart and had proved himself humble would the catastrophe wait until after his death (2 K 22, 14-20).

Josiah then summoned the elders of Judah and Jerusalem. The prophets and a great crowd of people answered his call. They came up into the temple where the "Book of the Covenant" was read publicly. The message was like a clap of thunder.[7] The king stood at the "pillar."[8] He renewed the covenant (*berît*) and swore to carry out the stipulations of that covenant (*dibrē habberît*). The discovery of the Book of the Law does not represent the beginning, but rather the conclusion of a reform program which was already well under way. It is generally agreed by scholars that the Book of the Law discovered in the temple coincides essentially with the fifth Book of Moses (Deuteronomy).[9] A view which was very popular in times past, namely that this was not a genuine discovery of the book, but simply an invention (*pia*

---

7. Bright, HistIsr 299.
8. Probably one of the two Temple pillars, Boaz and Yakin. Cf. III, 333.
9. Robert-Feuillet, IntrAT 367-371; Eissfeldt, EinlAT 278: "In the last analysis, the identity of Ur-deuteronomy with the book discovered in

fraus) on the part of the Jerusalem priesthood to establish some legal foundation for their prerogatives has been almost completely abandoned today. Deuteronomy actually contains the ancient Mosaic tradition, elaborated in the form of very pointed sermons. The vestiges of this Book's origin point to the Northern Kingdom of Israel where, after the destruction of Samaria, there certainly was ample reason to propose a national examination of conscience. The answer was simple: Israel had been destroyed because it had broken the covenant. It was very obvious that only by a return to the principles of the Mosaic legislation could the nation possibly experience a renaissance. We must not exclude the possibility that this book of reform had already been seized upon by Hezekiah's men and carried to Jerusalem.[10] During the reigns of the faithless kings Manasseh and Amon, however, there was no opportunity to apply the book's reform message. It thus passed into oblivion and, after the invasion of the pagan cults, it was probably relegated into a storage chamber in the temple. But with the reform and restoration, the time was ripe to listen to the message proclaimed so clearly in the Book of the Law.

While the battle against the invasion of paganism was already well under way when the Book of the Law was first discovered and could only receive additional impetus from the discovery, the centralization of the official cult, the new system for celebrating the pesach, might well have been introduced at that time. Josiah called the priests from all the cities of Judah, from Geba as far as Beer-sheba, and forbade the worship of the high places outside Jerusalem (2 K 23, 8). It is obviously the sacrificial sites in honor of Yahweh and the priests of Yahweh who are concerned here; they were to make common cause with "their brothers in Jerusalem" (23, 8). The law of one single cult site is clearly stated in Dt 12. Literary examination of this chapter reveals the existence of two strata.[11] The first part (12, 1-12) is composed in the plural number and enunciates a general law: the Israelites are obliged to destroy the

---

721, which motivated the reforms of Josiah, or which was at least a strong additional impetus, can be considered as proven. Whether it is to be dated at that precise time, or perhaps 5 or 10 years earlier is another matter. At all events, its effects are not earlier than 721."

---

10. R. de Vaux, *Les Institutions de l'AT*, II (1960), 186.
11. *Ibid.*, 185.

Canaanite high places; they are permitted to offer sacrifice only in one place, which Yahweh, your God, will choose out in order to let his name rest there. — The second section (12, 13-31) presents a series of ordinances phrased in the singular: "Take heed that you do not offer your burnt offerings at every place that you see; but at the place which the Lord will choose in one of your tribes, there you shall offer your burnt offerings, and there you shall do all that I am commanding you" (vv. 13-14). The first section seems to be the more recent composition. It contains the prohibition against visiting the pagan high places, and also commands that they be destroyed. Fundamentally, however, both sections are in agreement. Just as Israel has only one God, she must have also one single altar. This clear statement of the law obviously supercedes the provisions of the Book of the Covenant (Ex 20, 24) and the practice which was universally accepted as correct (1 S 14, 32-35). The idea of one cult cite is certainly bound up with the struggle for a political unity, but can still be said to have drawn its primary impetus from a reminiscence to the Ark of the Covenant and the days of the Exodus, in which there was only one single altar. Compliance with this law demanded a thorough-going reconstruction of the entire religious life and also the order of the priesthood in Judah. The sacrificial cult outside Jerusalem must simply cease. The priests who had formerly functioned at the sacrificial heights dedicated to Yahweh were now made subordinate to the central sanctuary in Jerusalem. The purity of the Yahweh faith was thus considerably strengthened; for from the sacrificial heights of Yahweh to the high places of Baal had been only a short and all too frequent step. The complete abolition of the outlying sacrificial sites did away with a very powerful temptation.[12]

The new order of things involved primarily the feast of pesach. "For no such passover had been kept since the days of the judges who judged Israel, or during all the days of the kings of Israel or of the kings of Judah" (2 K 23, 21). Up to this time, the passover had been simply a family festival. Josiah divorced it from the family frame of reference and raised it to the dignity of a pilgrimage festival (hag), which, from this time forward, could be properly celebrated only in Jerusalem.[13] The grounds for this were religious considerations; passover and covenant were a single unit. Through this annual pilgrimage and passover festival in Jerusalem, the forgotten covenant would be constantly renewed and indelibly impressed upon the memory of the people (2 K 23, 21-23).

The reform was not confined to the territory of Judah; it also spread to the provinces of the former Northern Kingdom which had been freed from Josiah from their Assyrian masters. In Bethel, he destroyed

---

12. There might be an allusion to the discovery of the Law on a jar stamp that has a picture of a scroll with wings.

13. R. de Vaux, l.c., 388.

the altar to the sacred bull (2 K 23, 15-18) which had been erected
by Jeroboam I. He did the same thing to the high places in Samaria.
As a symbol of perpetual desecration he had human bones burned to
ashes on the spot (2 K 23, 19-20).

3) THE BATTLE OF MEGIDDO

For a time it seemed as if Josiah would be free to assume the
abandoned Assyrian heritage of the Northern Kingdom without
opposition. The renewal of the covenant represented a religious
as well as a national high point. The country was once and for
all free of the Assyrian yoke. But then, at the last moment, Assyria
got help from a source that was totally unexpected. Egypt, who
had shaken off the Assyrian yoke in a great battle of liberation in
655, once again expressed a most surprising allegiance to her
former master. This move was not directed by pure idealism.
Quite the contrary: Egypt hoped to assume Ashur's dominion
over the western countries. In the year 616, as was described above,
an Egyptian auxiliary corps marched to the Euphrates. At the
final battle for Nineveh there is no mention of Egyptian forces.
Only when Ashur-uballit made his desperate attempt in Harran
did the Egyptians come to the aid. Despite Scythian and Egyptian
support, however, the king was driven from Harran in the year
610: "Ashur-uballit and the Egyptian army which came to his
assistance were smitten with terror in the face of the enemy . . . .
They abandoned the city . . . , crossed over the Euphrates . . . .
The king of Akkad made his way to Harran . . . . He conquered
the city and marched off with plunder from city and temple." [14]

Ashur-uballit departed from Syria only to return in the following year, 609, with a new contingent of Egyptian support, in
an attempt to reconquer Harran: "In the month of Tammuz
(July/August) Ashur-uballit, king of Assyria, crossed the Euphrates together with an Egyptian army . . . . They marched against
the city of Harran, in order to take it back." [15] This year of
609 was a fateful year for Judah as well, and its king Josiah.[16]

---

14. Wiseman, *Chronicles*, 63, 61-64.
15. *Ibid.*, 66ff.
16. M. B. Rowton, JNES 10 (1951), 128-130 suggests 608, but this is
    surely wrong. According to the Babylonian Chronicle, the Babylonians

In that same year, in Egypt, Necho II (609-593) succeeded his father Psammetich upon the throne. Following the established Egyptian Asian policy he sent an army to the Euphrates, not only to bring assistance to the heavily pressed Assyrian troops, but rather to reconfirm Egyptian dominion in Syria and Palestine. Josiah came to meet him along the high passes of Megiddo, in an attempt to bar his way. Necho was unwilling to wage battle with him. "What have we to do with each other, King of Judah? I am not coming against you this day..." (2 Ch 35, 21ff.). Josiah attacked, despite this warning. Hardly had the battle been joined when he was mortally wounded by an arrow. His servants lifted him from his chariot, laid him in his second chariot, and carried him to Jerusalem.[17] The prophet Jeremiah intoned a dirge over him. The Egyptian army thereupon made its way unhindered to the Euphrates.

It was not simply a stroke of rash presumption that prompted Josiah to undertake this desperate confrontation; it was rather a sober appraisal of the political situation. Nineveh had fallen. The destruction of what was left of Assyria could no longer be forestalled. The Pharaoh's campaign was obviously not motivated by genuine sympathy for Assyria. His forced march to the Euphrates (2 Ch 35, 21) was an attempt to seize whatever he could from the Assyrian heritage. Josiah realized that any Egyptian success would spell the end of Judah's recently won freedom. The defeat at Megiddo thus heralds the beginning of destruction for the kingdom of Judah. The reconquest of Harran did indeed fail and the Egyptian-Assyrian army was forced back across the Euphrates; but in the years 609-605 both Syria and Palestine found themselves under Egyptian rule. The murder of

---

were already in Urartu (Armenia) in this year. Wiseman, *Chronicles*, 46.

---

17. Since the Book of Kings does not explicitly mention any battle, many scholars have presumed that there was none, but that Josiah was simply taken and deported. But there is no grounds for doubting the evidence in Chronicles. Excavation has unearthed a level of destruction in Megiddo II which might well attest to the battle described in the text. Bright, HistIsr 303.

Ashur-uballit in the year 606 represents the inglorious end of the Assyrian world empire.

The territory of the great Assyrian empire had thus been divided into three spheres of influence who now fought among themselves to maintain a balance of power. The Medes had seized the ancient Assyrian heartland; in Mesopotamia the new Babylonian empire had established itself; the western countries were occupied by Egypt. The Euphrates formed the boundary between the Egyptian and Babylonian spheres of influence. The great river was, however, not so much a boundary as a line of confrontation. It was obvious that Nabopolassar did not mean to cede the western countries to the Pharaoh without resistance. The wheel of history, once set in motion, could not so easily come to a full stop.

What Josiah had hoped to prevent by his desperate measures now came to pass. Jerusalem, so recently liberated from the harsh scourge of Assyria, now lay under the hand of the Egyptian Pharaoh and, within a very short time, would feel the even harsher hand of the new Babylonian masters. Josiah's reforms seem to have occupied only a very brief episode; and yet their effects were felt long after the eventual destruction of the city and the kingdom. For the Jews returning from exile, Josiah's reform became a leitmotiv. In the second temple the reform work of Josiah finally became reality. It is no wonder, therefore, that the chronist (2 Ch 34, 1) ranks Josiah at the side of King David himself. Both kings had an effect that far outlived their own time and left their stamp upon the centuries to come.

In the midst of this disturbed and confused political picture falls the life of a prophet whom, it would seem, nature had not designed to bear such heavy loads. The prophet Jeremiah is a solitary and an individual, but, strengthened by Yahweh, he stands up as an iron wall against the trend of his times. His preaching makes it abundantly clear that it is God who directs human history unfailingly towards its goal, despite all temporal catastrophe.

CHAPTER XIII

THE PROPHET JEREMIAH

"ISAIAH has been called the greatest orator among the prophets, Jeremiah, the greatest poet. Style and form betray the poet. In his expression of feeling and mood, Jeremiah is a master. Everything is vital and gripping. Frequently the sentences are full of dramatic impact and force, overwhelming in their originality and directness." [1] Yet not a single verse was written for the sake of art alone. Against his will and against his natural inclination, Jeremiah was cast by God himself into the wine-press of time, trampled underfoot, and pressed to yield the last drop of his vitality. He did not want to be a prophet and yet he became one of the greatest; he did not want to be a poet and yet his words are among the most moving products of human composition. He was destined to be a herald of destruction in an era of universal collapse. The history of his life is woven into the history of the last decades of the kingdom of Judah and can thus be portrayed most simply in terms of the regnal dates of the last three kings: Josiah, Jehoiakim, and Zedekiah (1, 1-3).

---

1. Noetscher, EB III, 216.

A) JEREMIAH AND JOSIAH

1) "MOUTH OF YAHWEH" (15, 19)

Jeremiah ben-Hilkiah [2] comes from Anathoth, a small village in the tribal territory of Benjamin, two hours' journey from Jerusalem. His father, and thus he himself, belonged to the priestly clan of Anathoth (1, 1).[3] It is possible that the family belonged to the descendants of the high priest Abiathar who escaped Saul's blood bath in Nob (1 S 22, 20) and became David's priest, only to be set aside by Solomon and banished to Anathoth (1 K 2, 26). At all events, the family had a modest property (32, 6-15). Even though Jeremiah spent the greatest part of his activity in Jerusalem, his heart always longed for the tribe of Benjamin and the vanished glory of the Northern Kingdom of Israel. He thus has some spiritual affinity with the prophet Hosea, the herald of impending doom to the Northern Kingdom. Jeremiah refers to the destruction of the sanctuary in Shiloh, in the territory of the tribe of Ephraim (7, 12, 14; 26, 6, 9); he represents Rachel, the tribal mother of Benjamin, as singing a dirge for her lost children (31, 15). Her grave could not have been far from Anathoth.

Although he was thus sent by Yahweh into the capital of the kingdom of Judah, Jeremiah was no Judaean prophet in the strict sense of the word. His message is addressed to all the tribes. He looks to the salvation of "maiden Israel" (31, 15-22). He admits no split between north and south; he speaks only of one people of God, a people who, because of their breach of the

---

2. Derivation of the name uncertain. Two possibilities proposed: a. from the root *rāmah*, "throw, shoot"; *yirmeyāhû*, hence a prayer "May Yahweh shoot (with bow and arrow, Ps 78, 9) (the enemies)." — b. from the root *rām*: in its basic stem "high, exalted"; in its causative or "Yahweh, raise, make the child big," *EncMikr* III, 868. Septuagint and Vulgate read Jeremias and hence recommend the form chosen by us, Jeremiah, in which the ancient divine name is clearly evident.

3. That Jeremiah was a cult prophet is untenable! Rudolph, *Jeremia*, (1958[3]), 3.

Yahweh covenant, have been cast into the crucible of the nations. This raises his vision beyond the framework of human history. He is destined to be "the prophet of all peoples" (1, 5). This expression seems so audacious that many interpreters substitute the singular number: "For the people" (Israel). But there is no grounds for altering the text.[4] His predecessors, in their preaching, also spoke to the world beyond Israel. In the days of Jeremiah, Judah was so intimately bound up with the history of Asia Minor, first as an Assyrian tributary state, then subject to Egypt, and finally the vassal of Babylon, that Judah's fate was necessarily involved with the fate of the surrounding nations. It was a critical era in the history of the world.[5] By sending his prophet to the great peoples of the world, Yahweh revealed his claim to world dominion, to be Lord over the four ends of the earth. This is the programatic statement in the inaugural vision of Jeremiah.

In the 13th year of King Josiah (627) Jeremiah was called to be a prophet; he was torn away from the rustic peace of Anathoth. His vocation did not promise him a quiet life of mystical contemplation. From the fate of the earlier prophets he must have known that the prophet is a man of contradiction and persecution. He did not feel that he was born to be a warrior. When Yahweh called him to his service, he pleaded his absolute inability. "I am only a youth" (1, 7) "and am unfit for this vocation." There has been much discussion of a dual polarity in the character of Jeremiah.[6] By nature he is supposed to have been retiring and inclined to fear, an introvert with a strong emotional life. But after the finger of God had touched his lips (1, 9), he became suddenly "a fortified city, an iron pillar, and bronze walls, against the whole land, against the kings of Judah, its princes, its priests, and the people of the land" (1, 18). Yahweh set him "over nations and over kingdoms, to pluck up and to break down, to build and to plant" (1, 10). The heroic combat

---

4. Rudolph, *Jeremia*, (1958²), 5.
5. M. Buber, *Der Glaube der Propheten*, (1950), 238.
6. Pfeiffer, IntrOT 493. — Attempt at a "psychological biography," DBS IV, 876ff.

between natural disposition and divine vocation ends with the triumph of grace. All in all, Jeremiah resembles an oak more than a weeping willow. He became God's own warrior and threw himself into the violence of battle, paying no heed to the trembling of his knees or the chattering of his teeth. Impelled by God's own spirit, he waged a victorious battle against the hostile forces of the world around him. The general representation of a lamenting Jeremiah runs some risk of destroying the true picture of the man. He was indeed the lamenting prophet, deeply moved by the impending destruction of his people; but even more he was a warrior, a mighty citadel assaulted from every side, facing the ultimate destruction of city and people with the very sword of the word of God. His vocation itself had made him *paqid* (1, 10), overseer plenipotentiary and ambassador of God himself. His word is not an empty echo; it is filled with boundless power. He is "the mouth of God" (15, 19). Yahweh chose him for this mission,[7] and set him apart even before he was conceived in his mother's womb (1, 5).

2) ALMOND ROD AND BOILING POT

Two prophetic visions involving a play on words in the original Hebrew, set the tone for Jeremiah's times.[8] The Hebrew paronomasia can hardly be translated into English. Jeremiah is looking at a "rod of almond" (*maqqēl šaqēd*).[9] He is reminded of a second meaning of the word *šaqēd*, "to watch," and thus arrives at the interpretation that Yahweh is "watching" over his plans (1, 11-12). What God is planning becomes clear in the second vision. A pot boiling over. The seething water threatens to boil over any moment. The pot is facing away from the north; this means that the catastrophe will come from the north (1, 13ff.). Jeremiah, accordingly, must gird himself for a strenuous

---

7. Whereas the philosopher says, "I think, therefore I am," *Cogito, ergo sum*, the theme here is *"Cogitor, ergo sum."* Long before there was a Jeremiah he was a thought in the mind of God. Rudolf, Jr 4.

8. Noetscher, EB III, 218.

9. The pun is untranslatable in English.

battle. He must proclaim the imminent judgment without fear or
anxiety. Yahweh himself will stand beside his warrior (1, 17, 19).

As we have already pointed out,[10] between 630 and 625, if
we can trust the words of Herodotus, the Scythian storm broke
over the western countries. This is the somber background for
the prophet's early preaching. "The enemy from the north" (4,
5-8, 13-17, 19-31; 5, 15-17; 6, 1-7, 22-26) is never mentioned
by name. Everyone knew who was meant. If it was the Scythian
in the beginning, the later references are obviously to the Babylonians. Jeremiah apparently pointed to the threatening peril
from the north more than once. It is quite possible, as a result,
that these stormy chapters 4-6 contain elements from both the
earlier and the later years of his career. What is involved is not
primarily a description of the historical course of events, but
rather a prophetic foreknowledge of the catastrophe destined to
break from the north. This knowledge lay heavy on the prophet's
soul. There is war (4, 5-31). "My anguish, my anguish! I writhe
in pain! Oh the walls of my heart! My heart is beating wildly;
I cannot keep silent; for I hear the sound of the trumpet, the
alarm of war. Disaster follows hard on disaster; the whole land
is laid waste" (4, 19). At the approach of the enemy, the people
stream into the fortified city (4, 5). The enemy comes down like
a lion from the thicket (4, 7). Swifter than the eagles are his
horses, and his chariots are like the whirlwind (4, 13). The
daughter of Zion cries and wrings her hands: "Woe is me! I
am fainting before murderers." (4, 31).

Jeremiah does not only announce the coming of the catastrophe, he also interprets it. It comes as God's judgment. Hand
in hand with his preaching of God's judgment goes a thorough
examination of the national conscience. Just like his predecessors,
Jeremiah too unmasks the moral failings of his people. In mockery
he asks them: "Run to and fro through the streets of Jerusalem,
look and take note! Search her squares to see if you can find a
man who does justice and seeks truth" (5, 1). In the passion
of his intensity, the images flood into the prophet's mouth: Israel

---

10. Cf. above, p. 310.

is a stubborn ox (2, 20), a choice vine that has turned degenerate and wild (2, 21), a restive young camel (23), a harlot (20b, 25). He also compares her with a thief (26). All his images are taken from the daily life around him.[11] Perjury, violence, adultery — these are the order of the day. "They were all well-fed lusty stallions, each neighing for its neighbor's wife" (5, 9). But it is primarily the breach of covenant that is bringing God's judgment down upon them. Against God's legitimate demands their minds are set harder than stone. They refuse to take correction (5, 3).

In describing this sorry relationship between Yahweh and Israel, Jeremiah takes up the theme of marriage and adultery, a theme which Hosea had made the basis of his prophetic message. Judah and Israel are two sisters (3, 6-11). Israel was faithless and Yahweh gave her the letter of repudiation (3, 8); but Judah did not profit from the lesson. She too surrendered herself to unchastity. She desecrated the land by committing adultery "with stone and tree" (3, 9). Absolutely nothing is left of Yahweh's covenant. To make the whole tragic affair more concrete, Jeremiah does not simply have recourse to thundering words of rebuke; he puts a dirge into the mouth of Yahweh, a dirge which is more powerful than any threat: "What wrong did your fathers find in me that they went away from me?" (2, 5). It was Yahweh who led them out of the desert and gave them a fertile country. And yet what was absolutely unheard of in all the worlds about them, on the coasts of Cyprus or among the black tents of Kedar,[12] actually happened in Israel. The pagans never changed their gods, but Israel broke faith with Yahweh and followed foreign gods. They abandoned the stream of living water and dug for themselves cisterns that could not hold water (2, 9-13).

This was the beginning of Jeremiah's message of judgment and repentance, preached in the streets of Jerusalem. The young prophet was not very well received. When Josiah had discovered the Book of the Law and needed to consult the oracle of Yahweh, he sent not to Jeremiah but to the prophetess Huldah. At all

---

11. Rudolph, Jr 17.
12. *Kittaeans* is a term for the western island peoples from the city of Kition on Cyprus; *Kedar* is a Beduin tribe in the Eastern desert.

events, by the position he took, Jeremiah clearly meant to further the reform movement inaugurated by Josiah and he could only rejoice at the renewal of the covenant. The relationship between these two men is otherwise unknown. Only too soon Jeremiah was forced to the realization that the reform movement remained an external force and was unable to effectuate a radical conversion. In honor of the pious king Josiah, who had undertaken such great things, Jeremiah established a lasting monument in a dirge upon the king's tragic death at Megiddo (cf. 22, 15-16). After Josiah's death, the instincts that had been repressed broke out into the open. This was the time at which Jeremiah became "a man of strife and contention" (15, 10) and began to taste the full bitterness of his vocation. It is not without reason that this chapter in the prophet's life has been called Jeremiah's Gethsemani.[13]

B)   JEREMIAH UNDER JEHOIAKIM (609-598)

1) POLITICAL DEVELOPMENTS

The Egyptian relief forces had, as we have seen, been unable to check the destruction of what was left of Assyria. The Assyrians and Egyptians were defeated at Harran and thrown back across the Euphrates. Mesopotamia lay in Babylonian hands. Necho, therefore, needed to secure his position along the Euphrates and assert his dominion over Syria and Palestine. He summoned King Jehoahaz, who had been raised to the throne after the death of his father Josiah, to his headquarters at Riblah. After three months of rule, he deposed the king and had him deported to Egypt (2 K 23, 31-35; cf. Jer 22, 10-12). In his place he installed his brother Eliakim as king. As a reminder of the fact that he owed his kingship to the Pharaoh alone, Necho changed his name to Jehoiakim, and imposed a heavy tribute upon him which could only be raised by taxing the free citizens. Judah was once again under foreign dominion. Its independence, which had lasted only 20 years, was now a thing of the past.

---

13. DBS IV, 880.

The Egyptian rule over Judah, however, was only a brief intermezzo of four years (609-605). In the years 608-606, Nabopolassar and his son Nebuchadnezzar fought in the Armenian mountains, in an effort to secure the northern flank of the kingdom. When peace was established here, they turned to the Euphrates district. This had meanwhile been the scene of a small border dispute. Necho had attempted to build up the city of Carchemish as a bridgehead. In the year 605, the 21st year of Nabopolassar, his son and crown prince Nebuchadnezzar led the campaign. The aging King Nabopolassar remained in his country this year. Nebuchadnezzar marshalled his forces, marched up the Euphrates, crossed the river, and defeated the Egyptian army, which numbered some Greek mercenaries (46, 20), at Carchemish (May/June 605). What was left of the defeated army he pursued southwards as far as Hamath. There he defeated the army once again, so that not a single man survived.

He thus became master of all the country of Hatti, that is, master of Syria and Palestine.[14] But before he could assert his sovereignty, the news of his father's death reached him. He abandoned the victorious battlefield and made a series of forced marches to Babylon, in August of 605. On September 7, 605, he formally ascended the throne. The first year of his reign is reckoned only from the new year (March/April 604). Upon his accession to power, Nebuchadnezzar did not hesistate to follow up the successes of his campaign. At the end of 604 we find Babylonian armies in the Plains of Philistia. Ashkelon [15] was destroyed and the ruling class of that city was resettled in Babylon (47, 5-7). A letter from Ashkelon discovered in Egypt, an urgent appeal to the Pharaoh for help in their desperate crisis, might well have been composed during these days.[16] Judah herself was spared on this occasion. The approach of the Babylonian forces was sufficient to bring her to her knees. Jehoiakim did homage to the new master and was reconfirmed in his kingship

---

14. Wiseman, *Chronicles,* 67, lines 1-11.
15. *Ibid.,* 69, lines 15-20.
16. Bright, HistIsr 305.

(2 K 24, 1). The balance of world power had shifted only slightly. Judah was once again within the clutch of the great dragon, this time the dragon of Babylon.

But Judah bore the Babylonian yoke with a stiff neck, always waiting for a favorable opportunity to shake it off. The years 603 and 602 were filled with minor military actions throughout Syria. In the year 601, "the fourth year of his reign, the king of Akkad mustered his forces and marched into the land of the Hatti. They made their way through the land of the Hatti without encountering resistance. In the month of Kislev (November/December) he took over command of his army and marched against Egypt. The king of Egypt heard this and mustered his own forces. In open battle they met, breast to breast, and inflicted heavy losses upon each other. The king of Akkad and his troops turned around and marched back to Babylon." This is the sober account of the Babylonian chronicle.[17] It is obviously not the account of a magnificent triumph. The fight along the Egyptian frontier seems to have been a very hard one. The battle ended, if not in defeat, at least in a really Pyrrhic victory for Nebuchadnezzar.

Jehoiakim seized this opportunity to shake off the yoke of Babylon (2 K 24, 1), a political error which spelled the beginning of Judah's end. Nebuchadnezzar reorganized his army in 600 and prepared a huge number of horses and chariots. Before marching to the west himself, however, he commissioned his vassals, Judah's neighbors, to punish the rebellious cities. Armed forces from Aram, Moab, and Ammon, (2 K 24, 2; Jer 35, 11) began to invade Judah. In the 7th year of his reign, in the month of Kislev (December/January 598/97), Nebuchadnezzar himself left Babylon and undertook the subjection of rebellious Judah. In that same month, King Jehoiakim died in Jerusalem.[18] It is not impossible that he was murdered by a political faction who

---

17. Wiseman, *Chronicles*, 71, lines 5-7.
18. On the basis of a comparison with 2 K 24, 6, 8, 10ff., with the Babylonian Chronicle, Wiseman 73, lines 11-13. Kislev is the ninth month. In the twelfth month, Adar, Jerusalem was taken. Jehoiachin's reign falls in these three months.

thereby sought to secure more mild treatment for their country. His 18-year-old son Jehoiachin [19] was raised to the throne (2 K 24, 8). Three months later Jerusalem was entirely surrounded by Babylonians. "Nebuchadnezzar laid seige to the city of Judah (*al-ya-ahu-du*), and on the second day of the month of Adar he conquered the city and took its king prisoner. He established a king after his own heart (*šarra ša libbi-šu*), imposed a heavy tribute, and sent (them) to Babylon." [20] On the 2nd of Adar, that is March 15/16, 597, Jerusalem had fallen. Jehoiachin, the queen mother, the high court officials, and many of the more prominent citizens were deported to Babylon at the time of the "change of the year" [21] (2 Ch 36, 10). The new king, "after his own heart," was Jehoiachin's uncle Mattaniah, whose name was changed by the king to Zedekiah (2 K 24, 17). There had been no help from Egypt. Judah alone was forced to pay the final reckoning for her insurrection.

2) THE COLLAPSE OF THE REFORM

King Jehoiakim was not made from the same stuff as his father Josiah. Josiah had championed the rights of the poor and the commoner. Yahweh's law was the ultimate rule of his career. Jehoiakim, on the other hand, is more like a typical oriental despot. He used forced labor for his magnificent building projects, and refused to pay wages. The old palace was too modest for him; he meant to have a new one, more spacious, with windows and a broad balcony, paneled with cedar and painted vermilion (22, 13-17). The warning voice of the prophet was drowned in blood (2 K 24, 4). Jeremiah prophesied against him threatening

---

19. The name comes down in three different forms: Jehoiachin, Jeconiah, Koniahu. Cf. the Temple pillar named Yakin, III, p. 333.

20. Wiseman, *Chronicles*, 73, lines 12-13.

21. The new year began with the month of Nisan immediately following Adar (March/April). The deportation took place at the New Year. It is this circumstance that explains why it is dated in the 7th year of Nebuchadnezzar according to 2 K 24, 12 and in the 8th year according to Jr 52, 28. There are no grounds for arguing two different calendars here, Babylonian and Judaean.

that when he died people would not make the customary lament: "Alas my brother, alas my heart!" The burial of an ass would be his lot, cast forth beyond the gates of Jerusalem (22, 18-19). Circumstances such as these must sooner or later lead to a harsh confrontation between king and prophet.

a) *Against the Temple* [22]

One day, in the first year of King Jehoiakim (609), Jeremiah took a position at one of the Temple gates (26, 1) and delivered such a stirring sermon that the people would almost have lynched him except for the intervention of the authorities. What was his message? He robbed the people of the staff upon which they were leaning, and shattered all their false hope (7, 10). Since the days of reform, the Temple was the only legitimate place for sacrifice. Since it was here that Yahweh the Eternal had taken up his residence, it was commonly believed that the perpetual existence of the nation was guaranteed by the continued existence of the Temple. Now Jeremiah dared to assert that the Temple in Jerusalem would be destroyed just like the house of Yahweh at Shiloh, and Judah would be driven from her land just like Ephraim had been driven from hers (7, 11-14; 26, 9). The terrible force of his words must long have echoed in their ears:

qôl śāśôn weqôl śimḥah — qôl ḥatan weqôl kallah!
"I will silence the voice of mirth and the voice of gladness — the voice of the bridegroom and the voice of the bride" (7, 34). The mere presence of Yahweh's temple would not save them. They might cry "the temple of Yahweh, the temple of Yahweh" (7, 4) but what they needed was to do penance and be converted. The reform movement had not really taken hold of the people. The divine worship remained a matter of mere externals (7, 21-26). Actually, they were turning the Temple into a den of thieves (7, 11). The pagan abomination (*šiqqûsîm* 7, 30) had once again found its way into the temple itself. In the Hinnom Valley the

---

22. Chs. 7-10 are in the form of one single great address in which Jeremiah's words during the first years of Jehoiakim are the object of stylistic elaboration. Ch. 26 takes up the same context, but enlarges it with an account of the consequences of the prophet's words.

desecrated sacrificial high places had all been restored. Once again the people were sacrificing their children by fire (7, 31). On the roof tops they did homage to the queen of the heavens (*šarrat šamê*).[23] The moral demands of the Book of the Covenant were hardly recognized (7, 23).

b) *"You Must Die"*

The result of this tremendous sermon was not conversion and repentance. Priest and prophet alike attacked Jeremiah with a terrible threat: "You must die" (26, 8). The grounds for their attack was his alleged blasphemy. He had blasphemed the temple of Yahweh. Only by appealing to the example of the prophet Micah who had also prophesied the destruction of the temple and escaped without punishment (Mi 3, 12), was Jeremiah finally allowed to go free. A less happy fate awaited the prophet Uriah from Kiriath-jearim (forest city) who like Jeremiah, was a herald of destruction. In order to be rid of the unwelcome voice of conscience, the king arranged his murder. Uriah fled to Egypt, but the king's henchmen dragged him back to Jerusalem and put him to the sword. His corpse was cast among the graves of the common people (26, 20-23). Jeremiah was protected by a certain Ahikam, who protected him from the people's wrath (26, 24).

Whether it was this time or a few years later that Jeremiah's relatives from Anathoth attempted to have him murdered we can no longer accurately determine (11, 18-12, 6). The reasons behind this hostility are obvious.[24] The prophet's entire clan and relationship were under the same cloud of unpopularity as the prophet himself. In order to defend themselves, they held a family

---

23. Apparently one of the fertility goddesses (Astarte, Asherah, or Anat). The cakes baked in her honor might have had the form of a star (Morning and Evening Star, Venus). Rudolph, Jr 51.
24. It hardly seems probable that Jeremiah had won popular hatred for himself by going around preaching the law of Deuteronomy. That his relatives in Anathoth were high priests who had been done out of a job by the reform movements is also pure conjecture. Rudolph, Jr 76.

council and decided to get rid of the black sheep. Unsuspecting like a sheep being led to slaughter, Jeremiah continued his mission in the midst of mortal danger. How he escaped their attack is not recorded.[25]

c) *Herald of Doom*

The realization of the fact that the kingdom of Judah was ripe for destruction became clearer and clearer with the gradual rise of Nebuchadnezzar. The Egyptian defeat at Carchemish (605) is powerfully expressed in the stormy emotion of lines 46, 3-12: "The Lord God of hosts holds a sacrifice in the north country by the river Euphrates" (46, 10). In Jerusalem itself the prophet's constant warnings of impending doom grow more and more insistent. Since his words strike deaf ears, he has recourse to symbolic action.

One day he left his hiding and went into the house of a potter who was busy making vessels of various sizes on his wheel. When one vessel was spoiled, he simply reworked it into another. Jeremiah seized upon this figure to proclaim Yahweh's plan. Israel is like clay in the hands of Yahweh. The first form of the vessel was spoiled; Yahweh means to make a new and different one, if, and only if, Israel will be converted. But there is little likelihood of that. They are following their own designs and not the ones of Yahweh.

On another occasion Jeremiah received the command of Yahweh to buy an earthenware flask and go down with the elders of the people and some of the senior priests into the Valley of Hinnom, where they were sacrificing innocent children to the god Moloch. When he saw the valley, Jeremiah proclaimed that this place would everafter be named "Valley of Slaughter" (19, 6). He threatened further that city and Temple would both be destroyed. In a holy wrath, he then smashed the flask before the very eyes of his witnesses (19, 1-13). Upon his return to the

---

25. *EncMikr* III, 868 assigns this scene to the beginning of Jeremiah's activity. He was driven from his home and fled into the capital. But such a deadly enmity on the part of his relatives so soon after his public appearance is hardly likely.

courtyard of the Temple, the priest Pashhur had him arrested, beaten, and cast into stocks in the upper Benjamin Gate (19, 14—20, 6). On the following morning he was released but forbidden to enter the temple (36, 5).

d) *The Scroll* (36, 1-32)

Words were of no avail. Jeremiah took up his pen. In the fourth year of Jehoiakim (36, 1) the fateful year 605, Jeremiah had all the words he had spoken against Jerusalem, Judah, and the nations written on a scroll by his secretary Baruch (36, 1-4). Fundamentally this scroll must be identical with the first 25 chapters of the present Book of Jeremiah. The contents are a compendium of the 20 years of Jeremiah's prophetic activity. A year later, in the 9th month (November/December 604) a great festival was being celebrated in the Temple and Jeremiah sent Baruch with instructions to publicly read "the words of Yahweh out of the book." He continued to hope that the people would be converted and saved (36, 5ff.). This reading of the prophet's words, the first recorded instance of such a practice, made a great impression. Baruch first read the scroll at the "new gate," near the office of the state secretary Gemarriah. He took a stand in the open gateway of the Temple, while his audience gathered in the upper court of the Temple (36, 10). Gemarriah's son Micaiah brought word of the proceedings to his father who was sitting with the princes at council in the royal palace. Baruch was summoned. He read from the scroll a second time. They turned one to another in fear, as the Bible reports it, and asked him how he had written all these words. Was it at Jeremiah's dictation? (36, 16). These are very dangerous sentiments. The high council was familiar with the character of its king. He would want to be informed of these affairs. But they also recognized the great trust that prophet and secretary had in their God. On the one hand they advised Baruch to go and hide, together with Jeremiah, and let no one know where they were. On the other hand, they informed the king of what had happened (36, 19).

The king happened to be in the winter palace. It was the

9th month (November/December 605). A fire was burning in
the brazier before him. The scroll was brought into his presence.
As soon as Jehudi read three or four columns, the king cut them
off with a pen knife and threw them into the brazier until the
entire scroll was consumed in the fire. Neither the king nor any
of his servants who heard these words was afraid, nor did they
rend their garments before the threat of Yahweh's prophet. Instead, he issued orders for the arrest of both Jeremiah and Baruch.
"Yahweh, however, hid them " (36, 21, 26). Completely silenced
as far as public appearances were concerned, Jeremiah took advantage of his retirement to have the words in the destroyed scroll,
and many other words as well, written by Baruch on a second
scroll (36, 27-32).

3) CONFESSIONES JEREMIAE PROPHETAE

During these years of enforced silence (605-598), Jeremiah's
soul was in constant turmoil. He was constantly disputing and
arguing with Yahweh. When he emerged, he was "an iron column,
a bronze wall" (1, 18; 15, 19-21). The sufferings and struggles
of these seven years come to light in various passages of the
book,[26] particularly in the sections that have been collectively
referred to as "the confessions of the prophet Jeremiah." Trampled
in the winepress of God's purification, the prophet offers his most
precious possession, the record of his own personal experience.
Since open words, in preaching or in writing, were now forbidden, it must be his own inner soul, seven times purified, that
now gives witness to the God who called him to be a prophet.

In constant peril of being discovered, always in fearful anxiety
of his people's enmity, the prophet Jeremiah had to be a helpless
spectator as his beloved nation blindly brought about its own
destruction. The prospect cast him into the depths of despair
(15, 18). Knowing that his words would only bring him new
persecution and new desolation — "I did not sit on the company

---

26. 1, 4-19; 11, 18-23; 12, 1-6; 15, 10-21; 17, 14-18; 18, 18-23; 20,
14-18; Pfeiffer, IntrOT 497.

of merry-makers" (15, 17) — but that his words were fire and a hammer, destined to shatter and burn Judah (1, 10; 5, 14; 23, 29), he cursed the very day of his birth (20, 14-18). This is a bitter word, even more so than the bitter exclamation in Job 3, 1ff.: "Let the day perish wherein I was born." He accuses Yahweh of having made a fool of him and led him astray. He is like a deceitful brook whose waters have failed (15, 18). It was for his sake that he had chosen his solitary life. In order to be completely free for Yahweh's commands, he had abandoned the hope of marriage and family (16, 1ff.). Here we can see the prophet rising up against the burden God imposes upon him and doing his very best to shake it off. But if he refuses to prophesy, the words of God burn like fire in his bones (20, 9); and if he does proclaim God's word, he will reap only hate and deadly enmity (20, 8, 10). Whatever he does, the outcome is the same: it is the night of the soul, Gethsemani. The God whom he proclaims on earth has himself become the prophet's personal crisis.

The problem of God's rule of the world is the one insoluble question. "Why does the way of the wicked prosper?" (12, 1-6). There is no rational answer to this question. Just as in the Book of Job, the question is referred to the unfathomable depths of God's essence, its only final solution. "If you have raced with men on foot and they have wearied you, how will you compete with horses?" (12, 5). Man is simply too little for God's measure. God is always ineluctably greater. Left to himself, the prophet cannot understand the confused trail of his people's history.

In these years of quiet, however, Jeremiah found the road from crisis to certainty. Yahweh is the prophet's hope and Israel's hope as well (17, 13, 14). When the curtain rises and Jeremiah withdraws from his retreat, he is a different man. There is no more complaining, no arguing with God, but neither is there any intercession for the rebellious nation. He gives free course to God's stern hand. The years of enforced solitude could not break this man. It is only now that he appears as the man of iron, a bronze wall, prepared to endure and to suffer persecution, always in the realization that Yahweh is his strength: "I will make you to this people a fortified wall of bronze; they will fight against you, but they shall not prevail over you, for I am with you to save you and deliver you, says the Lord" (15, 20).

At the end of Jehoiakim's reign, Jeremiah once again entered the Temple, paying no heed to the former prohibition. He did not come alone. A few Rechabites, who had fled to Jerusalem at the approach of the Babylonians in the early winter of 598, accompanied him. He invited them to drink wine. They excused themselves on the grounds that their ancestor had forbidden it (35, 2ff.). How differently had Judah behaved! They had cast aside not only the rule of men, but God's own law; that is why they themselves would soon be passed aside (35, 12-17). This time Jehoiakim was unable to persecute this unflinching herald of death. Destruction was ready to take its course.

C) JEREMIAH UNDER ZEDEKIAH (597-586)

1) THE WEAK MAN AT THE HELM

Zedekiah [27] was not the man to provide strong and confident direction to the state in this time of catastrophe. Perhaps it was precisely for this reason that the Babylonians had raised him to the throne. Personally, he seems to have been possessed of the very best intentions (37, 37-21; 38, 7-28). But he simply did not have the energy to follow up his convictions in the face of hostile princes and people. One reason for this was the questionable position of his kingship. His nephew Jehoiachin was regarded by many of his contemporaries, even by the official Babylonian records,[28] as the legitimate "king of Judah." People were looking to his imminent return and the restoration of his rule (28, 4). Zedekiah's kingship rested on a weak foundation. It was to be expected that his reign would witness the terrible events that spelled the ultimate destruction of king and nation.

---

27. Hebr. *sidkî-yahû*, "my justice, i.e., the protector of my right is Yahweh." Cf. Sedekias. Also written Zedekia, or Zidkia. Following the ancient translations, I have chosen the form Zedekiah.

28. Jehoiachin in Exile, ANET 308. Jar stamp from Judah with the inscription: "Eliakim, servant of Jehoiachin" proves that the king's property was still administered in his name, Bright, HistIsr 307.

a) *"The Good Things Are All Gone"* (24, 1-10)

One might suppose that Jeremiah would lament the fate of his countrymen who had been resettled on foreign soil. Quite the contrary. Witness the vision of the two baskets of figs. The one basket contained fine and first-ripe figs, while the other had figs so bad they could not be eaten. The significance of the vision: a call of destruction. Judah is so evil that it has to be cast out. "I will send swords, famine, and pestilence upon them, until they shall be utterly destroyed from the land which I gave to them and their fathers" (24, 10). It was Jeremiah's conviction that the hope of the future lay with the expatriates in Babylon.

b) *Military Revolt in Babylon (595/94) and Its Effects in Judah*

Once again it was clear that Judah's history was most intimately connected with that of the world powers of her time. The effects of the political earthquake in Babylon could be felt even in Jerusalem. For the 10th year of Nebuchadnezzar (595/94) the Babylonian chronicle has the following laconic entry: "In the 10th year the king of Akkad was in his land. From the month of Kislev to the month of Tebet (mid-November to mid-January 595/94) there was revolt in Akkad . . . . With weapons he struck a blow to his own army. With his own hands he took his enemies." [29] The news of a military revolt in Babylon gave new impetus to the anti-Babylonian forces in the western countries. A political man-hunt began against Nebuchadnezzar.

At the king's palace in Jerusalem there appeared ambassadors from the kings of Edom, Moab, Ammon, Tyre, and Sidon (27, 3), to lay plans for a general revolution. One day the prophet Jeremiah made his appearance among these illustrious guests, a most comic figure (ch. 27). He had thongs and yoke-bars hanging from his neck.[30] He gave the ambassadors a message for their masters. Yahweh, the creator of heaven and earth, to whom

---

29. Wiseman, *Chronicles,* 73, 21-22.
30. The yoke of the plough-oxen is an oak board some 4½ feet long and 3 inches thick. It is positioned across the animals' necks and attached around the neck and horns.

all nations belong, had decreed that all nations and even all "beasts of the field" be given into the hands of Nebuchadnezzar. Every people that peacefully submitted their neck to the yoke of the king of Babylon would continue to live in peace in its own territory. But if a nation were to cast off the yoke, the only result would be sword, pestilence, and destruction.

These words and symbolic actions produced a near riot. The prophet Hananiah seized Jeremiah's yoke and shattered it, in an attempt to prove the emptiness of the words of threat (ch. 28). For his own part, he prophesied that Jehoiachin would return home in glory, within two years,[31] and with him all the vessels of the temple that had been carried away. Jeremiah had an answer: Hananiah had shattered a wooden yoke, but he would exchange it for an iron one.

Nebuchadnezzar managed to crush the revolt in short order and purge the military of its rebellious elements. In that same 10th year of his reign (595/94) he marched with his reorganized army into the country of the Hatti (Syria), in a demonstration of power, designed to intimidate any of his subjects who had future plans for rebellion.[32] The chronicle refers to a second campaign into the country of the Hatti, for the 11th year (594/93), but breaks off before recording the outcome.[33] Under these circumstances, Judah's only alternative was peaceably or stubbornly to lay its neck into the yoke of the King of Babylon (27, 8, 12). The external expression of this submission was the payment of tribute recorded in the Babylonian chronicle, a burden which Judah too was now forced to bear. Probably this payment was to be sent to Babylon on a yearly basis. According to the not uncontested evidence of Jeremiah 51, 59,[34] Zedekiah himself is supposed to have made a state visit to Babylon. At all events, embassies were

---

31. The formula means "a short time."
32. Wiseman, *Chronicles*, 73, 23-24.
33. *Ibid.*, 75, 25.
34. The text is not certain. According to MT Jeremiah wrote together with Zeriah, since "he went to Babel with (*'et*) Zedekian." LXX translates, however: "When he went to Babylon from (*para*) Zedekiah" (28, 59).

constantly being exchanged. Jeremiah took advantage of one such embassy to send a letter to the expatriates.

c) *Jeremiah's Letter to Babylon*

The exchange of messages between home and exile seems to have been very active. At all events, the spark of rebellion had leaped from Jerusalem to the expatriates in Babylon. Jeremiah's first letter (29, 1-23) has no precise date. It must have been shortly after King Jehoiachin and the queen, together with the eunuchs, the princes, the craftsmen and the smiths had all been deported from Jerusalem. The expatriates did not know how they should settle their affairs in the foreign country. Babylon too had its prophets, true prophets and false prophets alike. This is the question to which Jeremiah's letter is addressed. He unmasks the lies and deceit of the prophets who are always promising salvation. They are not proclaiming Yahweh's message. It is better to prepare for a long stay in the foreign country, to build houses, to plant gardens, to marry and rear a family. Only when 70 years are completed for Babylon will Yahweh bring them back home (29, 10). Why Jeremiah should have prophesied such a short span of power for the great Babylonian empire, then standing at its very zenith of world empire, cannot be explained on any rational basis. Yahweh himself had granted the prophet a glimpse into the future plan of history. Speaking as historians, we can, in hindsight, demonstrate that the number is reasonably close to the actual course of history.[35] But the number 70 was considered a round number — seven being a sacred number — and was meant to denote a reasonably long interval of waiting for the ultimate sentence to be passed by God. Isaiah, for example, used the same number with reference to the destruction of the city of Tyre (23, 5, 7). The same idiom is used in the case of Babylon. The Assyrian King Sanherib had destroyed Babylon in 689 and wanted to carry off the populace in chains. When

---

35. If we count from the fall of Nineveh (612) to the Fall of Babel (538), the total is 74 years; if we start counting with the year of Nebuchadnezzar's (605) accession, there are 67 years.

Esarhaddon, in the 11th year of his reign (670/69), wanted to rebuild the city, he first consulted the oracles. The destruction of the.city was interpreted as a divine judgment on the part of the god Marduk. In order to justify the early rebuilding of the city, the wise men of Babylon altered the numbers written upon the curse tablets (in cuneiform the number is written by two signs $\gamma\langle$ = 60 + 10 — by simply reversing the signs to read $\langle\gamma$ = 10 + 1 = 11 years).[36] Jeremiah has obviously made use of an expression from the religious vocabulary of his time and enlisted it in the service of his prophetic mission. The number 70 is thus a prophetic number, brim full of the wrath of Yahweh. But this too accounts for the fact that the message is bound up with time. If the people are converted and Yahweh's wrath is soothed, then the years will be shortened.

Just as in his homeland, among the expatriates too Jeremiah encountered the sharpest opposition. The prophets of freedom, Ahab and Zedekiah, who connected even sexual irresponsibility and "free love" with their objectives of political freedom, were stirring up support for a rebellion against Babylon. Nebuchadnezzar was not slow to react. He had the pair roasted over a fire, so that their fate became a warning and a proverb (29, 21-23). A certain Shemaiah of Babylon sent a letter of complaint to the temple police in Jerusalem, inquiring why they were taking no steps against this "madman" (29, 26). The captain of the temple police (Zephaniah) read this brief letter personally to Jeremiah. Was this a gesture of sympathy for the prophet? Or was it to serve as a warning? [37]

Jeremiah 51, 59-64 is concerned with a second letter from Jeremiah to the Babylonians. It is sent to the address of Seraiah ben-Neriiah, probably Baruch's brother (cf. 32, 12). Its content: "Babylon will be destroyed!" Seraiah was to read the letter aloud, thus proclaiming God's judgment at the very place it was destined to occur, and then sink the letter in the Euphrates River.

These letters afford a considerable insight into the development

---

36. E. Vogt, *70 anni exsilii*, Bibl 38 (1957), 236.
37. Rudolph, Jr 171.

of Jewish solidarity in the exile. This time of captivity must be pictured not as a life in prison or in a concentration camp, but rather a sort of forced settlement with considerable freedom to come and go within the limits of a determined territory.[38] Within these boundaries it was possible to achieve a measure of self-determination in civil as well as religious matters. The fact that this development took such a peaceful course is, ultimately, certainly the fruit of Jeremiah's advice.

2) DOOMED TO DESTRUCTION

a) *"A Beautiful Heifer is Egypt"* (46, 20)

Inevitably we are faced with the question of whether the ruling class of Jerusalem had merely been struck with blindness when they raised the banner of revolt against the Babylonian dragon, or whether there was somewhere some favorable prospect of success in this bold adventure. The word of Zedekiah, the weak man at the helm, was hardly the deciding factor. The uprising, however, was not simply the affair of a military clique either; priests, prophets, and the whole mass of the people were for the battle. If we examine the contemporary world politics, it does seem that the time chosen for revolt was not the most unfavorable opportunity. For the Babylonian kingdom, Judah represented the most isolated western border province. In Jerusalem there was a well-known proverb: "Babylon is far away, but Egypt is close." Egypt proved to be the anvil, Nebuchadnezzar was certainly the hammer (51, 20), and Jerusalem? Jerusalem was the iron that lay between both forces.

After the victorious battle at Carchemish, Nebuchadnezzar had thrown the Egyptians back from Syria and Palestine. Nonetheless, Necho (609-594) refused to give up the ancient dream of an Egyptian sovereignty over these territories. Since his efforts on land had failed, he turned to the sea in an effort to win back his losses. Herodotus (II, 159) reports that Necho had triremes

38. *Ibid.*, 166.

built, that is, ships with three banks of oars. The one fleet was to control the northern sea (Mediterranean Sea), the other the southern sea (Red Sea). In order to join both seas together, Necho undertook the construction of a great canal, which he meant to carry from the Nile River through the Wadi Tumilat into the Bitter Lakes, and from there into the Red Sea.[39] It was the Persian King Darius who first completed the project, which was actually nothing less than an anticipation of the modern Suez Canal. Necho was also the first to circumnavigate Africa. The military backbone of his army was formed by Greek mercenaries. The economic prosperity of the Nile country was also largely owing to the services of the Greek merchants.

Necho's successor Psammetich II (594-588) was certainly not the weak eunuch on the Pharaoh's throne that he has frequently been considered. On the basis of new sources [40] it appears rather that he was a self-awares conquering Pharaoh of the old style. He neglected Syria for a time and turned his attention to the southern part of his kingdom. With an army of mercenaries, consisting of Greeks from Ionia, Caria, and Rhodes as well as Jews, he made his way deep into the land of Cush as far as the fourth, and possibly the fifth, cataract. On this campaign the Greek mercenaries left their graffiti on the colossal pillars of Ramses II.[41] After his victorious return from the south, in the fourth year of his reign (c. 590), he sent an Egyptian fleet into the land of Haru, that is, Phoenicia; whether this was for purposes of war or simply demonstration of his newly acquired power is not made clear in our sources.

Psammetich's successor Apries (Hophrah 588-569) followed the route staked out by his predecessor. For the border country of Judah there was an ever present temptation to place its hope upon the newly rising Egyptian power, and be rid of the Babylonian yoke. The prophet Jeremiah, however, had a differ-

---

39. Drioton-Vandier, *Les Peuples de l'Orient Méditerranéen, II, L'Égypte* (1952), 582ff.
40. *Ibid.,* 594.
41. *Ibid.,* 595.

ent idea, one far too sober for his contemporaries. "A beautiful heifer is Egypt, but a gadfly from the north has come upon her" (46, 20).

b) *Ostraca Letters from Lachish*:

In the excavations at Lachish, in the year 1935, 18 Ostraca were discovered, with writing in the ancient Hebrew alphabet; in 1938 three more were unearthed.[42] The greater part of this treasure is, unfortunately, in poor condition; those which are still legible, however, provide a valuable, extra-Biblical insight into the conditions of the declining kingdom of Judah. The shards were discovered under the ruins of the city gate at Lachish. Since the gate was also the seat of judgment, Torczyner considers the material as the acta of a military court which took place there. This proposal has met with little enthusiasm.[43] Most scholars are convinced that these are true letters, addressed from various military outposts to the fortress commander of Lachish, whose name was Joash. Some of the letters come from Hoša-Yahu; the names of the other writers are unknown. The postal system seems not to have functioned very predictably. The commander had sent an earlier instruction to Hoša-Yahu, which was never received. Accordingly, he sent a second and more energetic letter. Hoša-Yahu writes back under oath: "May Yahweh punish me [44] if I have ever read or had read in my presence any letter from you." In letter three to Lachish he confirms his receipt and execution of the order, whose words were these: "General [45] Konyahu ben-Elnatan will depart for Egypt.[46] Accordingly, Hodayahu ben-Ahiyahu, together with his men, will be withdrawn from the outpost in question in order to escort him to Egypt." Together with these military affairs, we find one reference to a "letter from the prophet" (*sēpher ... mē'et hannabî*) which contains the strange warning "take care"; this letter was sent on to Lachish. We cannot exclude the possibility that this is a reference to the prophet of that day, Jeremiah. What was the content of this prophetic

---

42. Hebrew Text by Galling, TGI 63-65. — Translation of 3 Ostraca Commentary Literature and Photo: Winton Thomas, DOT 212-217. — ANET 321-322. — DBS IV, 411-417.
43. More on the problem in DBS IV, 413.
44. Oldest extra-Biblical verification of the full name Yahweh.
45. Literally, *sar hassāba'* "prince of the army."
46. The consonants *yrd* can be read as imperfect *yēred* "he will go down" (thus DBS IV, 414), and not as the perfect *yārad* "he has gone down." (Thus ANET 322; DOT 214).

letter? Was it a warning to the commander of Lachish not to turn to Egypt for help? Only conjectures can be advanced at this point.[47]

Letter six, which is poorly preserved, does provide some clear references to the internal crisis of that era, provided we are correct in our reading. Once again there is an exchange of letters and missives. "Read and see. The words (of the prophet) are not good to defeat the hands of the Chaldaeans."[48] The prophet Jeremiah had to listen to this same reproach in Jerusalem (38, 4). Letter four illustrates the contemporary system of military communications. In order to carry information over broad stretches of country, signal fires were lighted at predetermined points. The writer of this letter assures the commander of Lachish that, as ordered, they are monitoring all the signals he is sending, but can no longer see signals from Azekah. The writing does not make clear whether or not Azekah was already in enemy hands. It does, however, make it quite clear that the Judaic border fortresses were in a state of constant alert. Most of the letters are introduced with the salutation of peace: "May Yahweh let you hear the news of peace (šalôm)." This may have been simply the conventional manner of beginning a letter; but on the eve of the great war we may be assured that the words were taken at face value.[49]

c) *From the Ninth to the Eleventh Year of King Zedekiah* (588-586)

Neither king nor princes nor people listened to the advice of Jeremiah to put their neck into the yoke of Nebuchadnezzar (21, 1-10). The prophet had ordered them to choose between the way of life and the way of death (21, 8). Submission would have meant life. But Judah rebelled and thereby chose sword, famine, pestilence, and death. The time for revolt seemed favorable. In the year 588, Egypt was in the hands of the energetic Pharaoh

---

47. For Jeremiah, DBS IV, 415; against DOT 215, which supposes one of the itinerant prophets to be the messenger. Some scholars have supposed it to be the prophet Uriah (26, 20a), who did flee to Egypt. But this can hardly be the case, since Uriah's fall occurred ten years earlier.

48. DBS IV, 415.

49. The sender refers to himself as the "dog of his master," not so much in reference to his dog-like subjection, as to indicate his faithfulness. On the symbolism of "dog," cf. D. Winton Thomas, *Kelebh* "dog": its origin and some usages of it in the OT, VT 10 (1960), 410-427.

Hophrah, who made it abundantly clear that he meant to assert Egypt's hereditary claims in Syria and Palestine. Jerusalem revolted. Nebuchadnezzar reacted with the speed of lightning. There was more than Judah at stake.

In the 9th year of King Zedekiah, on the 10th month, on the 10th day (January 5, 587) Nebuchadnezzar, King of Babylon, marched to Jerusalem with all his army and laid seige to the city. He had a wall erected all around Jerusalem (2 K 25, 1; Jer 39, 1; 52, 4). At the same time he waged war against the Judaean fortresses which fell, one after another, before the enemy's tremendous power. Only Lachish and Azekah held out. It was then that Jeremiah came before the king and once again tried to persuade him of the stupidity of further battle; once again he begged him to bow his neck before the Babylonian yoke. Since the king remained obstinate, Jeremiah embarked upon a theme which must certainly succeed. If Zedekiah were to capitulate, then he might look forward to a peaceful life and especially to a solemn burial, one in which the people would take up the dirge "Alas my lord!" and burn the funeral pyre. The words of the prophet were without effect. The course of events seemed to prove him a liar; at the approach of the Egyptian army, the siege of Jerusalem was lifted (34, 21; 37, 5). This first phase of the war is remarkable also for the liberation of the slaves in Jerusalem, a measure designed to strengthen the common defense of the city. No sooner had the besieging army withdrawn that these newly liberated slaves were once again pressed into servitude. This unprincipled way of dealing earned Jeremiah's sharpest criticism (24, 8-22). He made it very clear that the Chaldaeans were going to return (37, 3-10). Words like this were not designed to win him friends.

In the 10th year of Zedekiah, that is, in the 18th year of Nebuchadnezzar (early 587 to early 586 — Jer 32, 1): The siege of Jerusalem had begun in the middle of winter (on the 10th day of the 10th month of the 9th year of Zedekiah — January 5, 587, 2 K 25, 1). There is no record of the precise date of the Egyptian troops' arrival; it probably was early summer of 587, since they had to hurry in order to save Jerusalem. Neither is there any record of where the decisive battle took place between Egyptian and Babylonian forces, if there actually was such a battle. It is possible that the besieging forces simply retreated in the face of the Egyptian advance. For Jerusalem, this was only a brief respite. Jeremiah took advantage of this opportunity to visit his home in Anathoth, to settle some business. When he appeared in the Benjamin gate, he was detained: "You are trying to escape to the Chaldaeans."

"No, that is a lie. I am not trying to escape." But all his protestations were of no avail. Jeremiah was beaten and thrown into the prison which had been established in the house of Jonathan the recorder. Probably the normal prisons were already overflowing with political prisoners. Jeremiah remained many days in the dungeon cell, in a reservoir which was normally used to collect rain water. Incarceration in this damp subterranean chamber was equivalent to a lengthy and unobtrusive execution (37, 11-16). This was simply the caprice of some minor officials. The degree to which the king's authority had already sunk is indicated by the circumstance that he had the prophet brought to visit him secretly in the palace, to determine whether there was some new word from Yahweh. Jeremiah could only repeat what he had said many times before: "You shall be delivered into the hand of the king of Babylon" (37, 17). At the conclusion of this strange audience, Jeremiah begged the king not to send him back into the dungeon where he would certainly die. The king committed Jeremiah to the court of the guard, where a loaf of bread was given him daily from the bakers' street, until all the bread of the city was gone (37, 17-21).

It was here that Jeremiah concluded the arrangements for the purchase of a piece of property in Anathoth (32, 1-15). The contract was sealed and put into an earthenware vessel, so it would last for a long time. This purchase marks a turning point in the prophet's preaching. The fact that he was purchasing a piece of property in the days of the city's impending destruction seemed to be senseless. But Jeremiah, from this moment on, becomes a prophet of salvation: "For thus says the Lord of hosts, the God of Israel: Houses and fields and vineyards shall again be bought in this land" (32, 15).

After his success over Egypt, Nebuchadnezzar withdrew into Syria and established his headquarters at Riblah. The conquest of Jerusalem he entrusted to his generals, who once again besieged the city, in an attempt to reduce the populace to starvation and thus prepare the way for the final storming of the walls (37, 21). In this desperate situation, only a united will to resistance, the common effort of all the people, could have promised any prospect of defending the city for more than a brief interval. Jeremiah, in the court of the guard, kept repeating the old refrain: "He who stays in this city shall die by the sword, by famine, and by pestilence; but he who goes out to the Chaldaeans shall live" (38, 2ff.). The princes reported to the king: "Let this man be put to death, for he is weakening the hands of the soldiers who are left in this city." Zedekiah abandoned the prophet to their power. They cast Jeremiah into the cistern in which there was no water, only mire, into which Jeremiah immediately sank. He would have perished miserably, were it not for the Ethiopian Ebed-Melech who immediately drew him out (38, 7-13). Shortly afterwards, Zedekiah had the prophet brought to the third gate of the Temple for a secret rendezvous, apparently by night and wearing a disguise. Jeremiah could only repeat the message from God: submission would save what could still be saved; continued resistance would bring destruction. But Zedekiah was too weak to follow this advice. This was the last confrontation between king and prophet. The threatened fate now ran its course (38, 14-23).

In the 11th year of Zedekiah, in the 4th month, on the 9th day (July 19, 586), a breach was made in the city wall (39, 2; 52, 7; 2 K 25, 3) and this led to a general panic. The king and his court fled the city by night, through the "gate between the two walls" [50] in the direction of the Hinnom and Kidron Valleys,

---

50. Probably what was later the Dung Gate, in the South of the city.

where the royal gardens were situated. From here he hoped to reach the Jordan and seek refuge in Transjordania. He was captured near Jericho and brought as prisoner into the headquarters at Riblah. Here he was forced to watch his two sons slaughtered before his very eyes. After this final grisly sight, he was blinded (39, 2-10; 52, 7-11; 2 K 3-7) and carried off to Babylon.

In the 5th month, the 10th day,[51] that is, the 19th year of Nebuchadnezzar (August 17, 586), Nebuzardan, commander of the bodyguard, made his way into Jerusalem and set fire to palace, temple, and homes; the city walls he tore down (39, 8; 52, 12; 2 K 25, 8). From the first breaching of the city walls until their final destruction one month had passed. It can hardly be assumed that the house by house defense of the inner city could have lasted so long. More likely the conquerors were simply awaiting new orders from headquarters. These came with Nebuzardan who arrived with the royal bodyguard and sealed the doom of the rebellious city. With bitterness and with a bleeding heart, both Jeremiah and the Book of Kings records everything that was carried out of the Temple before it perished in flames (52, 17-23; 2 K 25, 13-17).

Next came the procession of the captives. Nebuchadnezzar's orders to keep a special eye on the prophet Jeremiah (39, 12) apparently did not reach the subordinate officers. He too was forced into the procession of captives which was already making its way from Jerusalem northwards. Only at Ramah did Nebuzardan manage to rescue the chained prophet from the midst of the captives. He set him free, to go wherever he wished, either to accompany him to Babylon, or if he preferred, to remain in his own country (40, 1-6). Jeremiah chose the latter and joined the company of Gedaliah who, as Babylonian governor, with his headquarters at Mizpah, was beginning to assemble all the remaining citizens of good will in an effort to begin reconstruction of the

---

51. Thus Jr 52, 12; but 2 K 25, 8, "seventh day": there is no satisfactory explanation.

devastated land (40, 7-12). The fugitives began to return from Edom, Moab, and Ammon. They were greeted by an extraordinarily rich harvest of wine, fruit, and oil.

In the 7th month (November/December 586) however, Gedaliah was assassinated by Jishmael as being a collaborator with the enemy. The murderer made good his escape into Ammon. The people, bereft of their leadership, were in a state of panic. They were expecting a second Babylonian punitive expedition. Everyone wanted to flee to Egypt. Ten days after Gedaliah's murder, the word of Jahweh came to Jeremiah. He called together all the leaders of the troops and all the people, little and great, and demanded that they stay in their country and not take flight. Once again, the prophet's word was not received. The people would not be stopped, and they took both Jeremiah and Baruch with them to Egypt.

"In Egypt Jeremiah drops out of sight. The last thing we hear from him is a prophecy that Nebuchadnezzar would also make his way to Egypt (43, 8ff.), and a threat against his own compatriots that they could look forward to bitter suffering for having honored the queen of heaven on Egyptian territory (44). It is one sign of the tragedy of his life that at the end of his career he needs to raise his voice against the very sins of his compatriots that he first attacked at the beginning of his activity. Battle and failure are his companions to the very end. Upon considering the bitter confrontations described in chapter 44 it is certainly credible as the Jewish legends report, that Jeremiah was stoned to death in Egypt by his own compatriots." [52]

3) THE BOOK OF CONSOLATION AND THE NEW COVENANT

We would paint a most incorrect picture of the prophet Jeremiah if we see him only as a herald of death, although this he primarily was. At the climax of his suffering, a new light breaks through, to put all the dark side of his preaching into shadow. He is a prophet primarily by reason of the fact that he proclaims the destruction and announces a new era of salvation. In

---

52. Rudolph, Jr VII.

chapters 30 and 31, as well as 32 and 33, the message of expected salvation takes on the form of a book of consolation. Chapers 30 and 31 are addressed primarily to Israel, by which we must understand not only the northern kingdom, but the whole people of Israel. Chapters 32 and 33, on the other hand, record his purchase of property during the captivity and the prophecies of the future bound up with this occasion. Within the framework of this book of consolation, 30, 5 — 31, 22 form an independent prophetic poem, which stands out by its rhythmic form from the surrounding prose sections. This might be an independent scroll dating back to the time of Jeremiah (*sēpher* 30, 2), a section which, as we shall later demonstrate, was incorporated into the whole book by the final redactor. There is no agreement as to the time when Jeremiah composed this book of consolation (30-31). The beginning, the middle, and the end of his prophetic activity have all been argued as possible dates.[53] It is true that throughout the entire time of his prophetic activity, the consoling light of a future salvation broke through the somber tones of his message, but they were always overshadowed by the storm clouds of impending doom. Only after judgment was fulfilled over Jerusalem did his message of salvation come to light in all its power. The present book of consolation is thus a composite statement of Jeremiah's preaching of salvation. Genuine thoughts of the prophet have been further developed by his disciples.[54]

a) *Yahweh Savior and Lord*

Surprisingly enough, the book of consolation begins with images of terror. The prophet hears a cry of panic, every face turned pale, "every man with his hands on his loins like a woman in labor." The new era can, however, come about only by a complete transformation of the political situation. The coming of this era of salvation must be preceded by a time of terrible

---

53. Rudolph, Jr 172 argues for the time between the reforms and death of Josiah (622-609), since the inclusion of the Northern Kingdom of Israel makes particular sense here.
54. Particulars must be referred to the commentaries: there is no unanimity of opinion among the scholars.

crisis, the "woes of the messiah." This crisis is only a transition; salvation is waiting at the outcome. The end will see Yahweh himself, the savior. The vocabulary of this section is dominated by the verb *yāša'*, "to save, to redeem" (30, 7, 10, 11). Yahweh is thus the "Jesus" (*môšîa'* 30, 10b), the savior of Israel is Israel's healer, since he "heals" her wounds (30, 17).

b) *The Return*

Yahweh's first act of healing is the "gathering" of the scattered and dispersed elements of his people (31, 8).[55] To the exiles shall go out a call to be on their way, to set up waymarkers and guideposts for themselves, to consider well the highway, the road by which they went, and finally to come back home (31, 21). The faithless daughter Israel, however, continues to hesitate. In order to force a decision upon his hesitant countrymen, the prophet makes a bold statement: "The Lord has created a new thing on earth, a path through the breach,[56] along which the hero makes his way" (31, 22b). Jeremiah is here borrowing an image from his predecessor Micah (2, 13): "He who opens

---

55. The verb *kābas* is used by the modern Jewish repatriates as the name for their collective settlements, *kibûssîm*.

56. The Vulgate translates: "femina circumdabit virum" the woman will "surround" the man. This was interpreted as a prophetic symbolism for the marriage between Yahweh and Israel. In the years to come Israel will return to her husband Yahweh and remain perfectly faithful to him. The "woman" who thus "surrounds" (with her care and ministry) the man is none other than the virgin who gives birth. — But the Greek translation is so different from the Latin that there is no possibility of reconciling the two. The key word here is *nqbh;* if it is pointed *neqēbah,* it means woman; then the verb *tesôbeb* must be assigned some meaning that fits with man and woman. But if the consonants are read as in the Shiloh inscription, *niqbah* or *neqîbah,* then the meaning is "breach, way through." Since the whole section is a series of references to journeying, this would surely form the climax of the oracle. The text should accordingly read: "The Lord has created a new thing on earth, a path through the breach along which the hero makes his way." (*neqîbah, yesôbēh gāber*): we must note that "man" (*geber*) can be understood in the sense of "hero, warrior." For further discussion, cf. my article "Femina circumdabit virum 'oder' via salutis," ZkTh 83 (1961), 431-442.

the breach will go up before them; they will break through and pass the gate, going out by it. Their king will pass on before them, the Lord at their head." It is not to be explained on any human terms how this people rises again; it is entirely God's work and it is equivalent to a new creation.

c) *"The New Covenant"* (31, 31)

"Behold, the days are coming, says the Lord, when I will make a new covenant with the house of Israel and the house of Judah, not like the covenant which I made with their fathers . . . . But this is the covenant which I will make with the house of Israel after those days, says the Lord: I will put my law within them, and I will write it upon their hearts, and I will be their God, and they shall be my people" (3, 31-34). Basically both old and new covenants are alike. They are both the work of God alone. In terms of simple grammar, the acting subject in this entire section is God himself. It is he who strikes the covenant, he who gives the Torah, he who writes in the heart, he who will be God while they will be the people chosen by him. It is incorrect to distinguish between old and new covenant simply on the basis of the fact that it is man's activity that is at work in the law, while here it is God's grace alone. Both covenants are essentially the work of grace. The deciding element lies only in the fact that in the new covenant we are blessed with a greater measure of grace. "I have loved you with an everlasting love; therefore I have continued my faithfulness (*hesed*) to you" (31, 3). This greater measure of grace also effects a thoroughgoing transformation of the new people of God. Whereas Hosea was forced to complain: "There is no longer any knowledge of God (*da'at 'elohîm* 4, 1) in the land," in the days to come knowledge of God will be everywhere in evidence. No man will need to teach another man about God. From smallest to greatest, every man will know God as intimately as in paradise, where God walked with the first man. "All will know me" (31, 34). The new covenant has its climax in the "knowledge of God." As elsewhere in Scripture, the verb "know" (*yada'*) means not only the knowledge of the intellect and understanding, but rather to recognize, to accept, and to love. Once man as an individual and as the people of God is completely permeated with the reality of God's nearness, then sin and defection necessarily cease to be. The defection to the gods of Canaan can no longer be a question. The new covenant is so powerful that it is actually equivalent to a new creation: "A new thing has been created on earth" (31, 22). This new thing is the definitive and everlasting order created by God himself. As proof of this fact, there is a reference to the firm foundations of the cosmic order, as in the covenant with Noah: "If this fixed order departs from before me, says the Lord then shall the descendants of Israel cease from being a nation before me forever" (31, 35ff.).

The preaching of the new covenant does not, however, simply dissipate into the distant illusion of a new paradise. The next step of salvation will be a very concrete one: Jerusalem will be built up as the holy city (31, 38-40). The repatriates will return home and once again become a people in their own country. Kings after God's own heart will rule over them.

The prophecy of the new covenant thus takes on a sense of expectancy which can hardly be surpassed. His vision "into those days" into those final days of fulfillment, in which God will be all in all, is a most precious privilege; and still the next, sober step is not forgotten, the step which is inevitable in the painful history of the Ancient Near East. Jeremiah consigns the seed of his new hope to the earth, and confidently awaits its growth to become a mighty tree. He reveals God's new plan of history, a plan which cannot become reality until the fullness of time. The New Testament, the covenant concluded in the Messiah Jesus, is, in this respect, only provisional; it is not the perfect realization of the new covenant envisioned by Jeremiah. It is only a station along the way, although it is the final and eschatological station, preparing for the dawn of the definitive "new covenant."

d) *The Messiah from the House of David*

The preaching of the individual prophets exhibits a variety of tone and emphasis depending upon the concrete situation of their times. In the case of Jeremiah, who obviously lived in an era in which the crucial issue was the existence or demise of the house of David, the dynastic interest is much in the foreground. Isaiah thus becomes the herald of the Messiah king to come. There is a quite different tone and stress in Jeremiah. On the very eve of the destruction of city and nation he prophesies to a time beyond destruction, pointing to a new covenant which Yahweh would conclude with the remnant of his people. This new thing is so predominantly in the foreground that the concept of a Messiah king appears as only a secondary motif in this preaching of salvation. The messianic message is, however, clearly there. It grows from the concrete comparison with the kings and officials who are currently ruling over the people of God.

The somber background for the Messiah oracle (23, 1-8) is provided by the rejection of King Jehoiakim (22, 24-30). He is pushed aside like a shattered vessel. Yahweh's condemnation takes this form: "Write this man down as childless, a man who shall not succeed in his days; for none of his offspring shall succeed in sitting on the throne of David, and ruling again in Judah." Even if Jehoiakim were a signet ring upon the right hand of Yahweh, God will pluck him off and cast him into a foreign country. This threatened rift in the history of Yahweh and the house of David is brought to fulfillment by Jehoiakim's deportation during the first siege of Jerusalem (597). There was simply an end to this line of messianic expectation.

His successor, Zedekiah, was, as we have already seen, a weak man, a reed, buffeted by every breeze. The real power lay with the princes and officials. King Zedekiah did not effect right and justice (*sedeq*), and his princes were "bad shepherds." In this time of indecision and doubt, a time which meant a crisis in the face of many, Jeremiah preached the gospel of a "righteous branch of David" (*semah saddîq* — 23, 5). This message is both salvation and judgment. It is judgment on the officials (*peqîdîm*) who let the sheep to wander without care and pursued only their own advantage; that is why Yahweh visits them (*pāqad* 23, 2) and holds judgment over them. The remnant, the scattered sheep, he gathers from every country and puts over them shepherds after his own heart; particularly the shepherd from the house of David. Jeremiah here takes up the ancient dynastic prophecy and gives it a new and present meaning for his own day. Isaiah had already proclaimed that the battered stump would once again bloom (Is 11, 1). In like manner, Jeremiah refers to the expected Messiah simply as "a righteous branch" or "Yahweh is our justice" (*yahweh sidqēnû* — 23, 6). "Justice" is certainly not a formal juridic expression here; rather it is equivalent to "redemption, salvation." Salvation is accomplished only by the restoration of right and justice. Who is the subject acting in this work of salvation, even in terms of mere grammar? It is Yahweh. It is from him that the whole restructuring of people and world necessarily proceeds. In this total plan it is the new descendant of David who has a predominant role to play.

The divided kingdoms of Israel and Judah will once more be united, Jerusalem will be built anew (31, 38-40). The new ruler (*môšēl* — 30, 21) will be a second Moses who will approach God and dare to look upon his countenance (30, 21). This long awaited ruler chosen by God himself the prophet refers to as simply "David" (30, 9). This name joins the long departed golden age of David with the still more glorious time of the future, which will be ushered in by Yahweh's storm wind (30, 23).

Even though the dynastic-messianic oracles do not play such a decisive role in Jeremiah as they do in Isaiah, they are still very much in evidence. They are a leitmotiv in the confession of faith in the future salvation. In an hour of crisis, with destruction threatening from every side, Yahweh gave these truths of faith a new actuality and thereby restored the hope in a second "David" looking forward to a time beyond destruction of throne and kingdom.

e) *The Prophecy of Salvation is Sober and Pregnant With Future Promise* [57]

In the preceding chapter we have already looked to the

---

57. Cf. Rudolph, Jr 188.

horizon of the most distant future, the time at which this salvation is to become reality. Now we must call attention to the sobriety of this message. If it was actually to serve as a proclamation of salvation, then it must have had some concrete meaning for the contemporary generation. What is the prophet actually announcing as the immediately next step in God's dealings with his people?

His love for his firstborn (31, 9) impels Yahweh to put an end to this lamentable although richly deserved fate of his people (30, 12-15; 31, 15). By confessing their sin and by repentance (31, 18ff.), they can prove worthy of God's mercy (31, 3, 20). Only then will God's will of love have free hand to accomplish the work of redemption (31, 11, 35-37). Jeremiah was not a dreamer and neither was he an apocalyptic figure, losing his vision in the era of final fulfillment. In the political and material respect, his expectations were very sober. The woes which accompany the deportation and the return from exile, Yahweh could not possibly spare his people (30, 5-7). When they return to their native country they are not to expect any supernatural manifestations. The people must return home to rebuild their cities and villages (30, 18; 31, 4), where they will live as happy (31, 4, 13) and grateful (30, 19) people, under their own native rulers (30, 20; 31, 22) in peace and quiet (30, 10; 31, 2), unworried about their food supply (31, 5, 12) and protected from hostile attack (30, 20, 21). The people will multiply (30, 19) and celebrate the sacrifices and festivals of Yahweh undisturbed upon Mount Zion (31, 6).

Sober as this promise sounds, it was for the expatriates a strong bread of promise. The words pointed to a goal which could be reality in the immediate future. The fact that this prophecy was meant to point further, that it was pregnant with future reality, is evident in the proclamation of the eternity of this new covenant, an era in which the law of God will be written in every man's heart (31, 13-34) and a second David will be closer to God than any other king of Israel (30, 20).

Even though Jeremiah was thinking primarily of the abandoned vineyards and fields, the devastated cities and villages of Palestine, and the captives deported into Babylon, and promising that salvation would once again be theirs, there is still another, farther reaching horizon unfolding beyond this immediate step in the history of salvation and far surpassing the scope of present expectancy. In retrospect it is obvious that vineyard, city, village, even the holy city of Jerusalem itself are meant to refer to something more than the realities of earth. The promises made to the expatriates became a type for "those days" (31, 31, 38) or for "that day" (30, 8), when Yahweh will create all things completely new (31, 22). The precise import of this new creation is a reality granted not even to the mind of the prophet himself. His immediate concern is return and reconstruction. The manner in which Yahweh, as savior and healer, means to effectuate this "new covenant" (31, 31) in his "everlasting love" (31, 3) can be seen only in the further development of the history of salvation. Jeremiah, at all events, stands at a decisive turning point in this history. It is he who saw the earthly kingdom of God sink in ruin, while he looked to the "new covenant" that was to rise beyond this era of destruction. His picture of history seems to be bounded by the national element. He has indeed been called to be a prophet for the nations (1, 5), but the nations as yet have no active role to play in Israel's fortunes (31, 7, 10). They are, however, part and parcel of Yahweh's plan for human history, since it is in the midst of these nations that the fate of God's people is always fulfilled. Above all stands Yahweh, Lord of history, working his plan with or against the nations. The interpreter of God's ways in this dark era was his prophet, who, as herald of destruction and preacher of salvation, was nothing other than "the mouth of God" (1, 9). Only in this way could he possibly succeed in revealing the final and most intimate motivation behind the events of human history, the "heart of God" (31, 20).

D) THE BOOK OF JEREMIAH

From what has already been remarked, it must be obvious that the

Book of Jeremiah, in its modern form, has had a long and involved history. One more striking point is the fact that the Hebrew and Greek text are more at variance here than in any other book of the Bible. The Septuagint is almost one-eighth (approximately 2700 words)[58] shorter than the Masoretic text. There is no simple formula for deciding whether the Greek text has been abbreviated or the Hebrew text has been further augmented after the time of the Greek translation. The history of the text is too involved to permit of any comfortable solution. The decision as to which is the original reading must, in each individual case, be left to a thorough textual criticism.[59] The most obvious differences involve the sequence of the chapters. The Hebrew text and the translations based upon the Hebrew put the threat oracles against the nations at the end of the book in chapters 46-51; the Septuagint and its successors, on the other hand, have them after chapter 25, 13 — chapters 26–31.[60] The 52 chapters of the Book of Jeremiah are a combination of diverse literary genres: oracles in rhythmic form, confessions in the first person, prose accounts of the prophet's fate in the third person, annals in the form of the royal chronicles. In their present form, these sections are arranged in neither temporal nor thematic sequence. Chronologically earlier texts are put into later sequence, and vice versa. This alone would show that the book was not written at one single time. There is a long history. The evidence available from the book itself would suggest an approximate reconstruction of this process.

1) THE SCROLL FROM THE YEAR 605/604

Only when Jeremiah was forbidden to speak did he take to writing. He dictated to Baruch: "All the words that I have spoken to you against Israel and Judah and all the nations, from the day I spoke to you, from the days of Josiah until today" (36, 2). This first scroll was read three times and then burned by King Jehoiakim. Its content was the "words of Jeremiah," that is, a compendium of his preaching from the day of his first call to the time of actual composition. Eliminating those sections which concern the years after 605 (which we shall consider below), the following chapters thus form the original content of this first scroll: 1, 4–6, 30: vocation, preaching of repentance and divine punishment in the days of Josiah; 7–20: activity under Jehoiakim; 25 and 46–49, 33: threat oracles against the nations.

---

58. Rudolph, Jr XXI.
59. Critical edition of the Greek text, J. Ziegler in the *Göttinger-Septuaginta*, XV (1957), *Beiträge zur Jeremia LXX. Nachrichten der Akademie der Wissenschaften in Göttingen aus dem Jahre*, (1958).
60. The sequence of LXX could, however, go back to the sequence of the Hebrew original.

2) SECOND EDITION AND SUPPLEMENT OF THE ORIGINAL TEXT

After the first book was destroyed, "Jeremiah took another scroll and gave it to Baruch his scribe, the son of Neriah, who wrote on it at the dictation of Jeremiah all the words of the scroll which Jehoiakim King of Judah had burned in the fire; and any similar words were added to them" (36, 32). The text did not make it clear who added these other words, whether it was Jeremiah himself or Baruch speaking in the spirit of his master. The added material is, at all events, to be sought in the chapters identified above as containing the original message of the scroll. What can be recognized as addition? If we use chronology as an index, the answer will be all the words and events that date after the year 604: for example, 10, 17-22 (siege of Jerusalem), 12, 7-14 (the sword devours), 13, 12-19 (deportation), 15, 8-9 (the ravages of war), 16, 16-18 (the victorious enemy), 18, 1-12 (the potter) 46, 13-26 (campaign against Egypt), 49, 34-39 (threat oracles against Elam and Babylon). There are also the chapters about Jeremiah's personal fate, which read like a diary: 24 (bad figs), 27 (the Babylonian yoke), 35 (Rechabites). It was probably only after Jeremiah's death that Baruch published the "Confessiones Jeremiae Prophetae" and inserted them into the original text (11, 18-12, 6; 15, 10-12; 17, 12-18; 18, 18-23; 20, 7-18).

3) JEREMIAH'S PASSION AND SUFFERING

Together with this scroll, which, despite the supplements described above, remains the work of Jeremiah himself (first person), there is a bloc of anecdotes about the prophet (third person) which, by their style and language, are clearly the work of one single hand. They have been attributed to Baruch, Jeremiah's friend and scribe (32, 12ff.; 36, 4ff.; 45). But there is nowhere any express mention of his authorship. Internal grounds, however, would strongly suggest this answer. What is involved is not, as is frequently supposed,[61] a biography of the prophet in the strict sense of the word. Baruch is certainly not recording the life of his master from cradle to grave. Only one section of Jeremiah's life is actually described, the time of his suffering and persecution (608-586), the fate to which Jeremiah was exposed by reason of his prophetic vocation. These chapters can be perfectly described as the passion of the prophet Jeremiah. With only small exceptions, the following chapters can be included: 19, 1–20, 6 (speaking in the temple), 26 (the trial which followed), 36 (the scroll), 28 and 29 (the shattered vessel), 34, 8-22 (liberation of the slaves), 37-44 (on the occasion of the fall of Jerusalem,

---

61. Robert-Feuillet, IntrAT 523: "La biographie de Jérémie."

and afterwards). The fact that Baruch has left a small monument in this history of his master's suffering — he includes an oracle addressed to himself (45) and another to his brother in Babylon (51, 59-64) in his narrative — must not surprise us. It is simply the gratitude of the faithful servant and disciple to his lord and master. His style is quite distinct from that of the "words of Jeremiah." Pfeiffer [62] is of the opinion that Baruch was a good historian but simply not a poet. The words which, following the style of the ancient historians, he puts into his master's mouth, are poor shadows of the power of the original, a dreary and monotonous composition. While this might be an exaggeration, there is still a marked stylistic difference between the two. Baruch may have completed his work in Egypt (43, 6). It probably made its way very rapidly to Jerusalem and thence to Babylon, since there was considerable exchange between the expatriates and their home country. It has been presumed that Baruch most likely recounted these events in their historical sequence. But in our present book there is no guarantee that this sequence has been preserved.

4) THE WORDS OF JEREMIAH AND THEIR FURTHER ELABORATION

The prophet's original scroll and the history of his sufferings are recognized without any particular difficulty as two essentially compact literary units or "sources." [63] There is a third group of texts which exhibit an equally characteristic unity. These are the prose speeches of Jeremiah in which one and the same thesis is constantly treated in an undeviating and almost monotonous style: Judah and Jerusalem are condemned to judgment because they did not listen to Yahweh's words. The oracles begin with the formula: "The word which came to Jeremiah from Yahweh." Among them we might number: 7, 1–8, 3 (speech in the temple); 11, 1-14 (punishment for the breach of covenant) 16, 1-13 (the life of the prophet as a symbol for the nation); 17, 19-27 (sabbath rest); 18, 1-12 (potter and clay); 21, 1-10 (the way of life and the way of death); 22, 1-5 (social justice) 25, 1-14 (threat of exile); 34, 8-22 (resistance or capitulation); 35 (the Rechabites). — These are the texts which have earned Jeremiah the reputation of a tiresome and long-winded preacher.[64]

---

62. IntrOT 505: "A good historian but no poet."
63. Mowinckel, *Zur Komposition des Buches Jeremia* (1914) calls them source A and B, but in *Prophecy and Tradition* (1946), 62 and 105, he speaks of cycles of tradition, thus giving the fullest possible scope to oral tradition and elaboration: a purely literary derivation from his "sources" no longer seemed the answer.
64. Jerome in his prologue says: "Sermone aliis prophetis videtur esse

They exhibit a surprising similarity with the thought and content of the Book of Deuteronomy. This suggests the possibility that Jeremiah's sermons have come down to us in a Deuteronomic reworking. A careful evaluation of the vocabulary [65] would seem to confirm this conjecture.

The so-called "Deuteronomic style" might well represent the style of "rhetorical prose" in vogue in Judah at the end of the seventh and the beginning of the sixth centuries.[66] This argument, however, would presuppose the existence of literary-minded circles, which would pay attention to the development of style. We are thus directed from the composer's study into the stream of living tradition, into the *Sitz im Leben*. The scroll of Jeremiah and Baruch's history of the prophet would certainly have disappeared without a trace had they not been incorporated into the living tradition of the Old Testament "church" — not by the officials in power, who were all against the prophets, but rather by the spiritual guardians of the nation. The nucleus of this crystalization and the depository of this tradition after the destruction of the Temple was the divine service of the synagogue. It was here that the words of the prophet Jeremiah were read in the form that Baruch had handed them down. But they were constantly reworked and reinterpreted into a commentary on contemporary issues. As a result, the original substance of "the sermons of Jeremiah" is the work of the prophet himself, while its present form bears the stamp of an unknown link in the transmission of the word, a man who was also filled with the spirit. The clear, concise, and strikingly pithy words of the prophet permeated the soul of the man who read and contemplated them, and when they are handed down in turn, they have taken on, even in their external form, something of the individual character of the man who mulled them over in his heart.[67] These guardians and contemplators of Jeremiah's words in exile are responsible for the present state of the book. It is they who worked the individual sources they inherited (scroll, passion, independent traditions) into a literary unit. It would appear that the sequence was determined by the subject matter:[68]

a. Prophecy of destruction against Jerusalem and the nations (1, 1–25, 14);

---

rusticior." — Pfeiffer, IntrOT 511 however counts Jeremiah among the last great figures of the declining Golden Age of Hebrew Literature. He certainly does not approach the power of Amos or Isaiah.

---

65. Bright, JBL 70 (1951), 15ff.
66. *Ibid.*, 27.
67. Cf. the words of Jesus in John's Gospel, words which bear the personal stamp of the Evangelist.
68. The following divisions are from Rudolph, Jr XVIII.

b. Prophecy of destruction against the nations (25, 15—38; 46—51);
c. Prophecy of salvation for Israel and Judah (26—35);
d. Baruch's story of the suffering of Jeremiah (36—45).

The final redaction of the Book of Jeremiah took place during the exile; at all events, there is no compelling argument for a later date.[69] The book is, like most Biblical books, the work of the second generation. It was the school of disciples who received the heritage of their master with faithful hands, independently developing the content and forging the final literary form. Since this circle of disciples was not a mere private group, but rather a ruling class of the people of God led and directed by the spirit of the prophet, it is understandable that the books which are the product of their editing and tradition share in the spirit of God who is constantly directing the history of his chosen people. The inspiration of scripture thus becomes only a partial aspect of the spiritual direction of God's people in the Old Testament.[70]

---

69. *Ibid.*, XX.
70. Cf. Rahner, *Uber die Schriftinspiration,* ZkT 78 (1956), 137-168 for a new statement of the relationship between Church and inspiration.

CHAPTER XIV

JEREMIAH'S LAMENTATIONS AND BARUCH'S PROPHECY

A) THE LAMENTATIONS OF THE PROPHET JEREMIAH

THE catastrophe which dawned upon Jerusalem finds an imperishable echo in five elegies. In the Hebrew text, this short collection has no independent name of its own; its title comes from the opening words of the first, second, and fourth elegies: *"êkah"* — "O how!" Neither is there any reference to their author. What we have here, or so it would seem at least, is a collection of lamentations by an anonymous poet on the destruction of the holy city. The Septuagint translation prefaces these elegies by a brief introduction which is apparently based already upon the Hebrew model: "And it happened after Israel had been led into captivity and Jerusalem made a desert, Jeremiah sat down to weep and composed these lamentations." Hence the title of the book: "Lamentations (ϑϱῆνοι — *lamentationes*) of the prophet Jeremiah."

The first four elegies have 22 strophes, corresponding to the 22 letters of the Hebrew alphabet, each strophe beginning with the letter next in sequence. The poet has subjected the flight of his fancy to a strict, unvariable form of composition. Repetition is not excluded. But by casting his lamentation into the mold of the letters of the alphabet, he created a powerful aid to memory. The literary finds from Ugarit [1] have shown that alphabetical sequence was employed in instruction. The lamentations would thus appear to hark back to a very ancient popular form of poetry, a form which occurs in many of the Psalms as well.[2] Apart from some irregularities, it is the five-ictus line (3 + 2 *arses*), a Hebrew metrical form which has been called *qînah* (dirge or lamentation, dirge-form) precisely from its use in these songs.[3]

1) CONTENT OF THE ELEGIES

I: "How lonely sits the city" (1, 1-22): Jerusalem weeps bitterly, like a lonely widow, lamenting her abandonment and the fate of her children carried off into foreign lands. Her vanished glory stands like a dream before her eyes. She confesses her own guilt and wishes only that the enemies of Judah suffer a similar fate.

II: "How the Lord in his anger has set the daughter of Zion under a cloud" (2, 1-22): Jerusalem is besieged and destroyed. But by whom? By Yahweh himself. He drew his bow like an enemy, he shattered all her citadels, in the heat of his wrath he cut down priest and king. The altar was toppled, and the gates sank into the dust. The elders sit silent on the ground, strewing dust upon their heads and clad in sackcloth. Infants and babies are fainting in the streets; they are crying to their mothers, "Where is bread and wine?" — What can I say for you, to what can I compare you, O daughter of Jerusalem? What can I liken to you, that I may comfort you, O virgin daughter of Zion? Vast as the sea is your ruin; who can restore you? Cry aloud to the Lord! O daughter of Zion! Let tears stream down like a torrent

---

1. H. J. Kraus, *Klagelieder,* BK (Neukirchen), (1956), 6.
2. Pss 9/10; 34; 37; 111; 112; 119; 145; Pr 31, 10-31.
3. On the rhythm cf. Kraus, l.c. 7ff.

day and night! On the day of Yahweh's wrath no one survives. Jerusalem has fallen into the hands of God. Only the ruins are left.

III. "I am the man who has seen affliction" (3, 1-66): A primordial type of suffering arises, the man of sorrows, the incarnate fate of the city of Jerusalem and the people of Israel. Skin and flesh have wasted away, and the bones are broken; he is like a man attacked by a lion or by a bear. Surfeited upon bitterness and drunk with wormwood and gall. Sitting all alone, bowed down to the dust, his eyes sore from weeping, an object of mockery. But this man of sorrows has one hope left. God's grace never ceases and his mercy has no bounds; his fate will turn and a curse will fall upon his enemy.

IV: "How the gold has grown dim" (4, 1-22): A vision of the last days of Jerusalem. Hunger runs rampant in the city. The tongue of the nursling cleaves to the roof of its mouth; children beg for food but no one gives to them. The hands of compassionate women have boiled their own children. Zion is shattered like an earthenware vessel. Their eyes were watching vainly for help, for a nation which could save. But there is no help. Yahweh's anointed one lies captive in the dungeon. Jerusalem's guilt is greater than that of Sodom. Zion must drain the cup of Yahweh's wrath to the very dregs. But then there will be an end. "The punishment of your inquity, O daughter of Zion, is accomplished; but your iniquity, O daughter of Edom, he will punish."

V: "Remember, O Lord, what has befallen us" (5, 1-22): A prayer from crisis and shame. "Our heritage has fallen to the foreigner, our children are orphans, our mothers are widows, our women are dishonored. Water must be bought for gold. The hope in Egypt and Assur has proved illusion. Our young men must go off to forced labor; slaves rule over us. On Mount Zion, which lies desolate, the jackals prowl. But Yahweh abides forever. Shall he forever be mindless of our crisis? Restore us to thyself, O Lord, that we may be restored!"

2) AUTHOR AND DATE OF COMPOSITION

The chronist (2 Ch 35, 25) records that Jeremiah composed a funeral song for the death of King Josiah and that the song was performed by a choir of men and women. He also notes that it was written among the "dirges" (*qînôt*). Even though these five elegies have no author's name and no date of composition, it is a reasonable conclusion that they are the work of the one man who had a most vivid experience of the tragedy of Jerusalem's impending and actual destruction, the prophet Jeremiah. It is no wonder that this has been the traditional conception of both synagogue and Church. On the other hand, criticism has uncovered some mighty arguments to the contrary. These five elegies are far from being so unified in form as they first appear. They would suggest a variety of authors and a variety of dates for composition.

Pfeiffer [4] represents this opinion: On the basis of literary considerations, elegies two and four are among the best, clearest, and most ancient poems. The dramatic description of the horrors of the siege would suggest an eyewitness. They could both have come from the same author. Since there is a demonstrable linguistic relationship with Ezekiel, they could have been composed by a Jew in exile in Babylon around the year 560. Elegies one and three, on the other hand, are obviously much later in origin. In elegy I there is no longer any mention of a king, only "priests, elders, and princes" (1, 6, 19). The author was not an eyewitness; he has attempted to go back in spirit to the final days of Jerusalem and has composed these dirges only in retrospect, perhaps during the time in which the second temple was being built (c. 520-516). — Elegy III is an artificial piece of work incorporating commonplaces from the Psalter. The situation appears to presuppose liberation from crisis, and thus the author could have lived only after the time of Nehemiah, in the fourth, or even the third century.

Rudolph's [5] judgment is less radical. He dates song I in the year 598 (first destruction of Jerusalem!), songs II and IV in the year 587 (second destruction), songs III and V shortly after the catastrophe. Thus all five elegies were written very close to the events they lament. After examining the various propositions, the *EncMikr* [6] comes to this

---

4. IntrOT 723.
5. Eissfeldt, EinlAT 622.
6. *EncMikr* I, 262.

conclusion: "The Book of Lamentations is a collection of laments and dirges on the destruction of the first temple and the decline of Judah. All the elegies were written at the same time, which was very close to the events described. On the other hand, it is impossible to determine whether all are the work of one single writer. It is just as impossible to say who this writer or writers may have been. At all events it is clear that they were very close to the spirit of the prophet Jeremiah."

Finally, some attempt has been made [7] to fit these lamentations into the general body of Israel's songs. I, II, and IV would be political funeral songs, number III an individual song of lamentation, number V a popular dirge. This division, however, seems to have missed the *Sitz im Leben*. But these elegies were not produced as the freely fluctuating lyric products of a private poet; their spiritual home was certainly the divine service.[8] Upon the ruins of the destroyed temple or along the river of Babel the faithful used to assemble and recall the divine judgment that had struck down Jerusalem. Still under the sharp impression of this catastrophe, a poet took up the never ending lamentation in the spirit of Jeremiah. "It would be a wasted effort to attempt any identification of the poet or poets. We must rest content with the captivating beauty of the songs themselves." [9]

In the liturgy of the synagogue the lamentations are read every year on the 9th day of Ab, the day which commemorates the destruction of Jerusalem. The Church, too, has also taken the songs into her divine service and given them a new interpretation. In the lamentations over the destruction of Jerusalem there is an echo of the even more soul-shaking lamentation over the death of Jesus.

B) THE PROPHET BARUCH

According to the evidence of the Book of Jeremiah, the fate of his disciple, contemporary, and scribe, Baruch, was intimately bound up with that of his master.[10] With him he shared persecution and crisis, experienced the tragic fall of Jerusalem, and after the murder of Gedaliah was carried off together with

---

7. Eissfeldt, EinlAT 619. .

8. H. J. Kraus, *Klagelieder,* 11 counts Biblical lamentations as examples of the general type "lamentation over the destroyed sanctuary," and advances the destroyed sanctuary of Ur as his model. The external similarities, however, must not be allowed to conceal the inner theological variance. In pagan lamentations the confession of guilt is wholly absent.

9. Eissfeldt, EinlAT 623.

10. Jr 32, 12-16; 36, 4, 32; 43, 3, 6; 45, 1-5.

him to Egypt (Jer 43, 6). This is also the last information the Book of Jeremiah offers on the subject of the prophet and his scribe.

In the Book of Baruch we find Baruch no longer in Egypt, but in Babylonia. According to the title inscription (1, 1-2) he composed the "words of this book" in the 5th year after the destruction of Jerusalem, and sent them to Jerusalem to be read there on the festival day (festival of the booths). Considering the Book of Baruch in its present form, its magnificent interior compactness has earned it the description "masterpiece of original force, a drama about sin, conversion, and salvation." [11]

1) "THE WORDS" OR THE MESSAGE OF THE BOOK OF BARUCH

"Baruch, one of the smallest books of the Old Testament, can be divided, on the basis of literary history, into three quite different sections: I. Historical introduction (1, 1-14) and prayer of repentance (1, 15 — 3, 8); II. Song of wisdom (3, 9 — 4, 4); III. Songs of lamentation and comfort (4, 5 — 5, 9). All three sections, each in its own way, contain deeply moving religious thoughts which are closely bound up with the prophet Jeremiah in the first section, and, in the second and third sections, reach the heights of true lyricism." [12]

a) *The Nation's Great Confession*

The historical introduction takes us to Babylon. In the presence of the captive King Jehoiachin, the elders, and many of the exiles, Baruch publicly read "these words," then organized a collection of money and sent both money and "letter" to Jerusalem, the money for a holocaust and offering of expiation, the "letter" for the nation's confession. Silver vessels which Nebuchadnezzar had taken from the temple (1, 8) were also returned. This happened (1, 2) in the 5th year, the 7th day of the month of the destruction of the city (August 19, 581). During the following three months, up to the feast of booths in

---

11. Robert-Feuillet, IntrAT 735, 737.
12. V. Hamp, EB III, 423.

autumn (1, 14) a messenger could easily have carried the "letter" (*sēpher*) to Jerusalem.

The events of the exile have been unexpectedly illuminated by the discovery of the so-called Jehoiachin tablets.[13] They were excavated in the vicinity of the Istar Gate in Babylon and appear to have been part of the royal administration archives. They record deliveries of foodstuffs from the time between the 10th and 35th year of Nebuchadnezzar (595-570). Among these there is mention of a delivery of oil, grain, dates, and other supplies to "Ya'ukinu, the King of Israel, Ja'hu'du, and his son." Jehoiachin had freely surrendered at the approach of Nebuchadnezzar and was thus treated as a trusty (2 K 24, 11). In the 37th year of his reign, during the year of Awil-Marduk's kingship [14] he was granted full freedom (Jer 52, 31ff.; 2 K 25, 27). Under these circumstances there is no reason to doubt the existence of an assembly under the exiled king. It is certainly no wonder that such an assembly took place on the day which commemorated the destruction of Jerusalem. In the spirit of his master, Baruch proclaimed the national confession of his people's guilt (1, 14-30).

Baruch did not mean to be at all original in this prayer of repentance. Of the 51 verses, 22 are taken from Jeremiah, 5 from Deuteronomy, and 5 from the first Book of Kings. It can actually be called a prayer in the spirit of Jeremiah, who was tireless in proclaiming the collapse of the old covenant and the coming of the new. The prayer of repentance, accordingly, falls in with the idea of covenant. The history of the nation had, since the day on which Yahweh led them out of Egypt down to the present time, been one long chain of breach of covenant (1, 15-22). The catastrophes must be interpreted as just punishment (2, 1-10). Still, faith in God's invincible grace could raise up what was bowed to the earth (2, 11-18). Yahweh can raise even the dead to life (3, 4) and inaugurate an everlasting covenant (διαθήκη αἰώνιος, 2, 35).

This prayer of repentance might well have been taken into the liturgy of the commemoration of the destruction of Jerusalem

---

13. W. Thomas, DOT 84-86.
14. ZAW 74 (1962), 212.

as a great mirror of repentance reflecting the infidelity of the national history. This would explain its having been preserved. The fact that similar prayers of repentance had been formulated at other turning points' in the history of the Old Testament — for instance, by Nehemiah (1, 5-11; 9, 6-37), Ezra (9, 6-15), Daniel (9) — proves only that the seed of repentance sown by Jeremiah could always produce new fruit.

b) *"Wisdom Has Appeared Upon Earth"* (3, 8; 4, 4)

The solemn prose of the prayer of repentance is interrupted by a lofty hymn to wisdom. Here too we are dealing not so much with the cosmic and metaphysical but rather with the history of salvation. The agonizing question of why Israel must tarry in the enemy's country like an unclean corpse (3, 10) is pursued throughout. Even the song to wisdom becomes a sort of examination of conscience. This had been a people chosen before all others; not in Canaan and not among the sons of Hagar, not in Teman or Midian, not among the giants of the early days or the mighty kings has wisdom ever appeared (3, 16-28); wisdom is beyond the reach of any man (3, 29-31); the one God, beside whom there is no other, has revealed the ways of wisdom to his servant Israel. "She appeared upon earth and lived among men" (3, 38). The precise meaning of these words is explained by what follows: "She is the book of the commandments of God, and the law that endures forever" (4, 1). God's wisdom has thus taken on a form visible to man in the Law of Sinai. This tremendous honor shown to Israel above all other nations also explains Israel's dispersion throughout the world. Israel has rejected wisdom, and Israel is herself rejected. The hymn accordingly ends with a call to repentance: "Turn, O Jacob, and take her" (4, 2). In later reinterpretations of these words, the early Christian theologians already applied the apparition of wisdom to Christ and gave verse 3, 38 a messianic interpretation. The thought of the prophet was thus realized in the person of Christ.[25]

---

15. This is clearly expressed in the way the Vulgate translates. The

c) *The Consolation of Jerusalem* (4, 5 — 5, 9)

Three times the singer exclaims: "Take courage, my people" (4, 5, 21, 30). What is the purpose of this call? Jerusalem is destroyed and the people have scattered. Now is the time for examination of conscience: "You forgot the everlasting God and Father who brought you up: and you grieved Jerusalem your mother who reared you" (4, 8). Then Jerusalem herself takes up the dirge: "I was left desolate because of the sins of my children" (4, 12); "The Everlasting has brought about the capture of my sons and daughters" (4, 14). Only repentance can change the way of doom (4, 28). The singer already beholds a new Jerusalem arising (4, 30 — 5, 9). Jerusalem will set aside the garb of mourning and take on the cloak of God's grace. "For your name will forever be called by God 'peace of righteousness' (εἰρήνη δικαιοσύνης) and 'glory of godliness' (δόξα θεοσεβείας) (5, 4). From the rising of the sun even to the setting of the sun the dispersed will return home. The hills will be made low and the valleys will be filled up to make level ground for Israel's solemn return accompanied by the glory of God (5, 7). This concluding hymn is the answer to the prayer of repentance which stands at the beginning of the book. Repentance and grace go hand in hand.

2) THE LITERARY PROBLEM OF THE BOOK OF BARUCH

There is some question as to whether this little book has a long literary history behind it or whether it stands as the single outpouring of the prophet Baruch, a "letter of consolation" to Jerusalem.

a) *Text History*:

It is very clear that the text in the Book of Baruch has a long and involved history. It is preserved only in the Greek translation and in the Old Latin and Syriac translations which depend upon the Greek. It is just as obvious that the Greek text goes back to a Hebrew original.[16]

Greek verb ωφθη "appeared," which can, grammatically, be referred both to God and to wisdom, is unequivocally translated as *visus est*. "God or Christ has appeared."

16. Examples, Pfeiffer, IntrOT 412, 419, 423.

The Book of Baruch was not accepted into the Hebrew canon and thus it belongs to the Deutero-canonical writings. Because he placed too high a value on the *hebraica veritas*, St. Jerome refused to translate this book. The Old Latin translation was not included in the Vulgate. We are faced with the obvious question of why the synagogue allowed this ancient prophetic writing to perish. Is this to be taken as an indication of the fact that the book does not really stem from the prophet Baruch?

b) *Pseudepigraph*:

It has been argued that in the Hellenistic period more and more writers composed literary works and attributed them to the name of some famous personage from antiquity. This practice is in itself nothing new. With respect to the psalms of "David," the proverbs of "Solomon" and the Song of "Solomon," this problem has already been considered.[17] At the same time it is clear that the name of Baruch was very much in vogue during this era, as witness the Syriac and Greek Apocalypse of Baruch.[18] There is much evidence, accordingly, to suggest that Baruch is only a literary cover for this prophetic writing. There are certain historical discrepancies. Balthasar was not Nebuchadnezzar's son (1, 11), but Awil-Marduk's; Jehoiachin, since he was a prisoner, could not have been present at the reading of the scroll; the return of the temple vessels took place first under Ezra (6, 5); payments sent to the temple at Jerusalem point to a time in the later Jewish diaspora. It is claimed that the prayer of repentance exhibits a striking relationship with later writings. The song of wisdom is supposed to bear comparison with Greek thought; the song of consolation, finally, is supposed to be an excerpt from Deutero-Isaiah (43, 5; 49, 12; 60, 4). On the basis of these and similar facts, many scholars, even some Catholic exegetes, think that the Book of Baruch must be considered a pseudepigraph, and that it has nothing more than the literary name in common with the prophet. Accordingly, Hamp [19] assigns a general date from the Hellenistic era for the prayer of repentance, and dates the song to wisdom in the time between 300-200 B.C.; the songs of consolation, if they cannot be assigned, quite radically, to the time after Christ, are at least the product of the last centuries before Christ. In individual details, the datings of the three sections are extremely divergent. Pfeiffer [20] considers the hymn to wisdom as the last work of Palestinian wisdom poetry (around 100 B.C.). As a whole, one might speak of a *sententia quasi communis* [21]

---

17. Vol. III, p. 385ff.
18. Eissfeldt, EinlAT 775, 779.
19. EB III, 423.
20. IntrOT 419.
21. Robert-Feuillet, IntrAT 735: "construction artificielle ... histoire édificante."

which dates the book in the two centuries of the Hellenistic era, between 300 and 100 B.C., and thus admits that it must be considered a pseudepigraph. But this is certainly not the last word on the subject of the Book of Baruch.

c) *The Prophet Baruch's Share in His Book*:

Since all three sections of the book presuppose a Hebrew model, the clarification of the literary problem requires some recognition of this earlier stage. Prior to the Greek form of the book which is all we have today, the Book of Baruch obviously had a Hebrew form, and this consideration would move the dating back into the pre-Hellenistic, that is, the Persian era. Yet the entire book breathes the very spirit of the exile. It would certainly not be incorrect to suppose that the historical introduction (1, 3-14) records not simply "edifying stories," but real history. The discovery of the Jehoiachin tablets could only confirm this supposition. The fact that shortly after the destruction of Jerusalem the Easter liturgy was once again taken up as adequately as possible under the circumstances, is proved by the evidence of Jeremiah 40, 4, which describes people from Shechem, Shiloh, and Samaria making their way to Jerusalem with sacrificial offerings. A partial restitution of the Temple vessels would, accordingly, not be impossible, even though there is nowhere any explicit mention of the fact. Finally, Baruch's resettlement from Egypt to Babylon is certainly quite possible in view of the lively commerce between the exiles and the mother country. The "basic form" of the Book of Baruch could therefore have been a "letter of Baruch." This position is further advanced by the relationship, already described, with the thought and content of the master Jeremiah. Moreover, the concept of wisdom betrays few Hellenistic characteristics. It is much closer to the ancient Hebrew conception of *ḥokmah*.[22] Finally, the fact that the songs of consolation have such marked affinities with thoughts expressed in Deutero-Isaiah can easily be explained by the fact that both date from the same era.

What results from this literary-critical investigation is, accordingly, the conviction that, on the one hand, the Greek form of Baruch as we know it today took on its final form in the Hellenistic era, but that, on the other hand, there was a Hebrew original upon which the Greek Baruch was based, and that the Hebrew original was composed during the exile, a time at which the prophet Baruch undertook to examine his nation's conscience and to show it a new way to the future. The fact that his words were transmitted only in the Greek tradition is simply an accident. There is nothing to prevent us from identifying the author of these "words of Baruch" which have been handed down through the centuries and taken on a new interpretation as the actual prophet of that name, and not

---

22. Cf. Vol. III, p. 430ff.

some unknown Hellenistic writer who was hiding behind the name of the great Baruch of old. The last word on the subject of Baruch has not been written. His book may have suffered the same fate as the Book of Daniel which has come down to us in a Maccabean reworking, but still preserves the original Book of Daniel.[23]

C)   THE LETTER OF JEREMIAH

"A copy of a letter which Jeremiah sent to those who were to be taken to Babylon as captives by the king of the Babylonians, to give them the message which God had commanded him." — This inscription introduces the shortest "book" of the Old Testament. The Septuagint and the Syro-Hexapla count it as an independent work and locate it directly after the lamentations. The Vulgate and the Peshitta, on the other and, consider it as chapter 6 of the Book of Baruch. The letter has been preserved only in the Greek form, and thus belongs to the deutero-canonical books. Despite this title, however, it is not a real "letter" (ἐπιστολή) in the strict sense of the word; it is a "biting satire" [24] on the ridiculous character of the pagan gods.

1) "BY THIS YOU SHALL RECOGNIZE THAT THEY ARE NOT GODS"

In a bitter attack, repeated ten times over and ending with the obvious conclusion "How could anyone believe that they are gods?" (14, 22, 28, 39, 44, 51, 64, 68, 72) — the worship of pagan idols is unmasked as nonsense and faith in the gods is made fun of. The statues of the gods are indeed made of gold and silver which the priests have stolen from their worshippers, but they are worthless idols. They may indeed hold a sword in their hand, but they are incapable of defending themselves. They are lifeless and unfeeling wood; their eyes are covered with dust and their wood is eaten by worms and their face is black with rust and corrosion; bats and birds settle upon their heads and cats do likewise. But the gods notice nothing of all this. They are capable of no life or motion. The meat offered to them is eaten by the

---

23. Fuller treatment in Vol. V.
24. Pfeiffer, IntrOT 429.

priests; their wives preserve it. These gods can never go anywhere of their own volition; they must be carried back and forth. It is pointless to expect assistance from them, since they are but the product of an artist's hand who cast them together without a thought. Sun, moon, and stars all follow out their appointed course, but the gods know nothing of this. They are like a scarecrow in the cucumber field, watching and protecting nothing. Any bird who pleases is free to light upon them. Despite their gold and silver they are like an unclean corpse which will be cast out into the darkness.

A more biting satire against the heathen gods could hardly be written. We almost get the impression that a letter such as this deliberately making fun of the gods in an almost primitive manner, has hardly hit the essence of ancient religion;[25] for even the pagan divinities were capable of an ethical and cosmic universalism by virtue of which they were later able to make their triumphant way into the Roman Empire. The writer of this letter, however, did not have religion-history interests at heart. The rank and file of the people may actually have shared the magical belief that in the image of the god the divinity himself was present, and thus equivalenced god and image.[26] The battle against paganism would thus have been taken up at its weakest position. It was Israel's great privilege to be able to worship God without an image. This letter belongs, accordingly, to the polemics against paganism. It was probably written for pagans as well, perhaps as an answer to their attacks against the Jewish belief in God.

2) LITERARY GENRE OF THE LETTERS

By reason of its inscription, this polemical composition against the gods has been attributed to the prophet Jeremiah. Closer investigation[27] proves

---

25. Pfeiffer, IntrOT 428: "This Jewish denunciation of the religions of the ancient civilized nations, as a senseless adoration of inanimate images, is unfair and unfounded."

26. G. Furlani, *Le Religione babilonese e assira*, Bologna I (1928), 379: "The statue does not merely represent God; God himself is present in his image and is mysteriously identical with it."

27. Cf. A. Penna, *Lettera di Geremia*, GarBib (1954), 425ff.

the purely literary nature of this ascription. The "Letter of Jeremiah" is certainly written in the spirit of the ancient prophet, but it is not his work. It belongs to the pseudepigrapha and — since it is preserved only in Greek — to the deutero-canonical books. The present Greek version doubtless dates from the Hellenistic era. Since the letter contains few concrete points of reference, the dating fluctuates between the time of Alexander the Great and the era of the Maccabees. It was in the time of Alexander the Great that the cult of the Babylonian gods experienced a renaissance. The attempted reconstruction of the tower of Babylon came to grief only with the death of the great conqueror. But this did not mean the death of the gods. Their cult experienced a new popularity in the Hellenistic era. A warning against the pagan gods was more timely than ever before. The battle which the earlier prophets had led against the gods of the nations in a quite different manner, was now given new form and urgency. This accounts for the obvious affinities between this letter and the writings of Jeremiah (10, 3-16) and Isaiah (40, 19; 41, 7; 44, 9-20; 45, 16; 46, 6). The same motiv is to be found especially in the Book of Wisdom (13, 10-19; 14, 8-21; 15, 15ff.).

The Greek of this letter is among the choicest Greek of the Septuagint. Nonetheless, on the basis of errors in translation, it suggests a Hebrew or Aramaic original. It is possible that new discoveries will eventually bring the Hebrew text to light. No matter how involved the literary history of this tiny book may be, it is part of the canon of Sacred Scripture. It bears witness to the victorious faith of the Old Testament church surrounded by a storm of paganism. Despite all the external trappings of these idols, it is only the Lord God of Israel who deserves worship (5). It is no wonder that the church of the New Testament, in a like spiritual position, turned to this ready armory for its weapons in the battle against paganism.

CHAPTER XV

THE PROPHET EZEKIEL

"EZEKIEL is a poet, full of power and depth, gifted with an imagination and an abundance of imagery. His poetic power can burst out into the flames of passion and become so strong that it has an ugly, repelling effect. He is sometimes inclined towards the bizarre and immoderate, towards the gruesome and repulsive, qualities which make their appearance not only in his symbolic actions, but also in his words, which frequently go to the very limits of what can be borne, particularly in his unsparing openness with respect to sexual matters." [1] "The real Ezekiel was anything but a quiet teacher. Everything about him breathes passion and wild enthusiasm." [2] He is also been called "the first fanatic in the Bible." [3] Uncompromising zeal for the cause of Yahweh has wholly consumed him. A holy anger seizes him at the desecration of God's dwelling in Jerusalem. He is indeed capable of human feeling — twice he cries out in anguish at the thought of destruction that is to come (9, 8; 11, 13) — but he does not give in to these emotions. Unyielding, hard as a diamond (3, 9), he fought for the greater honor and glory of God.

1. G. Fohrer, *Ezechiel*, HAT 13 (1955), XXIV.
2. G. Hölscher, *Die Propheten*, 303.
3. Pfeiffer, IntrOT 543.

Some scholars have regarded Ezekiel as psychically abnormal; they have called him schizophrenic, or subject to cataleptic attacks.[4] His book has been called a better source for medicinal studies than edification. Still other scholars see him as "the father of Jewry," the first "apocalyptic."[5] The ancient learned Jewish tradition felt obliged to precede the reading of this book with a call-signal. Jerome[6] says that "the beginning and end of the Book of Ezekiel are completely dark. That is why, among the Jews, just as the first chapters of Genesis, they could be read only at the age of thirty." The argument over this book is further illustrated by a notice from the Talmud[7] according to which the Book of Ezekiel would almost certainly have been rejected from the synagogue as apocryphal, had not Rabbi Hananiah ben-Hizkiah studied and explicated the text in countless nights of work, a labor during the course of which he had said to have used 300 vessels of oil.

In the Gospels, we find few direct references to Ezekiel, although the symbols of the four Evangelists bear the clear stamp of his inaugural vision. On the other hand, the pattern of Ezekiel's thought finds new expression in the Book of Revelations of St. John. Almost every page makes it obvious how much the visionary of Patmos owes to the seer and prophet Ezekiel. There is hardly another Old Testament prophet who was so completely accepted into the Christian expression.[8]

Ezekiel's vocation (1, 2) is dated in the year 592/591, while his final appearance as a prophet (29, 21) can be assigned to the year 570/569. His prophetic activity thus spanned a period of more than 20 years. The first half coincided with the activity of the prophet Jeremiah. The question as to whether both prophets also worked together in Jerusalem has been much discussed by modern criticism. Ezekiel, it is argued, works not only in Babylon, but also in Jerusalem, or perhaps only in Jerusalem.[9]

---

4. Fohrer, l.c. XXIVff.

5. Robert-Feuillet, IntrAT 549.

6. *Epistola ad Paulinum* 53, 7 (PL 22, 547).

7. Sabbat 103, Hagigrah 13a.

8. P. Auvray, *Ezéchiel,* JerBibl (1949), 20.

9. H. G. May, *The Book of Ezekiel,* IntBib IV (1956), 51-53: Locality of Ezekiel's Activity. — Eissfeldt, EinlAT 446ff.

The possibility of his having spent some time in Jerusalem is advanced even today by many scholars,[10] but it would seem that the grounds for their argument are not convincing enough, as the following discussion should make clear. After a critical examination of the various opinions, Fohrer [11] comes to the conclusion that seems to correspond best to the actual course of events: "The argument for a two-fold activity of Ezekiel is just as improbable as its complete restriction to Jerusalem." The arena for the more than twenty years of Ezekiel's prophetic activity was, therefore, only Babylon. The fall of Jerusalem forms the decisive turning point in his preaching. The first half is a solitary call: "Jerusalem shall fall!" (*Jerusalem delenda est*). But after judgment broke upon Jerusalem, he turned into a herald of the new and everlasting Jerusalem. Like his predecessors, Ezekiel too is a herald of doom and the proclaimer of a new salvation.

Ezekiel's call is dated simply as the "30th year" (1, 1). What is the era in terms of which this number is to be reckoned? Is it the 30th year "after the deportation of King Jehoiachin"? This answer would set the final dating of the book (29, 17) as far as the year 567/566. Nor is it a satisfactory conclusion to regard this enigmatic data as referring only to the writing of the book. The clause in verse two: "that is, the 5th year of the exile of King Jehoiachin (*gālût*)," serves only to give a more precise date to the first verse. According to the context, both dates refer to the same event. Accordingly, the 30th year must be reckoned from a different point of departure. Eichrodt [12] argues that the number 30 is best interpreted as referring to the age of the prophet. Origen already expressed this opinion. This solution would provide some excellent insight into the life of the prophet. Five years earlier, in the 25th year of his life, he had been dragged away from his home. In this same year, as priest, he would have entered upon the service of the temple (Nb 8, 24; 4, 3, 30ff.). At that very age, accordingly, at which in his home country he would have been privileged to enter the sanctuary, he was uprooted and carried into the unclean land of the pagans — the first great disillusion of his life. It is quite understandable that he dated the vision of his first call from this decisive experience. — But this solution is not really satisfactory, since a system of counting based on the age of the individual is quite unusual.

The solution seems to be best arrived at on the basis of other double sets of dates recorded in the Bible, where an event is dated both according to the regnal year of the current king of Judah as well as that of the current king of Babylon (Jr 39, 8; 52, 12; 2 K 25, 8). Accordingly, the dating in verse one would refer to the regnal year of King Nebuchadnezzar.

10. P. Auvray, l.c. 14.
11. G. Fohrer, *Ezekiel*, HAT 13 (1955), XVIII.
12. W. Eichrodt, *Der Prophet Hesekiel*, ATD 22 (1959), 3.

His 30th year (574/575), however, is certainly not the 5th year of the exile. Accordingly, many scholars [13] presume a corrupt text and read instead of "30th year," the "13th year." Corrected in this manner, there is a surprising harmony between the two dates: the 13th year of Nebuchadnezzar is perfectly synchronous with the 5th year of the exile. The other dates in the Book of Ezekiel present no difficulty, since they are essentially determined down to the month and day.[14]

A) PROPHET OF DESTRUCTION

Ezekiel's vocation fell in a stormy and agitated era. Events were pressing closely upon each other. The 14 dates of the book (year, month, and day) make it possible to arrange the individual narratives within the larger framework of the tragic course of history that was pushing Jerusalem along the road to destruction. On the second day of Adar, in the 7th year of his reign (March 15/16, 597) Nebuchadnezzar had conquered Jerusalem; in his 8th year he carried off King Jehoiachin into captivity in Babylon (2 K 24, 12). This first year of exile is properly reckoned as "the beginning of the exile" (*rē'šît haggālût*),[15] while the "first year of the exile" is equivalent only to the 9th year of Nebuchadnezzar. Ezekiel's vocation fell in the 13th year of Nebuchadnezzar (the 4th month), the 5th day, that is, on the 5th year of Jehoiachin's exile, according to our calendar, July 21/22, 592.

---

13. P. Auvray, *Ezechiel I-III. Essai d'analyse littéraire*, RB 67 (1960), 481-502. In terms of paleography, the writing of the number 30 instead of 13 can be explained (498f.). The author does not, however, count these 13 years after Nebuchadnezzar, but after the Exile, arguing that there were two different datings that have been fused in the final redaction. The 5th year witnessed the inaugural vision, while the 13th year saw the vision of God's chariot — it is important to keep the two accounts separate.

14. The changes in calendar are explained in R. A. Parker and W. H. Dubberstein, *Babylonian Chronology 626 B.C. — A.D. 75*, Providence, Brown Univ. Studies XIX (1956).

15. Chronology: "Nochmals das Jahr der Zerstörung Jerusalems," ZAW 74 (1962), 211. The first eleven years of the deportation are synchronous with the eleven years of Zedekiah — a year of accession to power must be reckoned too.

1) VOCATION AND MANDATE

Like Isaiah and Jeremiah, Ezekiel has also described the experience of his call to be a prophet. No matter how individual his narrative may sound, in outline and in form it is the same as his predecessors. All three speak first of a vision; they then experience a consecration which elevates them from the anxiety of their vision and gives them a feeling of great power; finally all three record the mandate that is given to them.[16] Since Ezekiel gives a precise date for his vocation, this can be fitted into the history of his time. As we have already mentioned in speaking of the prophet Jeremiah,[17] the western countries were never in a settled condition after the military revolt in Babylon (595/594). The last entry in the Babylonian chronicle tells of Nebuchadnezzar's show of force in the rebellious west, a campaign which he undertook both in the 10th and 11th year; then the chronicle ceases. The spark of unrest had sprung from Jerusalem to the expatriates resettled in Babylon. Everyone was hoping for liberation and return home. It was at this point that Jeremiah intervened with his letter to Babylon and warned his countrymen against false hopes. He advised the exiles to build houses in their foreign country, to plant vineyards, to marry, to prepare for a long sojourn. The resettlement of the Judaeans did not simply scatter them to the four winds; it amounted rather to an internment outside their native land but in the near vicinity of the central rule of Babylon. This arrangement was intended to be only temporary, but actually no further settlement was ever effected.[18] The temporary internment camps thus turned to normal Jewish ghettos in Babylon, and within them life took on the same regulated form as in Judaea.

The settlement to which *Jᵉhezk'ēl ben-Bûzi* [19] was sent was

---

16. H. Schmidt, *Die grossen Propheten*, SAT (Gumkel), (1923²), 391.
17. Cf. p. 358.
18. Fohrer, *Ezekiel*, XVI.
19. The name of the prophet Ezekiel is composed of the imperfect of the verb *ḥāsaq* "to be strong" and the name for God *'ēl*. The meaning

located "in the country of Kasdim, on the river Chebar," and it was called "*Tel-'abîb.*" "The land of the Kasdim" (Chaldaeans)[20] comprised the southern Babylonian plateau, the real heartland of the Babylonian settlement. In this territory we must locate the "river" Chebar (Kobar). Excavation has actually unearthed two treaty documents from the days of Artaxerxes I (443-424) which refer to a *nār kabari,* a "great canal" (?). The Sumerians called it the "Euphrates of Nippur." This is probably to be located in the broad *Šatt en-nîl,* which leaves the Euphrates at Babylon and heads eastward, flowing through the site of ancient Nippur, then empties once again into the Euphrates.[21] That large Jewish settlements must have been located in this territory is evident from the later acta of the great Babylonian commercial and banking house *"Murašu and Sons,"* whose archives have been excavated in Nippur. Among the business partners there are many Hebrew names.[22] The place name *tel-'abîb* would be naturally interpreted by the Hebrew speaking settler as "hill of grain," but actually it most likely goes back to an ancient Babylonian place name, meaning something like "(ruin) hill of the deluge (*abûbu*)." The local Babylonian populace used the term in reference to an ancient city ruin which was currently uninhabited. It was this abandoned site that Nebuchadnezzar gave to the deportees as a place to settle.[23]

The expatriates attempted to somehow continue their religious

---

is either a confessional formulary "God is strong" or else a wish "May God show himself strong."

20. Originally, the Aramaean group of Kaldu who forced their way into the civilized country around the end of the first millennium B.C. were referred to as Chaldaeans. This ethnic group gradually overran ancient Babylonia and gave it the name "Land of the Chaldaeans." In Middle and Late Babylonia there is an observable shift from *ld* to *sd,* and hence both forms occur: Kasdim and Kaldim. Zimmerli, *Ezechiel,* BK XIII, 39.
21. E. Vogt, *Der Nehar Kebar: Ez 1,* Bibl 39 (1959), 211-216, identifies it with a canal in the neighborhood of Nippur. There is an outline map of the ancient river courses.
22. Text: W. Thomas, DOT 95-96.
23. Zimmerli, l.c. 83.

life even though they were far from the temple of their home.
It was not simply a romantic enthusiasm for nature that brought
our prophet to the riverside where he perhaps hoped to have
an encounter with God. From the New Testament times it is
a well-known fact that the Jews of the diaspora located their
prayer houses preferably along a water course, either on the
bank of a river or on the shore of the ocean.[24] This practice may
well have been prevalent in Babylon too. Witness for this are
the words from Psalm 136/37: "On the rivers (canals) of
Babylon, there we sat and wept . . . ." The water course was
important for a prayer site because it supplied the material for
the prescribed purifications. Accordingly, we must suppose that
Ezekiel's vocation, just like that of Isaiah, took place on a holy
site, not indeed in the Temple of Jerusalem, but probably in the
temporary house of worship erected by the expatriates.

a) The Vision of God's Heavenly Chariot (1, 4-28)

Since the Babylonians and the Hebrews reckoned the day
from evening to evening, it would be possible that the vision
dated on the 5th day of the month took place at the approach of
evening, perhaps at the time of the evening sacrifice in the
temple. As Ezekiel stood by the river praying, he raised his
eyes and saw a stormy cloud with flashes of lightning coming
upon him from out of the north.[25] With uncanny speed the storm
flew down upon him. The prophet studied it intently and realized
it was no ordinary storm cloud. He could make out several figures.
Drawing upon his memory, he attempts to describe them as accurately as possible, but he cannot find the words. Conscientiously
faithful to his vision, he tries again and again to describe its
substance. He can only use fragile comparisons to suggest the
ineffable wonder that his eyes have beheld. This accounts for

---

24. Acts 16, 13; Letter to Aristeas 304ff.; Flavius Josephus, ANT 14,
    10, 23.
25. Cf. Ps 47/48, 3: "The mountains of Zion, high in the north." The
    northern mountain is conceived of as the dwelling place of God; God
    accordingly comes from the "veiled" north. North (sāphôn), basic
    meaning "to veil."

his constant repetition of the indefinite formula: "something that looked like. . . ." "We must read everything that Ezekiel has written several times over before we are fully aware of the grandeur and power of his visions. At first the eye is confused by the abundance of conscientiously recorded detail." [26]

Ezekiel was looking upon a vision of the glory of Yahweh, approaching in a storm cloud upon the cherub chariot. There was nothing new or strange about this. As a priest he knew about the Ark of the Covenant and the description of God as "making his throne above the cherubim" (4, 13; 1 S 4, 4; 2 S 6, 2; Pss 98/99, 1; 79/80, 2). The ancient song of Psalm 17/18 sings of Yahweh's approach upon the cherubim. What is new is the fact that something the prophet had always believed now becomes a visible experience with overpowering impetus. No one before him had ever been treated to a like vision of God upon his flying chariot.

At first he attempts to describe the four creatures bearing up God's throne. Like the seraphim in Isaiah's vision, these creatures are surrounded by a fiery cloud. There are four of them, and they have a four-fold appearance. The number four is an expression of the fact that they are bearing up the Lord of the four corners of the earth, the ruler of the whole universe. Each of the four creatures has four wings and a four-fold "face"; that is, at all events, the normal translation, and then interpretation must attempt to imagine what is unimaginable. Did all four of the creatures actually have four faces, each of them facing one of the four corners of the earth? Quite apart from the fact that four-faced creatures very seldom make their appearance in the art of Mesopotamia prior to the time of Ezekiel [27] the prophets, after all, borrow their conception of things from the world around them — the text itself does not speak of four "faces," but four "*pānîm.*" The root of this word means "the side turned towards," and thus it is generally translated as "countenance, face." [28] There are, however, many passages which would suggest a broader range of meaning for *pānîm,* such as the general term "appearance" (Pr 27, 22; 2 S 14, 20), "surface" (Gn 1, 2; 2, 6; Is 14, 12). The Hebrew lexicon of synonyms [29] is quite right when it lists as synonyms for *pānîm* the words *mar'eh* (appearance), *demût* (likeness, similarity), *to'ar* (figure). The first two words, "appearance and similarity," Ezekiel particularly uses

---

26. Schmidt, *Die grossen Propheten,* 392.

27. Zimmerli, l.c. 53.

28. Köhler, LexVT 766.

29. EBEN-ŠOŠAN, *Millôn hādaš,* III (1956⁵), 1302.

in an attempt to make his vision understandable. Accordingly, the word *pānîm*, standing in this context, must not be translated in the narrower sense of "face, countenance," but in its more general meaning of "appearance, figure." This is the only clue to a proper understanding of the cherub creatures.

What is involved are creatures combined of four animals, such as are abundantly familiar from the pictorial art of Assyria and Babylonia.[30] Each individual cherub had the face of a man, while his body had "the appearance" of a lion and his four feet were like the feet of a bull. The creatures had four wings; two of them lay folded along the back and two were spread so that the ends of the wings of each pair of creatures met in the middle. On their outspread wings they bore something that had the appearance of a firmament (*rāqîa'*), a vault which was like the appearance of awesome crystal. Upon this firmament or vault they bore something like a throne, in appearance like sapphire. Seated above the likeness of a throne was a likeness as it were of a human form with the appearance of fire enclosed round about and both downward and upward from what had the appearance of his loins the prophet saw "as it were the appearance of fire, and there was brightness round about him" (1, 22). The whole was spanned by the appearance of a bow, looking like the rainbow on a cloudy day. This was the apparition of God's glory (*kᵉbôd yahweh*).

The four creatures are not simply a dead artistic adornment on the royal throne of God, they are living creatures. The spirit (*rûᵃḥ*), the "divine tumult" is in them driving them wherever God desires. They turn neither to the right nor to the left; they make their powerful way directly towards the prophet. The wings alone would be enough to bear them on their way. But each of the four creatures also has four wheels, indeed four double wheels, one inside the other, joined together by spokes and filled with eyes.

---

30. ANEP 644f. An excavation in the vicinity of ancient Esnunna unearthed two bronze statues of a four-figured god and goddess, dating from the days of Hammurabi. The discovery has no bearing on the vision of Ezekiel. Zimmerli, *loc. cit.*, 61.

The description of God's chariot is in itself nothing new. Solomon, when he built the temple, erected two cherubs in the holy of holies (1 K 6, 23-27). The chronist (1 Ch 28, 18) records that David entrusted to his son Solomon refined gold for the execution of the "chariot" (*merkabah*) and the cherubs (*kᵉrûbîm*). The concept of a divine chariot was not absolutely foreign to ancient Egyptian thought. Ezekiel seizes upon this image and, by way of contrast with the pagan world about him in which the chariots and processions of gods had an important role to play, endows it with a new and unheard of actuality. Yahweh's divine throne, the throne of the true God, is indescribably more splendid than the chariots and thrones of the Babylonian gods. But in the last analysis, we are here confronted with the mystery of mystical experience. Over and over again Ezekiel says that "the hand of the Lord was upon him." He was "lifted up," "seized away" (1, 14). But a man who is seized by a vision of God necessarily turns to the images and concepts at his disposal when he attempts to describe the ineffable. In terms of external appearances, Ezekiel is describing a heavenly throne chariot, borne by mixed creatures, an image which is sufficiently familiar from the pictorial art of that era. But a new meaning has been grafted onto this common form of description. Everything is tremendously big, gigantic; everything is alive. The bearers of the throne are living creatures, creatures who have incorporated the climax of creation and nature: the spiritual countenance of man, the majesty of the lion, the power of the bull, and the eagle's untiring wings that scale the very heavens.

What was at first simply the rush of the storm wind from the north becomes, now that the vision stands clearly before the prophet's eyes, the rushing of mighty wings. The whole thing appears to be surrounded by fire. There is a glow along the outside and in the center of the great cloud. Rich ore and precious stones are sparkling everywhere. And between the creatures there was something that looked like burning coals of fire, like torches moving back and forth. The figure of God himself, however, was like pure fire, surrounded by the shining hues of the rainbow.[31]

---

31. Schmidt, *Die grossen Propheten*, 393-394.

b) *Consecration and Mandate* (2, 1 — 3, 37)

Under the pressure of this mighty apparition — each of the four creatures had his face turned towards the prophet and none is turning aside: the threatening vision is coming inevitably towards him — Ezekiel fell upon his face. But God's hand was coming upon him not to annihilate him, but to raise him up and empower him with the divine mandate. After the terror of his vision and the mighty rushing of the winds, he suddenly hears himself addressed "the voice of one speaking," as "son of man" (*ben-'ādam*). He is still lying powerless upon the earth. The spirit (*rûᵃḥ*) must come upon him before he can rise up and speak with God face to face. The address "son of man" is used in the Book of Ezekiel 93 times, 23 times in the formula "you, son of man." The prophets Amos (7, 8; 8, 2) and Jeremiah (1, 11; 24, 3) were addressed by Yahweh in their personal names; Ezekiel, on the other hand, is only the "son of man," a creature belonging to humanity as such, a creation from the dust of the earth.[32] This is a supreme confrontation between divine majesty and human impotence. But here too the primary accent is not upon the essential unfolding of the secret of God's essence, but rather upon the concrete and historical mandate to the prophet. Yahweh is God of history. He seizes upon Ezekiel in order to proclaim his plan through him. The prophet is sent to announce God's claim to sovereignty over his rebellious and obstinate people. "The people are impudent and stubborn, a nation of rebels." This is the thankless mission, and one which promises little hope of success. But even though briars and thorns surround him and he sits upon scorpions, he is not to be afraid, since it is God's hand and spirit that will strengthen him (2, 6-8).

Just as the prophet Isaiah had his lips purified by a seraph, and Yahweh's own hand purified Jeremiah, Ezekiel too is introduced into his prophetic office by a sort of ordination.[33] A bizzare spectacle. He is to consume a scroll which is inscribed within and without with words of woe, lamentation, and mourning.

---

32. Further treatment of "son of man": Zimmerli, BK XIII, 70ff.
33. *Ibid.,* 75.

Even though the house of Israel to which he is sent is a people with a hard face and a stiff neck, the prophet's ordination makes his face harder than adamant, harder than flint (3, 9). The prophet's consecration has left no room for doubt: hardness will be repaid by hardness. But God's plan and will prove stronger than any human resistance.

The impression of what he had seen and experienced weighed so heavily on the prophet's soul that, when he returned to Tel-Abib, he sat there overwhelmed for seven days. Then Yahweh came to him with a new revelation. His ordination made him watchman over Israel. If the watchman sees disaster approaching and does not call out, the city will be destroyed, but the fault will rest with the watchman. If he calls out, however, and the city refuses to listen, he is himself without fault, even though the city sinks in ruins. Impelled by the knowledge of this divine mission and the necessity of his own conscience, Ezekiel breaks his silence and begins, in word and deed, to assert Yahweh's claims to kingship over Israel in the midst of an unparalleled crisis.

2) GESTURES OF THREAT (4, 1 — 5, 17)

The expression of God's word through symbolic signs and actions is quite in keeping with the general practice of prophetic preaching.[34] Hananiah made an iron yoke for himself, Elisha bade the king to shoot arrows of victory, and Isaiah went three years "naked." The symbolic actions of Ezekiel were designed simply to proclaim the judgment that was dawning over Jerusalem more forcefully than any words could express. It might indeed be true that, seen from the outside, there is a certain similarity with the practice of magic. We might think, for example, of the Egyptian execration texts. The names of the cities to be annihilated were written on clay tablets together with appropriate formulas of cursing, and then shattered. This was understood to be an effective blow against the distant enemy. The symbolic activities of the prophets, however, are sufficiently explained by the knowledge of their mission. Blind magic has no place here. Ezekiel's activity

---

34. G. Fohrer, *Die symbolischen Handlungen der Propheten*, (1953).

is a call to conscience. Interpreting his peculiar behavior as a symptom of a sick or unsound mental condition quite misses the heart of the matter.[35] It is not at all to be wondered that a man who has seen such a divine vision and was then commissioned to pronounce the judgment to come should in some way transcend the common norm of human behavior. Ezekiel bore the stamp of God and proclaimed God's will in symbols and actions that were destined to win him an audience.

Once he took a fresh brick — in Babylonia they wrote on fresh clay — and drew a picture of the city of Jerusalem (4, 1-3). Then he built a siege wall against it and cast up a mound against it and placed battering rams against it all about. The meaning? In precisely this way Jerusalem will be besieged. Next he had to lay on his left side for 390 days and 40 days on his right side (4, 4-8), in order to "bear the punishment of Israel and Judah." [36] He felt as if cords were binding him, the work of Yahweh himself, which is to say that he felt himself perfectly incapable of in any way interrupting this period of torturesome inactivity. For more than seven months of intense suffering, he was forced to experience, in his own body, the sentence of punishment that was inevitably breaking over the unrepentant people. The great catastrophe to come left its stamp upon his whole existence and made him stand out among his contemporaries as a most powerful sermon without words.

After passing through this period of bonds and inactivity, he was forced to ration his food, in imitation of a city under siege (4, 9-17), and finally to cut his hair with a sharp sword and not a barber's razor. One third of the hair he was told to burn in the city, a second third he was to cut up with the sword, and the remaining third was to be scattered in all directions. All this

---

35. Eichrodt, ATD 22, 29.
36. The interpretation of the number is not clear. Various points of departure have been attempted. Cf. Eichrodt, ATD 22, 28ff. — Possibly the symbolic number of 390 and 40 = 430 years is taken from Ex 12, 40 where it is mentioned as the number of years of the stay in Egypt.

was simply an image of the fate to come. The symbols required no words of explanation: they were enough by themselves. But Ezekiel was not satisfied with this. He also raised the sword of the word and proclaimed threats against the land and people of Israel (6, 1-7, 27). These words culminated in the statement: "An end has come, the end has come; it has awakened against you" (7, 6). Why this end had to come was made clear to the prophet in a state of visionary rapture into the temple of Jerusalem.

3) RAPTURE TO THE TEMPLE OF JERUSALEM (8, 1 – 11, 25)
(8, 1 — 11, 25)

In the 6th year of the exile, in the 5th month, on the 5th day (August 9, 591) Ezekiel was sitting in his house which he had built along the river Chebar. The elders of Judah, the leading citizens of the expatriate community, came to see him, apparently to ask for God's word on Jerusalem. They are sitting there and waiting. Suddenly the prophet feels as if something heavy is weighing down upon him. He experiences the "hand of Yahweh." Everything grows dark before his eyes. He must have sat there stiff and motionless. But his spirit was ranging abroad, his inner eye was open, and in vision he saw the abomination in the holy city, the cause for Jerusalem's impending destruction. He felt himself lifted up by a lock of his head, by the agency of a fiery creature, and carried into the holy city (8, 1-4). At the northern gate, where the gruesome tour began, he was forced to look upon the "image of jealousy" (*sēmel haqqin'ah*).[37] At the door of the courtyard, he saw a hole in the wall. The prophet had to dig into the wall; he did not trust his own eyes. "Upon the wall round about, were all kinds of creeping things, and loathsome beasts, and all the idols of the house of Israel. And before them stood seventy men of the elders of the house of Israel . . . . Each had his censor in his hand, and the smoke of

---

37. The expression is too general to suggest an Asherah image with any certainty. Possibly it may have been a sculpture of a goddess who kept watch over the gate. Such gate figurines were common in Northern Syria. Zimmerli, *Ezechiel,* 214 (BK XIII).

the cloud of incense went up" (8, 7-13). This mysterious cult scene is the counterpart of the mysterious policy of those days. Everyone looked for salvation not only from the strong arm of the Egyptian Pharaoh, but also from the pagan gods, fashioned in the form of animals, to whom the leading citizens of Judah were offering incense sacrifices. Coming out of the dark Egyptian sacrifice chamber into the light of the outer court, the prophet approaches the temple house itself. There, in the very shadow of the temple building, and thus on sacred ground, he sees a group of women weeping for Tammuz (8, 14-15).[38] This cult they could practice publicly because it was agreeable to the Babylonian powers. How little Yahweh himself was honored in his own sacred precinct is shown by the final scene of this strange tour. Between the temple and the altar of holocaust stood twenty-five men. They were prepared, however, not to fall down in worship of Yahweh who thrones above the cherubim, but quite the contrary, they turn their back upon him and turn their face to the sun god *Šamaš* in the east (8, 16). These "twenty-five" must have been among the leading citizens. Nor was it enough to refuse Yahweh honor in his own house; they were filling the temple with acts of violence (8, 17).

"From one holy place to another — from the northern part of the outer court across the inner court and into the sacred ground between altar and temple — our prophet has been led. What he witnesses is one abomination upon another. Now he is witness to the vengeance of Yahweh, the terrible judgment which is hanging over his city. Accordingly, his vision passes from the

---

38. The Sumero-Babylonian god of vegetation Tammuz (*dumu-zi* = "right child, proper son," Accadian *du'zu*) occurs only here in the OT. There has recently been considerable agitation on the subject of this god's name and early history. Cf. Vol. I, p. 73. The spread of the ancient Sumerian cult began only after Tammuz had already become a typical vegetation divinity. He was venerated as the god of the dying summer vegetation. The fourth month (June, July) is named after him. As a figure of a god who dies young he is lamented by his worshippers. Such laments are preserved in the words of their hymns. Cf. A. Falkenstein. W. v. Soden, *Sumerische und akkadische Hymnen und Gebete*, (1953), 185-187. AOT 270-273.

description of what he beholds at present to a consideration of what must come to pass.

Suddenly a voice sounds in his ear: 'Draw near, you executioners of the city!' Whose is the voice? Obviously someone who has power to proclaim this terrible punishment, obviously Yahweh himself. The awesome God who has brought his prophet in vision to become the witness of his terrible wrath now calls upon his executioners. We must suppose that the voice comes from the Holy of Holies, behind the twenty-five men who are worshipping the sun.

No sooner is the word spoken that a ghastly procession appears, solemn and silent. Following the same path that the prophet himself has walked, from the northern gate of the inner court they make their solemn way. They are seven giant men, their leader dressed in linen clothing, with a writing case at his side, the other six following behind him; each man had a 'weapon for slaughter' — perhaps a club — in his hand. The men took up their position beside the great altar. Meantime Yahweh has risen up upon the cherubim, that is, upon the wondrous chariot familiar to us from the inaugural vision which is here envisioned as present in the temple building, and has made his way from the interior of the house to the threshold. Standing above the heads of the twenty-five worshippers of the sun who have turned their backs on him, he spoke to his servants.

The orders he gives are terrible: all the men and women in the city, even the old men and the little children, are all to be killed. Only those who sigh and groan over all the abominations that are committed in the temple shall be spared. The recording angel is ordered to make his way through the city and mark everyone on their forehead with a Taw, the Hebrew letter which is like a cross (T or X) (9, 4). Then comes the judgment. The angel is to take the fire which is burning between the cherubim figures and the chariot of God and burn the holy city. The prospect is so terrible that the prophet has simply refused to record the execution of this command." [39] What was there left

---

39. Cf. H. Schmidt, *Die grossen Propheten*, 405ff. (SAT).

to depict, after the glory of Yahweh had disappeared towards the eastern gate over the throne of the cherubim?

In conclusion Schmidt says this: "No one can escape the powerful grandeur, the vivid beauty of this dream vision." Surely the dream is the illegitimate brother of visionary sight. Both meet each other on the same psychic plane, and yet the two of them are different in origin. In the dream the wild fantasy plays a game of free and unintelligible imagery with the mind that is sunk in sleep. The vision, however, takes place in a state of true consciousness, even though the person experiencing the vision may seem, externally, to be lost within himself, his mind miles away. The imagery involved in the vision is taken from the person's experience, although in the vision it becomes the type and image of a reality that transcends sense experience. Thus, the chariot of God and the mixed creatures are reminiscent of the Assyrian and Babylonian art. It might also be that the recording angel is patterned after the god Nabu [40] the lord of Borsippa, the "writer of the universe," the "writer of E-sag-il" (the Babylonian tower). Of this god it is said that "he has a writing instrument," that he "keeps watch over the whole of heaven and earth," that "he takes the stylus of the tablets of fate and lengthens the days of a man's life." Together with six angels of destruction, the recording angel makes up the number seven, all of them prepared to carry out the commands of God. The concept of seven creatures standing before God's throne comes up frequently in later Old Testament writings, and especially in the Revelations of St. John. In the Book of Tobit (12, 15) we hear of seven angels who have access to the glory of the All High. In the Revelations of St. John this conception is exchanged for others, seven torches standing before the throne of God (4, 5) or seven lamps (1, 12) or seven eyes (5, 6). Zechariah speaks of the eyes as looking over the whole world (4, 10). What are we to say of these creatures who, at one and the same time, are called angels or spirits, lamps or torches or eyes? Were they originally stars? Actually, the Book of Revelations (1, 16) does make explicit mention of the seven stars in the hand of the king of heaven. Are these seven powerful figures, in the last analysis, simply personified stars? (constellations)? As such, they are very fitting about the throne of God.

While Ezekiel, however, is indebted to the religious conceptions of the world about him, or, to put it more accurately, is stimulated by these conceptions, in his hands they become an entirely new and different thing. This practice of "borrowing" from extra-Biblical usages and symbols is to be found, in the

---

40. J. Ziegler, EB III, 475. Schmidt, l.c. 407.

course of Old Testament history, in various places: the *pesach,*
an ancient shepherd festival, becomes, under Moses, the feast of
Israel's salvation; the same thing is true of the ancient agricultural
festival of the unleavened bread (*massôt*). In the Solomonic
temple, the "borrowing" of pagan symbolism has been achieved
on a grandiose proportion. In Ezekiel, the same law is operative.
It is evidence of the overwhelming power of the religion of
revelation that it could attempt such a synthesis without sacrificing
any of its essential prerogatives.

The most moving element of the temple vision is not the
spatial aspect of the rapture, the prophet's being seized in the
spirit and taken to Jerusalem, after the manner of a second vision,
but rather in the religious reality that is the subject matter of his
vision. The God of Israel is the God of the universe. The Babylonian gods are not even mentioned by the prophet, since they
are a mere nothing. The God of Israel is not bound to any
single place. He can appear in even a foreign country, although he
has chosen Jerusalem as the place of his residence. Precisely in
Jerusalem, however, rebellion has flared up against his authority.
He has been forced from his own temple. The historian can
demonstrate that the kingdom of Judah is wholly subject to the
overwhelming power of Babylon. The prophet, however, delves
into the realities behind these political events and paints the
picture of the drama between God and man. History takes place
only as willed by God. Because Jerusalem has broken faith with
God it must be shattered under the hammer of Babylon. It would
be foolhardy to pronounce such a sentence over a nation. Only
in his prophetic vision are the events visible. Yahweh goes forth
from Jerusalem, leaving ashes and destruction behind — one
of the most moving passages of the Old Testament.

4) FLIGHT AND EXILE IN SYMBOL (12, 1-20)

Relentlessly the prophet takes up the same slogan: "Jerusalem must fall." It is only understandable that the expatriates
were clinging to the all but desperate hope that their native city
would survive. In an effort to portray the inevitable destruction
of Jerusalem, Ezekiel one day broke a hole into the wall of

his hut, shouldered a sack filled with only the most obvious necessities of life, and carried it out of the city in the dark, with his face covered. This would be the very fate of Jerusalem's king Zedekiah (cf. Jer 39, 1-7; 52, 4-11; 2 K 25, 7). Ezekiel then sang the fate of Zedekiah in an allegory song (*māšal*): "A great eagle with great wings and long pinions... came to Lebanon. He took the top of the cedar; he broke off the topmost of its young twigs and carried it to a land of trade, and sent it in a city of merchants" (17, 1ff.).

Such behavior must have seemed extremely erratic to many of his contemporaries. The proverb went around that "the days grow long, and every vision comes to nought" (12, 22); that is to say that Ezekiel's visions are only an illusion and will never be fulfilled. Besides Ezekiel there were many other preachers, prophets of their own choosing. They capitalized upon the wishes of the people and began to promise victory. They found a welcome ear. Ezekiel, however, unmasked them as lying preachers; he directed the curse of judgment both against the false prophets (13, 1-16) and the false prophetesses (13, 17-23).

5) THE DEFILED "TENT OF GOD" (20, 1ff.)

One year after the temple vision, in the 7th year of the exile, on the 10th day of the 5th month (September 1, 590), some of the elders of Judah came to Ezekiel to ask an oracle from Yahweh. They sat down before him and waited for his answer. The prophet had no new words for them, only the sentence of destruction. The history of Israel alone must make it clear that this would be the inevitable fate of constant rebelliousness and defection in the face of Yahweh's repeated acts of love (20, 1-41). Ezekiel is not about to glorify the history of his people. He is almost guilty of painting it rather too black. For him, the study of history is primarily an examination of conscience which must result in conversion. That is why he has to put his finger on the sore spot. In his description of the unchaste behavior of the two wicked daughters, Jerusalem and Samaria (23, 1-49), he reaches the limits of what can be borne. The history of the two kingdoms is simply harlotry with foreign gods, adultery and wantonness. Their names make it clear what their spirits are or should be. Samaria bears the name *'ohᵒlah,* that is, "her (own) tent." The Northern Kingdom had turned away from Yahweh and, following her own will, had set up images of bulls which had nothing to do with Yahweh. Jerusalem bears the name *'Ohᵒlibah,* that is, "my tent (is) in her." But this tent of Yahweh in Jerusalem had been defiled from top to bottom, as witness the temple vision. In the interpretation of the relationship between Yahweh and Israel as a marriage contract, Ezekiel is the disciple and pupil of the prophet Hosea. He has carried on the former's thoughts down to their ultimate conclusion. Ezekiel, as the champion of Yahweh's rights, must convict the two sisters of adultery. But the penalty for adultery, according to the Law, was death (23, 45): "The host shall stone them and dispatch them with their swords; they shall slay their sons and their daughters, and burn up their houses . . . . Thus will I put an end to lewdness in the land . . . . And you shall know that I am the Lord God Yahweh." The catastrophic history of destruction is, accordingly, nothing more than a revelation of God's reality. The smoking ruins of Jerusalem are witness to the fact that Yahweh is Lord and God.

6) "THE DELIGHT OF YOUR EYES IS TAKEN AWAY" (24, 15-17)

On the same day that Nebuchadnezzar laid his hand upon Jerusalem — Ezekiel was to write this date for himself (24, 2) — the hand of God made itself manifest in the life of his prophet. It was the 10th day of the 10th month in the 9th year of the exile (January 5, 587). He took the "delight of his eyes" (*maḥmad 'ēynôkā*) by a sudden death (24, 15). Ezekiel's wife had died unexpectedly. Reference to her as "the delight of his eyes" points to a very intimate and not simply a conventional marriage relationship. This made it all the harder for him to bear such a blow. Nothing would have been more natural than for him to break out into a violent expression of his terrible grief. But nothing like this happened: there was neither cry nor weeping nor taking off of the turban, nor taking off of sandals and going barefoot about the city (cf. 2 S 15, 30; Mi 1, 8), no veiling of the face and eating the bread of sorrow. Not a single tear ran down his cheeks. He was dumb and it was as if his grief had turned him into stone.

Such a strange behavior must have caused some notice. Was the prophet supposed to be a sign of something, even in his terrible suffering? When he found words once again he began to preach God's threat that he would cause a like fate to "the delight of their eyes and the desire of their soul" (24, 21). The holy city and the temple would be done away with. When the news reaches the exiles, the very incomprehensibility of the disaster will make them forget all signs of grief. Among the people destroyed in Jerusalem there were many relatives and acquaintances of the people who had been resettled in Babylon. But it is not the loss of friend and family that is so painful; it is the prospect of the destruction of the holy city that will make them dumb with grief, incapable of seeking the release of tears; for Jerusalem, the delight of their eyes, is dead.

7) DESTRUCTION AGAINST THE NATIONS (25 – 32)

Just as Isaiah (13 — 23) and Jeremiah (46 — 51), Ezekiel too is sent to preach judgment not only against Israel, but against the nations as well. His prophecies against the nations are found in the middle of the Book (25 — 32). Although this is a self-contained collection, the events described in it are most intimately bound up with events in the Holy Land. The nations have shared the guilt of Jerusalem's destruction. The fact that there are seven "burdens" is probably deliberate choice: Ammon, Moab, Edom, Philistia, Tyre, Sidon, and Egypt. The oracles are grouped into five smaller burdens and two larger ones (against Tyre and Egypt). Sidon is mentioned only briefly in connection with Tyre, probably in order to fill out the number seven. The sequence is not temporal, but rather geographical. Ezekiel turns to the east (Ammon, Moab), then to the south (Edom), and then to the west (Philistia). The great prophecies against Tyre and Egypt are at the end of the section. It is remarkable that there is not a single word directed against Babylon. The explanation is probably to be found in the fact that threats against Babylon would have been politically harmful to the exiles. Moreover, Ezekiel recognized Babylon as the rod of God's chastisement.[41]

If the dated oracles against Egypt and Tyre are removed from this more mechanical series, they take on a quite different color. From his place of banishment, Ezekiel closely followed the political events of Palestine. The fact that Jerusalem had been encouraged to attempt this disastrous adventure was primarily the fault of Egypt; Egypt kept fanning the fire of rebellion against Babylon and then, at the moment of crisis, simply abandoned the rebels. It was precisely in these fateful years of 586 and 585, where the desperate hope of Jerusalem looked to Egypt for help, that Ezekiel thundered forth his oracles against Egypt, in word and in poem.

"The song of the great dragon," the king of Egypt, is dated on the 12th day of the 10th month of the 10th year (January 26, 586). Yahweh will put hooks in the jaws of the dragon (*tannin*) and cast him forth into the wilderness, prey for the beasts of the earth and the birds of the air. Egypt was a broken reed upon which Israel sought to lean. The reed collapsed and wounded the hand of him who sought to lean upon it. — "Speech against the strong arm of Pharaoh" (30, 20ff.). Dated on the 7th day of the 10th month of the 11th year (April 19, 586). His arm will be broken, and the sword will fall from his hands. He can be of no help. — "The song against the glorious tree of Pharaoh" (31 1ff.), dated on the 1st day of the 3rd month of the 11th year (June 11, 586): "Whom are you like in your greatness? ... The cedars of Lebanon .... All the trees of Eden envied it." But foreigners will come and cut it down. Its proud glory will be destroyed.

One month from this date, it was obvious to everyone that Egypt could not help. On the 10th day of the 5th month of the 11th year (August 17, 586) Jerusalem had fallen and the temple had gone up in flames. Five months later, on the 5th day of the 10th month of the 11th year (January 8, 585) a fugitive made his way to Ezekiel with this news: "The city is taken"

---

41. J. Ziegler, EB III, 523.

(33, 21). It seems strange that the messenger took five months for the trip from Jerusalem to Babylon. Probably he set out on his journey only after the murder of Gedaliah in the 7th month, when what was left of the population of Jerusalem fled in panic in all directions. For Ezekiel, the terrible news was simply a confirmation of the truth of his preaching. He had spoken the truth. If his words had, prior to this time, been the hammer and sword of destruction, from now on they would be a balsam of healing for the grievous wounds. For Egypt he had now only a dirge to sing: "The great dragon is dead" (32, 1). The song is dated on the 1st day of the 12th month of the 11th year (March 3, 585). The same date marks the threat oracle against Tyre: "Ahah, the gate of the peoples is broken" (26, 1; 28, 19). It would be hard to find a more appropriate name for the mistress of the seas. Tyre had made common cause with Jerusalem in the rebellion against Nebuchadnezzar. The Babylonians had to continue their siege of the city for 13 years (585-572). The isle fortress could not be taken by battle, but eventually yielded to superior force (29, 17). — The last dated threat oracle against Egypt was delivered on the 15th day of the 1st month of the 12th year (April 16, 585). Jerusalem lay in ruins. Hope in Egypt had proved illusory. The prophet sings of the Pharaoh's final journey to the netherworld (32, 17ff.).

From these threats and oracles against the nations one thing becomes abundantly clear: Yahweh is not simply the God of the tiny people of Israel; he is Lord of all nations. History thus becomes a revelation of God; all the world can look to the course of human history and recognize that "I Yahweh, am your Lord and God" (32, 15).

B) PROPHET OF SALVATION

So long as Jerusalem stood, Ezekiel proclaimed with inexorable severity: "Jerusalem must fall." But now that Jerusalem had fallen, he suddenly changed his role. "The prophet's mouth is open wide, but no longer in words of threat. From this hour on it is only promises. There is a very fine distinction between threat and promise in Ezekiel. Yet, promise is much more characteristic of his preaching than threat. Despite his furious reproaches and the bitter quarrel with his countrymen, whom he opposed for so many years, Ezekiel is actually the prophet with whom the promise of the future takes on the so-called messianic character." [42] Ezekiel stands at a great pivotal point in Old Testament history. He can justly be called the architect of the future and, with some reservation, he can be considered "the father of Jewry." [43] Looking beyond the ruins, he can see a wholly new creation, the Israel of the believers, as a united people, thronging about the temple, standing in a holy land that is once again in full blossom.

The book does not say precisely when Ezekiel began his preaching of future salvation. The vision of the new temple is dated on the 10th day of the 1st month of the 25th year of the exile (April 17, 572 — 40, 1), that is, fourteen years after the destruction of Jerusalem. This would lead us to suppose that his awareness of the salvation to come was a gradual development during the course of these darkest years of his people's history, a time at which everything seemed inevitably lost. But his awareness of the future glory gradually matures into a majestic vision of the future.

I) *The New Israel* (34 — 39)

1) YAHWEH THE GOOD SHEPHERD (34, 1-31)

The comparison with the bad shepherds of Israel probably is to be dated close to the time of the destruction of Jerusalem. Yahweh revokes their shepherd's office and will henceforth himself be the good shepherd of his people. This section has been called "a model for shepherds." [44] First the bad shepherds are rebuked for what they have failed to do: they have not properly fed their weak animals, to make them strong; they have not cared for and healed the sick, but simply left them to die; the

---

42. Wellhausen, *Geschichte*, 145.
43. Robert-Feuillet, IntrAT 549.
44. J. Ziegler, EB III, 548.

wounded they have not attended to; those who wandered and strayed, or were scattered by the attack of wild animals they did not gather into the herd. The herd, as a result, perished, because the shepherds had failed. They have not cared for the flock, only for themselves. Accordingly, the flock is no longer theirs; it was Yahweh's flock that they allowed to perish. Now Yahweh, as owner of the flock, must take steps against the shepherds and hold them to a reckoning. Since they have played the part of beasts of prey, and the sheep had to be snatched out of their hands, they are no longer fit for their office. It is Yahweh's will that the ruling class resign their control. Yahweh liberates his people from their useless and selfish leaders.

But since the flock cannot be without its shepherds, Yahweh himself assumes the office of shepherd. As good shepherd he will make good all the harm done by the bad shepherds. First he will gather what had been scattered into the four corners of the earth. There will be a new and greater exodus than the exodus from Egypt. He will bring them back into the holy land. There he himself will pasture them with rich grazing land, and he will strike a "covenant of peace" (*berît šālôm* 34, 25) with the wild beasts so that they no longer harass the flock. There will be a new "plantation of prosperity" (*maṭṭā' šālôm* 34, 29).[45] The climax of this prophecy of salvation is found in the words: "They shall know that I, the Lord their God, am with them, and that they, the house of Israel, are my people, says the Lord God. And you are my sheep, the sheep of my pasture" (34, 30-31).

Yahweh will exercise his office of shepherd through a shepherd whom he will establish (34, 23-24). No longer will there be two kingdoms and two king-shepherds, Israel and Judah, but there will be one united people under one single prince from the house of David. Ezekiel does not refer to him as "king" (*melek*), but only "prince" (*nāśî'*), apparently because the title of king had been desecrated by the rebellious kings. The new prince (*nāśî'*) is equivalent with the "servant of God" (*'ebed*). His ruling office

---

45. MT reads *maṭṭā' le šēm*, "plantation unto glory." LXX reads φυτὸν ἠειρνης, "plantation of peace," which is preferable.

is a type and parable of the heavenly office of shepherd. Thus Ezekiel takes up the figures which were current in prophetic circles before the introduction of kingship. At that time the man chosen by God was not to be a "king" (*melek*) in his own right, in the sense of the nations around Israel, but rather a shepherd (*nāgîd*) in the full power of Yahweh.[46]

The picture of the future that Ezekiel sketches in describing the restoration of the lands (36, 1-38), is not at all utopian or eschatological. It is rather oriented towards immediate and concrete goals. The scattered people will return home again, settle on the mountains of Israel, after the land has been expiated and purified of all idols. This was a saving message that the exiles smarting under the Babylonian captivity could recognize and understand. Upon closer examination, however, we realize that this return home is not simply meant to restore the former borders; something entirely new will be established: "I will sprinkle clean water upon you and you will be clean from all your uncleannesses . . . . A new heart I will give you and a new spirit I will put within you; and I will take out of your flesh the heart of stone and give you a heart of flesh. And I will put my spirit within you, and cause you to walk in my statutes and be careful to observe my ordinances" (36, 25ff.).

What the prophet is describing is not the political future; he envisions a new people, a people living in the immediacy of God himself. God will be among them and they will be his people. Is this not perhaps a prospect which transcends the framework of history, a new horizon which is still awaiting its fulfillment? The prophecy of the future is at once messianic and eschatological. Its primary aspect is contemporary and historical. Only in this manner could it be a true message of salvation for those to whom it was first addressed.

2) THE RESURRECTION OF THE PEOPLE OF ISRAEL (37, 1-28)

The same depth of perspective is achieved in the vision of the cemetery and the reviving of the dead bones. The Fathers

---

46. Cf. Vol. III, 57, 290.

of the Church [47] refer to this chapter as a primary proof for
faith in the resurrection from the dead, and with perfect right.
On the basis of their fuller understanding of the faith, they had
realized a deeper interpretation of the Old Testament texts. The
vision presupposes faith in the fact that Yahweh is a God who
can kill and bring back to life. Faith in this God, in whose
power are the gifts of life and death, is also the foundation of
faith in the resurrection and the restoration of the flesh. Ezekiel's
vision, however, is not primarily addressed to the event that will
occur at the end of the days; it is directed towards his own time
and age. The "delight of his eyes" had been taken from him,
Jerusalem had been destroyed, and the people were dead. This
is the point of departure for his vision. The hand of Yahweh
came upon him once again and transported him in spirit into
the middle of a huge valley that was full of dead bones. Could
these ever come back to life? The prophet answered: "You know,
O Lord," which is to say that in human terms it is impossible.
But then Yahweh bade his prophet prophesy over the dried bones.
Thereupon the spirit of life (*rûaḥ*) came upon them and they
were living; they all stood up, a mighty host.

That these events are to be understood as symbolic of the
death of the people of Israel is clear from the words of interpretation that followed: "These bones are the whole house of
Israel" (37, 11). The exile was the grave into which the people
had been laid. If the people was to arise again, this can only be
in virtue of God's power to give life; for the "spirit" is that
power which emanates from God and works wonders in the
world. The restoration of the people of Israel will thus be a
most singular miracle effected by God. The unification of the
people will be experienced as a peculiarly powerful miracle.
Ezekiel calls attention to this fact by a symbolic act (37, 15).
He took two sticks and wrote upon them the names "Judah
(Southern Kingdom) and Joseph (Northern Kingdom)." Then he
joined them together into one stick. Just as they were now

---

47. Ziegler, EB III, 556 points to Justin Martyr, Irenaeus of Lyon, Ter-
tullian, etc.

destined to become one single people, one single king would rule over them. Only one shepherd would be recognized by all, the servant of God and prince from the house of David. Divided kingdom and divided faith are gone forever; the *Una sancta* is established. This is a promise that must have made the hearts of the exiles beat with joy. But the manner in which this promise would be realized was still hidden in the dimness of the future. Nonetheless, the way had been sketched, the figure of the new Israel had been outlined. This chapter has quite rightly been referred to as "a whole compendium of the theology of Ezekiel."[48]

3) YAHWEH'S BATTLE AND VICTORY OVER GOG (38, 1 – 39, 29) (38, 1 — 39, 29)

After Israel's return to its own country history has not come to an end. Ezekiel prophesies one final and terrible battle. From the north the wild horses of Gog will make their violent way into the unprotected holy land; but upon the mountains of Israel they will be dealt an annihilating blow. Then the land will be purified of their dead remains and all the world will know that Yahweh the Lord (God) sits in his throne in the midst of his people. No longer will he turn his countenance from them, but rather he will pour his spirit upon them and create a new Israel through whom his name will be sanctified among all nations (39, 28).

Various attempts have been made to interpret the enigmatic figure of Gog. The first recourse was to the contemporary extra-Biblical world, to see if there might not be some figure which corresponds to Gog. There is, for example, the name Gagi, which occurs in the cuneiform literature, prince of a country north of Assur.[49] In the Amarna letters there is mention of a land Gaga, which is probably to be identified somewhere in Northern Syria.[50] Closest to the name Gog would appear to be the name of a Lydian king Gugu (Gyges c. 607).[51] Scholars have also suggested kings who were to appear only after Ezekiel, for instance Cambyses, Alexander the Great, and Antiochus Eupator, Mithridates IV, or primarily the

---

48. Fohrer, *Ezechiel*, HAT 13 (1955), 202.
49. City prince of Median Sahi (Assurbanipal cylinder B IV 2).
50. Ziegler, EB III, 558.
51. Fohrer, *Ezechiel*, 212ff.

Parthians. But this later era is certainly not within the prophet's present field of vision.

Since the history of this era presents no figure that really corresponds to Gog, the name has been interpreted symbolically. Gog is supposed to be the equivalent of the Sumerian *Gug*, "darkness, gloom." The great prince of Gog would thus be the "prince of darkness," a sort of Old Testament Antichrist.[52] But none of these interpretations is really satisfactory and none of them really answers the riddle, simply because the point of departure for the name and figure of Gog is always based on insufficient evidence.

A far better methodology would use as its point of departure the names of the nations who owe allegiance to this prince or who enter into alliance with him. There is no further explanation required for the names of the allies *paras, kûš* and *put;* these are the Persians, the Egyptians, and the Libyans (38, 5), whose names probably found their way into the text only at its final redaction. Gog is also called "prince of *ro'š, mešek,* and *tûbal*" (38, 2); he is also joined by the northern nations *Gômer* and *Bêt-togarmah.* We are already familiar with the people of Gomer, the Cimmerians, who, under pressure from the Scythians who were forcing their way from the steppes of southern Russia over the Caucasus, and then in turn into the Assyrian empire where they severely pressed Sargon II (721-705) from the north. They were dealt a devastating blow by the united forces of Assyria and Lydia. It was this very defeat that paved the way for the Scythian invasion around 630. The name Gomer is to be identified with the country of Cappadocia in eastern Asia Minor. Armenia which lies to its west is equivalent with Bet-togarma.[53] In that same geographical area, south of the Black Sea, we must locate the peoples of Mesek and Tubal. Tubal is not well known, whereas Sargon II once had to fight against Mešek (*muški*). Whether these were Indo-Arian or Hurrite peoples cannot be determined. At all events, the names all point to the north. Ezekiel was thinking of the nations that formed a huge and compact bloc settling along the eastern half of Asia Minor south of the Black Sea. According to the contemporary conception of things, it was here that was located the margin of the earth, the extreme north, where the world simply ceased to be. It was precisely from this quarter that the great peril threatened. Jeremiah (4-6) already speaks of the enemy from the north. This "enemy from the north" is also mentioned in Joel (2, 20). It is an ancient element of the prophetic message that the peril "comes from the north" (Is 14,

---

52. *Ibid.,* 212.
53. Hittite, Tegarama, Accadian Tilgarímmu; between the Antitaurus and Euphrates. Cf. E. Fohrer, *Provinzeinteilung des assyrischen Reiches,* (1921), 81.

31; Jr 1, 13; 4, 6; 6, 1; 13, 20), "from a distant country" (Is 5, 26; Jr 4, 16; 5, 15). Familiar, too, is the great defeat that this enemy will suffer in the land of Israel (Is 14, 25; 29, 5-8). Ezekiel has here joined the various traits and produced a single eschatological image. Behind the recognizable names of these unimportant nations there lurks something more, something other. Experience had taught that it was from this unknown northern country that danger always threatened the contemporary civilized world. Ezekiel seizes upon this historical lesson in order to outline a picture of the future valid in a sphere that is both transcendental and eschatological.

From the ends of the earth, the great prince Gog from the land of Magog [54] will lead his hordes in an attack upon the holy land. But the power of the nations thus unleashed will be annihilated by Yahweh himself. Only after this final catastrophe of history can Israel dwell in security, as the holy people of God in the holy land. The new people will be holy. The concept of holiness is here understood in its real and not personal sense. All the dead bodies must be conscientiously removed after the battle. The weapons will be destroyed. Whatever of the spoils can be burnt must be used for fire. No longer will there be war, only great and everlasting peace.

The final note in this vision cannot help but remind us of Isaiah's proclamation of the kingdom of peace. Since Ezekiel also imitates his prophetic predecessors in his image of an enemy from the north, we might ask what is his own peculiar message. This message of Yahweh's battle and victory over Gog was primarily a message of salvation for his contemporaries. Israel, trodden underfoot by the nations, was looking to a great future; Yahweh will annihilate the nations attacking from the north, together with their numerous allies, and he will raise up a new Israel, free of the fear of its enemies; Israel will be a sign lifted up among the nations.

The point of origin for his vision must also be understood in terms of that time. The accomplishment is dated "on that day" (38, 10, 18; 39, 11), a time in the impalpable and distant future. That day, however, is the goal and end point of history. It is true that this vision appears in Ezekiel's predecessors, but it is only

---

54. *Magog* from *mat-gog* = land of God.

in Ezekiel that it is developed in terms of such overwhelming images (vision of the field of bones, the battle with Gog) and outlined with mathematical precision, measuring stick in hand (dividing the land, the new temple), so that he can properly be called the pioneer of eschatology and apocalyptic. St. John has taken over not only the vision of Yahweh's throne in his Book of Revelations, but also the vision of the battle against Gog, which he gives a new and important meaning (Rev 16, 14; 17, 12-14; 19, 17-19; 20, 7-10). According to him, Gog is the apocalyptic name of the prince of the end-time, who is destined to bring the people of God to the very brink of destruction, but who will then be destroyed himself. The prophecy is thus describing the final end-time; the words which express the prophecy, however, are taken from the concrete history of the Old Testament, just as in the Gospels the destruction of Jerusalem is described in terms which involve the destruction of the world.

II) *The New Jerusalem* (40 — 48)

Ezekiel did not have merely a general faith in the restoration of Israel; in chapters 40 — 48 he provides us with a very precise outline for the new era. These chapters have accordingly been called the Torah, that is, "the law of the prophet Ezekiel." [55] They have been compared with Plato's writing on the ideal state, or with other utopian constitutions which have never become reality. Ezekiel's outline for the future is not merely a vision that exists in the category of the ideal, simply another impossible Utopia; in an era in which the state had collapsed, the country had been lost, the temple destroyed, and the people scattered to the four winds, the prophet set about supplying his people with a constitution which could be realized as an immediate goal. Return home, rebuilding of the city and the temple, settlement of the land according to the twelve tribes, the gathering of the new Israel about its religious focus, — these are all immediate goals which could be realized in the foreseeable future. The composition of this torah is dated on the 1st of the 10th month of the 25th

---

55. P. Auvray, JerBib (1949), 144.

year of exile (April 17, 572). The entire world lay submissively at the feet of the mighty Nebuchadnezzar. Babylon had grown to be the political and religious center of the kingdom of the four ends of the world.

Babylon's growth to the position of world capital forms the background for Ezekiel's proposed constitution. Let us briefly examine some important moments from the history of Babylon's building. "In order to secure the city against hostile attack, the powerfully strengthened double wall about the inner city was further supported by a triple exterior wall at some distance from the double wall, so as to enclose large districts not yet covered with buildings. As a further precaution against attacks from the north — even Babylon feared the enemy from the north — Nebuchadnezzar built the so-called Median wall some 33 miles north of the city, a fortification extending from the Eu- phrates eastward to the Tigris and, according to the ancient records almost 100 feet high. In the city he raised temple and palace structures whose dimensions compare with the powerful palaces of the Assyrians. But there was one structure which outshadowed every building project heretofore attempted, the great central temple of Marduk, a raised temple situated upon a stepped terrace, a structure which had become world famous as the 'tower of Babel.' Smaller and somewhat less spectacular were the buildings with which Nebuchadnezzar adorned the other Babylonian cities; most of them were temples. The fact that he was able to undertake such an extensive building acti- vity, which is without parallel in ancient times, shows how quickly Babylonia had recovered her economy under his rule. Trade and economy blossomed as never before, since the king also addressed himself to the construction and maintenance of the canal system, and according to one report, even provided a huge catch basin for the spring high water level. All this made Babylon the greatest city of the contemporary Mediterranean world, while Babylonia became by far the richest country in all of western Asia." [56]

---

56. W. v. Soden, *Herrscher im Alten Orient,* (1954), 141-145.

Even the expatriate Jews began to experience the favorable effects of the Babylonian economic prosperity. They had established themselves on a more or less permanent residential basis. The loss of their home country was indeed a source of sorrow. There was always the danger that Israel would be absorbed ethnically and religiously into the foreign populace. With his grandiose constitution, the *magna carta* of the future, Ezekiel awakened the conscience of his compatriots and co-religionists, and showed them a new way to a new home. The new temple is, as it were, designed as a protest of faith against the architectural glories of the pagans.

1) THE NEW TEMPLE

"The great vision of the temple, the last of our prophet's great prophecies, is the brilliant counterpart to the vision of Gog. The story of Gog presents the peril from the nations culminating in the end-time, but here we see Zion with the temple rising high upon it as Yahweh's dwelling in the midst of a purified and holy country. What Isaiah (2, 2) and Micah (4, 1) refer to in these brief words:

'It shall come to pass in the latter days
    that the mountain of the house of the Lord
shall be established as the highest of the mountains,
    and shall be raised up above the hills'

here forms the content of nine long chapters. The other prophets speak in reverential awe, and from a distance, of this end of time. Ezekiel brings us closer. He is guided about in the sanctuary of the end-time and is concerned with making such a conscientious report of everything he sees and feels that we can actually experience what kind of vestments the priests are wearing and in what corner of the courtyard the hearth and sacrificial tables stand. The whole thing is put in the form of a vision, which has its closest parallel in the vision of chapter 8. Here too, the prophet feels borne in vision into the holy city. 'A man,' a heavenly spirit leads him twice through all the rooms of the Temple. In chapter 8 he saw Yahweh leaving his city, but here he sees him return in precisely the same way he left. Yahweh's return into his sanctuary — that is the true nucleus, the primary theme of the vision." [57]

As if he were pacing off the entire structure, Ezekiel provides accurate measures for the dimensions of the individual sections of the temple and their accompanying courtyards. The "man" who is accompanying him has a measuring reed in his hand (40, 5). They enter the sacred precinct from the outer eastern gate. The ground is accurately measured and recorded. The outer northern and southern gate was built in the same manner. Next they make their way through the outer court and enter the inner temple court through a new gate. In the midst of this court stands the altar of holocaust, built like a terraced tower.[58] They next turn to the "house of Yahweh," which was built on the western side of the inner court and consisted of the three elements familiar from the Solomonic temple, the outer court, the Holy, and the Holy of Holies. It was built upon a terrace, with ten steps leading up to it. For the other details, we must simply refer to the text of Scripture itself.[59]

On the basis of this precise description, many scholars have understood the vision of the temple as an actual building plan for the temple to be constructed by the community upon its return to the holy land. The returning Jews, however, were not in a financial position to carry out the plan. As in the case of many great building projects, the reality would simply have remained short of the original plans. It is true that, as a priest, Ezekiel was thoroughly familiar with the construction and dimensions of the Solomonic temple. In his outline of the temple structure the old memories are coming to life. But since we are here speaking of a vision, the outline presents us with a reality *sui generis*. "We have in this outline a mixture of reminiscences from the former temple and a visionary insight directed towards the future, a vision whose imaginations can be understood in terms of their architectural types, but not in their

---

57. Schmidt, *Die grossen Propheten,* 467.
58. Sketch of the holocaust altar, Vol. III, p. 338.
59. P. Auvray, *Ezechiel,* JerBib, 179.

ultimate realization in Jerusalem." [60] Ezekiel has taken the representations available to him and filled them with new meaning. His temple is a revelation of the inaccessible holiness of God. This is expressed, for example, in the steps and terraces. The outer court is reached by a series of seven steps, the inner court by eight, while ten steps lead up to the house of Yahweh. The wonder of the temple consists in the fact that Yahweh himself takes residence in the Holy of Holies and the whole city thus receives the name *"Yahweh šammah, —* God is there" (48, 35). In the very manner in which Ezekiel saw the cherubim and chariot of God disappearing towards the east, he sees him returning now through the eastern gate: "And behold, the glory of the God of Israel came from the east. And the sound of his coming was like the sound of many waters; and the earth shone with his glory.... The glory of the Lord (*$k^eb\hat{o}d$-yahweh*) entered the temple by the gate facing east" (43, 2, 4). Only by Yahweh's personal entry and residence in the temple at Jerusalem is it possible for the people of God to be gathered about this holy place as its center and sanctuary.

2) THE NEW LAW OF SACRIFICE (43, 13 — 46, 24)

The new Temple also has new cultic personnel. Jerusalem had been destroyed at an era in which the Old Testament priesthood was on the verge of a thorough-going transformation. Through the reforms of Josiah, the Levites who had been charged with overseeing the priestly services on the sacred heights dedicated from ages past to Yahweh throughout the country, had been relieved of their office and concentrated upon the one Temple at Jerusalem. Their recall to Jerusalem was equivalent to a degradation. It is true that a small percentage of the priestly revenues were still assigned to the priests of the former country sanctuaries, but the real priestly functions remained the special prerogatives of the priests from the family of Zadok. The rationale for this order of things lay in the fact that they had made themselves unclean by the cult of the high places. The deportation to

---

60. Fohrer, *Ezechiel* (HAT), 222.

Babylon had the same effects upon the priests of Zadok and Levites from the country. During the exile there must have been considerable discussion as to how the temple service should be reorganized after the restoration.

This is the *Sitz im Leben* presupposed by Ezekiel's vision; for his specifications for the new temple-torah (44, 5) are solemnly introduced by a vision, a sign of the importance attaching to these regulations.

The heavenly guide and escort brought Ezekiel from the northern gate to the front of the Temple which was filled with the glory of Yahweh. It is in the presence of God's glory that he proclaims the regulations for the priesthood. To approach God, that is, to see to the actual sacrificial services — this was the prerogative only of the sons of Zadok. Non-Israelites, who, in the first temple, were allowed to perform certain works as temple slaves, would have no access to the new Temple. Since the Levitical priests, by sharing in the syncretistic cult of the high places, had shared the guilt for the destruction of the Temple, they were indeed admitted to the new Temple, but only as priests of lesser degree; they were excluded from the sacrificial service.

Next, comes a great number of individual qualifications regarding clothing, wearing of the hair, marriage, abstention from wine during the time of service, duties towards the people, conduct in the case of death, and finally guidelines for personal property. "In all these prescriptions, Ezekiel is not so concerned with temple and cult as with the abiding presence of God who is, in the last analysis, the basis of the new salvation. That is why it is necessary for men who approach God to always be in a state of purity. For only those can approach God who are exteriorly clean and thus provide evidence of the fact that they are also pure in heart. For Ezekiel, as a typical ancient, both elements are intimately connected. External holiness is understood both to effect and to express the interior purity, and interior purity must express itself in fitting behavior." [61] Ezekiel, from his

---

61. *Ibid.*, 253.

exile, marked out the path that the priesthood of the Old Testament was destined to follow ever after.

3) THE NEW LAND (47, 13 — 48, 35)

Ezekiel describes not only the new Temple but also the new land, again with precise dimensions. The land into which the exiles are destined to return will no longer be divided into two kingdoms; it will be a single kingdom of twelve tribes. It is worth noting that Ezekiel does not hark back to the borders of the Davidic-Solomonic empire in describing his ideal. The country of Transjordania, so hotly contested in the course of history, he was willing to abandon completely. The holy land comprises only Palestine, bounded to the west by the Sea and the east by the river Jordan. The northern boundary runs from the Mediterranean across the sink between Lebanon and Hermon as far as Hauran; the southern boundary runs from the southern end of the Dead Sea to the Brook of Egypt. The assignment of territories for settlement to the individual tribes is a schematic device. From north to south, each tribe is assigned a strip of territory running from the Mediterranean to the Jordan: 1. Dan, 2. Asher, 3. Naphtali, 4. Manasseh, 5. Ephraim, 6. Reuben, 7. Judah. Next comes the special territory of the sacred precinct. Then 8. Benjamin, 9. Simeon, 10. Issachar, 11. Zebulun, 12. Gad. The specially reserved territory in the midst of the twelve tribes forms the political and religious center of the country. The middle of this territory, a square of some 25,000 cubits, forms the sacred precinct; the remainder of the territory to the right and left of the sanctuary belongs to the prince. The square itself, a symbol of perfection, is tripartite. From north to south comes first the territory of the Levites (25,000 by 10,000 cubits), the territory of the priests together wtih the temple (25,000 by 10,000 cubits), and finally the territory of the holy city (25,000 by 10,000 cubits). What thus appears to be a pedantically executed division of the land, by rod and rule, is in reality completely permeated with an invincible faith in the future of the people of God. "We need only to appreciate the time at which this prophecy is recorded: the temple at Jerusalem is in ruins, the city walls are torn down, the land is desolate and empty of inhabitants, the people are scattered among the four winds, the writer's immediate environment is broken in spirit, the prey of the foreign conqueror to whom they are subject, and he is at the very peak of his power — and nonetheless Ezekiel beholds the temple of the future, stone by stone, so precisely that he can measure it down to the least detail. He sees the country in full blossom and bloom, while the people of all the tribes return to their native home, . . . to possess it now forever: this implies a transformation in faith as well as in vision, and this is genuinely prophetic: to look, from the midst of all the woe and crisis of the world surrounding him, to the wondrous deeds of God who directs all human happenings. The new creation is his work, and it is close at hand — in a transcendent reality: but only he whose eyes God has opened to the vision can behold its glory. Only one element remains, the actual entry upon this new reality of world existence, and then it will be manifest to every man's eye." [62]

The fact that these pictures of the figure are actually meant to transcend the limits of history is, finally, abundantly clear from the account of the miraculous fountain issuing from the Temple (47, 1-12). It springs up from below the threshold of the Temple, flows through the eastern gate of the outer court, forms a small brook through the Kidron Valley, and finally becomes a mighty stream, too powerful to ford, before it empties into the Dead Sea. Since it is water from the sanctuary, coming from the throne of God himself, it transforms the wilderness into a fertile garden. Trees grow along its shore, and every month they bear fruit. Even the water of the Dead Sea becomes alive, and fishermen flock to its banks. The stream of life has overcome death.

Such a fountain and such a stream have never existed in Palestine. The Kidron Valley does form a natural water course between Jerusalem and the Dead Sea, but it drains water only during the rainy season. Otherwise it is a dried up and deserted

---

62. A. Bertholet, in Fohrer, *Ezechiel* (HAT), 260.

wadi.[63] These geographical data have been combined in Ezekiel with the description of the river of paradise, and the result is a statement of faith of unforgettable power. The dried up and deserted valley becomes a stream of paradise, issuing from the very point where God has established his dwelling. This figure, too, has been taken over by St. John in his Revelations (Rev 22, 1ff.).

Ezekiel's visions of the future are actually pursuing a goal meant to be realized in history: the return of the exiles, the reestablishment of government, the building of the temple, the reconstruction of the priesthood — but beyond all this we see a distant horizon which implies the end of history. This end is nothing other than the return of lost paradise, with God once again walking and taking his pleasure among men. The name of the city is "Yahweh, God is present." The *malkût haššamayim,* the royal rule of God, will then be perfectly realized. The vision is concentrated so directly upon God that the "prince" of the future comes in for only secondary consideration. So that he will not prey upon his people, as did the ancient kings, he has a strip of territory for his own possession (48, 21). Even in the cult he and the priests have only a subordinate role to play (46, 12). And yet, in earlier oracles, Yahweh had described the son of David who was to come as the servant of God and the shepherd established by God himself. But it is precisely in this subordination of the prince's position that the interior structure of God's rule is more and more clear. Yahweh guides his people, a nation which is to be called to new life in the storm of the spirit, and he guides this people through a Messiah king. The way of the Trinity is here anticipated: to the Father — through Christ — in the Holy Spirit. And thus the political kingship, which had failed, is transcended and a pure form of theocracy is reestablished. According to Ezekiel, the hope of the future lay not so much in the "messianic kingdom" as rather in the full realization of "God's kingdom and rule."

---

63. W. R. Farmer, *The Geography of Ezekiel's River of Life,* BA 19 (1956), 17-22.

C) THE BOOK OF EZEKIEL

"The Book of Ezekiel has been examined so frequently in the last hundred years and so many and different theories have been advanced regarding its composition, the date and place of its origin, that it is necessary to examine at least the primary contributions of this scholarship." With this statement as introduction, Eissfeldt [64] provides a thorough account and evaluation of Ezekiel scholarship over the last hundred years. It is not possible to examine all the particulars here. We must be content with looking into three points of view that function after the manner of thesis, antithesis, and synthesis.

1) EZEKIEL, COMPOSER AND RECORDER OF HIS OWN BOOK

The traditional point of view, that the Book of Ezekiel in its present form is the work of the prophet himself,[65] has been strongly argued by many scholars. Schmidt [66] describes this thesis in the following words: "We must picture Ezekiel as having spent many hours of his life concentrating on the scroll he was writing, making as precise and detailed a report as possible, forming the record of his experiences and thoughts on the subject of God and God's will into a carefully composed book.... Unlike the Book of Isaiah, it is not a succession of individual hands that have produced this work, gathering the recollected sayings of a great master. Nor do we have, as in the case of Jeremiah, one single devoted disciple, dedicated to the task of recording every least detail in the life of his hero. Here we have a prophet who has functioned as his own 'recorder,' writing his own book."

2) PROPHETIC WORD AND INTERPRETATION

This traditional thesis has been completely denied by G. Hölscher and Irwin among others.[67] Their antithesis centers about the assertion that of the 1273 verses handed down only 170 or perhaps 251 actually come from Ezekiel. Irwin distinguishes between the images and parables that are the genuine work of Ezekiel, compositions which involve only a few words, and their accompanying interpretations which, as a later elabora-

---

64. Eissfeldt, EinlAT 446ff.
65. *Ezechielem ipsum sua vaticinia litteris mandasse a nemine fere negatum aut in dubium vocatur.* – Höpfl, *Introduction,* Vol. II (1935), 350.
66. Schmidt, *Die grossen Propheten* (SAT), (1923), 472-473.
67. G. Hölscher, *Hezekiel. Der Dichter und das Buch,* (1924). – Irwin, *The Problem of Ezekiel,* (1943). – *Ibid., Ezekiel Research,* VT 3 (1953), 54-66.

tion, are clearly not the work of Ezekiel. What is more, he regards the alternate use of prose or poetry also as a measure of the genuinity of a passage, and thus regards everything as not genuine that cannot be fitted into the scheme of parallelism of members.[68] Accordingly, the gradual growth of the book would have required a rather long interval of time. Of the historical Ezekiel, determined according to the norms described above, there is little left. According to Torrey,[69] the Book of Ezekiel is pseudepigraph, that is to say that a writer from around the time 230-200 B.C. simply put his own ideas into the mouth of the ancient prophet in order to impress his contemporaries. As a result he dates the activity of Ezekiel in the reign of the rebellious King Manasseh. This violent approach to the text has not gone unchallenged. Even though the discussion cannot yet be regarded as finished, it does seem to be working towards a healthy synthesis.

3) THE PROPHET AND HIS DISCIPLES

According to the testimony of the book itself, a testimony which can hardly be doubted, some 22 years of prophetic activity are described between the 5th year of the exile (592/591) and the prophet's final appearance in the 27th year of the exile (570/569). The book, however, is obviously not a unified composition, memoirs written in the prophet's old age. The deliberately exact datings, in terms of month and date and year, all justify the conclusion that before the book appeared in its final form there were individual editions of the various chapters. These individual accounts, written on loose sheets, must be closely related to the time of the events they describe. They are certainly not the product of literary endeavors, but rather the clear precipitate of the living preaching of the word. Ezekiel's words, like those of his prophetic predecessors, are composed in rhythm. Fohrer [70] has thus attempted — not without argument [71] — to resolve the so-called prose passages into lively short verses. He claims to have uncovered a basic text made up of eight collections: 1, 1–3, 15 (vocation); 3, 16a; 4, 1–5, 17 (symbolic actions); 8, 1–11, 3 (ecstatic experiences, the vision of the temple and the judgment upon Jerusalem); 15, 1–16, 43 + 20, 1–32 (oracles on sin and judgment, the two harlots); 24, 1–24 (the delight of your eyes); 40, 1–48, 35 (Ezekiel's

---

68. Criticism in Fohrer, *Ezechiel*, IXff.
69. C. C. Torrey, *Pseudo-Ezekiel*, Yale Oriental Series, Research, Nr. 18, New Haven (1930).
70. Ezechiel, VIII: In the commentary the corresponding texts are translated into verse.
71. Critical evaluation of Fohrer's Commentary in: Zimmerli, TLZ 82 (1957), 333-340.

torah). He further distinguishes 24 briefer or longer sections which cannot be ascribed to Ezekiel.[72] What are involved are sections which "form a learned amplification of the text, reflecting and elaborating, inclined towards repetition particularly at the end of paragraphs." [73]

Fohrer thus presents the synthesis that the Book of Ezekiel is not a record of the prophet's preaching that dates only from post-Ezekiel days, but neither is it a unified work composed by the prophet himself. The prophet has recorded his words and experiences before or after his oral preaching and left them as individual records in this form. But he is not further responsible for the arrangement of these individual pieces and their eventual composition into the form of a book.[74]

Ezekiel would thus present the same literary type as Isaiah and Jeremiah. The master's literary heritage was taken over by his disciples' faithful hands, where it took on a new form and order and — since these were living words — sometimes a new reality as well. This hypothesis can at least claim to be most faithful to the literary customs of that age. The Book of Ezekiel exhibits the same fundamental outline as the Books of Isaiah and Jeremiah: a. threat oracles against Judah (Jerusalem, Israel) (1–24); b. threat oracles against the nations (25–32); c. prophecy of salvation (33–39 and 40–48).

We might raise the question as to whether Ezekiel himself was involved in the collection of his individual words recorded over the course of his prophetic activity. His torah (40–48) is actually the work of the "study," composed towards the end of his prophetic career. Here he is reckoning with the past and sketching the outline of things to come. In this stage of his career it would certainly have been possible for him to be occupied with collecting and arranging his earlier compositions.[75] But even granting this, the final form of the book must be ascribed to the community of disciples who preserved and reinterpreted its contents. If the testimony of Flavius Josephus is actually to be trusted,[76] there might have once been two collections, two "Books of Ezekiel"; the probable division would be into historical preaching (1–39) and apocalypse (40–49). The Book of Ezekiel, in its final form, would thus have passed down to us through the hand of the Old Testament "church."

Since the second temple did not at all coincide with Ezekiel's vision, some scholars have claimed that the Book must have been completed during the time of the exile. Textual criticism is here faced with a

---

72. L.c. X & XI.

73. *Ibid.*, XI.

74. *Ibid.*, XI.

75. Robert-Feuillet, IntrAT 538 takes over Fohrer's thesis, but leaves open the possibility that Ezekiel was responsible for the collection himself.

76. Ant 10, 51.

considerable problem, since the ancient Septuagint translation shows marked deviations from the Hebrew text of the Massorah. We must at all events remember that "the translation of the LXX is not to be considered as a scholarly philological piece of work; it grew out of the living piety and liturgical necessity, and is thus a sort of Targum in which the text received a new interpretation in keeping with the new language and culture, from a particular theological point of view." [77]

In the Christian canon the Book of Ezekiel stands between the Books of Jeremiah and Daniel, a fitting commentary on its position in history. Together with Jeremiah, Ezekiel belongs among the last prophets of the failing kingdom, and inexorable prophet of judgment, his vision of the future ties in with the prophet Daniel. Ezekiel is the founder of the "theocratic eschatology," [78] the forerunner of the apocalyptic. His ideas continue to work in the New Testament more than those of any other prophet, so that the Book of Revelations of St. John the Apostle can justly be called Ezekiel come back to life (*Ezechiel redivivus*).

APPENDIX

CHRONOLOGY

In the course of our discussion, we have considered individual questions at various points under the footnote title "chronology." [1] It would be well to briefly consider the fundamental problems of Biblical chronology as a whole.[2]

---

77. Fohrer, l. c. VII.
78. IntBib VI (1956), 54.

---

1. Cf. Chronology in the appendix.
2. For further information, consult the following system of constructing the history of Israel: a. Fr. X. Kugler, *Von Moses bis Paulus*, (1922). P. Heinisch, *Geschichte des AT*, (1949). — b. J. Begrich, *Die Chronologie der Könige von Israel und Judah und die Quellen des Tahmens der Königsbücher*, (1922). Taken over by M. Noth, *Geschichte Israels*, (1956³). — c. W. F. Albright, *The Chronology of the Divided Monarchy of Israel*, BASOR 100 (1945), 16-22. Taken over by J. Bright, *A History of Israel*, (1960). — d. E. R. Thiele, *The Mysterious Numbers of the Hebrew Kings*, (1951). Taken over by W. H. Hallo, *From Quarqar to Carchemish, Assyria and Israel in the Light of New Discoveries*, BA 23 (1960), 34-61. Albright's *Chronology* in S. Mowinckel, *Die israelitisch-judische Königschronologie*, NTT 56 (19-

1) *The State of the Problem*

St. Jerome [3] considers any involvement with chronology as the problem of a man who has more time for leisure than for study, *"non tam studiosi quam otiosi hominis."* According to R. de Vaux, chronology is a problem without a solution.[4] It is no wonder that Albright [5] is willing to adjust the data of chronology to fit the needs of individual hypotheses. Opposed to this skepticism, I share with Thiele a basic confidence in the Biblical tradition of numbers. What we have here is not a "Tohuwabohu," but a clearly ordered and faithfully transmitted system of numbers. In my opinion, only the numbers from the days of King Ahaz are corrupt, and even they can be set right by the simple expedient of correcting to tens — a system already described in detail — all the other dates are unassailable.

2) *Synchronisms*

The synchronisms between the kings of Israel and the kings of Judah for the time between the split of the kingdom and the destruction of Samaria form one positive foundation of chronology. The kings of Israel are always introduced with the formula: "In year x of King N.N. of Judah, N.N. became King of Israel." On the other hand, for the kings

---

55), 279-295. He accuses Thiele of juggling with the numbers. But I would be inclined to share Thiele's trust in the fundamental accuracy of the Biblical numbers. Thus my own figures generally overlap with his. e. The Hebrew *EncMikr* takes up the relevant chronological problems in the treatment of each king's reign. The solution varies with the individual author. In the article *'eres yisrael* (I, 667-741) there is a compendium of the history of Israel, done by Mazar, who goes his own way in the chronology. In dating the kings down to Jeroboam II he partially agrees with R. de Vaux in the Jerusalem Bible. f. Among the available chronologies, my own independent system agrees with that of de Vaux in the Israelite lists as far as the time of Jeroboam II. In the corresponding lists for Judah there are some differences of opinion. A thorough justification of my views is to be found in VT 12 (1962), 88-119, "Textkritische Bemerkungen zu den Synchronismen der Könige von Israel und Judah."

---

3. Ad Vitalem, epistola 72, 5. Migne, PL 22, 676.
4. *Les Institutions de l'AT*, I (1958), 295.
5. E. R. Thiele, *A Comparison of the Chronological Data of Israel and Judah*, VT 4 (1954), 187, has shown how many "adjustments" are required to bring the numbers advanced by Albright into harmony with the Biblical evidence. E.g., Rehoboam must rule 8 instead of 17 years, Omri 8 instead of 12, Ahab 20 instead of 22. This is not sober textual criticism, but the work of dubious intuition.

of Judah the formula is somewhat more explicit: "In the year x of the King N.N. of Israel, N.N. became king in Judah. He was x years old when he became king (*bᵉmolkô*) and he reigned x years as king." What appeared to be perfectly clear statements are, unfortunately, not quite so clear as we might hope; there is never any explicit mention of the system according to which the king's years are reckoned. In one system it is possible to count the year in which the throne changed hands as two years, the final year of the dead king and the first year of the succeeding king. In another system it is possible to count it only once, since the first year of the new ruler is reckoned only after the death of his predecessor. That the same system was not applied in the kingdom of Israel and in the kingdom of Judah is evident from the fact that, on the occasion of a new king's accession to power, there are differences in the official count which we arrive at by adding the recorded years of reign (cf. tables). The Israel list, for example, registers a plus of eight years, for eight changes in power, as opposed to the same interval of time for the kingdom of Judah; this is to say that in Israel it was customary to count the year in which the throne changed hands as two years, the last for the dying king and the first year for his successor. In Judah, on the other hand, it had always been customary to count this as only one year. This is evident, in my opinion, from the pedantically precise dating of the kings of Judah, which always inform us of the king's age at the time of his accession to power. This "year of accession," (Accadian: *rêš šarruti;* Hebrew: *rēš'it mamleket bᵉmolkô*) of a new king comprised the months from the death of the old king to the first new year festival (in our table this is marked by a zero). Only from the new year is the first year of N.N. officially counted. Thus the lists for the kings of Judah avoid the double counting of the year of accession to power. In Judah, accordingly, the system of reckoning in terms of a "year of accession" was not first taken over under Assyrian or Babylonian influence; it was in use from the beginning, as we can clearly see from the *bᵉmolokô* clause. It was under Babylonian or perhaps already Assyrian influence that the new year festival was transferred from autumn to spring but this transposition has exerted little influence on the lists. But since Jeroboam, after splitting the kingdom, made a deliberate attempt to organize Israel along different lines than Judah, he also introduced the Egyptian manner of dating — he had been in Egypt as an exile. If these facts are kept in mind, the synchronisms present no real difficulty.

3) *Coregents*

The existence of coregents is beyond argument. The most recent investigation of this office is the work of E. R. Thiele.[6] Coregencies cannot,

---

6. *The Question of Coregencies among the Hebrew Kings,* Papers, W. A. Irwin, Dallas (1956).

however, simply be postulated in an effort to explain difficult chronologies. Their existence is either directly attested (2 K 15, 5) or it is indirectly evident from the historical consideration and the overlapping of the dates. In my opinion, there were only four coregencies, one in Israel (Jeroboam II) and three in Judah, Jehoram, Uzziah, and Jotham. The individual cases have already been considered in the text.[7] Since the years of coregency as well as the years of sole rule are all reckoned together in the total number of a king's regnal years, the years of the coregency are given twice — both for the retiring king who now goes into private life as well as for the regent who actually has power. As a result, the final figures for the regnal years from the split kingdom to the destruction of Samaria exhibit a surprising discrepancy: 241 in Israel and 260 in Judah, although in reality there are only 209 years. The riddle is easily solved by recalling the fact that Israel counted the year of accession to the throne twice and also counted the years of coregency twice.

4) Extra-Biblical Synchronisms

The extra-Biblical texts of historical import provide a further support for Biblical chronology.[8] Among these we must enumerate primarily the Babylonian chronicle already described. It was with the help of this chronicle that we have succeeded in interpreting the system of reckoning so frequent primarily in the Book of Ezekiel: "In the X year after the exile," or "in the X year after the deportation of King Jehoiachin." [9] The year of deportation itself is not counted as the first year, but rather as the "beginning of the captivity." The same thing is true for the reckoning of years "after the destruction of Jerusalem" (cf. table). It might well be that further discoveries will add greater depth to our knowledge — and in many points this would be most desirable — but quite apart from this prospect the Biblical numbers must be seen to stand on a firm foundation. They are, in their way, an eloquent witness to the fidelity of the tradition. The way they mesh and overlap is not the result of some later historian's scholarly preoccupation, but the genuine precipitate of the actual confusion of history itself.

---

7. Cf. above, pp. 96 n. 16, 140 n. 21, 149 n. 36.
8. Cf. the synchronisms already treated in the footnotes: Battle of Qarqar (81 n. 99); Jehu's coup (109), Uzziah, Menahem, and Tiglath-Pilesar (194), Ahaz and Tiglath-Pilesar (207), Hosea and Salmanassar (234), Hezekiah, Sargon, and Sanherib (249ff.), Nebuchadnezzar and Zedekiah (358).
9. Cf. my article "Nochmals das Jahr der Zerstörung Jerusalem, 587 oder 586 v. Chr," ZAW 74 (1962), 209-213.

INDEX

REGNAL DATES OF THE KINGS

ISRAEL			JUDAH
Jeroboam I	931/30 — 910	931/30 — 914	Rehoboam
Nadab	910 — 909	914/13 — 912	Abijah
Bassha	909/08 — 886	912/11 — 871	Asa
Eiah	886 — 885		
Zimri	885		
Tibni	885 — 880	870 — 845	Jehoshaphat
Omri	885/84 — 874	845/44 — 841	
Ahab	874/73 — 853	CR	Jeohram (Joram)
Ahaziah	853 — 852	849/48 — 845	
Jehoram (joram)	852/51 — 841	841	Ahaziah
Jehu	841/40 — 814	841/840 — 836	Athaliah
Jehoahaz	814/13 — 798	836/35 — 797	Joash
Joash	798/97 — 783	797/96 — 768	Amaziah
Jeroboam II	782 — 754	768/67 — 740	
	CR·	CR	Uzziah (Azariah)
	794 — 783	792/91 — 768	
Zechariah	754		
Shallum	753	740/39 — 735	Jotham
Menahem	753/52 — 743	CR	
Pekahiah	742 — 741	751/50 — 740	
Pekah	740 — 731	735/34 — 722	Ahaz
Hoshea	730 — 722	738-699	Hezekiah
		698 — 643	Manasseh
		642 — 641	Amon
		640 — 609	Josiah
		609	Jehoahaz (3 mos.)
CR = coregency		609/08 — 597	Jehoiakim
When two dates are given, the first		597	Jehoiachin (3 mos.)
is the date of accession.		597/96 — 586	Zedekiah

GEOGRAPHY OF
THE OLD TESTAMENT

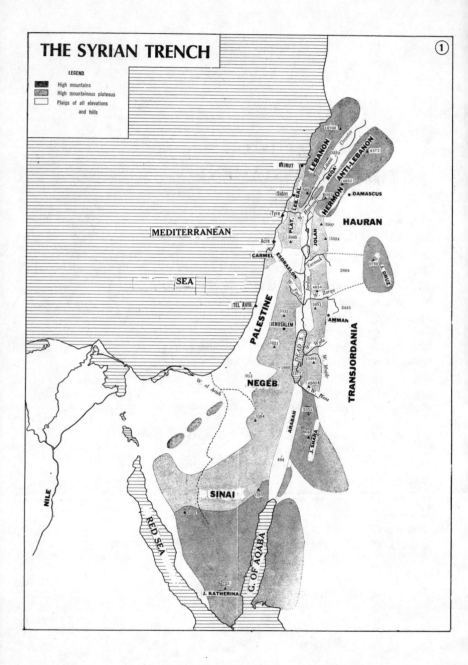

THE SYRIAN TRENCH

①

LEGEND
High mountains
High mountainous plateaus
Plains of all elevations
and hills

LEBANON
ANTI-LEBANON
10700
3239
8572
BEQA
HERMON
4092
BEIRUT
Litani
Orontes
Sidon
LEB. GAL.
5593
N. Ibrahim
3395
DAMASCUS
Tyre
4092
HAURAN
PLAT.
JOLAN
3907
MEDITERRANEAN
3960
3024
Acre
CARMEL
ESDRAELON
Yarmuk
2604
5750
J. DRUZ
SEA
W. Fara
Jordan
4054
TEL AVIV
3333
3651
2443
PALESTINE
JERUSALEM
AMMAN
3221
DEAD S.
W. Wala
TRANSJORDANIA
1660
3464
W. Mujib
913
1317
NEGEB
W. el Arish
4860
W. Hasa
3353
ARABAH
3364
6045
494
J. SHARA
SINAI
3183
NILE
3505
RED SEA
G. OF AQABA
8733
J. KATHERINA

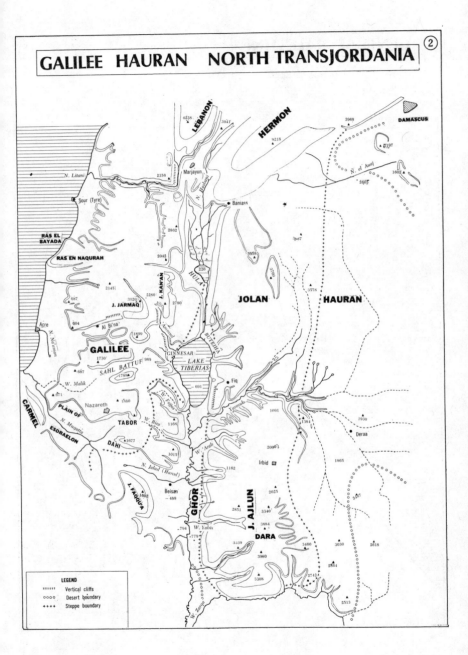

GALILEE HAURAN NORTH TRANSJORDANIA

②

LEGEND

|||||||| Vertical cliffs
ooooo Desert boundary
++++ Steppe boundary

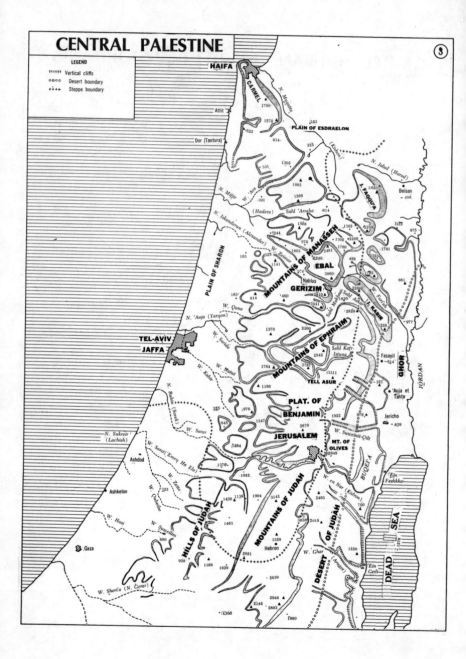

CENTRAL PALESTINE

③

LEGEND
- ⫿⫿⫿⫿ Vertical cliffs
- ∘∘∘∘ Desert boundary
- +∔+∔ Steppe boundary

HAIFA

CARMEL

N. Muqatta

Atlit

1780
1570
822

Dor (Tantura)

PLAIN OF ESDRAELON

163

834
325

(Kishon)

N. Jalud (Harod)

331
1302

1685
1268

Beisan
-488

J. FAQUA
1620

N. Mifjir *W. 'Ara*

391

1622

(Hadera)   *Sahl 'Arraba*   814

J.
N. Iskanderun (Alexander)

1568
1244
976
1603

2208
1302
1760

1302
2350

1791

163
W. Zeimar
325
141

2481
2240

488
2323

975

MOUNTAINS OF MANASSEH

EBAL
3060

J. KABIR

661

Nablus
Sahl Makhna
W. Fareh

163
814

GERIZIM
480
2910
2941

2284
1620

1238

977

W. Qana

N. 'Auja (Yarqon)

Sahl Askar

2820

W. Fareh

1370
2300

W. Sarida

TEL-AVIV
JAFFA

Sahl Kafr Istuna

2542

Fasayil
814

GHOR

JORDAN

W. Matul
W. Kobir

1784
2757
3311

1188

MOUNTAINS OF EPHRAIM

TELL ASUR

357

'Auja et
Tahta

N. Rubin (Sorek)

325
976

PLAT. OF
BENJAMIN

1922
979

Jericho
-839

N. Sukreir
(Lachish)

845
1247

2879

W. Suweinit-Qilt

JERUSALEM

1284

W. Samit ('Emeq Ha Ela)

MT. OF
OLIVES
2649

Ashdod
1370

BUQEI'A

1922

W. Zeita

Ashkelon
325

1904
3143

W. Qubeiba

W. en Nar (Kidron)

2463

'Ein
Fashkka

1430
1136

W. Hasi

W. Suweilim

1463

680

HILLS OF JUDAH

MOUNTAINS OF JUDAH

3085
2019

760

Gaza

920
1389
1629

2921

3329
Hebron

W. Ghar

1220

'Ein
Gedi

DEAD

SEA

-1270

W. Sheri'a (N. Gerar)

2639

DESERT OF JUDAH

Areuvi

2948
2142
2803

1300

980

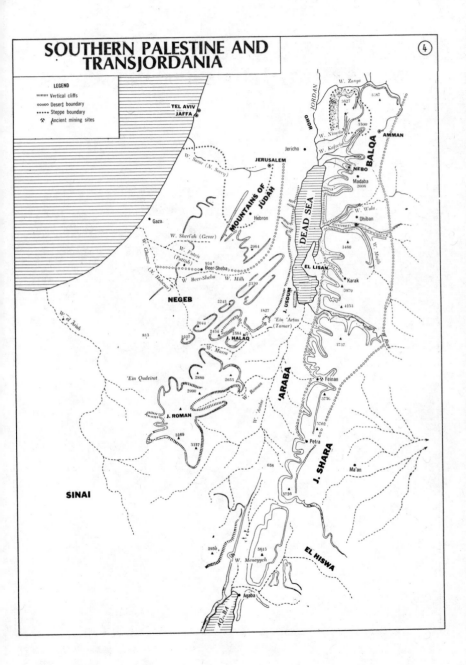

SOUTHERN PALESTINE AND TRANSJORDANIA

④

LEGEND
""""" Vertical cliffs
ooooo Desert boundary
••••• Steppe boundary
⚒ Ancient mining sites

TEL AVIV
JAFFA

JORDAN

GHOR

W. Zarqa

3027

3387

W. Nimrin

3500

AMMAN

Jericho

W. Kafrein

BALQA

JERUSALEM

NEBO

Madaba
2608

Gaza

W. Sheri'ah (Gerar)

MOUNTAINS OF JUDAH

Hebron

DEAD SEA

W. Wala

Dhiban

W. Futeis
(Pattish)

W. Churar
(N. Habeson)

934

2964

W. Beer-Sheba

Beer-Sheba

W. Milh

2330

EL LISAN

3460

W. Mujib

Karak

3979

NEGEB

2243

4233

W. el 'Arish

813

2044

2227

2434

1584

J. HALAQ

1827

'Ein 'Artus
(Tamur)

J. USDUM

3737

W. Murra

'ARABA

'Ein Qudeirat

2880

2653

Feinan

2990

W. Roman

3736

J. ROMAN

3269

5762

3337

Petra

J. SHARA

638

Ma'an

SINAI

3736

2950

5613

EL HISWA

W. Meneyyeh

Aqaba

RED SEA

ROADS BETWEEN BEER SHEBA AND SHECHEM

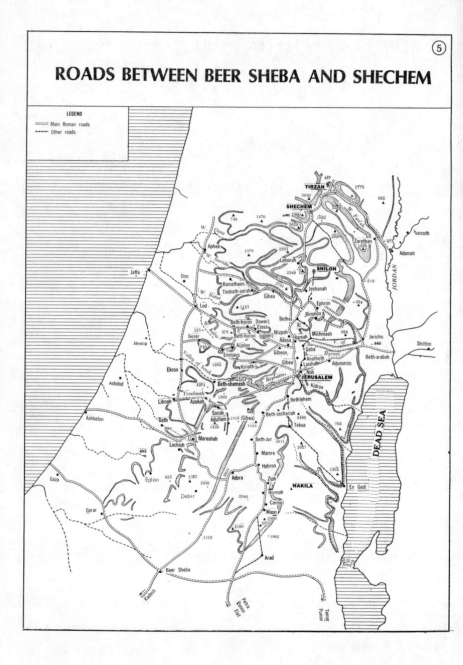

LEGEND
===== Main Roman roads
+++++ Other roads

TIRZAH
SHECHEM
SHILOH
Succoth
Adamah
Zarethan
Jaffa
Aphek
Ono
Lebonah
Jeshanah
Ephron
Ramathaim
Timhath-serah
Gibea
Rimmon
Lod
Bethel
Ai
Beth-horon (lower)
Elasa
Mizpah
Michmash
Jericho
Gezer
Beth-horon (upper)
Adasa
Ramah
Shittim
Aijalon
Geba
Emmaus
Gibeon
Anathoth
Beth-arabah
Ekron
Kiriath-j.
Gibea
Laishah
Adummim
Ashdod
Beth-shemesh
Rephaim
JERUSALEM
Libnah
Azekah
Terebinth
Kidron
Bethlehem
Ashkelon
Gath
Socoh
Adullam
Geb
Beth-zechariah
Gibea
Mareshah
Tekoa
Lachish
Beth-zur
Gaza
Eglon
Mamre
Debir
Adora
Hebron
Ziph
Gerar
Hormah
HAKILA
En Gedi
Carmel
Maon
Arad
Beer Sheba
Kadesh
Petra Punon East
Tamar Punon

DEAD SEA
JORDAN
W. Fer'ah
Valley of Sorek
Valley of Elah

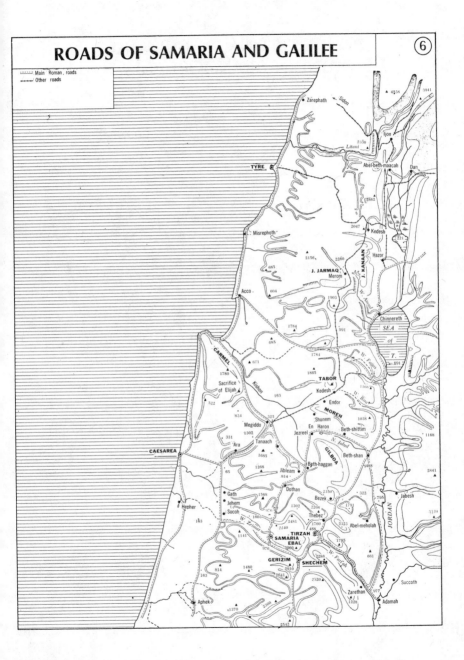

ROADS OF SAMARIA AND GALILEE

⑥

Main Roman, roads
Other roads

Zarephath
Sidon
4238
3941

2350
Litani
Ijon

TYRE

Abel-beth-maacah
Dan

2562

2047
Kedesh
221

Misrephoth

2156
3260
Hazor

685
J. JARMAQ
Merom

Acco
604
1903

1784
991

SEA
685
of

CARMEL
671
1784
T.
691

1780
1865
W. Fejjas

Sacrifice
of Elijah
Kishon
TABOR
1168

522
163
Kedesh

834
Endor
MOREH

Megiddo
323
Shunem
1038

1302
En Haron
Beth-shittim

331
Jezreel
1168

'Ara
Tanaach
N. Jalud

1683
GILBOA

CAESAREA
1268
Beth-haggan
Beth-shan

65
Jibleam
1488
2841

814
Dothan

Gath
1568
Bezek
2350
323
795
Jabesh

Hepher
Jehem
179
3320

Socoh
976
1302
3208
Thebez

183
W. Zeimar
2481
1760
3323
Abel-meholah

2240
488

1141
TIRZAH
1795
661

SAMARIA
1060
EBAL
W. Farah

976
3286

GERIZIM
1480
2910
SHECHEM

163
814
2641
2320

Aphek
1370
2200
Zarethan
975
Succoth

1328
Adamah

2543

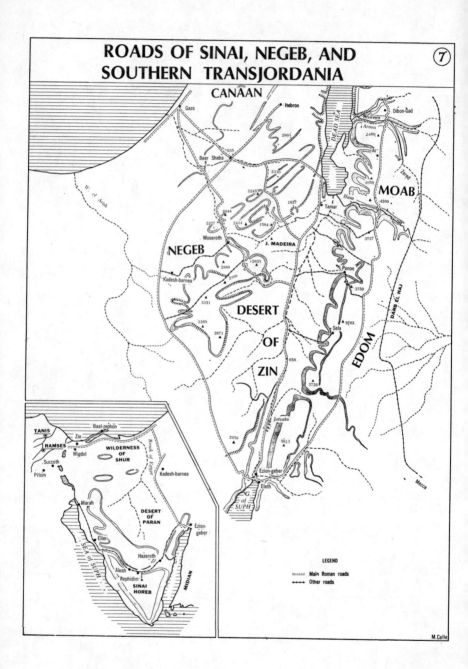

ROADS OF SINAI, NEGEB, AND SOUTHERN TRANSJORDANIA

⑦

CANAAN

Gaza • Hebron

2803

935

Beer Sheba

2310

2247

3044

1827

2227 2434 1384

Moseroth

J. MADEIRA

NEGEB

2880 2655

Kadesh-barnea 3590

3351

DESERT

3269

2871 OF

ZIN

658

3726

DEAD SEA

Dibon-Gad

Arnon 3460

4058 4260

MOAB

Hasa

Tamar

3737

Punon

3750

3762

Sela EDOM

DARB EL HAJ

Jotbata

2950 5013

Ezion-geber

Elath

G. of SUPH

Mecca

TANIS Baal-zephon

Zin

RAMSES Migdol WILDERNESS OF SHUR

Succoth

Pitom Kadesh-barnea

Marah DESERT OF PARAN

Elim Ezion-geber

Hazeroth

Alush MIDIAN

Rephidim

SINAI HOREB

SEA OF SUPH

W. el Arish

Brook of Egypt

LEGEND

═══ Main Roman roads

+++ Other roads

M.Celle

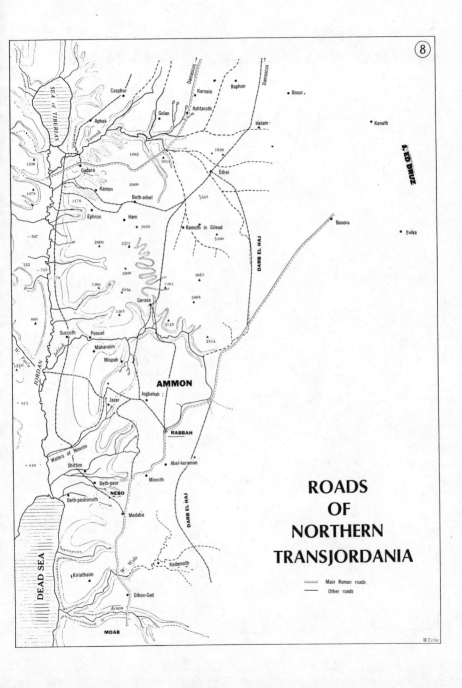

ROADS
OF
NORTHERN
TRANSJORDANIA

‑‑‑‑‑ Main Roman roads
——— Other roads

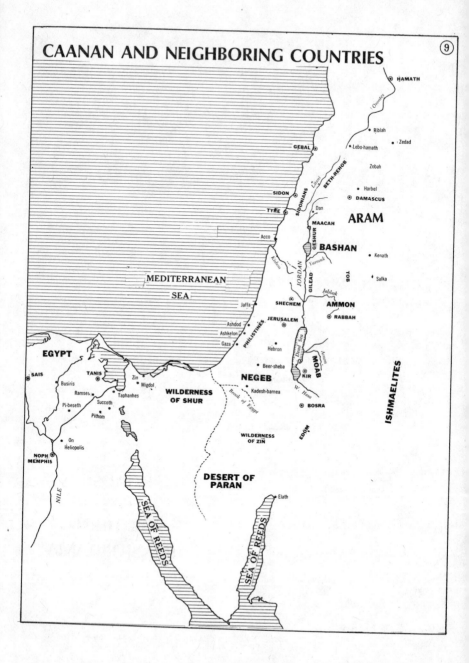

CAANAN AND NEIGHBORING COUNTRIES

⑨

HAMATH

Riblah • Zedad

GEBAL • Lebo-hamath

Zobah

• Harbel

SIDON ◎ DAMASCUS

TYRE Dan

MAACAH **ARAM**

Acco GESHUR **BASHAN** • Kenath

TOB • Salka

MEDITERRANEAN SHECHEM GILEAD **AMMON**

SEA Jaffa JERUSALEM ◎ RABBAH

Ashdod **PHILISTINES**

Ashkelon Hebron

Gaza •

EGYPT Beer-sheba KIR **MOAB**

SAIS **NEGEB**

Busiris Zin Kadesh-barnea **ISHMAELITES**

TANIS Migdol **WILDERNESS** ◎ BOSRA

Ramses Taphanhes **OF SHUR**

Pi-beseth Succoth **EDOM**

Pithom **WILDERNESS**

OF ZIN

On

Heliopolis

NOPH

MEMPHIS **DESERT OF**

PARAN

NILE • Elath

SEA OF REEDS

SEA OF REEDS

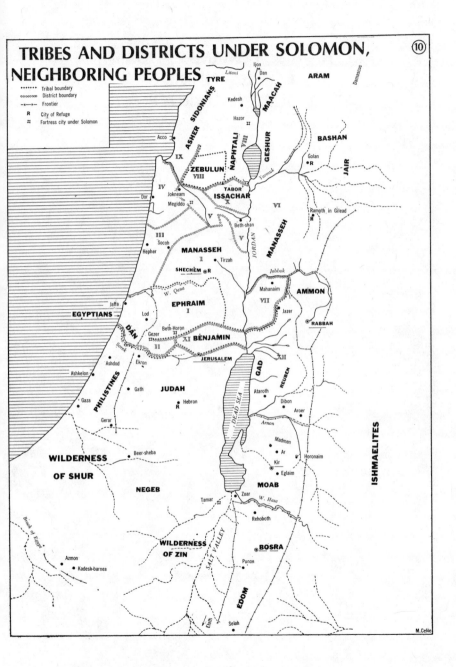

TRIBES AND DISTRICTS UNDER SOLOMON, NEIGHBORING PEOPLES

⑩

Tribal boundary
District boundary
Frontier

R City of Refuge
⊓ Fortress city under Solomon

ARAM

Damascus

TYRE
Litani
Ijon
Dan

SIDONIANS
Kedesh
Hazor
MAACAH

Acco
ASHER
IX
NAPHTALI
VIII
GESHUR
BASHAN
Golan
R
JAIR

ZEBULUN
VIII
Yarmuk

IV
Jokneam
Megiddo
TABOR
ISSACHAR
X
VI

Dor
V
Beth-shan
V
Ramoth in Gilead
R

III
Socoh
Hepher
MANASSEH
I
Tirzah
MANASSEH

SHECHEM
R
Jabbok
Mahanaim
AMMON

Jaffa
W. Qana
EPHRAIM
I
VII
Jazer

EGYPTIANS
Lod
Beth-Horon
RABBAH

DAN
Gezer
XI
BENJAMIN
Sorek
II
JERUSALEM
GAD
XII

Ashkelon
Ashdod
Ekron
REUBEN

Gath
JUDAH
Ataroth
Dibon

Gaza
Hebron
R
Aroer

PHILISTINES
Gerar
DEAD SEA
Arnon

Madmen
Ar
Horonaim

Beer-sheba
Kir
Eglaim

WILDERNESS
OF SHUR
NEGEB
MOAB
Tamar
Zoar
W. Hasa

ISHMAELITES

Rehoboth

Brook of Egypt
WILDERNESS
OF ZIN
BOSRA

Azmon
Kadesh-barnea
Punon

SALT VALLEY

EDOM
Edith
Selah

M.CeHe

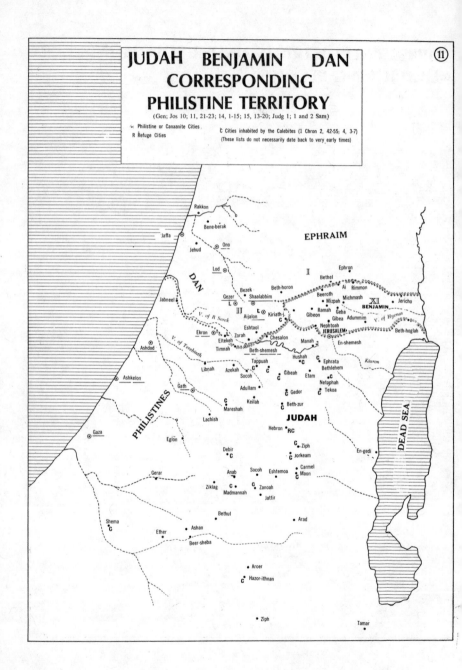

JUDAH   BENJAMIN   DAN
CORRESPONDING
PHILISTINE TERRITORY

(Gen; Jos 10; 11, 21-23; 14, 1-15; 15, 13-20; Judg 1; 1 and 2 Sam)

⊙ Philistine or Canaanite Cities
R Refuge Cities

C Cities inhabited by the Calebites (1 Chron 2, 42-55; 4, 3-7)
(These lists do not necessarily date back to very early times)

⑪

EPHRAIM

Rakkon

Bene-berak

Jaffa

Jehud

Ono

Lod

Ephron

Bethel

Ai Rimmon

II

Bezek Beth-horon

Beeroth

Gezer Shaalabbim

Mizpah Michmash

Jericho

Jabneel

Ramah Geba

XII
BENJAMIN

V. of R Sorek

Aijalon Kiriath

Gibeon Gibea Adummim

V. of Hyena

III

Eshtaol

Nephtoah

Ekron Zorah Chesalon

JERUSALEM

Beth-hoglah

DAN

Eltekeh

Ashdod

Timnah Beth-shemesh

Manah

En-shemesh

V. of Terebinth

Hushah

Kidron

Tappuah

Ephrata
Bethlehem

Ashkelon

Libnah Azekah

Gibeah Etam

Socoh

Netophah

Gath

Adullam

Gedor Tekoa

PHILISTINES

Keilah

Beth-zur

Mareshah

JUDAH

DEAD SEA

Lachish

Hebron RC

Gaza

Eglon

Ziph

Debir

Jorkeam

En-gedi

Gerar

Anab Socoh Eshtemoa Carmel

Ziklag Zanoah Maon

Madmannah

Jattir

Bethul

Arad

Shema

Ether Ashan

Beer-sheba

Aroer

Hazor-ithnan

Ziph

Tamar

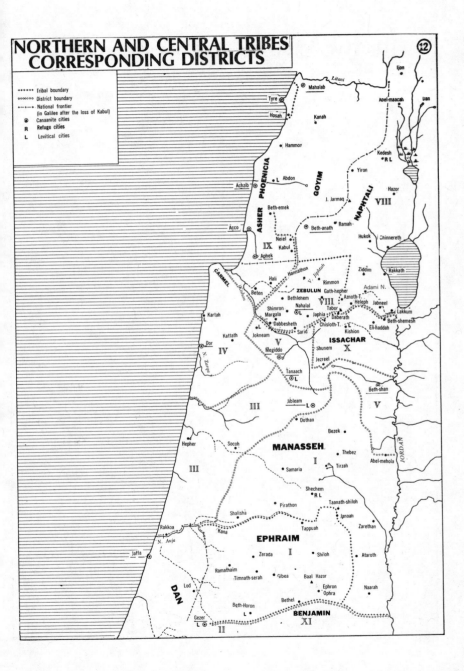

NORTHERN AND CENTRAL TRIBES CORRESPONDING DISTRICTS

42

Tribal boundary
District boundary
National frontier
(in Galilee after the loss of Kabul)
Ⓐ Canaanite cities
R Refuge cities
L Levitical cities

Litani
Ijon
Mahalab
Tyre
Abel-maacah
Dan
Hosah
Kanah
Hammon
Kedesh R L
Abdon
Achzib
GOYIM
Yiron
PHOENICIA
J. Jarmaq
Hazor
Beth-emek
NAPHTALI
ASHER
VIII
Acco
Ⓐ Beth-anath
Ramah
Hukok
Chinnereth
Neiel
IX
Kabul
Aphek
Ziddim
Rakkath
Hali
Hannathon
V. Jiphtah
Rimmon
Adami N.
CARMEL
Beten
ZEBULUN
Gath-hepher
Aznoth-T.
Bethlehem
VIII
Heleph
Jabneel
Shimron
Nahalal
Tabor
Lakkum
Kartah
Margala
Japhia
Daberath
Beth-shemesh
L
Dabbesheth
Chisloth-T.
En-haddah
Jokneam
Sarid
Kishion
Kattath
V
ISSACHAR
Dor
Megiddo
X
IV
Shunem
N. Zarqa
Jezreel
Tanaach
Beth-shan
L
V
III
Jibleam L
Dothan
Bezek
Hepher
Socoh
Thebez
MANASSEH
I
Tirzah
Abel-mehola
III
Samaria
Shechem
R L
Taanath-shiloh
Pirathon
Janoah
Shalisha
Tappuah
Zarethan
Rakkon
Kana
EPHRAIM
N. Auja
Zerada
I
Shiloh
Ataroth
Jaffa
Ramathaim
Lod
DAN
Timnath-serah
Gibea
Baal Hazor
Ephron
Naarah
Ophra
Bethel
Beth-Horon
L
Gezer
BENJAMIN
L
XI
II

JORDAN

THE TWO DIVISIONS OF TRANSJORDANIA

⑬

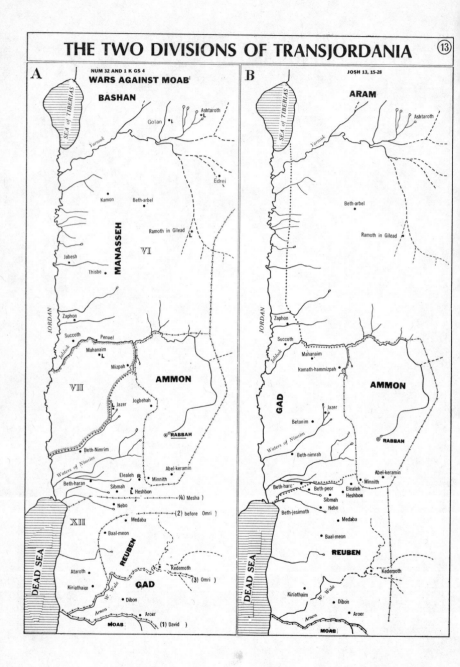

A

NUM 32 AND 1 K GS 4
WARS AGAINST MOAB

BASHAN

SEA of TIBERIAS

Golan • L • Ashtaroth L

Yarmuk

Edrei

Kamon • Beth-arbel •

MANASSEH

VII

Ramoth in Gilead • L

Jabesh •

Thisbe •

JORDAN

Zaphon •

Succoth • Penuel •

Mahanaim • L

Mizpah •

VIII • AMMON

L Jazer • Jogbehah •

◎ RABBAH

• Beth-Nimrim

Waters of Nimrim

Beth-haran • Elealeh • R • Minnith • Abel-keramin

Sibmah • L Heshbon

——————— (4) Mesha)

• Nebo

——·——·—— (2) before Omri)

XIII • Medaba •

• Baal-meon

DEAD SEA

REUBEN

Ataroth • • Kedemoth

Kiriathaim • GAD ———— (3) Omri)

W. Wala

• Dibon

Arnon • Aroer

MOAB ———— (1) David)

B

JOSH 13, 15-28

ARAM

SEA of TIBERIAS

• Ashtaroth

Yarmuk

Beth-arbel •

Ramoth in Gilead •

JORDAN

Zaphon •

Jabbok

Succoth •

Mahanaim •

Kamath-hammizpah •

GAD • AMMON

Jazer •

Betonim •

◎ RABBAH

Waters of Nimrim

• Beth-nimrah

Abel-keramin •

Beth-hare • Beth-peor • Elealeh • Minnith

Heshbon

Sibmah •

• Nebo

Beth-jesimoth •

Medaba •

• Baal-meon

DEAD SEA

REUBEN

• Kedemoth

Kiriathaim •

• Dibon

Arnon • Aroer

MOAB

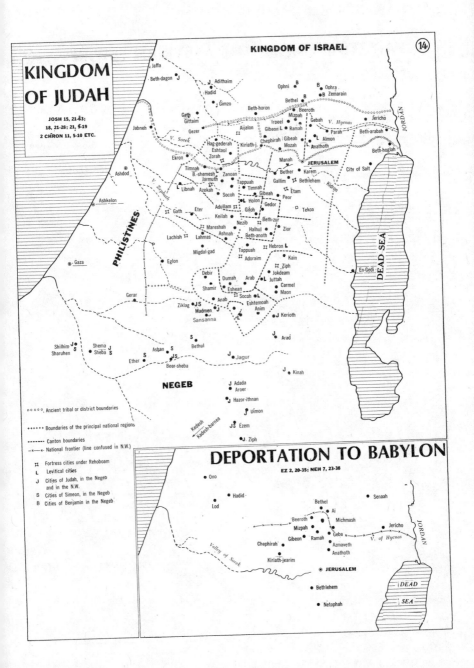

KINGDOM OF ISRAEL

KINGDOM
OF JUDAH

JOSH 15, 21-63;
18, 21-28; 21, 9-19
2 CHRON 11, 5-10 ETC.

Jaffa
Beth-dagon
J. Adithaim
Hadid
J. Gimzo
Ophni   B
Bethel   B   Ophra
B   Zemarain
Beth-horon   Beeroth
Mizpah   Gibeah
Gath   Irpeel   Gebah   V. Hyenas   Jericho
Gittaim   Aijalon   Gibeon   Ramah
Jabneh   Gezer   Chephirah Gibeah   Parah   Beth-arabah
V. Sorek   Hag-gederah   Kiriath-j.   Mozah   Anathoth
Ekron   Eshtaol   Manah   Beth-hoglah
Ashdod   Zorah   JERUSALEM
Timnah   Bether   Karem   City of Salt
B.-shemesh Zanoah   Bethlehem
Ashkelon   Tappuah   Gallim   Kidron
V. Zephiah Libnah Azekah   Timnah
Gath   Eter   Socoh   Gibeah   Etam
Adullam   Holon   Gedor   Peor
Keilah   Giloh   Tekoa
Gaza   Nezib   Beth-zur
Mareshah   Halhul   Zior
Lachish   Ashnah   Beth-anoth
Lahmas   Hebron
Eglon   Migdal-gad   Tappuah   Kain
Adoraim   En-Gedi
Debir   Ziph
Dumah   Arab   Jokdeam
Gerar   Shamir   Eshean   Juttah
Anab   Socoh   Carmel
Ziklag   JS   Eshtemoah Maon
Madmen   Anim
Sansanna   J. Kerioth
J. Arad
Shilhim J   Shema   Bethul
Sharuhen   S   Sheba   S   Ashan   S
Ether   S   JS   Jagur
Beer-sheba
J. Kinah
NEGEB   J. Adada
Aroer
J. Hazor-ithnan
J. Dimon
Kedesh   JS. Ezem
Kadesh-barnea   J. Ziph

○○○○○ Ancient tribal or district boundaries
++++++ Boundaries of the principal national regions
------- Canton boundaries
—x—x— National frontier (line confused in N.W.)

⊄ Fortress cities under Rehoboam
L Levitical cities
J Cities of Judah, in the Negeb
  and in the N.W.
S Cities of Simeon, in the Negeb
B Cities of Benjamin in the Negeb

DEPORTATION TO BABYLON

EZ 2, 20-35; NEH 7, 23-38

Ono
Hadid   Senaah
Lod   Bethel
Beeroth   Ai
Mizpah   Michmash
Geba   Jericho
Chephirah Gibeon Ramah   V. of Hyenas
Azmaveth
Kiriath-jearim Anathoth
JERUSALEM
Bethlehem
Netophah

JORDAN

DEAD SEA

Valley of Sorek

PALESTINE UNDER THE ASSYRIAN EMPIRE

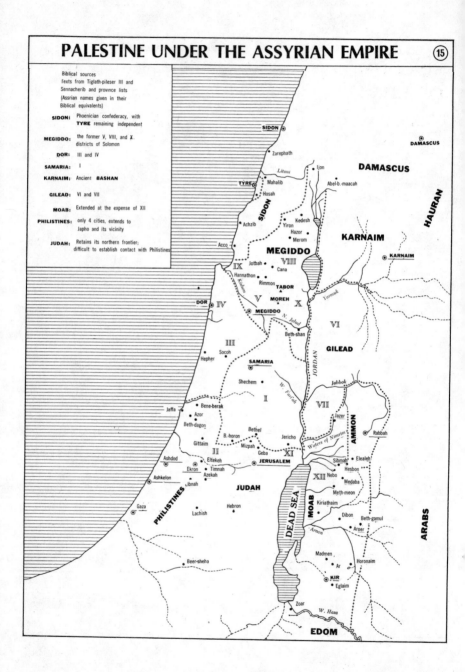

Biblical sources
Texts from Tiglath-pileser III and
Sennacherib and province lists
(Assrian names given in their
Biblical equivalents)

SIDON: Phoenician confederacy, with
TYRE remaining independent

MEGIDDO: the former V, VIII, and X.
districts of Solomon

DOR: III and IV

SAMARIA: I

KARNAIM: Ancient **BASHAN**

GILEAD: VI and VII

MOAB: Extended at the expense of XII

PHILISTINES: only 4 cities, extends to
Japho and its vicinity

JUDAH: Retains its northern frontier;
difficult to establish contact with Philistines

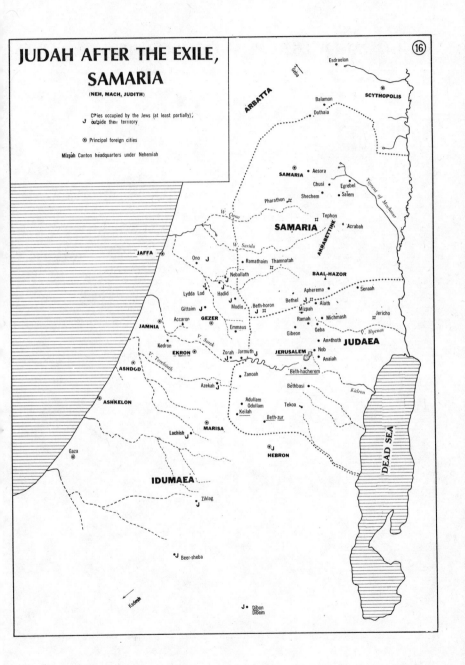

JUDAH AFTER THE EXILE, SAMARIA

(NEH, MACH, JUDITH)

Cities occupied by the Jews (at least partially),
J outside their territory

⊙ Principal foreign cities

Mizpah Canton headquarters under Nehemiah

⑯

Esdraelon

Geba

ARBATTA

SCYTHOPOLIS ⊙

Balamon

Dothaia

Torrent of Mochmur

SAMARIA ⊙ Aesora

Chusi Egrebel

Shechem Salem

Pharathon

Tephon

SAMARIA

AKRABETTINE Acrabah

W. Qana

W. Sarida

JAFFA ⊙

Ono J

Ramathaim Thamnatah

Neballath

BAAL-HAZOR

Apherema Senaah

Lydda Lod Hadid J Bethel Alath

Gittaim J Modin Mizpah Jericho

J Beth-horon Michmash

Accaron GEZER ⊙ Ramah Anathoth

JAMNIA ⊙ Emmaus Geba V. Hyenas

Kedron Gibeon JUDAEA

V. Sorek Nob

EKRON ⊙ Zorah Jarmuth JERUSALEM Anaiah

ASHDOD ⊙ V. Terebinth Zanoah Beth-hacherem

Azekah J Bethbasi Kidron

Adullam Tekoa

ASHKELON ⊙ Odollam

Keilah Beth-zur

Lachish J MARISA ⊙

Gaza ⊙ HEBRON ⊙

IDUMAEA

Ziklag
J

DEAD SEA

J Beer-sheba

Kadesh

J Dibon
Dibom

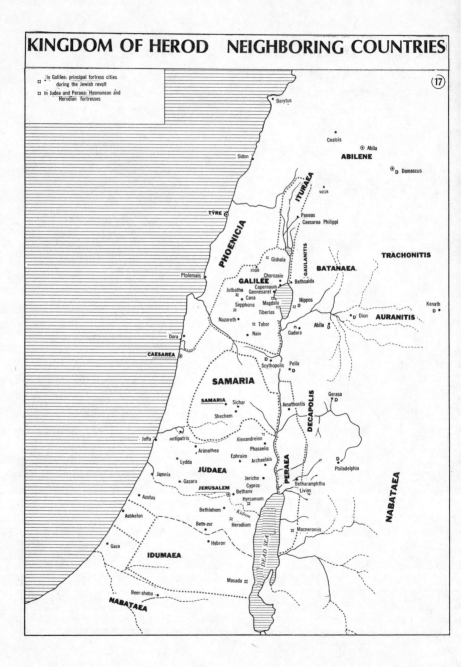

KINGDOM OF HEROD NEIGHBORING COUNTRIES

In Galilee: principal fortress cities during the Jewish revolt

In Judea and Peraea: Hasmonean and Herodian fortresses

(17)

Berytus

Cnalcis

⊙ Abila

ABILENE

□ Damascus

Sidon

ITURAEA

9218

Tyre ⊙

PHOENICIA

Paneas
Caesarea Philippi

GAULANITIS

TRACHONITIS

Gishala

BATANAEA

Ptolemais

3920

Chorozain
Capernaum
Gennesaret
Cana
Magdala
Tiberias

Bethsaida

GALILEE

Jotbatha

Sepphoris

Hippos □

Kenath □

Nazareth

Tabor
Nain

Gadara

Abila □

□ Dion

AURANITIS

Dora

Scythopolis □

Pella □

CAESAREA ⊙

SAMARIA

SAMARIA Sichar
Shechem

Amathontis

Gerasa □

DECAPOLIS

Jaffa Antipatris

Alexandreion

Phasaelis

Arimathea

Ephraim Archaelais

Lydda

PERAEA

Philadelphia

JUDAEA

Jamnia

Gazara

Jericho
Cypros

JERUSALEM ⊙ Bethany

Betharamphtha
Livias

Azotus

Hyrcanium

NABATAEA

Bethlehem

Kidron

Ashkelon

Beth-zur

Herodium

Macnerontis

Gaza

Hebron

DEAD SEA

IDUMAEA

Masada

Beer-sheba

NABATAEA

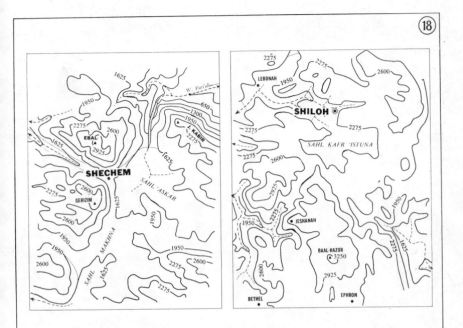

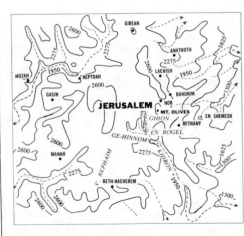

THE THREE CAPITALS

SHECHEM: Good soil, easy communications to North, East, and West; no natural defenses.

SHILOH: Good soil, difficult communications in all directions; natural defenses.

JERUSALEM: Mediocre soil, easy communications to North and South, difficult in other directions; natural defenses.

Geological Morphology

Hard Limestone: vicinity of **SHILOH** and West of **JERUSALEM**

Soft Limestone: East of **JERUSALEM**

Soft Limestone with overlying nummulite: West of **SHECHEM**

Plains or alluvial valleys.